Potato Health Management

edited by

Randall C. Rowe

Department of Plant Pathology
Ohio State University, Wooster

Steering Committee

David Curwen
Department of Horticulture
University of Wisconsin, Madison

David N. Ferro
Department of Entomology
University of Massachusetts, Amherst

Rosemary Loria
Department of Plant Pathology
Cornell University, Ithaca, New York

Gary A. Secor
Department of Plant Pathology
North Dakota State University, Fargo

in cooperation with
The Potato Association of America

APS PRESS
The American Phytopathological Society

Mention of various pesticides is made throughout this book. To
the best knowledge of the editor, these pesticides were registered
for use on potatoes in the United States or Canada at the time of
this writing. Pesticide labels are constantly changing, and thus
current labels must be in hand at the time of pesticide use, and
applications must be made in strict accordance with these labels.
Mention of specific pesticides in this book is to be construed not
as a recommendation or endorsement of their use but rather as
information for readers of this book to consider when devising
their own potato health management plans.

Front cover photograph by
David Curwen, University of Wisconsin, Madison

Back cover photographs by
Randall C. Rowe, Ohio State University, Wooster

Library of Congress Catalog Card Number 93-70663
International Standard Book Number 0-89054-144-2

Printed in the United States of America on acid-free paper

The American Phytopathological Society
3340 Pilot Knob Road
St. Paul, Minnesota 55121-2097, USA

Potato Health Management

Dedication

Floyd I. Lower
Pioneer Educator in Potato Health Management

This book is dedicated to the memory of Floyd I. Lower. The first time I met Floyd Lower was in August of 1974. I had been on the job for 3 weeks as a new assistant professor of plant pathology at Ohio State University and had been invited to participate in harvesting a potato cultivar test plot near Marietta, in southern Ohio. Upon arriving at the farm, I was surprised to see a man who looked to be in his early 70s working along with staff from the university and the Ohio Potato Growers Association. He was certainly doing his share of the work, picking up potatoes and putting them in baskets and lifting 100-pound sacks. Later I was shocked to learn that in fact Floyd was 82 and had retired in 1963 at 70 years of age. I thought at the time that it was interesting to meet such a person in the last few years of his career. Little did I know then that Floyd would be with us another 17 years and continue to contribute actively to potato research the entire time.

Floyd Lower was involved with potatoes all his life. Both his father and grandfather had raised potatoes. Floyd was educated in one-room rural schools and then, following high school, took a 3-year short course in agriculture at Ohio State University. Following service in World War I, he became an agricultural agent in Carroll County, Ohio. In 1925 he transferred to Columbiana County, where he served as agricultural agent until his retirement in 1963.

Potatoes were a major crop in Columbiana County. The use of certified seed potatoes was just beginning in Ohio in the early 1920s, and Floyd pioneered their use. He set out demonstration plots for growers to see the benefits of planting certified seed rather than tubers left from their own farms. He even collected seed potatoes from various growers and planted test plots to examine differences in sources. Local growers became interested and wanted to go to Michigan to visit seed production farms. Beginning in 1926, Floyd led groups of growers to Michigan every year. They spent a week driving around the Lower Peninsula in a Model T Ford touring car. In those days that was a major undertaking, as there were no paved roads north of Lansing.

In an account of early potato production in Ohio, Floyd wrote in 1990 that "there were no lodging facilities in those early days in northern Michigan, so each car carried camping equipment. It was set up in a grower's field or a village camp area. In some areas getting off the gravel road meant getting stuck in the sand and being pulled out with a farm team of horses. The roads were very dusty."

His description of seed production in 1928 shows just how far things have come: "Most of the better certified growers plowed down a legume sod (alfalfa, sweet clover, vetch). Many also used manure. Fertilizer ranged from 400 to 600 pounds of the low analysis then available (2–12–6). Some of the best growers plowed sods in the fall and replowed in the spring.

Most planted in early June. Field sizes varied from 4 to 20 acres which yielded about 200 bushels per acre. Seed potatoes were stored in cellars, pits, and some storages. A few of the best growers hill-selected the seed to plant the next year's crop. Some used seed plots away from their potato fields."

The importance of diseases and insects in limiting potato production was not well recognized then. Floyd recalled, "At that time most potato diseases and insects were not yet well known. Some of the small insects such as aphids and flea beetles were not recognized. Most of the virus diseases except leaf roll were not known by growers. Verticillium wilt was unheard of. Even early blight was seldom recognized. Late blight, Fusarium wilt, and blackleg were the diseases known and recognized by most growers. Of the tuber diseases, scab was the major problem. Of course growers knew soft rot and dry rot. In the 1930s Michigan had a severe outbreak of potato

Floyd I. Lower (1893–1991), pioneer educator in potato health management.

yellow dwarf. Seed from one grower had 75% yellow dwarf when planted in Ohio the next year."

Floyd worked closely with potato growers throughout northeastern Ohio to improve potato production. By the late 1920s most were using certified seed. He pioneered the formation of industry advisory committees and used them to help develop special educational programs. In the 1930s he helped organize a bi-county potato growers association to cooperate in potato marketing. His tours bringing growers to seed production areas continued through the 1940s and 1950s and included visits to farms in Pennsylvania, Michigan, and New York. Through the years he sponsored hundreds of local tours, which included demonstrations of spraying, roguing, and grading along with comparisons of seed sources and cultural practices. Winter meetings were established, and well-known speakers from other areas were invited. Floyd believed that letting growers see and hear about results of changes practiced on other farms would inspire them to try these on their own farms.

Floyd is best known in the potato industry for his efforts in evaluating cultivars under Ohio conditions. In the 1930s he began cultivar trials on various commercial farms. This was needed because, as Floyd noted, "new names were sometimes applied to old cultivars or unknown seed stocks and orders for seed of new cultivars were sometimes filled with common varieties." On-farm testing continued into the 1950s. When Floyd retired in 1963, he was asked to help with the statewide cultivar evaluation trials sponsored by Ohio State University and the Ohio Potato Growers Association. For over 25 years he provided day-to-day supervision of these plots in six to eight locations across the state. He cooperated closely with many research and extension professionals and potato breeders from both the United States and Canada.

After retirement, Floyd traveled widely across North America and visited potato growers, breeders, and extension specialists wherever he went. He led several tours to Europe with farm groups. Floyd was elected an Honorary Life Member of the Potato Association of America in 1978. He rarely missed an annual meeting of the PAA and was honored at its annual banquet in Oregon in 1989.

Floyd Lower lived to see the North American potato industry develop from its preindustrial roots into the dynamic agricultural enterprise it is today. He was truly a pioneer educator in potato health management who spent his entire life serving the potato industry and its people.

Randall C. Rowe   March 1993

Preface

This is the second in a series of books on plant health management published by APS Press. Planning for the book began in 1987. An interdisciplinary steering committee met in Chicago and spent a day discussing and debating issues involved in the management of healthy potato crops. Various chapter outlines were proposed, and finally the basic idea took shape. The group decided that potato health would be considered in the broad sense to include mineral nutrition, water relations, and effects of various pests and pathogens. The concepts of holistic management would be stressed to encourage those in the potato industry to adopt management systems that promote overall crop health, maximize profitability, and maintain environmental quality. It was decided to limit the geographic scope of the book to North America, emphasizing Canada and the United States. Exact production plans would not be given, because of the great diversity of conditions across North America. Rather, overall principles of potato health management would be put forth, coupled with detailed chapters on management of specific problems. The concept was that individual readers could assemble their own customized management plans by incorporating into the generalized plan details for the management of specific problems important to them.

The steering committee realized that no one person could write this book. Authors were secured to prepare various chapters, and some of them invited co-authors to work with them. I am particularly indebted to all the chapter authors who wrote and rewrote their chapters several times. It was especially challenging for a group of professionals to write with a single style, audience, and philosophical goal in mind and to subject themselves to the continual editing of myself and other reviewers.

For all their efforts in finding and working with chapter authors, meeting several times, making many suggestions, and serving as reviewers for portions of the final text, special thanks are due to the members of the steering committee:

David Curwen, Department of Horticulture, University of Wisconsin, Madison

David N. Ferro, Department of Entomology, University of Massachusetts, Amherst

Rosemary Loria, Department of Plant Pathology, Cornell University, Ithaca, New York

Gary A. Secor, Department of Plant Pathology, North Dakota State University, Fargo

Outside reviewers read each chapter and made editorial comments. Thanks are due to the following reviewers:

K. Duane Biever, U.S. Department of Agriculture, Agricultural Research Service, Yakima Agricultural Research Labs, Yakima, Washington

Oscar Gutbrod, Department of Crop and Soil Science, Oregon State University, Corvallis

Donald E. Halseth, Department of Vegetable Crops, Cornell University, Ithaca, New York

Melvin R. Henninger, Department of Horticulture, Rutgers University, New Brunswick, New Jersey

Casey Hoy, Department of Entomology, Ohio State University, Wooster

Alvin R. Mosley, Department of Crop and Soil Science, Oregon State University, Corvallis

John Nalaweja, Department of Crop and Weed Science, North Dakota State University, Fargo

Gregory A. Porter, Department of Plant, Soil and Environmental Sciences, University of Maine, Orono

Mary L. Powelson, Department of Botany and Plant Pathology, Oregon State University, Corvallis

Karen A. Renner, Department of Crops and Soil Science, Michigan State University, East Lansing

Steven A. Slack, Department of Plant Pathology, Cornell University, Ithaca, New York

Terry Wheeler, Department of Plant Pathology, Ohio State University, Wooster

Thanks are especially due to R. James Cook, U.S. Department of Agriculture, Agricultural Research Service, Department of Plant Pathology, and Robert E. Thornton, Department of Horticulture and Landscape Architecture, both of Washington State University, Pullman. They each reviewed the entire manuscript and made numerous, very useful comments and suggestions. The final version of this book is the result of many ideas offered by writers and reviewers. In some cases content has been altered from that submitted by the originating authors, and final responsibility for the text rests with the editor.

I am also grateful to Jo Hershberger and Bonnie Littleton for considerable assistance with word processing and correspondence related to this process and to Ken Chamberlain and Cindy Gray for help with several illustrations. Finally, a special thank you is due to Sandra Rowe, my wife, for all her patience during the many months when I was shut in the upstairs study working on this book.

Randall C. Rowe   March 1993
Department of Plant Pathology
Ohio State University, Wooster

Contents

Part One

Integrating Production Strategies
for a Healthy Potato Crop

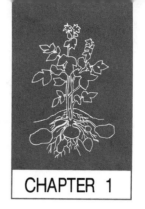

Randall C. Rowe
Department of Plant Pathology
Ohio State University, Wooster

CHAPTER 1

Potato Health Management: A Holistic Approach

Holistic is a word that is not commonly used in discussing the management of potato crops. It expresses the view that when we select among various management strategies, we must consider the big picture. Each management practice must be evaluated not only for its direct effects but also with regard to its effects on the overall agricultural enterprise. Not only production but diverse factors such as economics, law, land stewardship, and water pollution must be considered as well.

North American agriculture is currently undergoing many fundamental changes that require new approaches to crop management. Emphasis has shifted from maximizing total yield and control of pests to maximizing total economic return, food safety, and environmental protection. Production economics in a global market is now the bottom line. The quality of the final product is of utmost importance in marketing. Environmental and legal issues are dictating that production practices be modified to protect human health and the environment as well as attain agricultural production goals. All these factors are pushing today's agriculture toward more management-intensive systems.

Potato farming is no exception. In order to thrive in this new age, production management skills must be improved at all levels. A better understanding of the potato plant itself and the underlying principles of modern pest and disease management is needed, as well as an appreciation of how these factors interact to affect the overall health of the potato crop. With this knowledge, current production practices can be evaluated to determine the role of each one in the overall goals of improving crop health, ensuring economic returns from production, and maintaining environmental quality. Alternative practices must be given careful consideration. A comprehensive strategy for potato health management can then be devised that will result in a quality product produced with due regard for environmental and legal guidelines and yielding a reasonable profit for the producer. This is *holistic health management*.

The goals of this book are twofold: first, to provide the most current information on potato production practices, with an emphasis on pest and disease management; second, to explain how these practices can be integrated into a comprehensive potato health management scheme in the context of today's agriculture.

There is no one correct way to raise potatoes. Local conditions and requirements vary greatly. Our goal, therefore, is to provide the principles and basic information needed to understand various management options and how they interact to affect the health of a potato crop. This book is written for all *potato health managers*—producers of commercial and seed potatoes, extension specialists, commercial and private farm advisors and consultants, university and industry plant scientists, and students. The information pertains to potato production in the United States and Canada, but much of it should be useful worldwide.

Importance and History of the Potato and Its Diseases and Pests

The potato (*Solanum tuberosum* L.) originated in the Andean highlands of South America. Analysis of ancient living sites has confirmed that potatoes have been cultivated there for at least 8,000 years. Of some 2,000 known species in the botanical genus *Solanum*, 160–180 are tuber-bearing plants. Eight species are cultivated as food plants, but only *S. tuberosum* is extensively grown throughout the world.

Domesticated *Solanum* species were a staple crop of the native peoples of Peru when the Spanish explorers arrived in the mid-1500s. Potatoes were introduced into Europe around 1570 but did not become widely established as a food crop there for some time. Eventually, the crop became a staple in many areas of northern Europe, especially in Ireland, where by the mid-1700s most of the peasant population was living almost exclusively on a diet of potatoes and milk. As production spread throughout Europe, explorers and settlers took potatoes to many other parts of the world, including North America. The English introduced them into the Bermuda Islands in 1613 and into Virginia in 1621, but the crop was not widely grown in the more northerly American colonies for another century.

Today, potatoes are a crop of major significance in human nutrition, ranking fourth in world production, after wheat, corn (maize), and rice. Potatoes are grown on over 44 million acres in more than 125 countries, with annual production of about 250 million tons. Russia and the western countries of the former Soviet Union produce about 25% of the world's potatoes, China 19%, and Poland 12%. Potatoes are grown across North America, with production concentrated in several areas of the northern United States and southern Canada (Fig. 1.1). North American production is significant (Table 1.1) but accounts for less than 10% of the world total.

The potato has hundreds of recognized pests and pathogens (disease agents), including many weeds, insects, nematodes, fungi, bacteria, and viruses. Some of these were transported to new locations along with the crop. Others were already present in locations where the potato was introduced and then proliferated on this new host plant. Because a potato crop is vegetatively propagated from tubers, which easily carry some pathogens and pests, many disease and pest problems have followed potatoes to wherever they are grown.

The late blight organism is a prime example of a pathogen introduced on seed tubers. Recent evidence indicates that the fungus originated in central Mexico and was spread throughout the eastern United States and Canada and northern Europe in the early 1840s. Late blight was unknown in Europe until it devastated the Irish potato crops in 1845 and 1846. The Irish Potato Famine resulted in a million deaths and the emigration of 1.5 million people to North America.

Virus diseases, though not initially understood, have long been associated with potato planting stock. "The curl"—the disease we refer to today as potato leafroll—was mentioned by English writers of the late 18th century. This disorder and the condition that we now know as mosaic were not recognized as diseases, but rather were thought to be symptoms of cultivars that had progressively declined and become unproductive, a condition then referred to as "running out."

One of the pests already present before the introduction of potatoes into North America was a native insect, the Colorado potato beetle. These beetles were first noticed in the early 1800s in the central region of the continent, where they fed on native plants such as buffalobur and silverleaf nightshade—members of the same plant family to which potatoes belong. As potatoes were cultivated in the insect's native area, the beetles reproduced rapidly on this new food supply. They ate their way east and had become established on the Atlantic coast by the 1870s. The Colorado potato beetle was accidentally introduced into Europe in the early 1900s, probably in food relief shipments after World War I, and by the middle of this century had become well established there.

What Is a Healthy Potato Plant?

In order to manage a potato crop in a state of optimal health, it is necessary to understand what constitutes a healthy potato plant. The potato is a member of the plant family Solanaceae, which also includes tomato, pepper, eggplant, and tobacco, as well as weeds such as nightshade, groundcherry, and buffalobur. Unlike these other crops, however, potatoes are not produced from true seeds but rather are grown vegetatively from tuber "seed" pieces (Fig. 1.2). It is convenient to divide the growth and development of the potato plant into five distinct life stages (Fig. 1.3), described below.

Growth Stage I: Sprout Development. Sprouts develop from eyes on seed tubers and grow upward to emerge from the soil, and roots begin to develop at the base of the emerging sprouts. The seed piece is the sole energy source for growth during this stage, because photosynthesis (the process by which plants manufacture food using solar energy) has not yet begun.

Growth Stage II: Vegetative Growth. Leaves and branch stems develop from aboveground nodes along emerged sprouts. Roots and underground stems called stolons develop at below-ground nodes. The plant still obtains some energy from the seed tuber in the early part this growth stage, but photosynthesis begins during this period, and by this process the plant produces carbohydrates (fixed carbon) as a source of energy for further growth and development. This stage, in which all vegetative parts of the plant are formed, begins at emergence and lasts until tubers start to develop at the tips

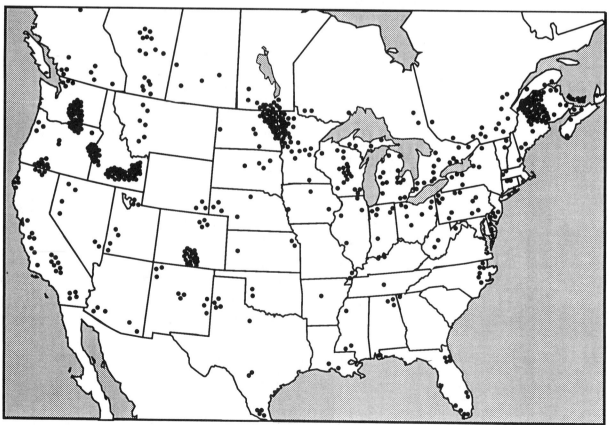

Fig. 1.1. Potato production areas of the United States and Canada.

Table 1.1. Production of commercial potatoes in the United States and Canada in 1990

	Area harvested (acres)	Average yield (cwt/acre)	Production (1,000 cwt)
United States			
Winter production			
Florida	7,700	140	1,078
California	5,500	230	1,265
Spring production			
Florida	37,000	236	8,714
California	22,500	375	8,438
North Carolina	16,200	200	3,240
Arizona	6,900	260	1,794
Texas	6,800	165	1,122
Alabama	5,700	150	855
Summer production			
Michigan	11,500	250	2,875
Virginia	11,000	180	1,980
New Mexico	10,000	340	3,400
Texas	10,000	195	1,950
Delaware	8,200	245	2,009
Colorado	6,900	280	1,932
Alabama	6,800	160	1,088
Minnesota	6,100	300	1,830
Missouri	5,800	165	957
California	5,600	330	1,848
New Jersey	4,400	230	1,012
Illinois	3,100	270	837
Nebraska	2,700	260	702
Maryland	1,800	180	324
North Carolina	1,400	100	140
Iowa	1,000	160	160
Fall production			
Idaho	393,000	286	112,340
North Dakota	145,000	115	16,675
Washington	132,000	515	67,980
Maine	76,000	270	20,520
Minnesota	68,000	210	14,280
Colorado	65,000	340	22,100
Wisconsin	65,000	355	23,075
Oregon	52,000	443	23,014
Michigan	33,000	280	9,240
New York	28,500	277	7,890
Pennsylvania	22,500	240	5,400
California	16,400	380	6,232
Nebraska	9,300	305	2,837
South Dakota	9,000	220	1,980
Montana	8,900	280	2,492
Ohio	7,800	245	1,911
Nevada	7,000	335	2,345
Utah	6,200	265	1,643
Indiana	3,900	220	858
Massachusetts	2,600	250	650
Wyoming	2,200	255	561
Rhode Island	1,200	245	294
Alaska	600	234	138
Total	1,359,700	290	394,005
Canada			
Prince Edward Island	75,000	250	18,750
New Brunswick	49,000	255	12,495
Manitoba	47,000	165	7,755
Quebec	43,200	197	8,488
Ontario	33,000	244	8,036
Alberta	25,500	240	6,120
British Columbia	7,500	153	1,150
Nova Scotia	4,500	195	878
Saskatchewan	4,000	203	811
Newfoundland	600	130	78
Total	289,300	223	64,561

of underground stolons. Growth stages I and II last from 30 to 70 days, depending on the planting date, soil temperature and other environmental factors, the physiological age of the seed tubers, and the characteristics of particular cultivars.

Growth Stage III: Tuber Initiation. Tubers form at stolon tips in growth stage III but are not yet appreciably enlarging (Fig. 1.4). Tuber initiation is controlled by growth-regulating hormones produced in the plant. This stage is a short period, lasting 10–14 days, and in most cultivars the end of this period coincides with early flowering, when a few open flowers are visible. It is generally believed that most tubers of harvestable size are initiated during this period. Early-maturing cultivars usually begin tuber initiation earlier than late-maturing cultivars. Late-maturing types may continue to initiate tubers during growth stage IV, but they usually do not reach harvestable size and may even be resorbed by the plant.

Growth Stage IV: Tuber Bulking. Tuber cells expand with the accumulation of water, nutrients, and carbohydrates. Tuber bulking occurs in a nearly linear fashion if no growth factor becomes limiting. During growth stage IV, tubers become the

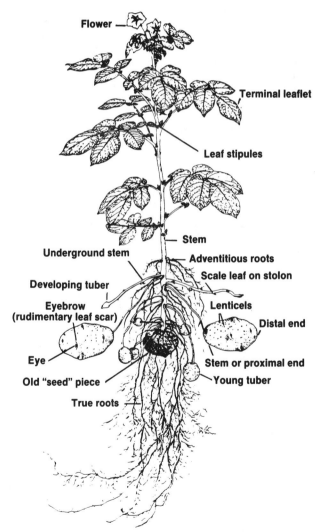

Fig. 1.2. A potato plant developing from a seed piece cut from a tuber. Tubers develop from the enlarged tips of stolons (underground stems). Tubers have eyes (dormant buds), which can develop into shoots, and lenticels (pores), through which air penetrates to interior tissues. (Reprinted, by permission, from R. E. Thornton and J. B. Sieczka, 1980, Commercial potato production in North America, American Potato Journal 57, supplement)

dominant site for the deposition of carbohydrates and mobile inorganic nutrients within the plant.

Growth Stage V: Maturation. Vines turn yellow and lose leaves, photosynthesis gradually decreases, tuber growth rate slows, and the vines eventually die. The dry matter content of tubers reaches a maximum at growth stage V, and the skins of tubers thicken, or "set."

In theory, a healthy potato plant is one that can carry out all its physiological functions to the limits of its full genetic potential as it develops through these five growth stages. The characteristics of a completely healthy potato plant would include rapid emergence of sprouts, development of strong root and foliage systems, efficient use of mineral nutrients and water, optimum rates of photosynthesis, uniform growth and development of tubers, and maximum movement of photosynthetic products to the tubers by the end of the growing period.

In the real world, however, perfect plant health is never achieved, because of interference from various factors. Potato growth and development may not proceed uninhibited through the five growth stages. Various environmental factors, such as temperature, soil conditions, and the availability of water or plant nutrients, may limit the growth of the plant or the rate of photosynthesis. Weeds may compete with potato plants for available resources, and insects may eat roots or leaves, thus limiting plant processes such as nutrient uptake, water movement, and photosynthesis, and diverting resources from the tubers. Diseases may destroy roots or foliage, interfere with plant processes, or damage the tubers themselves. If left uncontrolled, diseases, insects, and weeds can destroy an entire crop.

The potato health manager must evaluate various constraints on crop development as they appear and change throughout the production cycle and then decide when to implement appropriate management strategies. Several concepts have been devised to aid in making these management decisions. A simple concept is the *damage level*. This is the point at which a particular constraint, such as the population of a certain weed or insect or the amount of a certain disease, reaches a magnitude great enough that it will limit crop yield or quality. One Colorado potato beetle chewing on a potato leaf will not affect the yield of that crop, but some larger population of beetles will do significant damage. The point at which the population is large enough to affect the yield or quality of the crop is the damage level for this pest.

> **From a practical standpoint, a healthy potato plant is one in which growth and development are not limited by any factor to such an extent that the economic loss level for that factor is exceeded.**

A second, more practical management concept is the *economic loss level* (Fig. 1.5). This is the point, usually somewhat beyond the damage level, at which the potential financial loss due to a certain production constraint exceeds the cost of managing that factor. Thus, to avoid a net financial loss, corrective action must be taken sometime before the economic loss level is reached. The point at which action should be taken is called the *action threshold*. Figure 1.5 illustrates

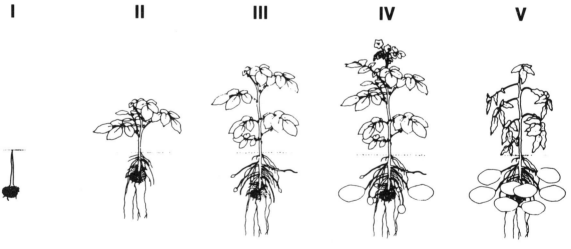

I	II	III	IV	V
GROWTH STAGE I **Sprout development**	**GROWTH STAGE II** **Vegetative growth**	**GROWTH STAGE III** **Tuber initiation**	**GROWTH STAGE IV** **Tuber bulking**	**GROWTH STAGE V** **Maturation**
Sprouts develop from eyes on seed tubers and grow upward to emerge from the soil Roots begin to develop at the base of emerging sprouts	Leaves and branch stems develop from aboveground nodes along emerged sprouts Roots and stolons develop at belowground nodes Photosynthesis begins	Tubers form at stolon tips but are not yet appreciably enlarging In most cultivars the end of this stage coincides with early flowering	Tuber cells expand with the accumulation of water, nutrients, and carbohydrates Tubers become the dominant site for deposition of carbohydrates and mobile inorganic nutrients	Vines turn yellow and lose leaves, photosynthesis decreases, tuber growth slows, and vines eventually die Tuber dry matter content reaches a maximum, and tuber skins set

Fig. 1.3. Growth stages of the potato. (Adapted from Western Regional IPM Project, 1986, Integrated Pest Management for Potatoes in the Western United States, Publication 3316, Division of Agriculture and Natural Resources, University of California, Oakland)

the relationship between the economic loss level and the action threshold. As the crop develops, the population of a particular pest or the amount of a particular disease may go up or down. Beginning treatment too early results in an unnecessary production expense. Treatment provided when the action threshold is reached prevents the potential loss from exceeding the cost of the treatment. From a practical standpoint, then, a healthy potato plant is one in which growth and development are not limited by any factor to such an extent that the economic loss level for that factor is exceeded.

Factors That Limit Potato Health

The health of a potato crop can be limited by environmental factors, competition from weeds, insect and nematode pests, and disease.

Limitations imposed by the environment may be associated with soil, water, temperature, light, air quality, or mineral nutrition.

Weed competitors include annual broadleaves, such as pigweed and lambsquarters; perennial broadleaves, such as Canada thistle and bindweed; and grasses, such as barnyard grass, foxtail, quackgrass, and nutsedge.

Insect pests are of three general types. The most obvious are those that damage leaves or stems, such as the Colorado potato beetle, the European corn borer, and flea beetles. Less obvious are those that damage tubers or roots, such as wireworms, cutworms, and the potato tuberworm. Aphids and leafhoppers cause damage by feeding on plant sap, and some are vectors (carrying agents) of viruses that infect plants.

Nematodes are tiny, round worms that are extremely common in most soils. Some species, such as root-knot and root-lesion nematodes, feed on roots and tubers, thereby retarding plant growth and sometimes causing direct damage to tubers. Some nematode species also transmit certain viruses or interact with certain root-infecting fungi, increasing the severity of root diseases.

Potatoes are susceptible to many diseases. Unlike weeds and most insects, which compete with or cause direct damage to crop plants, disease results from a disruption of the plant's physiological processes. This usually appears as some type of symptom. Diseases are caused by microorganisms, including fungi, bacteria, mycoplasmas, viruses, and viroids. Diseases can affect foliage, roots, and tubers. Early blight and late blight are primarily diseases of foliage. Scab, Fusarium dry rot, and bacterial soft rot affect tubers. Ring rot, potato early dying, and some virus diseases (mosaic and leafroll) are systemic, affecting the entire plant.

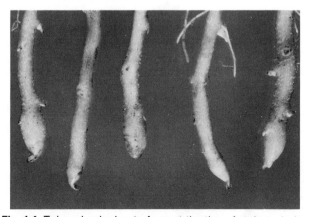

Fig. 1.4. Tubers beginning to form at the tips of stolons during growth stage III.

Principles of Holistic Potato Health Management

A management strategy that integrates several techniques for improving plant health into a unified crop production system that benefits the overall agricultural enterprise is a *holistic plant health management system.* Holistic plant health management is based on a view of the crop as an *agricultural ecosystem.*

Natural ecosystems, such as forests, prairies, and ponds, form a web of life. All the organisms interact with each other and the environment through complex, interrelated natural cycles, to form relatively stable, self-sustaining, and continuous life systems. Agricultural ecosystems are similar, but they differ from natural ecosystems in two key ways. First, they contain much less diversity of plants and animals. Second, though they are also biologically complex, agricultural ecosystems are not self-sustaining and can be maintained only by human management. When developing a management strategy, the potato health manager must always keep in mind the biological

> **Recognizing that management practices are all interrelated is the first step in understanding holistic plant health management.**

complexity of agricultural ecosystems and remember that manipulation of one part of a system can cause rebounding effects throughout the system. Recognizing that management practices are all interrelated is the first step in understanding holistic plant health management.

Management of plant health within an agricultural ecosystem consists of manipulating production factors to provide conditions that optimize the crop environment and minimize the effects of pests and diseases. The potato health manager must first understand the requirements of the crop and the

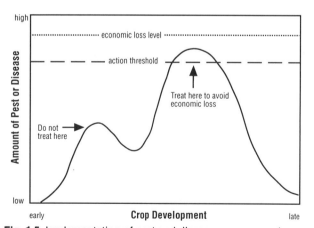

Fig. 1.5. Implementation of pest and disease management practices based on the concept of an economic loss level. The economic loss level is the point at which the potential financial loss due to a factor (such as a pest or disease) that limits the yield or quality of a crop exceeds the cost of managing that factor. The action threshold is the point at which corrective action (such as pest or disease management practices) should be implemented to avoid exceeding the economic loss level. (Adapted from C. S. Hollingsworth, D. N. Ferro, and W. M. Coli, 1986, Potato Production in the Northeast: A Guide to Integrated Pest Management, Publication C-178, Massachusetts Cooperative Extension Service, Amherst)

Devising a holistic health management plan for potatoes

STEP 1

Identify and prioritize potato health problems at the site

STEP 2

Identify the manageable factors in the production process

STEP 3

Select appropriate management practices and integrate them into a holistic health management system

production limitations of the site and then exercise management options that will minimize stresses throughout the production cycle (Fig. 1.6). A holistic health management plan includes decisions about site selection and land preparation, crop rotation, tillage, seeding practices, water management, fertility, and many harvest and postharvest procedures. After these needs have been handled, decisions must be made about pest and disease management to protect the crop, so that the plants can produce to the limits attainable at a given site.

The components of a viable pest and disease management strategy can be visualized as several shells of protection around the crop (Fig. 1.7). The first shell consists of practices intended to *exclude or evade pests and disease organisms*. The goal here is to avoid contact between the crop and damaging pests and pathogens—for example, by preventing the distribution or establishment of a new weed, insect, or pathogen in a region not yet infested. Exclusionary procedures are particularly effective in avoiding introductions of pests and disease organisms on planting stock. These procedures include micro-propagation (a technique for obtaining pest- or pathogen-free planting stock), sanitary precautions designed to prevent the introduction of soilborne and waterborne pests and pathogens into uninfested lands, and governmental regulation of quarantines, seed certification, seed use, and mandatory inspections. Techniques for evading existing pests and pathogens include selecting uninfested production sites and adjusting planting and harvest times.

The second shell of protection consists of practices intended to *limit initial populations of pests and disease organisms that cannot be avoided*. The aim of these practices is to keep populations of weeds, insects, and pathogens at the beginning of the season well below the economic loss level. Crop rotation,

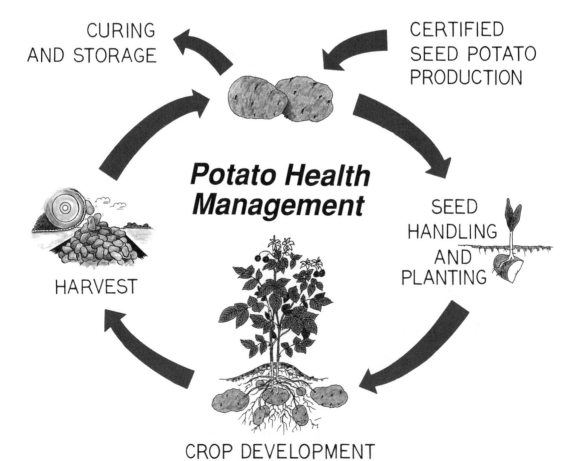

CURING AND STORAGE

CERTIFIED SEED POTATO PRODUCTION

Potato Health Management

HARVEST

SEED HANDLING AND PLANTING

CROP DEVELOPMENT

Fig. 1.6. Holistic potato health management integrates appropriate practices that are compatible with the entire agricultural enterprise. (Adapted from a drawing by Newell Hartrum)

soil fumigation, removal of overwintering sites, preventing weeds from going to seed, deep plowing of crop residues, and sanitation of equipment and storage facilities all help limit or reduce initial pest and pathogen populations.

The third shell consists of practices that *minimize the development of pest outbreaks and diseases in the crop.* The use of resistant cultivars, most pesticide applications, and cultural practices such as adjustment of soil pH, row spacing and orientation, cultivation, and fertility and water management are in this category.

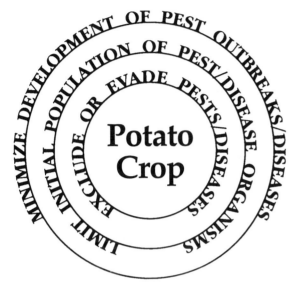

Fig. 1.7. Pest and disease management strategies visualized as shells of protection around a potato crop.

The challenge for the potato health manager is to select an appropriate set of management practices that results in the production of a quality crop and maximizes total economic return. Since all management options have associated costs, economic loss levels and action thresholds must be considered before implementation. The successful manager understands the genetic potential of the crop and the limitations of the site being managed and then makes a series of decisions that take into account the changing weather and pest or disease situations. Economic, legal, and social constraints must also be considered as they affect management options (Fig. 1.8).

Devising a holistic potato health management system that is appropriate for a particular production situation can best be approached in a systematic fashion, as outlined below.

Step 1. *Identify and prioritize potato health problems* that historically have affected the crop at a particular production site. What is most likely to limit the quantity and quality of potato production? Which of these limiting factors are of major importance, and which are more tolerable?

Step 2. *Identify the manageable factors in the production process.* Some limiting factors may not be manageable in certain locations, because of physical, economic, or legal limitations.

Step 3. *Select a set of appropriate management practices and integrate them into a holistic health management system.* Individual management strategies must be compatible and cannot be implemented without consideration of their effects on the entire agricultural enterprise (Fig. 1.6). In most cases, various trade-offs must be evaluated. Certain options aimed at managing one problem may aggravate another, and the priorities of step 1 must be considered. The economics of various management options must be evaluated in terms of input costs and effects on the profitability of the production enterprise. Legal constraints and concerns for environmental stewardship also affect choices among management options.

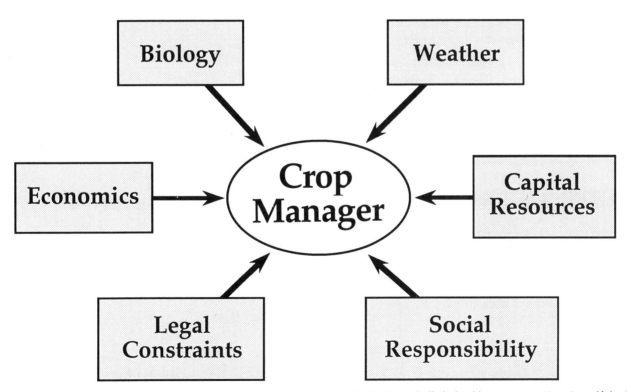

Fig. 1.8. The potato health manager must consider numerous factors in developing a holistic health management system. (Adapted from N. D. Stone, 1989, Knowledge-based systems as a unifying paradigm for IPM, Proceedings: National Integrated Pest Management Symposium/Workshop, National IPM Coordinating Committee)

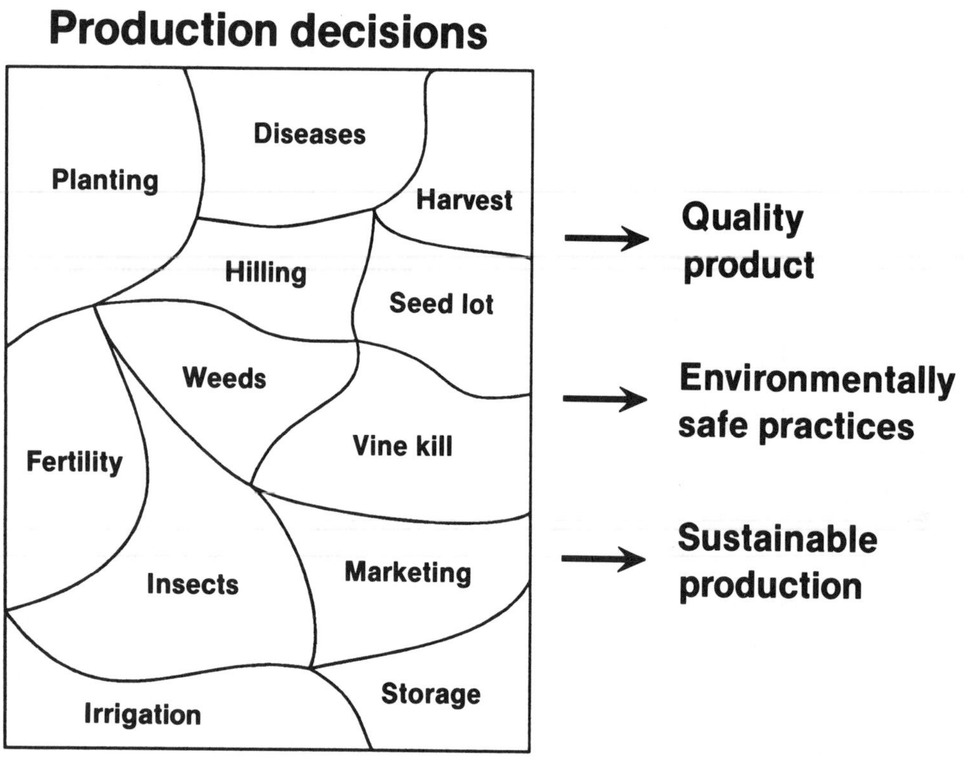

Production decisions

Fig. 1.9. All the production decisions in a holistic health management system must fit together well, like the pieces of a jigsaw puzzle. (Adapted from a drawing by W. R. Stevenson)

The overall goal in developing a holistic potato health management system is to adjust the total production inputs so as to produce a quality crop in a manner that optimizes

> **The overall goal is to adjust production inputs so as to produce a quality crop in a manner that optimizes financial returns and minimizes undesirable impacts on human health and the environment.**

financial returns to the grower and minimizes undesirable impacts on human health and the environment. To accomplish this, all production decisions should fit together well, like the pieces of a jigsaw puzzle (Fig. 1.9).

Chapters 2–6 present a generalized, comprehensive plan for producing a healthy potato crop, starting before planting and proceeding through production, harvest, and storage. A checklist of important potato health management practices is presented at the end of Part One. The chapters in Part Two provide detailed information on management strategies for specific production problems. Rather than trying to cover every pest or disease problem that might occur, these discussions focus on the most important ones. Further information can be obtained from the references listed at the end of the book. By selecting relevant information from Part Two and incorporating this information into the management plan presented in Part One, the potato health manager can devise a holistic health management plan that is locally adapted to any production situation.

Robert E. Thornton
Department of Horticulture and Landscape Architecture
Washington State University, Pullman

Robert G. Stevens
Department of Horticulture and Landscape Architecture
Washington State University, Pullman

Max W. Hammond
Cenex / Land O'Lakes Agronomy Company
Ephrata, Washington

CHAPTER 2

Selecting the Site and Preparing It for Planting

A holistic plan for potato health management begins with several decisions that must be made before the crop is actually planted. These include 1) selecting an appropriate planting site, 2) choosing rotational crops to be included in the cropping scheme, and 3) preparing the site, which involves crop residue management, fertilization, pest and disease management, and tillage. These decisions are influenced by the geographical location of the production site as well as by personal preferences, past experience, the availability of alternative locations, land ownership, the size of the operation, and many other considerations. Because each situation is unique, management procedures must be tailored to local conditions and designed to optimize potato production at a given site.

Site Selection

Characteristics to be considered in selecting a field for potato production include topography, soil properties, cropping history, and the presence and populations of soil pests and pathogens. No site is perfect in every respect, so the question to be answered is, What are the pros and cons of raising potatoes here? If potatoes have previously been raised at a potential site, the answer will come from experience. If a new site is being evaluated, however, careful consideration of the characteristics discussed in this section is very important for identifying and avoiding potential problems. Potatoes are a crop that demands intensive management. Yield and quality can be affected by relatively minor stresses. If problems have occurred in a particular field with crops such as corn or alfalfa, it is reasonable to anticipate that related problems may develop if potatoes are grown there.

Topography

Potato production is not well suited to highly erodible soils, because of tillage requirements and the lack of plant cover during the early part of the growing season. Also, in fields with slopes greater than about 10%, equipment such as planters, cultivators, and harvesters tends to slip sideways and therefore cannot be kept aligned properly. This creates a hazard for equipment operators and makes accurate row spacing difficult. Uneven row spacing often results in excessive damage to plants during cultivation and to tubers during harvest. The slope also affects air drainage from the field, by concentrating cooler air in low areas. In these so-called blight pockets (Chapter

16), there is greater risk of late blight and also frost damage in early spring or before harvest.

The slope of a field greatly affects irrigation practices. Surface irrigation of slopes greater than 5% is difficult without causing excessive erosion and nutrient losses. Sprinkler irrigation can be used successfully on slopes in excess of 5%, although erosion may be severe in wheel tracks of center-pivot or linear-move systems. Even with sprinkler irrigation, successful potato production on slopes this steep requires modification of tillage and cultivation practices. One example is reservoir tillage, in which specialized equipment is used to form a series of small depressions and ridges across the bottom of each furrow (Fig. 2.1). The small reservoirs formed down the rows hold water against runoff and greatly increase the rate at which water infiltrates the soil. In nonirrigated production systems

Fig. 2.1. Reservoir tillage, a potato cultivation technique in which special tillage equipment is used to create small holes in the furrows to serve as reservoirs, intercepting water and slowing runoff. (Used by permission of Ag Engineering and Development Company, Kennewick, Washington)

in which contour farming can be used (Fig. 2.2), potatoes can be grown successfully in fields of somewhat greater slope.

Selection of an appropriate site and the production practices to be used should take into account the potential for soil erosion, nutrient and pesticide leaching or carryover, and interference with local commercial or residential activities. Because of increasing concern for non-point-source pollution, drainage patterns must be evaluated from the standpoint of possible contamination of surface water and groundwater with nutrients or pesticides. Irregularly shaped fields may be difficult to spray with pesticides, especially if bordered by trees or power lines. Pesticides may be difficult to apply on fields located close to residential areas or other public facilities, because of potential problems with aerial drift.

> ## Selection of an appropriate site should take into account the potential for soil erosion, nutrient and pesticide leaching or carryover, and interference with local commercial or residential activities.

Soil Properties

Potatoes are adapted to a wide range of soil conditions, but not all soils consistently produce economic yields of high-quality tubers. Soil properties that influence potato productivity include chemistry (pH, soluble salts, and inherent fertility), texture (the proportion of clay, silt, sand, and organic matter), and physical condition, especially compaction.

Preplant soil testing is necessary to determine the chemical status of a soil. Although potatoes are adapted to a wide range of soil pH, it may be necessary to modify the pH to optimize production, as this property can affect nutrient availability (Fig. 9.2) and the activity of certain soil pathogens.

Both saline conditions (soils high in soluble salts) and sodic conditions (soils high in sodium) can affect the physiology of potato plants. High salinity makes it more difficult for roots to obtain water from the soil solution. More frequent irrigation with high-quality water (low in soluble salts) is required for optimal plant growth in saline soils. High concentrations of

sodium can cause physical sealing of the soil, which reduces the infiltration of water. Sodic soils typically have a high pH, which affects nutrient availability.

Because potatoes require a high level of soil fertility, soils with low inherent fertility must be given high inputs of nutrients from organic or inorganic sources. Before planting, every field should be extensively sampled to determine inherent fertility and variations in fertility throughout the field. Laboratory analyses to determine inherent fertility and fertilizer requirements should be based on realistic yield goals and local information on expected responses to fertilizer.

Potatoes can be produced in soils with a wide range of textures. Soil texture determines the water infiltration rate and the ability of the soil to store water available for plant growth. The availability of soil water is a major factor determining potato yield and quality (Table 8.1). Inadequate water at critical times during the growing season may increase the severity of some diseases, such as scab and early dying (Chapter 17), and certain tuber disorders (Chapter 10). Excess water may also reduce tuber yield and quality and accentuate disease problems associated with wet soils, both in the field and in storage. Excess water also leaches nutrients out of the root zone, which can affect the growth of a shallow-rooted crop such as potatoes.

Fine-textured soils, those with a high percentage of clay or silt, have lower water infiltration rates than coarse-textured soils, those with a high percentage of sand (Fig. 2.3). The water infiltration rate of a soil is important in determining the method, application rate, and duration of irrigation. Fine- to medium-textured soils also store more water that is available to plants than coarse-textured soils (Fig. 8.3) and therefore are better suited to nonirrigated, rain-fed production in areas where rainfall may be irregular. Such soils, however, are prone to waterlogging, and therefore adequate surface or tile drainage is critical. Fine- and medium-textured soils also require less frequent irrigation.

The amount of organic matter and the presence of stones also affect the suitability of a soil for potato production. Both water infiltration and the water-holding capacity of soils increase with increasing amounts of soil organic matter. Plant residues left on the soil surface can increase water infiltration by slowing runoff and also reduce erosion by wind and water. Rocky or gravelly soils often present tillage problems and may require specialized harvesting equipment. Other problems associated with such soils include unacceptable amounts of

Fig. 2.2. Contour farming used in nonirrigated production of potatoes and wheat in alternate strips on moderately sloping fields. (Courtesy R. C. Rowe)

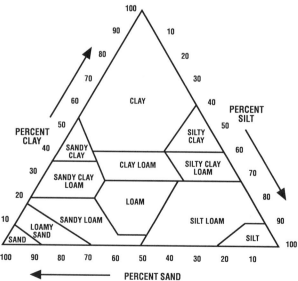
Fig. 2.3. A textural triangle showing various soil textures and their percentage composition of sand, clay, and silt.

foreign matter in the harvested product and increased bruising of tubers during harvesting and handling.

The physical condition of the soil must also be considered in selecting a site for potato production. Compacted layers within the soil profile, often called plow pans, are usually the result of past tillage practices, but natural pans also occur. These compacted layers inhibit root penetration and growth as well as water movement through the soil profile. Compaction increases the energy required for root extension and tuber expansion—energy that would otherwise go into plant growth and tuber yield. It often causes shallow rooting and the formation of tubers too close to the soil surface. Lack of adequate root growth limits the ability of the plants to obtain needed nutrients and to withstand periods of moisture stress, resulting in less vigorous plants and lower tuber yield and quality.

A compacted layer or natural pan can also form a perched water table, where water is held above the compacted area (Fig. 2.4). Plants in this poorly drained area may take up fewer nutrients, because of poor root aeration, and may have more problems with root diseases associated with saturated soil. Perched water tables are also produced by textural layering of soils, which occurs where soils with distinctly different textures occur in layers with sharp boundaries between them. For example, where a layer of fine-textured soil overlies a coarse-textured layer, water can be held up in the fine material, because of the reduced rate of percolation through it. Similarly, where a coarse-textured soil overlies a fine-textured layer, water accumulates above the fine-textured material.

If compacted layers are detected in soils to be used for potatoes, they should be removed to the extent practical by subsoiling, or ripping below the plow layer. This is especially important in nonirrigated production and in areas where irrigation may be limited, because storage of soil moisture and extensive development of roots are more critical in these situations. Subsoiling is generally most effective in sandy soils. It should be done when the soil is relatively dry, so that the pan is well fractured or disrupted. The most suitable time for subsoiling is usually just after a harvest of potatoes or another crop. Subsoiling when the soil is too wet may be detrimental to its physical condition and may even result in lower yields from future crops. Subsoiling can also make it more difficult to obtain uniform distribution of water across a field under surface irrigation. Some natural pans may be very difficult to disrupt, because of their depth and strength. Fields with such pans may not be suitable for potato production.

Production sites where the soil has uniform chemical and textural characteristics and physical condition can be managed better than those having considerable variation. The production of uniform, high-quality tubers requires a site on which the potato health manager can provide the best possible conditions for uniform plant growth throughout the growing season. Potatoes can be successfully produced on sites with less than ideal uniformity of topography, soil texture, fertility, and physical conditions, but successful production on such sites usually requires more careful management and greater economic inputs.

Previous Crops, Pests, and Diseases

When a potential production site is being evaluated, consideration must always be given to the cropping history of the field. Potatoes are relatively sensitive to the influence of previous crops in the rotation. Under most conditions potatoes should not follow potatoes closely in the cropping sequence. The dominant consideration in cropping history is the effect of previous crops on disease organisms and insects in the soil. Crops grown prior to potatoes should not be hosts of fungal pathogens such as *Verticillium* and *Sclerotinia*

(Chapter 17) and insects such as wireworms and white grubs (Chapter 12). Crops that favor the development of plant-parasitic nematodes (Chapter 18) should also be avoided.

Residues from previous crops can affect the availability of plant nutrients, especially nitrogen. Crops that leave high residual nitrogen in the soil may complicate proper nitrogen management in a subsequent potato crop. Residual nitrogen is difficult to manage in potato production; it tends to be leached out of the shallow root zone and thus can contaminate the groundwater. This may be especially important in nonirrigated production areas where periods of high rainfall normally occur during noncropping portions of the year.

Large amounts of crop residues with a high ratio of carbon to nitrogen, such as wheat straw and cornstalks, if deeply incorporated, may temporarily immobilize nitrogen and make it unavailable to the potato crop while the residues decompose. In contrast, residues with a lower ratio of carbon to nitrogen, such as bean straw, alfalfa hay, and residues of green manure crops, release nitrogen into the soil for use by the potato crop during the season. Both situations can complicate nitrogen management. On the other hand, crop residues can significantly improve soil tilth, by adding organic matter, and thus improve both the water and the oxygen environments of the root and tuber zone. The positive aspects of crop residues usually override difficulties they may cause in managing nitrogen. Problems can be handled by incorporating residues well ahead of planting, banding fertilizer below and to the side of the seed pieces at planting, and avoiding the placement of excessive amounts of residues in the vicinity of the seed pieces.

Volunteer plants from previous crops, especially corn, can be a serious weed problem in a potato crop. They may pose difficulties since they are not controlled by many herbicides used in potatoes. In addition, some volunteers develop within crop rows and are not controlled by cultivation. Volunteers may also serve as hosts of certain pathogens and insect pests that affect potatoes.

Particular attention must be paid to the history of pests and diseases and the previous use of pesticides at a potential production site. It is important to keep records of the occurrence of significant soil pests and diseases caused by soil pathogens. If a field history is not available, laboratory tests can identify nematode pests and estimate their populations and can identify some disease organisms. If a potential site has just been in sod or pasture, soil should be checked for wireworms and white grubs. The validity of laboratory test results depends on adequate, thorough sampling and reliable laboratory procedures. Consult local agricultural advisors for instructions on sampling, handling samples, and contacting a reliable testing facility. Lab test results may indicate the

Fig. 2.4. Water standing in tractor wheel tracks as a result of compaction of the underlying soil. (Courtesy N. Fausey)

potential for serious problems with nematodes, insects, or diseases for which current control methods are inadequate, in which case the correct decision may be to not use that field for potato production.

Knowledge of past weed problems is also important in deciding whether to plant potatoes in a specific field (Chapter 11). Perennial weeds can be a serious problem in potato fields, because many herbicides used with potatoes have a narrow spectrum of activity and do not adequately control these weeds. Nonchemical control methods may also be inadequate during

> ## Particular attention must be paid to the history of pests and diseases and the previous use of pesticides at a potential production site.

the production of a potato crop. Useful control practices for perennial weeds include tillage in the fall following the harvest of the previous crop, tillage in the spring before planting potatoes, and application of broad-spectrum herbicides prior to planting or emergence of potatoes. Many problem weeds can be controlled most effectively with a combination of herbicides and tillage during the production of the crop preceding potatoes in the rotation. In some fields with severe problems with perennial weeds, it may be advisable to delay potato production 1 or 2 years and plant other crops in which appropriate weed management programs can be implemented. Certain perennial weed species can be especially troublesome in potatoes. Fields heavily infested with Canada thistle, bindweed, or Russian knapweed should be avoided completely. Rotation-wide strategies for controlling perennial weeds are discussed in Chapter 11.

Herbicide carryover from previous crops can be a significant problem for potatoes, especially after a dry winter. Some herbicides applied to cereal crops at labeled rates, particularly sulfonylurea and imidazolinone products, can remain in the potato root profile the following year at concentrations high enough to affect potato plants. In some cases yield and tuber quality can be adversely affected. The potential for herbicide carryover can be minimized by following label directions carefully, particularly specifications on rates and the time interval between application and planting a sensitive crop.

Details of all pest and disease control practices should be written in the permanent records for each field. This information should include at least the following: materials applied; rates, times, and methods of application; soil texture (including organic matter content); and soil pH. The cropping history prior to potatoes and the climatic conditions during the growing season should also be recorded. Important climatic information includes soil temperature (winter and summer), the amount of soil moisture, and the movement of water through the soil profile. This information is needed to determine the degradation rate of previously applied pesticides. If accurate records are not available, soil can be sampled and tested to detect residues of potentially damaging herbicides. Potatoes should be planted on the site only if it can be determined that no potentially damaging pesticide residues are present and that no pesticides have been applied whose label instructions prohibit planting potatoes the following year.

Crop Rotation

After a site is identified, an appropriate cropping sequence that favors the production of a healthy potato crop must be selected. When establishing a long-term rotation for commercial potato production, the potato health manager must recognize that the maximum advantage from a particular rotational sequence can be gained only by implementing a rotation-wide management strategy. This strategy may differ from one selected to provide the highest cash return from each individual crop. In rotation-wide management, direct economic returns from each crop or sequence of crops must be weighed against potential indirect returns that may yield long-term benefits, such as improvements in soil structure or fertility and improved management of certain pests or diseases. Various alternate crops should be considered for inclusion in a rotation, as each may have economic, agronomic, or environmental value, or any combination of these.

Although potatoes are commonly grown in the same field every other year, a rotation that includes potatoes only every third or fourth year is much more effective in long-term management of land resources, pests, and diseases. Appropriate rotations can be very effective management tools for some soil pathogens, the Colorado potato beetle, and some soil insects (Chapters 12 and 17). Crops that host potato pathogens or insects should not be grown in rotation with potatoes, or at least not immediately before a potato crop. An appropriate crop rotation can help reduce or prevent soil erosion during potato production and throughout the entire rotation. Residues from alternate crops should be managed so as to maintain or improve the organic matter content and aeration of the soil, as well as water infiltration and retention. Cereal crops, including corn, are commonly used for this purpose in rotations with potatoes. Legumes in a rotation provide both nitrogen and organic matter, and their roots penetrate and break up deeper soil layers, thus helping to reduce the effects of compaction.

> ## The maximum advantage from a particular crop rotation can be gained only by implementing a rotation-wide management strategy.

Crops that tend to volunteer and become weeds later in a rotation should be spaced two or more growing seasons ahead of the potato crop. Volunteer potatoes also can become perennial weeds in subsequent crops. These may then carry over into the next potato crop, possibly resulting in cultivar mixtures or providing a reservoir for pathogens and insects. An appropriate crop rotation scheme should allow opportunities in the production cycle for the control of volunteer plants, weeds, and other potato pests and pathogens when the field is not planted with potatoes. A rotation-wide management strategy can include such practices as well-timed applications of broad-spectrum herbicides, the use of herbicides that cannot be used during potato production but can be applied when other crops are in production, and irrigation timed to stimulate the germination of annual weeds or waste grain after harvest, followed by timely tillage to remove them (Chapter 11). Rotation-wide management of potato pests and diseases should also include management of nearby uncropped areas. Especially important are the destruction of cull piles (Fig. 2.5) and the management of ditch banks and fencerows to minimize sites where important insects and pathogens might overwinter.

Establishing and maintaining a proper crop rotation and using rotation-wide management of soil resources, pests, and pathogens are key components of a holistic health management plan. With proper rotations, the potato health manager is better able to handle the crop, raising the potential for increasing profits through higher yields and quality, and minimizing detrimental impacts on the environment.

Preplant Tillage
and Soil Moisture Adjustment

Proper preparation of the field before planting is essential for maximum yield of high-quality tubers. Tillage equipment brought in from another area should be cleaned of all soil before use, to prevent the introduction of weed seeds and disease organisms not present in the field. Preplant tillage incorporates residues from the previous crop and promotes microbial decomposition of them. It can also serve to distribute fertilizer nutrients throughout the root zone and incorporate herbicides. Preplant tillage is often an important part of an effective weed control program. It is most effective against annual weeds but can also be useful in controlling perennial weeds and volunteer potatoes when combined with appropriate herbicide treatments (Chapter 11). The timing of tillage operations to achieve maximum destruction of weeds is critical for peak effectiveness.

Tillage can also improve water infiltration, by disrupting surface seals or crusts. Deep tillage before planting can improve infiltration by disrupting compacted areas formed by previous tillage operations, field traffic, or natural layering or pans. Preplant tillage can break up clods, if done properly and at the appropriate time, but may promote clod formation in excessively wet soil. The timing of tillage operations should be based on climatic and soil conditions.

Management of soil compaction is an essential part of potato health management. Excessive compaction slows emergence, restricts root growth, and results in stunted plants. Soils with a high clay content tend to compact more readily than sandy soils. Practices that lead to increased compaction include tillage and other field operations done when the soil is excessively wet, transporting heavy-axle loads with large equipment, repetitive and excessive tillage, excessive and random traffic patterns, and continuous production of row crops.

To minimize compaction, avoid tillage operations as much as possible when the soil is wet. Fall tillage may be more appropriate than spring tillage in some areas. The depth of tillage should be varied from year to year, to avoid creating a pan just below the plow layer. Light equipment should be used whenever possible, and the load should be distributed over many axles, rather than mostly on a single axle. Four-wheel-drive tractors generally cause less compaction than comparable rigs with the load concentrated on a single rear axle with dual wheels. One disadvantage of four-wheel-drive tractors, however, is that operators may be tempted to work soils that are too wet, thus promoting compaction.

Sandy soils may need to be partially prepared in the fall to reduce wind erosion in the spring. On these coarse-textured soils and in areas where water erosion is a problem, some form of minimum or conservation tillage may be appropriate (Fig. 2.6). These techniques leave crop residues on the surface or incorporate them only slightly into the soil. The residues may be from a previous crop, such as cereal stubble, or a cover crop, such as rye, intentionally seeded to anchor the soil in place. Tillage implements designed to cause little disturbance of the surface layer are available. Often a deep-tillage implement is used either before seedbed preparation or after planting to break up areas of compacted soil below the surface. Combination tillage and planting implements have been developed for minimum-tillage operations.

Management of soil compaction is an essential part of potato health management.

Several concerns about minimum tillage often arise. One is the reluctance of some growers to accept trashy-looking fields. Another is the difficulty in applying preplant, broadcast-incorporated fertilizers. Incorporation of preplant herbicides is also difficult, but there are alternative herbicides that can be used after planting.

In some areas land preparation is done entirely in the fall. This includes plowing, disking (subsoiling, if desired), and forming planting beds. Fall bedding facilitates earlier planting in the spring and minimizes clod development, by eliminating traffic on the beds, thus taking full advantage of the effects of winter freezing and thawing. It may also eliminate over-wintering sites for some pests, such as the European corn borer in corn stubble. The main disadvantage of fall bedding is exposure of land to wind and water erosion during the winter. Fall bedding is not commonly practiced, but in some areas preplant bedding, or "marking out," is done in the spring to ensure accurate row spacing. This is especially desirable with large, multirow planting equipment.

Factors to be considered in selecting a method of preplant tillage include the amount of crop residue to be incorporated, the depth of tillage desired, and the condition of the soil surface required. Excessive crop residue should not be left in the vicinity of potato seed pieces. A large amount of undecomposed organic matter, especially a recently incorporated green manure crop or animal manure, may favor the development of tuber diseases, such as scab and Pythium seed piece decay (Chapter 17). It may also increase the incidence of the seedcorn maggot in seed pieces after planting. As mentioned previously, deep

Fig. 2.5. Potato cull pile—a primary source of certain disease organisms and insect pests. (Courtesy R. C. Rowe)

Fig. 2.6. Conservation tillage program in which potatoes are planted directly into a cover crop of rye. The rye is killed prior to potato emergence and then tilled out during growth stage II, as shown on the left. (Courtesy R. W. Chase)

incorporation of large amounts of crop residue affects the amount of nitrogen in the soil and its availability to the crop. Layering plant residue may impede the movement of water in the soil and thus should be avoided.

Soil moisture is another important preplant factor. The desirable amount of moisture in a seedbed at planting time is 70–80% of available soil water (Chapter 8). In nonirrigated areas, if rainfall is not adequate to provide this amount of moisture, planting may need to be delayed if historical records indicate that rain is likely to occur in time to allow planting by a reasonable date. If spring rainfall is usually inadequate, tillage practices that conserve winter moisture, such as fall bedding, should be considered. In irrigated production, preplant irrigation in the fall or spring can be used to increase soil moisture appropriately. Enough water should be applied before planting that further irrigation is not needed until after the plants emerge. Preemergence irrigation should be avoided, as it may promote seed piece decay. In areas with fine-textured soils and abundant winter and spring rainfall, soil moisture at planting is often excessive. Fields in these areas must be equipped with appropriate drainage tiles.

Management of soil moisture and management of nitrogen fertility are integrally related. Water moving into and through the soil transports water-soluble nutrients, mainly nitrogen. If fall rain or irrigation is adequate to bring the soil in the root zone to field capacity or near it, then additional water (from either rain or irrigation) will leach out residual and applied nitrogen and carry it below the root zone. Since nitrate nitrogen is easily transported by water, it can be adequately incorporated by irrigation or rainfall. Split applications of nitrogen are more efficient and minimize the possibility of polluting surface water and groundwater with leached nitrogen (Box 9.2).

Soil Fumigation

In some production areas, soil pests and pathogens are limiting factors affecting tuber yield or quality on most land available for growing potatoes. Preplant soil fumigation is commonly practiced in these situations, especially in areas with coarse-textured soils and a relatively long growing season. It is most often used for suppressing nematodes (Chapter 18) and *Verticillium*, the fungus that causes potato early dying (Chapter 17). In some areas, it is also used to reduce tuber damage from wireworms (Chapter 12). Some fumigants reduce annual weed populations by reducing seed viability and perennial weeds by weakening or destroying rhizomes or stolons.

Soil fumigation has significant advantages and disadvantages. Properly done, it may be very effective in managing soil pathogens and insect pests. It is an expensive procedure, however, requiring special equipment and well-trained applicators, and fumigants are highly toxic to humans and other animals. Furthermore, fumigation completely alters the community of living organisms in the soil and thus may have unintended side effects, such as a change in the response to applied fertilizers or an increase in herbicide residues. These effects occur because soil microorganisms that normally play a role in nutrient cycling or herbicide breakdown are killed. Another potential problem is a rebound effect in which the target pathogen rapidly reestablishes itself after fumigation because of decreased competition from other microorganisms in the soil.

The objective of fumigation is to inject or incorporate the fumigant into the soil, where it or gases that form from it can disperse throughout the expected root zone of the crop. Fumigants move in the spaces between soil particles or in moisture films surrounding them. The injected materials form gases that disperse sideways and upward. For fumigation to be effective, the target organism must be exposed to a sufficiently high concentration of the fumigant for enough time to reduce its population to a point well below the economic loss level.

The potato health manager must remember that soil fumigation is not a cure-all. It can reduce populations of pests and pathogens, but these organisms are rarely, if ever, eradicated. Following fumigation, pest populations are likely to increase again to damaging levels, possibly after only one season of a susceptible crop. Because of these limitations, fumigation should always be done in conjunction with appropriate soil sampling and analysis for populations of target organisms. Treatment should be applied only if an established action threshold is exceeded.

> ## Soil fumigation is not a cure-all. It can reduce populations of pests and pathogens, but these organisms are rarely, if ever, eradicated.

Soil fumigation can be accomplished in several ways. Some fumigants are injected into the soil by a shank injection applicator, plow-sole applicator, or blade applicator. On coarse-textured soils, products containing metham sodium can be applied directly through irrigation systems if this use is stated on the label. In some areas, these products are more appropriately applied by shank injection or by mechanical incorporation with a disk or rotary tiller. Several types of fumigant products are available for nematode control. When *Verticillium* is the target organism, fumigants containing chloropicrin or metham sodium are generally used.

Successful soil fumigation is based on several principles. Soil moisture and temperature are both important. The optimal soil temperature for fumigation is 50–70°F. Nematodes are in a more active state and thus are more easily killed when the soil is warm. At temperatures above 80°F, fumigant gases escape too quickly from the soil to achieve the desired results. Fumigants should not be applied when the soil temperature is below 45°F. Gaseous fumigants do not disperse properly in cold, wet soils, and uneven results usually occur.

For best results, fine-textured soils should contain 65–75% of available soil water, and coarse-textured soils should contain a slightly higher percentage. The cooler the soil, the more important that it not be too wet. Excessively dry soils, however, can also be a problem, since fumigant gases may escape too rapidly from them, especially in warm weather. Dry soils do not allow adequate penetration of a fumigant applied by sprinkler irrigation, because the fumigant is generally tied up in the upper soil layers, where most of the moisture is absorbed.

Because most fumigants are toxic to plants, a waiting period is required after application, before planting the crop, to allow time for the gases to dissipate. This period may be longer for cool soils. As with all pesticides, it is essential to *read and follow all label directions*. Suitable soil conditions and application procedures are detailed on the product label. Certain products must be applied at different rates on soils of different textures.

Fumigation is usually done after tillage, because good soil preparation and proper application procedures are important in achieving the desired results. Before a soil-injected fumigant is applied, the soil should be in good seedbed condition, prepared by deep plowing followed by disking or rotary tilling. It is important that clods are broken up and crop residues are finely chopped and thoroughly incorporated. If this is not done, target organisms in soil clods and large pieces of plant debris may survive, because they are not exposed to the fumigant. Fall fumigation is easier to accommodate if the crop grown ahead of potatoes produces a small amount of residues or produces residues that are removed from the field early in the fall. Perennial and annual weed populations can be reduced if the crop rotation allows fumigants to be applied at the appropriate time.

Wind may prevent uniform application of fumigants by sprinkler irrigation systems. In areas subject to wind erosion, treatment with irrigation-applied fumigants has been successful when the land was prepared only by ripping through the crop residue or standing crop, all other tillage being delayed until just prior to planting.

There are some nonfumigant materials that can be used in combination with soil fumigants to control some nematode species when they are present in large numbers or are deep in the soil.

Preplant Fertilization and pH Adjustment

The goal of any fertilizer program is to provide plant nutrients in a form and at a rate that will meet the crop's needs throughout the season. As yield potentials change and new cultivars are grown, fertilizer programs must be continually evaluated and modified to ensure adequate full-season availability of nutrients and minimal application of excess nutrients.

A fertilization program that provides basic fertility needs (other than nitrogen) by preplant applications is generally superior to one dependent on foliar applications. This is especially true of phosphate and potassium. However, with the development of fertilizers with better water-solubility and the availability of sprinkler irrigation systems equipped with injection equipment, it is possible to establish a fertilizer program combining preplant, irrigation-applied, and foliage-applied nutrients. To be used for this purpose, a sprinkler system must be capable of making a uniform application. Such specialized fertility programs are not adapted to every situation. They require appropriate equipment, adequately trained personnel, and readily available soil and plant tissue analyses for timely decision making.

In nonirrigated production areas or where only supplemental rather than full-season irrigation is used, untimely rainfall may delay a needed fertilizer application. Preplant application is especially important in these situations. Generally, the entire phosphate and potassium needs of the crop can be met from residual nutrients in the soil and fertilizer that is either broadcast and incorporated prior to planting or band-applied at or following planting.

The amount of fertilizer nutrients applied should be based on a soil test. The soil sample must be taken and managed so that the results of laboratory tests on it are representative of the area of the field that was sampled. In many cases, this requires intensive sampling to determine areas of different fertility levels within a field, which could require differential applications of fertilizer nutrients. Modern sampling techniques and application equipment make this a viable management tool for optimizing productivity and minimizing the problem of adding excess nutrients to the soil. Details of soil testing and overall fertility management are discussed in Chapter 9.

Nitrogen

Nitrogen fertilizer is almost always required for a successful potato crop. Crops grown without it must rely on nitrogen-fixing and green manure legume crops in the rotation or on the addition of animal manures. When potatoes are to be pro-duced without applied nitrogen, the cropping sequence necessary to provide adequate nitrogen must be well planned and implemented in advance to ensure the timely availability of required nutrients throughout the growth of the crop.

When the need for preplant nitrogen fertilizer for each field is being determined, several factors must be considered, including preplant soil analysis, cropping history, production history, and data from foliar analysis of previous potato crops. Foliar analysis is used during the growing season to monitor the nitrogen content of the tissues and help determine the need for additional nitrogen during plant growth. The total nitrogen requirement for the crop can be determined quite accurately for any given yield goal under a specific management system. The amount of nitrogen to be added is then the difference between the total amount required and the amount expected to be available in the soil during the growing season. The rate and timing of nitrogen applications are influenced by soil texture, irrigation management practices, anticipated rainfall, and available options for applying nitrogen.

Generally only one-third to two-thirds of the total nitrogen requirement is applied preplant in most areas, to avoid losses due to leaching and possible contamination of surface water or groundwater. Split applications usually reduce the movement of nitrates out of the shallow root zone due to leaching and the loss of nitrogen in irrigation water or rainfall.

Phosphorus and Potassium

Both phosphorus and potassium must usually be added for successful potato production. Application rates should be based on the results of soil tests, because there may be considerable amounts of these nutrients remaining in the soil. Since water transports phosphorus and potassium very slowly through the soil profile, these nutrients are usually applied preplant. They may also be banded below and to the side of seed pieces at planting instead of or in addition to being broadcast before planting. Banding below seed pieces may limit early access to the fertilizer, because of the time required for roots to grow down to where the fertilizer is placed. These nutrients may also be applied as side-dressings along the row before emergence or before row closure. Side-dressing must be done with great care to avoid root damage. In some situations on coarse-textured soils, phosphorus or potassium or both can be successfully applied midseason by sprinkler irrigation systems.

Whether fertilizer is broadcast before planting or banded at planting depends on soil texture, soil temperature, fertilizer formulation, cost, and available equipment. Banding near seed pieces ensures more rapid access for the growing roots and improved uptake under adverse conditions. Broadcasting distributes the nutrients more completely throughout the root zone. In general, a greater yield response can be obtained from banded fertilizer than from the same amount applied broadcast.

Other Nutrients

Supplemental calcium and magnesium are sometimes needed for potatoes, especially in acid soils. Zinc may be required on some calcareous, alkaline soils in the Pacific Northwest, where it is broadcast as zinc sulfate or chelated zinc. Sulfur supplements are required where the available sulfur in the soil or in irrigation water is insufficient for the crop. Muck or peat soils may benefit from additions of copper and manganese.

Considerable research has been conducted on foliar application of nutrients, especially micronutrients, but there is no clear evidence that it is superior to soil application. Although there are reports of the superiority of each method, preplant application is generally recommended.

Adjustment of Soil pH

Soil pH may need to be modified for optimal production.

The availability of phosphorus can limit plant growth at both high and low pH. Some micronutrients, especially iron, manganese, and zinc, become less available above pH 7.5 (Fig. 9.2). Acid soils are a major problem in some potato production areas, primarily in eastern North America. In soils with low pH (below pH 5.5), the concentration of available aluminum and manganese may increase to phytotoxic levels. Low pH may also indicate low levels of calcium and magnesium in the soil and may alter relationships between soil nitrogen and the nitrogen status of the plant by affecting the activities of soil microorganisms.

Soil pH may also influence the development of some potato diseases. Common scab is most severe in soils in the range of pH 5.5–7.5. Another form of scab, called acid scab, found mostly in the northeastern United States, can be a problem at pH 5.0–5.5 (Chapter 17). To control common scab, the soil may need to be adjusted to pH 5.5 or slightly below. Soils already slightly acidic may be further acidified by applications of sulfur or acid-forming fertilizers. Although it is not practical to lower the pH of a highly alkaline soil uniformly throughout the root zone, the addition of elemental sulfur can result in tiny zones of low-pH soil, which can reduce the incidence of common scab.

In some locations in the western United States there has been a downward trend in the pH of soils that were originally neutral to alkaline. This decline has resulted from intensive farming practices over the last 30 years, primarily long-term use of large amounts of nitrogen and extensive irrigation. These practices have changed the pH by removing calcium and magnesium from the soil via crops, leaching, and soil acidification due to fertilizers. In some cases values below pH 5.5 have been found in soils that once were in the range of pH 7.0–8.0. In soils that have recently been acidified, the acid condition is generally confined to the upper 6 inches. This distinguishes them from native acid soils, which are acidic throughout the profile. Available aluminum in newly acidified soils usually remains below phytotoxic concentrations, whereas native acid soils potentially have much higher levels of available aluminum.

Lime is usually applied to raise soil pH. Application rates should be based on a soil test and the neutralizing equivalent of the material to be applied. In the cropping sequence, lime should be applied prior to planting potatoes. If the soil pH of a field intended for potato production is below the range normal for the area, local soil experts should be consulted on the amount and type of liming material to use. Dolomitic lime can be used to provide magnesium as well as raise soil pH. Gypsum has been used to supply nutrient sulfur and as an amendment for sodic soils. Gypsum should be applied on saline-alkali soils to prevent them from becoming alkali soils, but it is not effective in raising soil pH.

Alvin R. Mosley
Department of Crop and Soil Science
Oregon State University, Corvallis

Richard W. Chase
Department of Crop and Soil Science
Michigan State University, East Lansing

CHAPTER 3

Selecting Cultivars
and Obtaining Healthy Seed Lots

After selecting and preparing the planting site, the next step in holistic potato health management is to select appropriate cultivars and secure top-quality seed tubers. The health and performance of a potato crop are influenced by many factors. Of those directly controlled by the producer, none are more important to crop health than the selection of cultivars and the choice of planting stock. Maximum profits from potato production can be realized only by starting with healthy, vigorous seed stock of highly adapted cultivars that are well suited to the intended market.

Cultivar Selection

Potato cultivars differ in time to maturity; in resistance to pests, diseases, and physiological disorders; and in the appearance, storage, uses, and marketing characteristics of the tubers (Table 3.1). Each cultivar has unique requirements for optimum performance. For good crop health and maximum profits, a cultivar must be well adapted to local soil, weather, and cultural conditions and meet the demands of the intended market. Because of these requirements, only a few of the dozens of available cultivars are well suited to most individual farming operations. In 1990, 10 cultivars accounted for over 80% of the total acreage of certified seed in the United States and Canada (Table 7.2). In the United States, Russet Burbank alone accounted for nearly 40% of seed acreage and half of commercial production in 1990.

Market acceptability must always be considered first in cultivar selection. Desirable traits such as high yields, tuber quality, and resistance to pests, diseases, and physiological disorders are of little importance if the crop cannot be sold. Relationships between physical characteristics of cultivars (specific gravity, dry matter content, and texture) and their optimal use are outlined in Table 3.2.

The choice of cultivars may be severely limited by market restrictions (Box 3.1). Producers of potatoes for processing into frozen french fries, for example, may have a choice of only two or three cultivars. If the crop is under contract, the cultivar may be specified by the buyer. Similar restrictions apply to potatoes grown for processing into chips. By comparison, market requirements are less precise for fresh-market potatoes, and most are not produced under contract. In recent years, significant changes have occurred in the fresh market for early russets, because of the increasing availability

of new early-maturing cultivars, such as Russet Norkotah.

After the list of potential cultivars has been narrowed to those acceptable for the intended market, other factors should be considered, including yield potential, quality and storability of tubers, time of maturity, and resistance to pests, diseases, and disorders. Yield potential is genetically controlled and varies widely among cultivars. Low-yielding cultivars should be avoided unless other traits such as early maturity, high quality, or specific types of resistance are considered more important. Because tuber quality is such a critical marketing factor, producers should be aware of potential quality limitations characteristic of cultivars, such as poor storability or a tendency to hollow heart, second growth, or other physiological disorders. Cultivars highly susceptible to specific tuber disorders should be avoided, if possible. Sensitivity to certain herbicides, such as metribuzin, varies among cultivars, and this may be a consideration. The perfect potato cultivar has not yet been developed, so the potato health manager must be aware of limitations on a cultivar in advance of production and must design a management program accordingly.

Genetic resistance can be an important part of a holistic health management program. Currently available cultivars have no significant resistance to important insect pests, but cultivars with resistance to some nematodes and diseases are available (Table 3.1). Cultivars vary considerably in susceptibility to many viruses (Table 14.3) and soilborne pathogens. Highly susceptible cultivars should be avoided, especially if specific diseases are expected to be a problem. For example, if either potato early dying or common scab has been troublesome in the past, it might be worthwhile to select a cultivar with some resistance to *Verticillium* or scab (Figs. 17.2 and 17.4). Cultivars vary considerably in susceptibility to early blight and late blight (Figs. 16.1 and 16.2). In some production areas, selecting a cultivar with greater resistance to these diseases can significantly reduce the rate and frequency of fungicide applications needed and the associated costs (Chapter 16). Unfortunately, improved resistance to diseases and insects has not been a top priority in most potato breeding programs, because of demands for improved market adaptability, high yields, and tuber quality. In the future, however, genetic resistance will probably be increasingly substituted for chemical control of pests and diseases, as a result of growing public concern over pesticide use and new biotechnologies available to plant breeders.

Because of the overriding importance of cultivar selection

Table 3.1. Characteristics of the 25 most important potato cultivars approved for certification in the United States and Canada in 1990

Cultivar	Tuber type	Primary uses	Maturity	Strengths[a]	Weaknesses[b]	Rank in total production	Year released	Agency	Published release data[c]
Atlantic	Round white	Chip processing	Medium-late	Good chip color; high solids content; some res. to Verticillium	Sus. to hollow heart, internal brown spot; poor storability	4	1976	USDA–Beltsville	APJ 55:141-145 (1978)
BelRus	Long russet	Fresh market	Early	Res. to PVA, net necrosis, leafroll, heat necrosis	Poor expression of ring rot symptoms; sus. to early blight tuber decay	21	1978	USDA	APJ 58:111-116 (1981)
Centennial Russet	Oblong russet	Fresh market	Medium-late	Some res. to Verticillium	Sus. to common scab, leafroll; high sugar content	12	1976	Colorado	APJ 54:603-605 (1977)
Irish Cobbler	Round white	Fresh market Chip processing	Early	Res. to PVA; moderate res. to blackleg, Fusarium dry rot	Sus. to common scab, late blight, leafroll, PVX, PVY, Verticillium	22	1876	Unknown	USDA Circ. 741 (1946)
Katahdin	Round white	Fresh market	Late	Res. to PVA; some drought tolerance	Sus. to common scab, Fusarium dry rot, late blight, leafroll	14	1932	USDA–Maine	APJ 8:121-125 (1931)
Kennebec	Oblong white	Frozen processing Chip processing	Medium-late	High yield; wide market use; res. to PVA, PVY	Poor storability; high sus. to Verticillium, pink eye, bruising	5	1948	USDA–Maine	APJ 25:351-361 (1948)
Krantz	Oblong russet	Fresh market Processing	Medium-late	Res. to common scab, late blight, hollow heart	Sus. to growth cracks, early blight	24	1985	Minnesota–Texas	APJ 65:387-391 (1988)
LaRouge	Round red	Fresh market	Medium-late	Res. to common scab	Sus. to late blight	16	1962	Louisiana	APJ 40:130-132 (1963)
Monona	Round white	Chip processing	Medium-late	Good chip color; res. to PVA; some res. to PVY, Verticillium	Sus. to blackleg; low solids content	11	1964	Frito-Lay	APJ 42:253-255 (1965)
Norchip	Round white	Chip processing	Medium-late	Good chip color; some res. to common scab, Fusarium dry rot, Verticillium	Irregular tuber shape; poor storability	3	1968	North Dakota	APJ 46:254-258 (1969)
Norgold Russet	Oblong russet	Fresh market	Early	Res. to common scab; good cooking quality	Sus. to hollow heart, blackleg, Fusarium dry rot, late blight, leafroll, PVX, PVY, Verticillium	17	1964	North Dakota	APJ 42:201-204 (1965)
Norland	Round red	Fresh market	Early	Smooth appearance; res. to PVA	Lack of intense red color; sus. to ozone damage	9	1957	North Dakota	APJ 36:12-15 (1959)
Onaway	Round white	Fresh market	Early	Res. to common scab, late blight, PVA	Sus. to blackleg, early blight tuber decay, Fusarium dry rot, PVX, PVY	19	1956	Michigan–USDA	APJ 38:353-355 (1961)

Cultivar	Type	Market use	Maturity	Resistance	Susceptibility / comments	No.	Year	Origin	Reference[c]
Ontario	Oblong white	Fresh market	Very late	Res. to common scab; some res. to late blight, Fusarium wilt	Tubers set late; very late maturity; some after-cooking darkening	15	1946	USDA–New York	APJ 23:315-329 (1946)
Red LaSoda	Round red	Fresh market	Medium	High yield; good red color; heat and drought tolerance	Oversized, misshapen tubers	13	1953	USDA–Louisiana	APJ 31:40-43 (1954)
Red Pontiac	Round red	Fresh market	Medium	High yield; some drought tolerance	Deep eyes; lack of intense red color; sus. to common scab, PVY	10	1949	North Dakota	...
Russet Burbank	Long russet	Frozen processing Fresh market Dehydrated products	Late	Wide market use; good storability; some res. to common scab; res. to blackleg	Low percentage of U.S. No. 1's; sus. to most diseases; uniform soil moisture required	1	1914	Private breeder	...
Russet Norkotah	Long russet	Fresh market	Medium-early	Smooth appearance, high percentage of U.S. No. 1's	Sus. to *Verticillium*; low solids content	7	1987	North Dakota	APJ 65:597-604 (1988)
Sangre	Round red	Fresh market	Medium	Res. to net necrosis, hollow heart, black-spot	Sus. to early blight, late blight, *Verticillium*	18	1982	Colorado–USDA	APJ 59:435-437 (1982)
Sebago	Round white	Fresh market	Very late	Res. to PVA, late blight, early blight; some drought tolerance	Sus. to blackleg, Fusarium dry rot, leafroll	8	1938	USDA–Maine	USDA Circ. 503 (1938)
Shepody	Long white	Frozen processing	Medium-late	Good processing quality for french fries	Sus. to common scab, pink eye, PVY	6	1980	Agriculture Canada–New Brunswick	APJ 60:109-113 (1983)
Sunrise	Round-oblong white	Fresh market	Early	Res. to golden nematode, PVX, net necrosis	Sus. to pressure bruise	23	1985	Maine–Campbell Institute	APJ 62:221-226 (1985)
Superior	Round white	Fresh market	Early	Excellent type and general appearance; res. to common scab; high percentage of U.S. No. 1's	Sus. to Pythium leak, *Verticillium*	2	1961	Wisconsin	APJ 39:19-28 (1962)
Viking	Round-oblong red	Fresh market	Medium	Res. to common scab; some drought tolerance	Sus. to blackleg, Fusarium dry rot, late blight, leafroll, PVX, PVY, *Verticillium*	20	1963	North Dakota	APJ 41:253-255 (1964)
White Rose	Long white	Fresh market	Medium	Bright skin	Sus. to blackleg, common scab, Fusarium dry rot, late blight, leafroll, PVS, PVX, PVY, *Verticillium*	25	1893	New York	USDA Circ. 741 (1946)

[a] Res. = resistance.
[b] Sus. = susceptibility.
[c] APJ = American Potato Journal.

to potato health and returns from production, inexperienced producers should thoroughly discuss their needs and available choices with established local growers and other knowledgeable persons. As a general rule, most of the acreage should be planted with locally accepted cultivars, and only a small portion planted with promising alternatives. Cultivar evaluations are conducted annually in most potato-producing areas. Results of local trials are usually available through offices of the Cooperative Extension Service and are a valuable source of information.

Cultivar failure is sometimes confused with crop failure caused by inappropriate management inputs. Poor performance of seed stock is a leading cause of failure of new cultivars, for at least two reasons. First, the supply of high-quality seed stock of a new cultivar is usually limited. Second, a new cultivar may require seed-handling and production methods that are unfamiliar to both seed growers and commercial growers. Traditional cultural practices for spacing, fertilization, or irrigation of new cultivars often lead to disappointing results. Growers wishing to determine the true potential of a new cultivar should begin by selecting the highest-quality seed stock available, handling it carefully, and modifying production inputs as needed to maximize performance. Lists of seed sources for most cultivars and advanced selections are available from seed potato certification agencies, grower cooperatives, and offices of the Cooperative Extension Service.

Obtaining Healthy Seed Lots

Once appropriate cultivars have been selected, a supply of high-quality certified seed potatoes must be obtained. Planting healthy seed is a basic component of any holistic health management program for potatoes. Inferior seed stock limits cultivar performance and may result in complete crop failure if seed is heavily infected with disease organisms.

Healthy seed is the essential foundation of management programs for virus diseases and bacterial ring rot (Chapters 14 and 15) and helps to minimize the introduction of some other pathogens, such as the fungus causing late blight, and certain nematode pests. Once present in the soil, most nematodes and many pathogens cannot be eradicated, and expensive control measures may be required to suppress them. Despite the use of fumigants, for example, some Pacific Northwest fields have been lost to potato production because of the introduction and spread of the Columbia root-knot nematode.

Table 3.2. Physical characteristics of potatoes related to their culinary uses

Specific gravity	Total solids (%)	Texture	Best use
Below 1.060 (very low)	Below 16.2	Very soggy	Pan frying, salads, canning
1.060–1.069 (low)	16.2–18.1	Soggy	Pan frying, salads, boiling, canning
1.070–1.079 (medium)	18.2–20.2	Waxy	Boiling, mashing; fair to good for chip processing and canning
1.080–1.089 (high)	20.3–22.3	Mealy, dry	Baking, chip processing, frozen french fry processing; some cultivars tend to slough when boiled
Above 1.089 (very high)	Above 22.3	Very mealy or dry	Baking, frozen french fry processing, chip processing; tendency to produce brittle chips and to slough when boiled

Because of the critical importance of healthy seed tubers, the selection of quality certified seed lots from quality seed growers must be a top priority for the potato health manager.

The choice of whole or cut seed tubers for planting may affect crop health and productivity. Most potato crops in North America are grown from seed pieces cut from larger tubers. Cutting disrupts apical dominance, the characteristic of whole tubers by which the eye nearest the tip of the tuber predominates in sprouting, and thus all eyes on cut seed pieces have the ability to sprout. Seed tubers for cutting, often referred to as A-size, should weigh 4–10 ounces. Each tuber is then cut into several blocky seed pieces weighing 1½–2 ounces.

Healthy seed is the foundation of management programs for virus diseases and bacterial ring rot.

In the European potato industry, only small, whole, uncut tubers are used as seed. These whole seed tubers, usually called B-size, B's, or single-drop in North America, are generally less than 2 inches in diameter and weigh under 4 ounces. The intact skin of uncut, whole tubers is an effective barrier against organisms in the soil that can cause decay in seed tubers. Eliminating the cutting operation also reduces the spread of seedborne bacteria, especially the ring rot pathogen, and some viruses, notably potato virus X.

Whole seed tubers are particularly desirable in nonirrigated areas where spring rains often cause excess soil moisture after planting and lead to subsequent problems with seed piece decay. Cultivars that are highly susceptible to seed piece decay, including most white- and red-skinned types, benefit the most from whole-tuber seeding. For these reasons, whole seed is more popular in the eastern and central production areas of North America than in irrigated western areas, where drier conditions and the predominant use of Russet Burbank usually favor a relatively low incidence of seed piece decay. Whole seed can be especially important in the production of organically grown potatoes, on which no chemical seed treatments or other pesticides may be used.

Compared to cut seed pieces, whole seed tends to produce more stems and set more tubers per hill, which often leads to smaller tubers at harvest. This tendency can usually be offset by wider spacing of whole seed within the row. Apical dominance in whole seed is not interrupted by cutting, and whole seed tubers usually have more eyes than cut seed pieces. Thus, sprouting from whole seed within individual hills occurs over a longer period, so that emergence is often less even across the field than with cut seed. Differences between whole seed and cut seed in the number of stems and emergence rates may favor the use of one type over the other with certain cultivars. In most situations, however, the overall performance of whole seed is equal or superior to that of cut seed. Although growers often choose not to use whole seed because of its price and limited availability, it is usually well worth the slightly higher cost if the required amounts can be obtained.

Selecting the best planting stock available involves more than simply studying certification records and purchasing lots with low disease ratings, although these steps are important. Certification records typically emphasize amounts of viral and bacterial ring rot symptoms observed in seed production fields or winter test plots. These records typically contain little or no information about other aspects of quality, such as the seed grower's reputation for dependability and honesty; field and storage conditions to which the seed has been exposed; the physical condition, grade, size distribution, and physiological age of the seed tubers; the incidence of tuber decay; and the incidence of pests and diseases not considered in the certification process. Because many aspects of seed quality are not addressed in certification reports, selection of healthy seed lots clearly requires considerable interaction between commercial growers and seed producers.

Characteristics of a Healthy Seed Lot

Seed quality is difficult to define, but it is generally accepted that the most important characteristics of a healthy seed lot are that it should be

- Free of cultivar or clonal mixtures
- Within established certification tolerances for certain diseases and pests
- Free of bacterial ring rot, late blight, and root-knot nematodes

- Physically sound, with minimal mechanical and cold injury
- Properly sized and classed as A-size or B-size (single-drop):

    A-size tubers, which are intended to be cut into seed pieces, weigh 4–10 ounces and are 1½–3¼ inches in diameter (no more than a total of 5% may weigh more than 12 ounces or be less than 1½ inches in diameter)

    B-size tubers, which are intended to be planted whole, generally weigh less than 4 ounces and are 1½–2¼ inches in diameter

- True to grade, with few knobs and second growth
- Free of excess soil, stones, and other debris
- Of the desired physiological age
- Properly inspected and certified
- Winter-tested, when applicable

Box 3.1

Selecting Cultivars for Specific Markets

Cultivars for Fresh Consumption

Although taste and cooking quality are important attributes, tuber appearance is the key to fresh-market sales. Cultivars for the North American fresh market consist of four major types—long russets, long whites, round whites, and reds—and a few specialty types with unusual characteristics, such as yellow flesh or purple skins. Currently, the leading long russet cultivars are Russet Burbank, Russet Norkotah, Centennial Russet, and Norgold Russet. These are not adapted to all production areas, however, and several other russets are of regional importance. The most popular long white cultivar is White Rose, grown mainly in the southwestern United States. The leading round white cultivar is Superior. Other important round whites include Katahdin, Kennebec, Monona, Onaway, Ontario, and Sebago. Important red cultivars are Red Norland, Red Pontiac, and Red LaSoda.

Yellow-fleshed fresh-market cultivars have become increasingly popular in North America since the early 1980s. Important cultivars in this class include Yukon Gold, Golden Finn, and Yellow Finn. Other yellow choices include Delta Gold, Saginaw Gold, Bintje, and Donna. Several other specialty cultivars of European or South American origin are popular in local areas. Desiree, a red-skinned, yellow-fleshed cultivar, is increasing in popularity. Rose Gold and Red Gold also have pale red skins and yellow flesh. Yellow-fleshed and other novelty cultivars are presently sold only in selected markets, but volume is increasing.

Cultivars for Potato Chips

Cultivars grown for processing as potato chips must have specific tuber characteristics. The most important are high specific gravity (high total solids content) and low reducing sugar content, giving chips a light color when fried. The ideal specific gravity for chipping potatoes is in the range 1.080–1.095; the corresponding total solids content is 20–23% (Table 3.2). Cultivars producing tubers with a specific gravity that is characteristically below 1.080 produce lower chip yields, require more frying time, and absorb more oil during frying. Excess oil is an added expense for processors and tends to cause sogginess in chips. Cultivars producing tubers with a specific gravity characteristically above 1.095 are more susceptible to bruising during handling and produce chips with associated defects. Tuber specific gravity is a cultivar characteristic, but it is also strongly influenced by climate, soil, and cultural factors. Specific gravity may vary within a range for a given cultivar; for example, the specific gravity of Norchip tubers ranges from 1.070 to 1.095.

The cultivars most commonly grown for the North American chipping industry are Atlantic and Norchip. Atlantic is broadly adapted, and thus chip processors can obtain supplies at harvest from most production areas. It is moderately resistant to common scab, is susceptible to hollow heart and internal brown spot, and stores relatively poorly. Norchip is less widely adapted than Atlantic and generally yields less and has a lower specific gravity. Monona has been an important chipping cultivar, but its low specific gravity has reduced the demand for it by chip processors. A significant number of chipping cultivars have been developed by private breeding programs, but most are grown under contract and are not generally available to the public. Potato breeding programs of the U.S. Department of Agriculture and state agricultural experiment stations are emphasizing the development of cultivars for the chip market, and improved cultivars for chipping should become available.

Cultivars for Frozen Processing

Cultivars grown for frozen processing must have internal characteristics similar to those required by the chip industry—at least 20% total solids and light fry color (Table 3.2). In addition, those intended for french fry production must have long, blocky tubers, as opposed to the round types used for chip processing. Russet Burbank is presently the predominant cultivar grown in North America for frozen processing. Kennebec and Shepody are other important cultivars, used primarily for processing directly from the field.

Most of these characteristics can be evaluated by either physical examination of the seed lot or consultation with the seed producer or certification agency. However, the most important attribute of healthy seed—satisfactory field performance—can only be determined by planting and producing a crop. Healthy seed emerges uniformly and forms vigorous plants that produce high yields of quality tubers. High-quality, healthy seed, if properly handled and managed with good production practices, will maximize profits. The old adage "Good seed doesn't cost, it pays" is absolutely true.

Physiological age is one characteristic of good seed stock that is not well understood. Evidence suggests that it plays an important role in determining the number of days to emergence, number of stems and tubers per hill, tuber size distribution, crop maturity, total yield, and market grade. No objective preplant measure of physiological age has yet been devised. Aging of seed lots seems to depend on the combined effects of the seed-growing environment, date and conditions of harvest, conditions of seed storage, cutting and handling conditions, and field conditions at the time of planting. High seasonal temperatures and stresses caused by lack of adequate moisture or fertility during seed production hasten tuber aging. High temperatures, bruising, and dehydration during storage also age seed.

High-quality, healthy seed, properly handled and managed, will maximize profits. The old adage "Good seed doesn't cost, it pays" is absolutely true.

Compared to physiologically "old" seed, "young" seed is characterized by slower emergence, fewer stems and tubers per hill, larger plants, a longer tuberization and bulking period (growth stages III and IV), larger tubers at harvest, delayed senescence, and higher yields in long-season areas. Production of seed in short-season locations tends to favor physiological youngness in seed potatoes. Youngness is enhanced by harvesting when tubers are slightly immature—conditions that unfortunately also tend to favor mechanical injury and storage decay.

The desirability of physiologically young or old seed depends on production objectives. French fry producers and those growing small-tubered cultivars, especially in long-season areas, may prefer young seed, because it produces larger tubers. Seed potato producers, on the other hand, may choose to produce smaller tubers and therefore prefer to plant physiologically old seed.

Locating a Healthy Seed Lot

Dealing with reputable seed growers is probably the single best guarantee against catastrophic crop losses. Finding and establishing long-term relationships with two or three reputable seed growers is highly desirable. These individuals usually have consistently good certification records, which they willingly reveal. Their customers recommend them highly. They deliver a good product on time, and they rectify any losses related to poor seed performance for which they are responsible.

After potential seed suppliers have been identified from certification records and customer recommendations, periodic on-farm visits are advisable. Prior to a visit, it is wise to become familiar with seed potato certification procedures in general (Chapter 7) and the regulations that govern certification in the production area where the supplier is located. If possible, selected seed growers should be visited twice annually, preferably in August and again in January or February. The August visit should be timed to allow observation of production conditions. Seed fields should have uniform stands of healthy plants and be relatively free of weeds and volunteer potatoes. Different seed lots should be clearly separated and identified. Cull piles and rogued plants should not be evident. Ideally, the operation should be geographically isolated from commercial potato production areas and devoted solely to seed production.

Dealing with reputable seed growers is probably the single best guarantee against catastrophic crop losses.

The August visit should include an inspection of equipment and storage facilities and provide an assessment of the seed grower's technical expertise and past inspection records. Equipment should be clean, well maintained, and not shared with other operations. Storage facilities should be clean, free of old potatoes and other debris, and designed to provide a proper environment for seed tubers. The entire seed production operation—fields, equipment, and storage—should be well kept and orderly. In discussions, it should be evident that the seed grower is knowledgeable and enthusiastic about disease and pest control, roguing, sanitation, field rotation, antibruise techniques, and recommended storage practices. Participation in limited-generation, virus-tested, or tissue-cultured programs (Chapter 7) is highly desirable, but a grower may use compensating practices that allow the production of excellent nongeneration, non-virus-tested seed. Because of obvious advantages associated with the limited-generation concept, however, most areas are eliminating nongeneration programs.

The midwinter visit should focus on the condition of stored seed tubers and evaluation of available certification records. Storage facilities should be inspected carefully. The ideal storage environment should be about 38–40° F with a relative humidity of 90–95%. Minimal condensation should be visible on the ceiling and walls, and no hot spots or sunken areas should be evident in the piles. The air system should be adjusted to provide for recirculation or ventilation as needed. The pile surfaces should be relatively smooth, to prevent the formation of dead air spaces. If multiple seed lots are stored, each should be clearly identified and adequately separated from all others by suitable physical barriers.

The condition of the seed tubers should be carefully evaluated. Tubers should be physically sound, firm, and turgid, with minimal bruising and mechanical injury; unsprouted; and relatively free of dirt and debris. They should show minimal evidence of scab, Fusarium dry rot, soft rot, or the black scurf stage of Rhizoctonia canker (Box 4.1). The storage atmosphere should be free of the smell of ammonia or decaying potatoes.

By midwinter, the seed grower should have records of field and bin inspections required for certification of the current crop and, possibly, results of winter grow-out tests. Winter tests are usually done in the field in Florida or California or in local greenhouses. Records for all seed lots should be examined, and the reasons for rejection of any lot should be discussed. Rejection of any lot for bacterial ring rot or Columbia root-knot nematode is of special concern and is generally a sufficient reason for purchasing seed elsewhere. If possible, certification records for the two or three preceding years should also be examined, and the reasons for any rejection should be discussed. Certification records should be readily available from the seed grower, but they can also be obtained from appropriate certification agencies.

Using seed from at least two or three good growers is recommended, to avoid excessive losses sometimes associated with a single source of seed. Many seed growers offer more than one seed lot of major cultivars. Some maintain seed lot identities to distinguish between clones thought to be well suited to specific production areas or uses. Maintaining separate seed lots also permits growers with multiple storage units to manipulate storage environments and thus physiologically age seed for specific growing areas. Individual numbering of seed lots also provides access to information such as the lot origin, certification history, and current certification classification.

Dealing with the Seed Grower

Your goal should always be to buy the best seed available at a price fair to both parties. Never purchase uncertified or "year-out" seed. Quality should not be sacrificed for price, because cheap seed may be extremely expensive in the long run. A suitable contract should be developed and signed, to protect both parties against misunderstandings. While transactions between long-established trading partners can be based largely on trust, precise agreements should be considered mandatory in dealing with new suppliers. So-called universal seed contracts are available from seed certification agencies and most established seed growers. Among other considerations, a contract should specify the cultivar or clone, lot number, seed class or generation, tag color, state seed grade, minimum and maximum tuber sizes, quantities, and method of shipment (bulk or bagged). It should also define price, payment schedule, shipping methods and responsibilities, delivery points, and delivery schedule.

The potato health manager should always keep in mind that certification is not a guarantee of seed quality. The certification process warrants only that systematic inspections were made and that the crop was found to be within specified standards at the time of the inspections. Be certain that you understand the certification requirements that apply to the seed growers you deal with. In some areas, certification procedures may not require tuber and bin inspections. Because seed quality can be destroyed by improper storage, tubers should be examined prior to shipment, especially those from a new supplier. Federal and state shipping-point inspections, if properly performed, help to ensure that tubers meet size and grade specifications and are relatively free of decay, mechanical and cold injury, and other disorders. A shipping-point inspection should also identify obvious cases of bacterial ring rot and other deficiencies. All inspection reports and tags should be retained for possible future use in resolving conflicts.

Upon delivery, you should expect to receive seed of the quality, grade, and tuber size distribution specified in the contract, shipping-point inspection report, or other written or oral agreement. If, after careful examination, the product received does not meet your expectations, the seed grower should be notified and allowed to rectify the situation. In most cases, conflicts between reputable trading partners can be resolved informally. If a resolution is not achieved, however, local experts may need to examine the seed and circumstances and assist in resolving the problem. Keep in mind that seed quality can be totally destroyed by improper handling during and after unloading. Do not create problems for yourself and your supplier by handling, cutting, and planting seed carelessly. You are liable for any mistakes you make.

Taking time to follow these steps carefully when purchasing seed tubers (Box 3.2) will consistently pay dividends in the production of a healthy potato crop and is a key factor in ensuring profitability in commercial production.

Box 3.2

Steps for Obtaining Healthy Seed Tubers

- Deal only with well-established or highly recommended seed growers with good reputations for proper grading, timely delivery, and seed that consistently performs well in your production area.

- Visit seed growers and examine seed lots in the field and in storage before agreeing to buy them.

- Examine complete certification records for *all seed lots* produced by a prospective supplier, and discuss the reasons for the rejection of any lots.

- Purchase seed from two or three different growers to avoid problems sometimes associated with a single source.

- Never purchase uncertified or "year-out" seed.

- Thoroughly discuss details of the transaction, including price, seed class, delivery date, and payment; universal seed contracts are recommended.

- Request a third-party federal or state inspection of loads prior to shipment, if appropriate.

Gary A. Secor
Department of Plant Pathology
North Dakota State University, Fargo

Neil C. Gudmestad
Department of Plant Pathology
North Dakota State University, Fargo

Handling and Planting Seed Tubers

Once a high-quality seed lot has been purchased, management procedures implemented after seed delivery determine seed performance to a great degree. How seed tubers are handled, prepared, and planted is just as important as the quality of the seed itself. Proper handling and planting promote optimum stand establishment by minimizing exposure to disease-causing organisms, reducing mechanical and stress damage to the seed, and providing favorable conditions for rapid plant development. Establishing a good stand of healthy, vigorous plants is a big step toward the dual goals of high tuber yields and quality.

Preparing the Seed Storage

After a seed lot has been selected and a price and delivery time negotiated, storage facilities should be prepared to accept the seed. Seed potatoes should not be placed in a storage treated within the past 6 months with the sprout inhibitor CIPC (isopropyl *N*-chlorophenylcarbamate) unless the entire ventilation system, including plenums, flumes, fans, and ducts, has been thoroughly cleaned with soap and water applied with a high-pressure washer. CIPC is applied to tubers in the pile as a very fine aerosol that is injected into the ventilation system and carried throughout the storage by air movement. Even a small amount of CIPC residue in the storage can retard or prevent sprouting of seed tubers. Field-applied sprout inhibitors, such as maleic hydrazide, do not contaminate storages.

Cleaning and sanitizing storages and seed-handling equipment each year to eliminate carryover of disease-causing organisms on surfaces or in potato debris are essential steps in potato health management, even if disease has not been a problem in previous crops. Pathogens of major concern are the soft rot and blackleg bacteria, the ring rot bacterium, and the *Fusarium* fungi. Ring rot bacteria can persist for 2–5 years on dry surfaces and can survive freezing temperatures. All trash left from previous seasons, including tubers, vines, soil, broken boxes, and old bags, should be removed from the storage and properly discarded or burned. Discarded potatoes should not be left near the storage or in a cull pile, which could be a source of disease organisms. They should be burned, buried, or completely removed from the farm. In northern areas, if none of these methods are feasible, cull potatoes can be spread sparingly during the winter on the surface of fields not intended for potato culture the following spring, where they are allowed to undergo several cycles of freezing and thawing.

After cleanup, storage bins, walls, and floors should be thoroughly washed with a high-pressure washer using hot, soapy water and then rinsed well. After washing, a disinfectant should be applied according to the manufacturer's instructions (Table 4.1). It is critical to wash these surfaces before applying a disinfectant, because most disinfectants are not effective on dirty surfaces, as they are rapidly inactivated by organic matter and soil. To kill bacteria, disinfectants generally must be in contact with the surface to be sanitized for a minimum of 10 minutes. Porous surfaces retain larger populations of bacteria than smooth surfaces and require extra attention. Adding a foaming agent to some disinfectants helps retain the chemical on vertical surfaces, such as walls, for the required time.

> ## How seed tubers are handled, prepared, and planted is just as important as the quality of the seed itself.

Before a new seed lot is handled, all containers, tools, and equipment such as seed trucks, planters, seed cutters, and conveyors should also be sanitized (Fig. 4.1). Special attention should be given to open-cell foam rubber rollers. These may carry ring rot bacteria deep in the foam from one season to another and cannot be properly sanitized. To avoid this problem, it is preferable to replace them with closed-cell foam rubber rollers. After the sanitation process, all treated surfaces should be rinsed well with clean water, and any excess water removed.

Important characteristics of a good disinfectant are high germicidal activity, rapid action, effectiveness in the presence of organic material and in hard water, long shelf life, low human toxicity, noncorrosiveness, and ease of use. Several types of disinfectants are available, marketed under many brand names. Each type has certain characteristics that affect its use (Table 4.1). Hypochlorite bleaches are extremely sensitive to inactivation by organic matter, and hence thorough prewashing is especially important when these compounds are used. Hypochlorite bleaches and iodine compounds are corrosive to metal. Alcohol disinfectants are especially suitable for small jobs, such as sanitizing tissue culture tools, vessels, and equipment. If properly used, most commercially available disinfectants are effective sanitizers and kill residual ring rot bacteria.

Most disinfectants are aimed at killing bacteria, but many also inactivate viruses. Because viruses are inactivated under alkaline conditions (pH 8.5 or higher), high-pH disinfectants, such as bleach, are most effective. Calcium hydroxide (slaked lime) and 3% trisodium phosphate effectively inactivate viruses, but their activity against bacteria is unknown.

Live steam also can be used to kill ring rot bacteria, but the temperature of the steam contacting the surface to be sanitized must exceed 180°F. *Caution: Do not confuse condensed water vapor (fog) with colorless, and therefore invisible, steam.* The temperature of condensed water vapor may be lower than that required to kill bacteria. Steam must be used properly to be effective. The surface to be sanitized must be exposed to live steam for 15–30 seconds. *Steam cleaning cannot be rushed.* Steam is more useful for sanitizing equipment than for entire storages, because of the need for high temperatures, the time involved, and the small surface area that can be covered at one time with the steam appliance.

An alternative sanitizing method is space fumigation with chloropicrin (tear gas). This procedure should not be used annually, but only under extreme circumstances (for example, if ring rot bacteria are known to have contaminated a storage). Space fumigation must be done in a warm storage (at least 50°F) that has been sealed to prevent the escape of the gas. All surfaces must first be thoroughly wetted with a solution containing a wetting agent (surfactant). Fumigation for 12 hours with 0.3 pounds per 1,000 cubic feet kills ring rot bacteria, as well as other bacteria, fungi, insects, and rodents. *Chloropicrin is extremely toxic to animals and people, and this procedure must be done only by a certified fumigant applicator.* Chloropicrin is registered for use in empty potato warehouses only.

Nonchemical alternatives can be used to eliminate pathogens in some situations. Painting wooden surfaces can cover and seal in disease organisms and prevent them from causing infection. Special measures may be necessary for sanitizing earth cellars, because soil and organic material inactivate chemical disinfectants. It may be necessary to cover earthen walls with plastic sheeting to prevent direct contact with the potatoes. For earthen floors that are contaminated, removing the top few inches of soil or adding a few inches of new soil may effectively remove or seal in pathogens.

Table 4.1. Types of disinfectants used for sanitizing potato-handling equipment and storage facilities

	Inactivated by organic matter	Inactivated by hard water	Corrosive to metal	Safety	Recommended concentration for use	Recommended exposure time	Shelf life	Comments
Quaternary ammonium compounds	Slightly	No	Slightly	Relatively safe; use caution (see labels)	Follow label directions	10 min	1–2 yr	Poisonous in concentrated form; relatively safe when diluted Stainless
Hypochlorites (including 5.25% household bleach and other chlorine-based disinfectants)	Yes	Affected by iron only	Yes	Irritant, caustic	1:50 to 1:200	10 min	5.25% bleach stable 3–4 mo at 70°F; once diluted, it should be used within hours	Quick-acting Inexpensive Caustic to skin and clothing More effective at pH 7–8 than at normal pH 10–11 To use, mix 1 part 5.25% bleach, 200 parts water, and 0.6 part white vinegar; the chlorine concentration of this mixture is 256 ppm
Iodine compounds	Yes	Affected by iron only	Yes	Relatively safe; use caution (see labels)	Follow label directions	10 min	1–2 yr	Do not take internally No longer effective if it loses yellow-brown color Tamed iodophor compounds work best
Phenolic compounds	Moderately	No	No	Oral poison	Follow label directions	10 min	1–2 yr	Residual action Phenol listed as ingredient on the label
Alcohols	Slightly	No	No	Oral poison, flammable	Ethanol Dip or spray, 70% Flaming, 95% Isopropanol, 50% Methanol, 50%	10 min	1–2 yr	Best suited for small applications (tissue culture facilities, utensils) Can be used to flame utensils for immediate sanitizing

Accepting Delivery and Handling Seed

A separate storage, or at least separate bins, should be available and prepared for incoming seed prior to delivery. Individual seed lots should be kept in separate bins to maintain their identity and to prevent transmission of pathogens. An important potato health management principle is that the manager must maintain the seed pedigree—that is, know the identity, generation number, grower, and certification record of every seed lot. This identity should be preserved throughout storage, cutting, planting, and field operations in order for seed performance to be evaluated. Records of seed pedigree allow a seed lot to be traced back to its origin if problems develop later.

Certain procedural and legal details should be taken care of before delivery. A signed confirmation or contract for the purchase should be in hand. Assurances should have been obtained that the seed will be delivered in clean, sanitized containers and trucks. The seed should have been inspected at the shipping point at the time of loading; if not, it may be advisable to request a federal or state inspection prior to unloading. Bulk handling and shipping are common today, because of reduced costs. Each bulk load should have its own tag and seal. Seed, especially cold seed, should not be held in tightly sealed, unventilated trailers or rail cars for more than 12 hours. These conditions tend to create a low-oxygen environment as a result of respiration by the tubers and condensation that may form on them. Exposure to these conditions may increase the physiological aging of seed and trigger the development of bacterial soft rot.

Seed deliveries should be received by an experienced person capable of determining that the load meets contract specifications. When the seed arrives, this person should inspect the truck to be certain that the seals are intact and examine the shipping-point inspection report. The shipment should be inspected before unloading to be sure that it complies with the order—that it contains the correct cultivar, seed lot, and tags and that it has not been damaged or frozen in transit. Both external and internal inspection of tubers is necessary to detect diseases and disorders. If the seed is clearly out of compliance, the supplier and shipping-point inspector should be contacted before unloading. Reinspection of the load by a federal or state inspector may be advisable. It is important to maintain a good working relationship between buyer and seller. The seed grower should be informed of any problems before the seed is unloaded. Copies of tags and all paperwork associated with each load should be retained for future reference. Remember that *once the seed is unloaded, it is your property.*

If seed tubers are not to be planted right away, store them in cool (38–40° F), well-ventilated bins at 90–95% relative humidity. Take steps to minimize bruising during unloading and handling. Bruised seed is more susceptible to bacterial and fungal decay, and breaks in the tuber skin can act as entry sites for disease organisms. If possible, the tuber pulp temperature—the temperature of internal tissues measured with a pulp thermometer (Fig. 4.2)—should be above 45° F before unloading, as tubers sustain increased bruise damage when handled at lower temperatures. Conveyors should be adjusted so that the tubers drop no more than 6 inches. Seed delivered in bags should not be piled higher than 8–10 feet, and the bags should be arranged to allow for good ventilation. As seed is put into storage, it is a good policy to examine it for disease. There are several diseases to watch for and some simple tests that may be used to help evaluate seed lots for disease potential (Box 4.1).

Managing the Seed-Cutting Operation

Because of potential hazards associated with seed cutting, careful management of this process is an important part of a holistic health management program.

Seed tubers should be allowed to warm to 50–55° F before handling. Their pulp temperature should be monitored carefully (Fig. 4.2) and, beginning 7–10 days prior to cutting, should be raised slowly, about 0.5–1° F per day. Warming the seed tubers serves three purposes: it reduces bruising during handling, promotes rapid healing after cutting, and initiates sprouting before planting. Ideally, seed and soil should be

Fig. 4.1. Cleaning a planter with a high-pressure washer prior to sanitizing the machine with a disinfectant. (Courtesy R. W. Chase)

Fig. 4.2. Measuring tuber pulp temperature with a pulp thermometer. (Courtesy R. C. Rowe)

Box 4.1

Diseases to Watch For on Seed Tubers

Virus Diseases. Certification records, including field inspections and results of winter grow-out tests, are the best gauge of the amount of virus infection in a particular seed lot. Virus symptoms are generally not visible in tubers, except for current-season leafroll, which causes net necrosis (Fig. 14.1) in tubers of certain cultivars, notably Russet Burbank (Chapter 14).

Rhizoctonia Canker. Look for the black scurf stage on tubers (Plate 63). Ideally, seed should be free of visible sclerotia, but as much as 2–5% coverage of the surface can be tolerated. Coverage greater than this may result in yield and quality losses (Chapter 17).

Fusarium Dry Rot. No more than 1–2% of the tubers should have obvious symptoms of Fusarium dry rot (Plates 66 and 67). A 2% incidence is allowed under most certification standards and should not be exceeded in most years. Seed tubers with dry rot have the potential to develop Fusarium seed piece decay, and an appropriate fungicide treatment should be applied to seed pieces after cutting (Chapter 17).

Bacterial Ring Rot. When examining seed tubers, watch closely for the presence of ring rot. Look for characteristic sunken cracks in the skin (Plate 47). As a precaution, cut about ½ inch of tissue from the stem ends of at least 100 tubers selected at random, and examine the cut areas for discoloration of the vascular ring. This is visible as a slight to dark discoloration appearing as a ring or partial ring located about ¼–½ inch from the skin (Plates 47 and 49). Squeeze any suspected tubers and check for bacterial ooze emerging from the vascular ring at the cut surface

No seed lot confirmed to have any amount of bacterial ring rot should ever be planted.

(Plate 48). Any tubers with suspected symptoms should be sent out for laboratory confirmation, since other tuber problems can be mistaken for this disease. The presence of bacterial ring rot should be verified by a pathologist acceptable to all parties involved, including the seed grower. If any tubers suspected of having the disease are found in a seed lot, delay planting that lot until laboratory confirmation is received. No seed lot confirmed to have any amount of bacterial ring rot should ever be planted (Chapter 15).

Soft Rot and Blackleg. If more than 1% of the tubers in a seed lot show visible symptoms of soft rot (Plate 45), there is a possibility that excessive bacterial seed piece decay or blackleg, or both, may develop. The *Erwinia* bacteria that cause these diseases are likely to be present in additional tubers that do not show symptoms. The percentage of tubers infested with these bacteria is an indicator of the potential for bacterial seed piece decay and blackleg to develop after

the seed is planted. This can be determined by wrapping 100 randomly selected tubers in wet paper towels and then in clear plastic wrap and holding them for 5–7 days at 50–60° F. The number of tubers that decay is an estimate of the percentage of infected tubers. A more stringent test is to puncture 10 lenticels per tuber with a toothpick (a separate toothpick for each tuber) prior to wrapping. Soft rot is an odorless, mushy, wet decay. A sticky, stringy decay with a bad odor indicates Clostridium rot, which should not be confused with soft rot. *These tests indicate only the potential for bacterial seed piece decay and blackleg to develop if conditions following planting favor these diseases.* Extra care should be given to seed lots in which more than 50% of the tubers develop soft rot during this test. If they are handled carefully, seed lots with high levels of symptomless contamination with *Erwinia* can produce acceptable stands and yields, unless conditions after planting (primarily, excess soil moisture) are highly favorable for disease development (Chapter 15).

Early Dying. Tubers infected with *Verticillium* often have a tan discoloration of the vascular ring, visible when they are cut at the stem end. Inoculum of this pathogen within seed tubers is not as important in current-season disease as inoculum in the soil. However, internal tuber-borne inoculum is an important source of contamination of uninfested fields (Chapter 17).

Scab. Look for scab lesions on the tubers (Plate 65). Because inoculum of the scab pathogen is both seedborne and soilborne, seed tubers should be free of the disease, or nearly so, to prevent the introduction of the pathogen into the field. Excessively scabby seed should not be purchased (Chapter 17).

Late Blight. Seed tubers infected with the late blight fungus, when cut, show a coppery-colored, granular-appearing discoloration of tissues just under the skin, penetrating as deep as ½ inch (Plate 55). Infected seed tubers can serve as an important source of the pathogen and may lead to an epidemic later in the season. If the presence of late blight is suspected, a sample of tubers with symptoms should be evaluated by a pathologist for confirmation (Chapter 16).

Nematodes. Seed potatoes known to be infected with plant-parasitic nematodes should not be planted. Certification agencies inspect seed potatoes for symptoms that indicate nematode feeding (Plate 69). Some species of root-knot nematodes cause small bumps on the skin of tubers or pinpoint discolorations just under the skin. Careful inspection for evidence of nematodes is especially critical if the seed tubers originated in a production area where the Columbia root-knot nematode is prevalent (Chapter 18).

Chapters 15–18 and some references listed at the end of this book provide additional descriptions of tuber symptoms of these diseases. Universities, certification agencies, and private labs may offer some of the tests described here as part of their services.

close to the same temperature at planting time. Bruising seed potatoes before planting significantly increases the occurrence and severity of seed piece decay, often resulting in a poor stand. Healing of cut surfaces, which is accelerated at temperatures above 50°F, retards infection by disease organisms.

Bruising seed potatoes before planting significantly increases the occurrence and severity of seed piece decay, often resulting in a poor stand.

However, warming seed tubers for periods longer than 2 weeks or to temperatures higher than 55°F can result in excessive sprouting and physiological aging, which may lead to lower yields and quality.

Controlling the size of seed pieces is an important management objective. Most seed tubers are cut with mechanical cutters that produce seed pieces of various sizes. The desired size is 1½–2 ounces. Smaller seed pieces may result in weak plants, while seed pieces above 3 ounces produce plants with excessive numbers of stems, possibly leading to lower yields. A wide variation in size results in skips and doubles when the seed pieces are planted, because of inconsistent feeding through the planter.

Seed piece size is controlled by adjustments on the cutting machine and by the size distribution of the tubers being cut. If the machine is set to cut tubers in the 6- to 8-ounce range, those below 5 ounces or above 9 ounces may yield a lot of seed pieces below the 1.5-ounce minimum. Large tubers of some cultivars, such as Russet Burbank, also yield a significant number of blind seed pieces, without eyes. For these reasons, it is best to avoid seed lots that have excessive amounts of very large or very small tubers.

Seed cutters should be cleaned and sanitized at least daily while cutting, and definitely before cutting a different seed lot.

Seed tubers should be cut in a clean, relatively humid area, preferably indoors. Many types of seed cutters with various advantages and disadvantages are commercially available. Regardless of the type used, it is essential that cutters be cleaned and sanitized prior to use each season. To reduce the spread of disease organisms, the equipment should be cleaned and sanitized again at least daily while cutting, and definitely before cutting a different seed lot. Cutters with water-impermeable (closed-cell) sponge rollers are recommended, since open-cell rollers may harbor ring rot bacteria. Workers should be provided with disinfectants and washing facilities, to minimize bringing disease organisms, especially bacteria, into the seed-cutting area. A daily change of plastic disposable booties and new gloves is advisable. Disinfectant dip pans for boots are effective only if the boots are soaked in them for about 10 minutes—a quick dip may not work. A good technique is to keep a pair of rubber boots soaking in fresh disinfectant and change boots when entering the warehouse.

The flow of seed potatoes into the cutters should be adjusted so that they are not more than one tuber deep. Keep the blades sharp and adjusted to deliver seed pieces in the appropriate size range. Periodic examination of the cut seed is advisable. A 12-pound sample should contain about 100 pieces. It is also a good idea to sort the sample into size categories to determine maximum and minimum sizes being produced and the distribution of various sizes. Adjustments to the cutters can then be made.

Watch for diseased tubers during the cutting operation, especially tubers with ring rot (Box 4.1). *If the presence of ring rot is suspected, stop all cutting operations immediately.* Remove the suspected seed lot, and thoroughly clean and sanitize all cutting equipment and facilities before continuing. If the presence of ring rot is confirmed by laboratory analysis, do not plant that seed lot.

Differences between cultivars may dictate differences in handling and cutting procedures. It is important to consider cultivar characteristics such as the number and placement of eyes, dormancy, and recommended seed piece size. For example, Russet Norkotah has many eyes spirally distributed on the tuber. Seed pieces of this cultivar can be cut smaller, with each seed piece still having an eye. Nooksack has a long dormancy period and may require a longer warming period than other cultivars. Consult local advisors or Cooperative Extension Service specialists for recommendations on seed cutting for particular cultivars.

Immediately after seed potatoes are cut, a natural wound-healing process begins. When completed, this prevents both

Wound healing is favored by fresh air, 95–99% humidity, and temperatures of 55–60°F.

moisture loss and infection of the cut surfaces by bacteria and fungi. The healing process is favored by abundant oxygen (fresh air), high relative humidity (95–99%), and temperatures of 55–60°F. This humidity range is critical, because lower humidity causes death of cells on the cut surfaces and prevents proper healing. Although high humidity is required, the formation of free water (condensation) on tuber surfaces must also be avoided, because a water film acts as an oxygen barrier to cells on the cut surface. Free water on seed pieces interferes with wound healing and may allow soft rot bacteria to become established.

The cut surface of a potato tuber heals by a twofold process. The first phase is suberization: a waxy, fatty compound called suberin is produced by cells just below the cut surface. This seals the wound, prevents water loss, and blocks entrance by pathogens. Suberization occurs in 1–3 days and is usually complete in 4–7 days. The second phase of healing is the formation of wound periderm. The periderm is a permanent, protective layer of cells that replaces the epidermis (skin) when it is destroyed. The new periderm is a corky layer, which serves as the final covering to prevent infection and desiccation. Periderm formation begins shortly after suberization and is complete in about 1–2 weeks.

Following cutting, seed pieces are either planted immediately or held in storage under conditions that favor wound healing, a practice known as precutting. If seed is planted immediately, wound healing takes place in the soil, provided that soil conditions favor the process. The best results are usually obtained when both the seed pieces and the planting soil are around 55–60°F. Planting unhealed seed pieces in cold, wet soils or hot, dry soils usually results in a poor stand. Because properly healed seed pieces seldom decay, the best practice is to plant when soil conditions encourage wound healing and rapid emergence.

When seed pieces are to be planted immediately after cutting, it is best to cut no more seed than can be planted the same day. To avoid bruising, conveyors used to load seed pieces onto trucks and planters should be managed so that the seed pieces drop no more than 6 inches. It is important not to expose cut seed to direct sunlight, since even a brief exposure may dry out the cut surfaces and delay or prevent suberization. Cut seed should be hauled in covered trucks, but not stored there for long periods, because of potential overheating resulting from poor aeration.

Precutting, in which seed is cut and held for a period of time before planting, is an alternative to planting immediately after cutting. Many growers successfully use precut seed, especially for cultivars that lack quick emergence and uniform growth, such as Shepody, Yukon Gold, and Nooksack. Because the seed-cutting operation is done before planting begins, more time is available for attention to details of the cutting process, and the cut surfaces have time to heal properly prior to planting. The disadvantage of precutting is an increased risk of seed piece decay prior to planting if the precut seed is not carefully stored under the right conditions.

Successful use of precutting depends on careful management of the operation. It is essential to avoid condensation on freshly cut seed pieces, as this retards wound healing. The extent of this problem may vary with different cultivars. To avoid condensation, whole seed tubers should be warmed to approximately 55° F for several days before precutting. Do not cut seed outdoors on rainy days or in extremely humid areas. The best plan is set up the seed-cutting operation in the same area where the cut seed pieces will be stored.

Following cutting, it is critical that precut seed be stored in an environment that favors rapid wound healing—temperatures of 55–60° F, relative humidity at 95-99% (but no free water!), and air movement adequate to provide oxygen and prevent the accumulation of carbon dioxide. Some growers use pallet bins or boxes to hold precut seed, while others place it in piles no more than 4–6 feet deep. Blowing air through ventilation ducts, as for normal storage management, may provide too much air for freshly cut seed and result in excess dehydration. If so, over-the-pile fans are preferable. It may be best not to humidify the air in the storage during the first 24–48 hours after cutting, to ensure the removal of any condensation and surface moisture that may develop, but this may vary with the cultivar and with local storage conditions. In any case, humidity should be monitored carefully, and humidification should be provided as needed to keep the relative humidity of the air above 95%.

Under proper conditions, suberization of cut surfaces should occur in a few days. A layer of dry, dead cells on the cut surface can be mistaken for a suberized layer. This nonprotective layer can be differentiated from a suberized layer by holding a seed piece in the hand and applying gentle pressure across the cut surface with the thumb. A layer of dead cells is usually pushed off the cut surface, while a suberized layer remains in place.

Precutting seed tubers can be a useful management practice if handled properly. However, improper storage of precut seed, especially at temperatures above 60° F, can result in severe problems with seed piece decay, particularly from Fusarium dry rot. *If appropriate curing and storage conditions cannot be provided before planting, precutting is an extremely risky procedure and probably should not be attempted.*

Using Seed Piece Treatments

Seed piece decay can be a major problem in some years in most production areas. Bacterial seed piece decay is usually caused by the soft rot *Erwinia* bacteria (Chapter 15) and is favored by wet soil. These bacteria can enter through cut surfaces and wounds, but more importantly they may already be present in the tuber lenticels. Under the low-oxygen conditions that develop in waterlogged soils, these bacteria become active and can rapidly decay seed pieces. Fungal seed piece decay is usually caused by several species of the fungus *Fusarium* (Chapter 17). These pathogens need wounds to enter the seed piece, and decay is favored by a wide range of temperature and moisture conditions. Seed tubers with Fusarium dry rot in storage continue to decay when planted.

As a preventative measure against seed piece decay, various treatments in the form of dusts or mists are often applied to cut seed. Seed piece treatments can be applied to seed that is cut and planted or to precut seed before healing begins. Serious problems with seed piece decay are often related to adverse weather during the planting season. If high-quality seed stock is used and properly healed after cutting, seed piece decay is usually minimal if soil conditions at planting and in the first few weeks following planting favor rapid emergence. There may be little benefit from seed piece treatments if soil conditions are optimal at planting and until emergence. However, if unfavorable environmental conditions develop soon after planting, treated seed usually produces a better stand. Because environmental conditions are not always optimal at planting and may change afterward, application of a seed treatment is a valuable precautionary measure. Seed treatments may also be of some use in managing other seedborne diseases, including Rhizoctonia canker, Pythium leak, Phytophthora pink rot, and scab (Chapter 17). These diseases are not major causes of seed piece decay, but chemical treatments can reduce the amount of inoculum of disease organisms carried on the surface of seed pieces.

Seed treatments provide two general benefits. First, they eliminate most fungal pathogens from the surface of the seed tubers and protect them from infection by fungi in the soil. Second, they may promote wound healing of the cut surfaces. Materials labeled for potato seed treatment are primarily fungicides. These fungicides are not systemic and do not affect fungi already inside seed pieces (especially *Fusarium*). They affect only those on the cut surface and in the soil close to the seed piece. Seed piece treatments do not control viruses and provide little direct control of bacteria. None of the treatments affect lenticel-borne *Erwinia* soft rot bacteria. However, because *Fusarium*-infected seed is more susceptible to blackleg (caused by *Erwinia*), controlling *Fusarium* indirectly helps control blackleg. The point to remember is that seed treatments do not cure existing infections. They only prevent new infections. *They cannot make bad seed good!*

Several products are available for seed piece treatment, and most contain the fungicides captan, thiophanate-methyl, thiabendazole, or maneb. The selection of a treatment should be based on product label information, results of local professional evaluations, and personal experience. Thiabendazole is not labeled for use directly on cut seed, except for some dust formulations that are labeled for use on Russet Burbank only. Multiple treatments of seed potatoes with thiabendazole (when they are placed in storage, when they are removed from storage, and when they are cut into seed pieces) may cause abnormal sprouting disorders, such as tuber formation on seed pieces (Plate 3) and may result in reduced stands. This is especially true of round white cultivars, particularly Monona, and with seed lots that are physiologically old.

Some growers successfully treat cut seed with dilute chlorine solutions, but wet treatments of cut seed are always risky and may result in increased amounts of bacterial seed piece decay if the seed pieces are not dried rapidly. It is generally best to avoid any type of liquid treatments for seed pieces.

Seed piece treatments may affect wound healing. Recommended products should not interfere with normal suberization as long as environmental conditions are appropriate. The inert ingredients of seed treatments are usually finely ground minerals (talc, gypsum, diatomaceous earth, or mineral clays) or finely ground bark of trees such as fir or alder. Mineral carriers may absorb moisture under wet conditions and become like wet plaster on the cut surfaces. This reduces the availability of oxygen to the seed and may promote bacterial seed piece decay. Bark carriers tend to make the seed flow more easily through planting equipment, and they wick away moisture from cut surfaces. Fir bark has been reported to enhance wound healing. Because of the advantages of bark, some growers use bark treatments that do not contain any fungicide. The disadvantages of bark-only treatments are that they do not kill fungal pathogens on the surfaces of seed pieces, and they may encourage the growth of nonpathogenic molds on cut surfaces, especially if treated seed pieces are held for more than a few days before planting.

The fungicides used in seed piece treatments are not highly toxic, but like all pesticides they must be handled and applied with care to ensure safety. Seed treatments are usually dusted onto cut seed as it flows by on a conveyor directly from the cutter. The seed is often then moved through a rotating drum apparatus to distribute the treatment more evenly. It is important to check the applicator often to be certain that the treatment is being applied at the labeled rate. Because of the proximity of the cutting and treatment operations, dust control can be a problem, and personnel should wear appropriate dust masks or other protective devices. Improved applicators that contain and recirculate dusts are being developed and will greatly facilitate seed treatment. As with all pesticides, *use only materials registered for use as potato seed piece treatments and apply them according to the label directions.*

Planting the Crop

Proper seedbed condition, especially soil temperature and moisture, is one of the most important factors in ensuring a healthy stand of potatoes. The ideal soil temperature for planting potatoes is 55–60°F. This temperature encourages quick emergence without promoting the growth of seed piece decay organisms. The seedbed should be neither too wet nor too dry—70–80% of available soil water (Chapter 8) is ideal. Planting in either hot or cold soil wetter than this favors bacterial seed piece decay and may result in a poor stand. Planting cut seed pieces in dry, hot soil (especially sandy soil) immediately after cutting results in poor wound healing and thus excessive seed piece decay. Cold seed planted in warm

> **The ideal soil temperature for planting is 55–60°F. This encourages quick emergence without promoting the growth of seed piece decay organisms.**

soil often sweats after planting, and the moisture film increases the potential for bacterial decay. Some physiological disorders may also result from planting in excessively wet or dry soil (Chapter 10). Where center-pivot irrigation is used on extremely sandy soil, preplant irrigation may be necessary to provide appropriate soil moisture and to prevent wind erosion during and after planting. This is preferable to irrigation after planting, which may induce seed piece decay.

Deciding when to plant is an important management decision that can have significant implications for crop health. Try to plant when soil conditions favor rapid emergence. In nonirrigated areas where spring rains are often plentiful, planting is usually a waiting game controlled by the weather. Many growers try to plant early, since early planting may result in greater yield and quality. Because of problems with planting in cold, wet soil, however, it is usually a good

management decision to wait for warmer, drier weather. Other factors affecting the choice of a planting date include the maturity class of the cultivar and the timing of harvests needed for certain markets. Planting should be delayed at least 2 weeks after plow-down of a green manure crop, since the undecomposed residue may favor Pythium seed piece decay.

Potato planters are of four general designs: the picker planter, cup types, the assist-feed planter, and the tuber-unit planter. By far the most commonly used is the picker planter. It operates by forcing sharp metal picks into the seed pieces to carry them out of the hopper and then drop them into the planting shoe (Fig. 4.3). The picks must be of appropriate length, straight, sharp, and spaced to obtain the desired spacing of the seed. A major liability of this type of planter is that punctures are made in the seed pieces. Disease organisms can be carried on the picks and injected into healthy seed. This can be very significant in the spread of the ring rot and blackleg bacteria and some viruses.

Cup planters use a series of cups instead of picks to convey the seed to the soil (Fig. 4.4), thereby lessening the hazard of disease spread. With cup planters, seed size must be quite uniform to avoid skips and doubles and to obtain even spacing of the seed pieces. These planters are well adapted for use with whole seed.

Assist-feed planters are sometimes used in seed-growing operations or in small-acreage production. Seed pieces are mechanically fed onto a rotating spacing disk before being dropped into the furrow. With this type of planter, additional labor is usually needed to place seed in skipped seed pockets and remove excess seed to prevent planting doubles.

The tuber-unit planter combines the cutting and planting operations. It is used mainly for seed potato production. Whole tubers are placed in the seed box, and a pick transports each

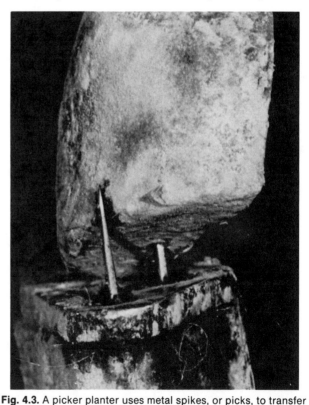

Fig. 4.3. A picker planter uses metal spikes, or picks, to transfer seed pieces from the hopper into the seedbed. Picks can spread pathogens from infected to uninfected seed pieces during planting. (Reprinted, by permission, from Western Regional IPM Project, 1986, Integrated Pest Management for Potatoes in the Western United States, Publication 3316, Division of Agriculture and Natural Resources, University of California, Oakland)

tuber to the cutting knife, where it is cut into four seed pieces. Each seed piece is then planted separately. Equipment may be added to sanitize picks and cutting knives between tubers. The machine has a small capacity, and proper sizing of tubers is essential.

Appropriate spacing of rows and seed pieces within rows depends on several factors, including the cultivar, fertilization program, availability of irrigation, soil type, and expected market. Spacing requirements vary with cultivars, and local recommendations should be obtained. Row widths generally range from 30 to 36 inches, with 34 inches being most common. Spacing within the row may affect the development of some physiological disorders; for example, in highly susceptible cultivars, hollow heart may be minimized by closer plant spacing (Chapter 10). In cultivars with a tendency to develop oversize tubers or set few tubers, such as Katahdin and Kennebec, seed pieces should be spaced 6–9 inches apart within the row. Closer within-row spacing is appropriate where irrigation is used or where moisture is not expected to be a limiting factor. In cultivars that generally produce a heavy set, such as Norchip, seed pieces should be spaced farther apart in the row, up to 11–14 inches in some areas.

Market considerations also affect spacing. Frozen french fry processors prefer large tubers, within limits, and often pay a premium for them if a high percentage is over 10 ounces. Production of large tubers is enhanced by wide within-row spacing. The seed market, however, prefers tubers less than 10 ounces and under 3¼ inches in diameter, and whole B-size tubers often command a premium. Production of tubers in this range is best accomplished with close within-row spacing. Table 4.2 lists seed requirements for several spacings and seed piece sizes.

Appropriate planting depth and soil cover vary in different production areas, because of variations in soil and moisture conditions and established practices. A general practice in northern regions to encourage rapid emergence is to plant 2–4 inches below the surface, with a total soil cover of only 2–3 inches. This helps minimize seed piece decay and the development of Rhizoctonia stem canker. In the West and in any area where moisture may be limiting, seed pieces are usually planted 3–5 inches deep, to ensure that they are covered at all times with moist soil. In some cases, they are planted 6 inches deep in preformed beds. In areas with fine-textured (clay-type) soils, some growers install rippers behind the planter wheels, to allow early-season rains to drain below the planted seed pieces.

Fertilizer may be applied preplant, at planting, postplanting, or at all of these times, depending on the production area and cultural systems used (Chapter 9). Some starter fertilizer is usually applied before planting or banded at planting (or both). Proper fertilizer placement is important, to avoid burning or stressing young sprouts, which may increase their susceptibility to disease.

Herbicides are usually applied either pre- or postplant, but not at planting (Chapter 11). Where preemergence herbicides are used, minimizing field operations between planting and emergence prevents excess soil mixing and thus maximizes the effect of the herbicide.

A systemic insecticide is sometimes applied at planting to control aphids, leafhoppers, and Colorado potato beetles during the first 30–60 days of growth, although this practice is less common now than in the past. Partial control of nematodes may be accomplished in this manner. The needs for early-season insect and nematode control and the potential for groundwater contamination should be taken into account if this practice is under consideration.

Methods of application of all of these materials vary considerably throughout North American potato-producing areas, and various simple and sophisticated methods have been developed. Individual requirements and markets dictate their use and necessity.

Fig. 4.4. A cup planter uses metal cups to transfer seed pieces from the hopper into the seedbed. Since the surfaces of the seed pieces are not broken or penetrated by picks, pathogens are not readily spread during planting. (Reprinted, by permission, from Western Regional IPM Project, 1986, Integrated Pest Management for Potatoes in the Western United States, Publication 3316, Division of Agriculture and Natural Resources, University of California, Oakland)

Table 4.2. Quantity of seed potatoes required per acre for different seed piece sizes and spacings

Row spacing (in.)	Seed piece spacing (in.)	Quantity of seed potatoes (cwt/acre) with average seed size (oz) of:		
		1½	1¾	2
30	8	24.6	28.6	32.6
	10	19.6	22.8	26.1
	12	16.3	19.0	21.8
	14	14.0	16.4	18.7
	16	12.3	14.3	16.3
32	8	22.9	26.8	30.6
	10	18.4	21.4	24.5
	12	15.4	17.9	20.5
	14	13.1	15.2	17.5
	16	11.5	13.4	15.3
34	8	21.6	25.2	28.8
	10	17.3	20.2	23.0
	12	14.4	16.8	19.2
	14	12.4	14.4	16.5
	16	10.8	12.6	14.4
36	8	20.4	23.8	27.2
	10	16.3	19.0	21.8
	12	13.5	15.8	18.1
	14	11.6	13.6	15.5
	16	10.2	11.9	13.6
38	8	19.3	22.6	25.8
	10	15.5	18.1	20.6
	12	12.9	15.0	17.2
	14	11.1	12.9	14.7
	16	9.7	11.3	12.9

Randall C. Rowe
Department of Plant Pathology
Ohio State University, Wooster

Gary A. Secor
Department of Plant Pathology
North Dakota State University, Fargo

CHAPTER 5

Managing Potato Health from Emergence to Harvest

At this point, the foundation for a healthy potato crop has been laid by planting high-quality, certified seed tubers in an appropriate manner on a properly prepared site. A holistic strategy for potato health management includes many practices that have already been implemented by this time and several that begin at harvest. While the crop is growing, however, attention must be focused on changing nutritional and environmental needs and on the development of insects, diseases, and other factors that may limit yield and quality.

Active Management of Potato Health

Managing a potato crop as it grows is a complicated undertaking, because conditions are constantly changing. The potato health manager must be very knowledgeable in order to recognize problems as they develop and deal with them in a timely manner. An effective manager is in the field often throughout the season. A growing potato crop cannot be managed properly from a desk or a pickup truck! Spend time looking at the crop—dig, cut, probe, pull, and examine what you see (Fig. 5.1). Study any plants that look unusual, and

> **An effective manager is in the field often throughout the season. A growing potato crop cannot be managed properly from a desk or a pickup truck!**

try to identify the cause of any problems. If you cannot identify the cause, take representative samples to a reliable and competent expert who can offer ideas, identification, and advice on solutions or management options. It is a wise practice to develop a professional working relationship with several such people before you need their services.

Although many things must be done as the crop grows, all of them focus on three important management objectives:

Objective 1. Provide the best possible conditions for *uniform and continuous growth* of the crop throughout the season, minimizing extremes and excessive fluctuations in soil moisture and fertility.

Objective 2. Monitor weed growth, insect populations, and disease incidence within the crop, and implement appropriate measures when action thresholds are exceeded.

Objective 3. Prevent detrimental environmental impacts that may affect future crop production or environmental quality, such as pesticide drift, groundwater contamination, erosion, soil compaction, and herbicide carryover.

The goal in managing moisture and fertility is to maintain uniform plant growth. If possible, soil moisture should be controlled to avoid excessively wet or dry conditions at any time. Allowing a field to become too dry (less than 60–65% of available soil water) or maintaining the soil too near saturation may induce several tuber disorders. In irrigated production, a precise irrigation management plan should be followed, so that water is applied strictly in accordance with crop demands (Chapter 8). Measures should also be taken to provide for the continuous nutritional needs of the crop, so as to avoid nutrient stresses as well as excesses that may induce growth spurts. A proper nutrient management program should be aimed at maintaining nutrient concentrations in the sufficiency range throughout the growth cycle (Chapter 9).

Not all moisture and nutrient stresses can be avoided, but the more closely this goal is approached, the better the final crop. Failure to achieve this goal has various consequences (Table 8.1). Excess or improperly timed irrigation may cause leaching of nitrates out of the root zone, which adversely affects crop growth and may result in contamination of groundwater

Fig. 5.1. An effective manager is in the field often throughout the season, spending time looking at the crop. (Courtesy D. T. Westermann)

or surface water. Water and fertility management are interrelated with disease management. Most tuber disorders are associated with periods of moisture or temperature extremes that alter tuber growth rates. If vines remain wet too long, because of overirrigation or excessive rainfall, the microenvironment maintained in the crop canopy favors the development of several foliar diseases. Lack of a balanced nutritional program or excessive leaching of nitrate results in undernourished plants with low vigor, which are more

> ## Not all moisture and nutrient stresses can be avoided, but the more closely this goal is approached, the better the final crop.

susceptible to certain diseases. Conversely, excess nitrogen usually results in overgrowth of foliage. A lush canopy maintains a protected, moist microclimate within the soil profile, at the soil surface, and within the canopy—conditions favorable for several foliar and tuber diseases.

Fields should be scouted regularly to accurately monitor weed growth, insect populations, and disease development. Timely cultivation and herbicide application are critical in preventing large weed populations from becoming established within the crop (Chapter 11). Controlling weeds in uncultivated

Plant health management objectives in the growing crop

OBJECTIVE 1
Provide the best possible conditions for uniform and continuous crop growth throughout the season

OBJECTIVE 2
Monitor weed growth, insect populations, and disease incidence, and implement appropriate measures when action thresholds are exceeded

OBJECTIVE 3
Prevent detrimental environmental impacts

areas, fencerows, roadsides, field borders, and ditch banks helps reduce weed populations in the crop and minimizes sites for insect reproduction. Potato foliage should be examined for the presence of key insect pests, especially Colorado potato beetles, aphids, leafhoppers, flea beetles, and psyllids, where appropriate. Because of the devastating potential of bacterial ring rot, growers should always be vigilant for any signs of this disease. Field assessment is also an important component of management programs for early blight and late blight, for which early detection is the key to successful control.

Management programs for key diseases and insect pests have been developed in most production areas. Once the action threshold for any pest or disease has been exceeded, specific management options should be implemented. During crop growth, this usually involves the application of pesticides according to labeled procedures. Other than adjustments in irrigation and fertility, most nonpesticide management options have already been implemented by the time the crop is established. Pesticide application schedules should be based on current field scouting reports or information from disease-forecasting or insect-monitoring devices located in the field or operated regionally. Care must always be taken to avoid nontarget effects when pesticides are used.

It is never a wise practice to apply pesticides routinely, as so-called insurance sprays, without regard to actual pest populations or disease incidence. Aside from the unnecessary expense, routine applications often result in increased pesticide use, which may lead to environmental contamination, development of pesticide-resistant populations of pests or pathogens, and outbreaks of certain nontarget pest species. Keep in mind that specific herbicides, insecticides, and fungicides are active against specific weeds, insects, and diseases. Do not expect pesticides targeted against specific pests to control all other pests at the same time. Some insecticides targeted against specific pests may actually promote outbreaks of other insects previously present in low populations. This usually happens when the pesticide reduces the population of a beneficial nontarget insect that had been holding another pest population in check naturally (Fig. 13.3).

> ## It is never a wise practice to apply pesticides routinely without regard to actual pest populations or disease incidence.

Selection of pesticide-resistant strains of insect pests or disease organisms from the general population, followed by a large increase in their numbers, is another problem associated with overuse of some insecticides and fungicides. This eventually results in a population that is no longer affected by that chemical (Fig. 12.3). The use of several pesticides, representing different chemical classes, in rotation during the season can minimize many of these problems (Chapter 12).

Details for managing water, fertility, and specific pests and diseases are covered in Part Two of this book. The following discussion focuses on the integration of management practices during each of the five stages of potato growth and development (Fig. 1.3). Strategies for management of potato health vary considerably with geography, local practices, the availability of irrigation, management style, and economic considerations. The goal here is to discuss potato health management during crop growth in a logical progression, in order to aid crop managers in devising a holistic management program useful in their own situations.

Planting to Emergence: Growth Stage I

Prior to emergence, sprouts and roots develop from seed pieces. During growth stage I, the seed pieces are the sole energy source for the developing plants. Management operations within the first 2–3 weeks after planting generally focus on weed control. Little can be done at this stage to manage insects or disease.

Drag-off cultivation, using a flex-tine or spike-tooth harrow, is often performed at this time, to level off ridges left at planting and thus encourage rapid emergence of sprouts. Any practice favoring rapid emergence is useful in the management of Rhizoctonia stem canker, because potato stems are much less susceptible to attack after green tissue has developed. Drag-off cultivation also uproots and kills newly sprouted weeds. To prevent injury to developing potato sprouts, this must be done before the sprouts are within 2 inches of the soil surface.

Most weed control practices involve the use of herbicides and timely cultivation. These two practices, integrated effectively, complement one another and overcome certain disadvantages of either used alone. Herbicide usage and cultivation practices vary widely among production regions and between irrigated and nonirrigated systems. Preplant, postplant, and postemergence herbicides can be used effectively (Chapter 11). Local advice should be sought for optimal results.

Herbicide application techniques must be chosen to fit the local situation. If used properly, ground sprayers are the most precise, with the least off-target drift. Aircraft application is suitable in some situations. This method offers several advantages, including rapid treatment of large areas and avoidance of soil compaction, but precautions must be taken to prevent off-target drift. A few herbicides are registered for application through irrigation equipment. In some areas this practice is becoming more common and offers several advantages (Chapter 11).

Water management prior to crop emergence is important. Postplant irrigation is usually not advisable before sprouts emerge, because saturated soils favor seed piece decay caused by bacteria and by *Pythium*. In some areas with very light sandy soil, preemergence irrigation may be necessary to prevent wind erosion or replenish soil moisture. Even in this situation, an increase in seed piece decay may result. In nonirrigated production, the lack of control over soil moisture prior to emergence must be compensated for by careful attention to preplant seed handling and by the use of seed piece treatments.

Vegetative Growth: Growth Stage II

During growth stage II, leaves and branches form aboveground while roots and stolons develop in the soil. Roots begin to take up nutrients from the soil, either from applied fertilizer or from the residual nutrient base. Except in the early part of this stage, the plant is now independent of the seed piece, and energy is supplied by photosynthesis.

As the plants emerge, any problems with stand establishment should be noted and investigated (Fig. 5.2). These may be disease-related (bacterial or fungal seed piece decay or Rhizoctonia stem canker), or they may result from planter skips. The only solution for poor stands during the current year is replanting, but evaluation of these problems may be useful in preventing their reoccurrence in the future.

Managing Nitrogen and Water

Previously applied nitrogen, phosphorus, and potassium should ensure rapid, continuous growth of the developing crop and help suppress diseases favored by nutrient stresses. Except where the growing season is quite short, nitrogen fertilizer is most efficiently used when applied in split applications. Generally, one-third to two-thirds of the total nitrogen requirement can be side-dressed after plant emergence or applied more frequently, but in smaller amounts, with several sprinkler irrigations spaced over the growing season. Split applications of nitrogen generally result in more even growth of the crop and fewer tuber disorders, such as hollow heart, brown center, and knobby or misshapen tubers. Nitrogen fertilizer may be satisfactorily side-dressed at the last hilling operation or at any time until 60 days after planting. Care must be taken to ensure that application equipment does not damage plant roots. Root injury may also occur if high concentrations of ammonia are present or develop in the fertilizer band. Side-dressing fertilizer materials other than nitrogen is generally not recommended (Chapter 9).

Adequate water should be available throughout the growth and development of a potato crop, and wide fluctuations in soil moisture should be avoided whenever possible. Uniform soil moisture minimizes plant stresses that usually lead to lower tuber yield and quality. Irrigated fields should never be allowed to drop below 60–65% of available soil water, and 75–85% is preferable during growth stage II. Soil moisture can be monitored by various direct indicators, such as squeezing a ball of soil, checking lenticel proliferation on tubers, or using an instrument such as a tensiometer. An indirect approach involving a water budget is more commonly used (Chapter 8).

Steps should be taken to avoid excess soil moisture as the plants develop, because this may stimulate blackleg or promote infection by *Verticillium*. Excess or improperly timed irrigation may result in nitrate leaching, which leaves the crop without adequate nitrogen in the root zone and may lead to contamination of surface water or groundwater. Irrigated sands in areas prone to occasional heavy rainfalls should be maintained at slightly lower soil moisture levels, in order to leave enough water storage capacity to reduce the potential for nitrate leaching (Box 9.2).

Hilling and Weed Control

Cultivation during growth stage II involves hilling. Regardless of planting depth, seed pieces should ultimately be about 6–8 inches below the top of the final hill. To accomplish this, ridging or hilling is usually done as the plants develop (Fig. 5.3). A wide, flattened hill is preferable to a sharp, peaked hill. Adequate hilling before row closure is important, so that when tubers develop they are covered with sufficient soil to

Fig. 5.2. As the plants emerge, any problems with stand establishment should be investigated. These evaluations may be useful in preventing similar problems in the future. (Courtesy A. R. Mosley)

avoid sun damage (greening and sunscald) and to minimize infection by the early and late blight fungi. In some production areas, multiple hilling operations are part of the weed control program. Others recommend hill formation all at one time when sprouts have completely emerged, followed by herbicide application and then no further cultivation unless absolutely necessary (Chapter 11).

To effectively kill newly emerged broadleaf weeds while hilling, they must be cultivated before they get past the two-true-leaf stage (Fig. 11.1A). The driest part of the field should be cultivated first, so that uprooted weeds are killed by drying prior to scheduled irrigation or expected rainfall. Cultivating moist soil may allow cultivated weed seedlings to reroot, and it increases soil compaction. Avoid completely covering potato plants during cultivation, as this retards their growth.

The last cultivation, often called lay-by, must form the final hill and mound enough soil around the base of the potato plant to cover and kill any small weeds. This operation must be performed well before row closure. Cultivation and other postemergence field operations done when the plants are so large that significant contact occurs between vines and tractor tires or machinery may result in mechanical transmission of certain viruses, especially potato virus X and potato virus S, and bacterial pathogens, particularly *Erwinia*, which causes blackleg. Because of this, weeds in seed production fields should be controlled with herbicides alone, whenever possible. Cultivating large plants may also cause excessive pruning of roots. Root pruning is commonly a contributing factor to tipburn (Plate 11), a climate-induced disorder caused by excessive water loss from young leaves during hot, dry, windy weather that follows cooler, moist conditions (Chapter 10). Tipburn symptoms are often mistaken for late blight lesions (Plate 54).

Scouting Fields and Treating for Insects

Once the crop is well emerged, insect scouting and disease monitoring should begin. From this point until harvest, each field should be visited at least weekly by the crop manager or by hired specialists to evaluate the development of the crop and to scout for pests and diseases. Proper scouting involves careful examination of plants, especially their lower leaves and the undersides of leaves, where disease symptoms and insects are usually first detected (Fig. 5.4).

Key insects to scout for are Colorado potato beetles, aphids, leafhoppers, flea beetles, and psyllids. Management decisions about control of these insects should be based on accurate estimates of their population densities at each stage of plant development. Action thresholds for these pests are discussed in Chapters 12 and 13. Because these vary considerably among potato-growing regions, at different crop growth stages, and with different insecticides, growers should seek local advice on insect management.

One method of scouting for Colorado potato beetles (Plates 15–18) is to sample 50 whole plants selected randomly throughout the field during the first beetle generation and 50 primary stems during the second generation. Insecticides should not be applied for beetle control until the population exceeds the action threshold. Potato plants can withstand up to 20% defoliation without loss in yield, and excessive insecticide applications often result in a buildup of insecticide-resistant strains of the beetle. Because of the widespread development of resistant strains, the effectiveness of insecticides against the Colorado potato beetle varies throughout North America.

> ## Proper scouting involves careful examination of plants, especially their lower leaves and the undersides of leaves.

Aphid populations should also be monitored during routine scouting. With customary pest management practices, aphids seldom become numerous enough to cause direct injury to potatoes in commercial production. However, they can spread several important potato viruses, and thus special considerations apply to seed potatoes and to commercial production of cultivars (such as Russet Burbank) that are susceptible to net necrosis of tubers (Fig. 14.1) as a result of current-season infection by the potato leafroll virus. Local advice on aphid management should be sought, because appropriate action thresholds and management techniques for aphids vary according to the production area, the cultivar, and the intended use of the crop.

The development of large aphid populations in potato crops is usually associated with the use of insecticides. Insecticide-induced outbreaks (Fig. 13.3) may occur, and insecticide resistance is common in aphid populations, especially in the green

Fig. 5.3. Potato plants are hilled after they are well established, so that the developing tubers will be covered with enough soil to avoid sun damage and to protect them from infection by the early blight and late blight fungi. (Courtesy A. R. Mosley)

Fig. 5.4. When scouting for insects and diseases, scouts must examine the plants carefully, especially the lower leaves and the undersides of leaves, where disease symptoms and insects are usually first detected.

peach aphid. Systemic insecticides applied to the soil at planting may provide good early-season control of aphids but lead to outbreaks later by preventing the establishment of their natural enemies. The first application of almost any foliar insecticide often gives acceptable aphid control. With subsequent foliar applications, however, the density of insecticide-resistant aphids on treated potatoes may increase to a level many times greater than that on untreated potatoes, because of the virtual immunity of the new population. Aphid outbreaks can usually be prevented by delaying insecticide applications until the aphid action threshold has been exceeded and by rotating use of several insecticides of different chemical classes.

The potato leafhopper (Plates 34 and 35) is of great concern to commercial potato producers in eastern North America because of feeding damage to the crop referred to as hopperburn. Other leafhoppers are of less concern, although the aster leafhopper spreads the mycoplasmalike organism that causes purple top (Chapter 14). Leafhopper populations are relatively easy to scout. Adults are best sampled with a sweep net. Nymphs can be counted on randomly selected leaves taken from the middle of the plant. If the number of leafhoppers exceeds the action threshold, insecticides provide the only effective control. Insecticide resistance is not a problem with the potato leafhopper, and almost any registered insecticide is usually effective.

Flea beetle populations are monitored by checking foliage for feeding damage, namely, the number of shotholes per leaf (Fig. 12.7). Sprays for controlling the Colorado potato beetle and aphids usually keep flea beetle populations in check, and specific controls for this pest are rarely needed.

In areas where psyllids occur (Fig. 12.8), it is very important to scout for this pest before initiating any specific control measures, because their occurrence is quite sporadic. Production losses due to psyllid yellows result only from nymph feeding. Feeding by adult psyllids has little effect on production. Scouting should focus on the lower leaves of early-planted potatoes and on solanaceous weeds (such as nightshade, buffalobur, and matrimony vine) growing near or in potato fields. Insecticides provide the only consistent control of psyllids, and treatment should commence when the action threshold is exceeded. It is important to cover the foliage thoroughly and to get spray penetration into the canopy, to control nymphs feeding on the undersides of leaves.

In areas where tuberworm is a problem (Fig. 12.4), it is best to use pheromone traps and base control decisions on the growth stage of the crop and the number of moths caught. Examine the traps every 3–4 days to count the trapped moths (Plate 22). Insecticides should be applied when the number trapped exceeds the appropriate action threshold, which may vary with the potato cultivar and field conditions. It is extremely important to control this pest prior to harvest. However, if moth activity does not reach the threshold before vine kill, treatment is unnecessary, since insecticide application after vine kill is not effective.

Monitoring for European corn borer moths is essential before beginning any control program for this pest. Effective techniques include blacklight traps, pheromone traps, and observation of the emergence of moths from infested cornstalks placed in a screened cage. Potato foliage should be sampled to check for feeding damage (Plate 24) beginning 7–10 days after the first moths are found. Insecticides should be applied only when 15% of the stems are infested. Thorough coverage of the foliage is necessary, since the objective is to kill the larvae while they are still feeding on the foliage and before they bore into the stems.

Monitoring and Treating Diseases

Unlike insect scouting, disease monitoring is primarily aimed at judging the effectiveness of disease control procedures rather than triggering pesticide applications. In monitoring for foliar blights, special emphasis should be given to areas of each field most prone to disease development. These areas, often called blight pockets, are usually located near windbreaks, shelterbelts, woodlots, or other obstructions to air movement, where foliage tends to remain moist for longer periods. Blight pockets also occur in continually wet areas near the center of pivot irrigation systems; in low, poorly drained areas; and in areas adjacent to water, such as farm ponds or streams.

Implementation of control procedures for early blight and late blight (Plates 50–55) is usually based on weather patterns and, to be effective, must be initiated before disease has become well established. Several computer programs have been developed for blight prediction and can help determine if weather conditions have been favorable for disease and when foliar blights are likely to appear (Chapter 16). Weather-monitoring instruments for these must be in place in the field before the crop has completely emerged. Disease prediction programs are especially useful in timing the initiation of fungicide sprays in areas where early blight is the main foliar disease and late blight rarely occurs. Application of fungicides for early and late blight control is usually necessary, especially in eastern North America. Most fungicides registered for blight control are protectant materials, which must be applied before infection has occurred and then reapplied regularly during the season as the plants grow. Complete coverage of foliage is the key to successful use of protectant fungicides. The systemic fungicide metalaxyl has been effective in managing late blight when integrated into a program of protectant fungicide treatment (Chapter 16). Use of this material must be limited, and it must be applied in conjunction with protectant fungicides to avoid the development of metalaxyl-resistant strains of the late blight fungus.

Where Sclerotinia stem rot (white mold) is a significant problem (Plates 58–60), nitrogen applications and irrigation patterns should be managed so as to avoid the development of a dense plant canopy and long periods of leaf wetness. Foliar fungicides may also be necessary to control this disease. Although a single application at row closure may be sufficient, repeated applications are required in some situations (Chapter 17).

Tuber Initiation: Growth Stage III

Growth stage III is a short period, 10–14 days, when tubers form at stolon tips but are not yet appreciably enlarging (Fig. 1.4). Tuber initiation is best monitored directly, by pulling plants and examining the stolons. In many cultivars the end of growth stage III generally coincides with early flowering, when a few open flowers are visible. Proper water management during growth stage III is especially important to the health of the developing crop. Maintaining 80–90% of available soil water during tuber set and enlargement favors rapid plant growth and limits the development of scab (Plate 65) and some tuber disorders, especially translucent end (Plate 8).

Weekly petiole analysis is often begun during growth stage III to monitor the nutritional status of the growing crop (Chapter 9). Foliage is sampled by collecting the petiole of the fourth leaf down from the top of the plant (Fig. 9.4). All leaflets should be stripped from the petiole immediately after sampling. Sometimes foliar applications of nutrients are made in response to petiole analysis. However, only a small portion of the total requirement for nitrogen, phosphorus, potassium, calcium, magnesium, and sulfur can be applied in foliar sprays. Micronutrients should only be applied in response to the results of a soil test or plant tissue analysis. Sufficient amounts of zinc, manganese, copper, boron, and molybdenum can be applied in foliar sprays to satisfy the crop's requirements, particularly with repeated applications. Symptoms of nutritional deficiencies (Box 9.1) are usually not visible when petiole concentrations are in the marginal range, but nutrient applications may be needed if a significant amount of the growing season remains. Details of nutrition management are discussed in Chapter 9.

In irrigated production, nitrogen is often applied with irrigation water throughout growth stage III and much of growth stage IV. Nitrogen applications should be adjusted according to petiole analysis and local recommendations. Heavy applications may lead to excessive vegetative growth, resulting in an extensive foliar canopy and delayed tuber initiation and development. This situation should be avoided, as a continually moist microclimate underneath the canopy may promote the development of aerial stem rot, Sclerotinia stalk rot, late blight, and several tuber rots associated with wet soil.

Scouting for insect pests and monitoring for diseases should continue along with application of appropriate pesticides as needed. If foliar fungicides are directed mainly against early blight, applications can usually be delayed until growth stage III. If the systemic fungicide metalaxyl is used as part of the fungicide program to control late blight or to control leak and pink rot, it should be applied only twice during the season, as specified on the label.

Tuber Bulking: Growth Stage IV

Tuber bulking occurs in a nearly linear fashion following tuber initiation, provided no growth factors become limiting. The majority of the plant nutrients used during the entire growing season are taken up during growth stage IV. Application of nitrogen with irrigation water is most effective at this stage. Prior to the latter part of growth stage III, root systems are generally not sufficient to capture enough sprinkler-applied nitrogen for this method of application to be effective. Foliar application allows nitrogen to be applied according to crop needs and places this nutrient into the root zone for rapid uptake.

Careful irrigation management is essential during tuber bulking to maintain 80–90% of available soil water and to apply nutrients uniformly. Moisture stress during growth stage IV may increase the severity of potato early dying. Over-irrigation must also be avoided, to prevent excessive movement of nitrates below the root zone. Nitrogen-deficient plants are more susceptible to early blight, which is most significant during tuber bulking. Petiole nitrate analysis should be continued throughout this period, to ensure that excess irrigation or rainfall does not lead to undernourishment of the plants.

Excessive irrigation or rainfall promotes several other diseases, by keeping the soil moisture high and vines wet for long periods. Management of the plant canopy and manipulation of the environment within the canopy to reduce the duration of leaf wetness can limit the development of early and late blights, aerial stem rot, Sclerotinia stalk rot, tuber rots such as pink rot and leak, and enlarged lenticels, which may lead to tuber soft rot. Excessive irrigation can also erode hills, thus exposing shallow-set tubers to greening or sunscald and infection by the early and late blight pathogens.

In some production areas, maleic hydrazide is applied in a foliar spray during growth stage IV to inhibit sprouting when the tubers are in storage. The proper time for application is when most tubers are at least 2 inches in diameter, vines are green and actively growing, and no irrigation or rainfall is expected for 24 hours. Read and follow the label directions carefully.

Scouting fields for insects and monitoring for diseases should be at peak activity during growth stage IV. Insecticide applications should be made only when action thresholds are exceeded. Fungicide applications are most critical during this period, to prevent loss of foliage and infection of tubers. Application intervals should be shortened as disease-forecasting programs or actual disease development in the crop warrants. In order to monitor populations of nematode pests that may require treatment after the potato harvest or in future crops, soil samples for nematode analysis should be collected in the root zone no later than 1 month prior to harvest.

Tuber Maturation: Growth Stage V

During maturation the vines slowly senesce and lose leaves, photosynthesis decreases, tuber growth slows, and the skins set. At the end of growth stage V, the vines die or are killed with an herbicide. As the crop matures, the amounts of water and nitrogen applied should be reduced. However, appropriate pesticide applications should be continued until all vines are dead. Details of vine killing and management of crop maturity in preparation for harvest are discussed in the next chapter.

CHAPTER 6

Edwin S. Plissey
Department of Plant, Soil and Environmental Sciences
University of Maine, Orono

Maintaining Tuber Health During Harvest, Storage, and Post-Storage Handling

After producing a healthy crop, the potato health manager has the final task of harvesting the tubers and storing them properly. Thousands of dollars are lost every year by each potato producer because of excessive mechanical damage to crops during harvest and handling operations. For some producers, financial losses due to mechanical damage may exceed 20% of gross income during seasons with adverse harvest and storage conditions.

Three types of mechanical damage occur during harvest: skinning, shatter bruise, and internal blackspot (Chapter 10). In addition to directly reducing the value of the crop, mechanical damage during harvest affects tuber health by facilitating the entry of disease organisms and thus increasing the susceptibility of tubers to breakdown in storage. In severe cases, harvest injury may lead to the complete loss of all tubers in a storage bin. The last stage of a holistic potato health management plan—the maintenance of tuber health through harvest, storage, and post-storage handling—demands dedicated management and a thorough understanding of the potato's vulnerability to its environment.

The Importance of Tuber Quality

Commercial potato marketing is rapidly changing because of consumer demand for quality in both fresh and processed potatoes. A high-quality, healthy tuber commands a high market price and can be sold in a high-value market. A potato sold as a foil-wrapped, premium baker is of far more value than one in a load of culls delivered for cattle feed or starch. Growers should always view the cull box as the Grim Reaper of their operation.

A supply of healthy, damage-free tubers is the first priority for potato processors. To remain competitive, they require a high ratio of finished product to raw product. Accordingly, processors often provide premiums to contract growers to encourage production and delivery of high-quality tubers. These premiums usually include financial incentives for disease- and damage-free tubers, in addition to grade and size incentives.

Producers of seed and fresh-market potatoes must also manage their operations closely to ensure tuber health through harvest, storage, and marketing. Breakdown of tubers during storage makes grading and packing nearly impossible. Producing a healthy potato to harvest and store is the best insurance to enable delivery of a quality product to seed and fresh-market buyers.

A healthy potato crop not only maximizes profits but also minimizes problems and expenses associated with cull disposal. Disposal of cull and waste potatoes raises environmental concerns and can be a significant problem for both growers and processors. In some areas, regulations have been enacted that severely hamper the disposal of cull potatoes. Water and air quality standards may also limit disposal techniques and sites.

Preparing for the Harvest

Managing Crop Maturity

During growth stage V, potato plants must be properly conditioned for harvest if mechanical damage to tubers is to be minimized. In some areas, crops are harvested while the vines are still green and the tubers immature. These potatoes are usually shipped directly to a fresh or processed market, where they are used immediately—before the full effects of harvest damage develop. However, even under these conditions, unhealthy tubers reduce crop quality and user satisfaction.

In most production areas of the United States and Canada, most of the harvested crop is stored before marketing. To facilitate this, growers must produce mature potato tubers that resist mechanical damage during harvest and handling operations. A mature tuber is one that has been managed to achieve full physiological maturity, either naturally or artificially. Physiologically mature tubers are high in total solids and low in reducing sugars and have good skin set.

Timing of operations is critical in managing for a healthy, damage-free potato crop. Early-maturing cultivars, such as Irish Cobbler, Norland, and Superior, are frequently ready for low-damage harvest with minimal preharvest treatment. In many northern production areas, however, damaging frost occurring before all fields are dug frequently complicates planning for tuber maturity and a damage-free harvest, especially with mid- or late-season cultivars. In these areas, early planting and early emergence are essential, to allow time for the crop to approach physiological maturity.

In most situations it is necessary to induce maturity artificially, by careful management of fertility, irrigation, tillage, and vine killing. Nitrogen fertility must be carefully managed, because excessive nitrogen delays maturity, reduces specific gravity, and raises the reducing sugar content. Nitrogen should be applied in amounts that do not exceed the crop's needs, and it should not be applied within 4–6 weeks of vine killing.

In irrigated production, the frequency of irrigation and the amount of water applied should be reduced during tuber maturation to promote skin set. During growth stage V, the percentage of available soil water can be allowed to decline to 60–65% (Chapter 8). High soil moisture should be avoided during maturation, to prevent problems with pink rot, Pythium leak, and enlarged lenticels, which often lead to increased bacterial soft rot in storage. Excessively dry soils should also be avoided, to prevent tuber dehydration, which increases the sensitivity of tubers to blackspot during harvest (Chapter 10). As they dry out, soils with a high clay content also form more clods.

Tillage affects harvest bruising primarily by influencing clod formation. Clods are a significant source of bruising during harvest, and thus tillage and other field operations should be managed to minimize soil compaction and clod formation. In some production areas, deep-tillage root pruning is being tried to encourage partial crop maturity prior to the application of a vine-desiccating herbicide. In this operation, care must be taken to avoid tuber damage and soil cracking, which may expose tubers to dehydration or sunburn. Timely application of vine killer is also essential, to avoid excess tuber dehydration.

Vine Killing

Killing potato vines before harvest is essential in most situations. Vine killing stops tuber growth, stabilizes tuber solids, and promotes skin set (the formation of the outer periderm layer). A mature tuber with a well-set skin is considerably more resistant to injury during harvest, and thus the potential for infection by fungal and bacterial disease organisms through wounds is minimized.

> **A mature tuber with a well-set skin is considerably more resistant to injury during harvest, and thus the potential for infection by fungal and bacterial disease organisms through wounds is minimized.**

Much loss due to disease in storage is directly attributable to failure to achieve proper vine kill and tuber maturation before harvest. Vine killing also helps stop the spread of spores of the early and late blight fungi from foliage to tubers at harvest (Chapter 16), and it limits late-season spread of viruses

---

Box 6.1

A Checklist for Preharvest Storage Inspection

Insulation

The insulation in a potato storage should be inspected to be sure that it is intact in ceilings, walls, and doors. Adequate insulation must be installed in each component to avoid condensation and heat loss. The greater the expected differences between inside and outside temperatures during the storage season, the more insulation needed. For most potato storages in northern areas, a minimum of R-30 in walls and R-40 in ceilings is recommended. Condensation on walls and ceilings and excessive heat loss along perimeter walls are frequently major factors leading to breakdown of tubers in storage. These conditions are favorable for the development of bacterial soft rot and other types of deterioration of processing quality that can result in rejection of entire lots.

Vapor Barrier

The vapor barrier serves two purposes: it maintains the high–relative humidity atmosphere needed to prevent water loss and shriveling of stored tubers, and it prevents water vapor from penetrating the insulation and thereby altering its ability to insulate. To be effective, it must be continuous over all interior storage walls. The preharvest inspection should include a thorough examination and repair of all exposed surfaces of the vapor barrier. In some storages the vapor barrier is an integral component of the insulation.

Fans and Humidifiers

Fans and humidifiers exchange air and add water vapor to the storage environment. Both functions are critical to the maintenance of tuber health in storage. Stored tubers require frequent air exchanges through the pile to remove undesirable products of respiration, namely, carbon dioxide, heat, and excess water vapor. Fans should provide uniform temperature and even distribution of water vapor throughout the storage. The fans and humidifiers should be sized to deliver maximum output during the most difficult storage situations. Fan capacity is rated in cubic feet of air per minute (cfm). At least 1 cfm should be provided for each 100 pounds of stored potatoes.

Before filling the storage, be certain that all bearings are properly lubricated and drive belts are in good repair. After the storage is filled, a smoke bomb may be used to check for proper air distribution through the storage pile. In storages equipped only with perimeter air distribution, a careful inspection must be made to ensure that airflow is uniform throughout the facility and that excess condensation is removed from walls or ceilings by the airflow. Consult with local Cooperative Extension Service advisors or other experts to determine procedures for optimal fan operation in specific storage facilities.

Duct System

The duct system includes a plenum chamber, which usually houses the fan and humidifier, and several ducts, which distribute air uniformly to all storage areas. Ducts usually consist of galvanized culverts, wooden sections, or concrete troughs in the floor covered with boards (see the photograph). Plugged or broken ducts interfere with airflow, which may result in damage to adjacent tubers in the pile. During the preharvest inspection, make sure that

by aphids or mechanical means. Immature tubers are easily infected with dry rot *Fusarium* fungi and soft rot bacteria during harvest if these pathogens are present on tuber surfaces when damage occurs during handling (Chapters 15 and 17).

Timely vine killing also improves the harvest operation by reducing the total vine mass moving through the harvester and by weakening the abscission layer at the point where each tuber connects to its stolon. This allows easier separation of tubers from vines, thus reducing the loss of tubers from the harvester with the devining chains. Vine killing is also useful in controlling tuber size, if that is desirable.

The timing of vine-killing operations is best determined by digging a few hills in several places across a field and examining tuber development (Fig. 6.1). In most production areas, vine killing is done by mechanical or chemical means (using vine-desiccating compounds) or by a combination of these. Flaming is still used to kill vines in a few areas. However, this method is slow, expensive, and environmentally unacceptable. Mechanical vine-beaters are available that are very efficient in shredding vines with minimal physical injury to tubers. Partial vine shredding or rolling of vines frequently enhances the efficacy of chemical desiccants. Very rapid vine killing occasionally induces a discoloration of the tuber vascular ring, often called stem-end browning. This is usually more severe when chemical desiccants are applied at high temperatures when the soil is dry. Stem-end browning may reduce tuber

grade sufficiently to affect the quality of french fries or chips.

Most potato cultivars require at least 10–14 days, and often more, after vine-killing treatment for tubers to mature sufficiently to resist bruising and skinning damage at harvest. During this time it may be tempting to cease applications of pesticides. Fungicide applications should be continued until all vines are dead, to minimize late-season development of spores of the early and late blight fungi, which can infect tubers during harvesting. Cultivars that are susceptible to net necrosis (Fig. 14.1), such as Russet Burbank, should also continue to receive insecticide applications to prevent late-season spread of potato leafroll virus by aphids. Ideally, vines should be dead and dry before harvest begins. Delaying harvest more than 4 weeks after vine kill is also unwise, however, because tubers left in the ground this long are more likely to have excessive numbers of *Rhizoctonia* sclerotia develop on their surfaces (Chapter 17) and may be exposed to cold injury.

Managers unfamiliar with proper vine-killing methods and materials and the appropriate timing of application for their production areas should consult local crop advisors or Cooperative Extension Service specialists.

Preharvest Storage Sanitation and Systems Inspection

A well-designed and operational potato storage facility is necessary for maintaining tuber health after harvest. To keep all ducts are in good repair and are properly sized to provide uniform air distribution.

Doors

Storage doors must function as walls when the storage is in operation. Thus they must be equipped with adequate insulation and vapor barrier to maintain the necessary environment. Doors must seal tightly when closed, to avoid

> **Because of their heavy use, doors are the storage component most often in need of maintenance and repair.**

excessive heat loss during winter and to avoid heat gain from the outside air during warm periods. Because of their heavy use, doors are the storage component most often in need of maintenance and repair. The preharvest inspection is not complete until all doors have been repaired and function properly.

Sensors and Control Panels

In an automated potato storage, the control panel and environmental sensors are critical to successful storage management. An improper installation, malfunction, or sensor failure can quickly lead to a compromised storage environment and subsequent losses in tuber health. All thermocouple

wires should be inspected for proper placement and function. Be certain that automated controls function properly and that all storage systems are well integrated. Determine that dampers and damper motors function properly on demand from the control panel to maintain the storage environment within allowable tolerances.

Potato storage with under-the-pile air ducts in the floor covered with boards. (Used by permission of Spudman magazine)

potatoes healthy for long periods, the storage must be clean, with all systems in good repair. An improperly cleaned and sanitized storage may harbor disease organisms and other pests, such as rodents. Before harvest begins, the walls, plenum areas, air ducts, and floors of the storage should be thoroughly cleaned and sanitized. Details of cleaning and sanitizing storages are discussed in Chapter 4.

Fig. 6.1. The timing of vine-killing operations is best determined by digging a few hills in several places across a field and observing tuber development. (Used by permission of Valley Potato Grower magazine)

After the storage is cleaned, all operating systems should be inspected carefully and repaired as needed (Box 6.1). The insulation, vapor barrier, fan and humidifier components, duct-work, sensory and regulatory components, and doors must all be functional and coordinated to ensure maintenance of the proper environment for long-term storage.

Preharvest Equipment Inspection

Before harvest begins, all harvesting and handling equipment should be inspected to ensure that it is mechanically ready to perform the harvest with a minimum of damage to the crop. Mechanical damage occurs at all points of the harvesting and handling operations (Fig. 6.2). The condition and operation of harvesting equipment greatly affect tuber bruising. Significant bruise damage to more than 3–4% of the crop is excessive; it can be considerably reduced by identifying problem areas and making "low-bruise" modifications to harvest equipment (Box 6.2).

All harvesters, windrowers, bulk trucks, bin pilers, and other equipment used during harvest should be tested and serviced to ensure proper operation during periods of peak use. Worn and damaged parts should be replaced. During each lubrication, equipment should be carefully examined for worn bearings. Gearboxes, transmissions, hydraulic lines, and reservoirs should be checked for leaks and repaired. Electrical systems should be inspected and repaired as needed. Rubberized chains that have become hard and brittle from being stored outside and exposed to bright sunlight should be replaced, because they will no longer protect tubers from bruising during harvest. Before use, all equipment should be thoroughly cleaned and sanitized, to prevent potential contamination of freshly harvested tubers with disease organisms. Steam cleaning is especially effective for this job (Chapter 4).

Managing the Harvest Operation

Training Personnel in Low-Bruise Philosophy

Personnel involved in the potato harvest are just as important as the equipment in minimizing harvest damage. A properly trained crew working together with bruise control as a common

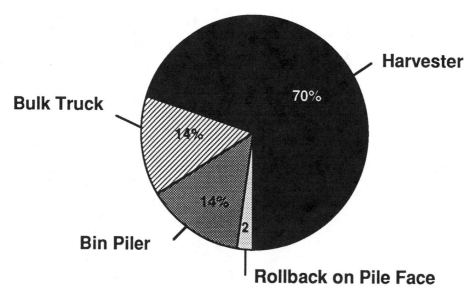

Fig. 6.2. Sources of mechanical injury to potato tubers. Mechanical injury occurs at all points of the harvesting and handling operation. (Adapted from G. D. Kleinschmidt and M. K. Thornton, 1991, Bruise-Free Potatoes: Our Goal, Bulletin 725, University of Idaho Cooperative Extension System, Moscow)

objective is necessary to ensure the delivery of healthy potatoes into the storage. The entire harvest staff must understand that even though the best management practices have successfully readied the crop for harvest, tubers remain very susceptible to skinning and bruising when handled. A team attitude should be developed, with each member of the crew constantly striving to protect quality at each step as the potatoes move from the field into the storage bin.

> ## A properly trained crew working together with bruise control as a common objective is necessary to ensure the delivery of healthy potatoes into the storage.

Operators of harvesters, windrowers, bulk trucks, and bin pilers are key staff in minimizing tuber damage during harvest. They should ensure that all drops are held to a minimum, preferably less than 6 inches. They should be made aware of the damage that can result from improper operation of their equipment, inattention, and neglect of maintenance. The potato health manager should train all staff to examine equipment during routine maintenance and lubrication shutdowns and to identify and correct any problems that may cause tuber damage.

Harvester and windrower operators should be instructed to maintain enough soil on the primary beds to cushion the tubers and ensure an even flow onto the secondary beds. Remind them that agitation of the primary bed chains should be held to the absolute minimum necessary to achieve adequate separation of the tubers from the soil. Bulk truck operators should be instructed to coordinate field operations closely with the harvester operator, to avoid dropping tubers into the truck from excessive heights or allowing the loading boom to plow into the potatoes piled on the truck (Fig. 6.3). Once loading is complete, the truck operator should carefully tarp the load and avoid walking on the potatoes. Truck and bin piler operators must work together to ensure that the flow of potatoes out of the truck box and the capacity of the bin piler are matched in order to keep the conveyor on the piler filled to capacity at all times. Several instructional videos are available to assist in training personnel in low-bruise operations and general harvest safety procedures (see Sources of Additional Information, at the back of this book).

Using Bruise Detection Techniques

Some bruise damage to potato tubers is obvious upon inspection, but fresh bruises often involve hairline cracks or internal shatter bruises that are difficult to detect visually. Tissue bruises may also occur beneath unbroken skin and develop into blackspot, which cannot be detected without peeling. Details of bruise damage are discussed in Chapter 10.

Techniques are available for monitoring bruise damage at harvest and pinpointing operational and mechanical adjustments needed to minimize bruising. Fresh bruises that break the skin can be detected with a solution of catechol (Box 6.3). The percentage of bruised tubers and the amount and severity of bruising per tuber in a sample can be determined by the catechol test. In large operations, managers frequently collect 20- to 30-pound test samples at regular intervals and determine the amount of damage as a percentage by weight.

Internal blackspot does not begin to develop in bruised tissues for 6–8 hours after the damage has occurred, and it does not fully develop for a day or so. To detect blackspot

bruising, tuber samples can be held at room temperature for at least 24 hours and then peeled. Blackspot is readily apparent as a bluish gray to black discoloration just under the skin (Plate 10). The holding period can be shortened to 8 hours if the tuber sample is maintained at 100°F in a hot-water bath. Blackspot can also be detected with a solution of triphenyltetrazolium chloride (Box 6.3).

When tubers are being checked for blackspot, the first sample should come from the storage pile. If blackspot is found, samples should be collected at other harvesting and handling points, to determine where the damage is occurring. Large tubers are most susceptible to blackspot and should be selected for the first sample. If significant bruising is found, progressively smaller tubers should be tested.

Many processors include a bruise-damage clause in their contracts and penalize commercial producers for delivery of potatoes with excessive mechanical damage. Processors frequently collect samples from delivered loads, hold them for 1 or 2 days, and then steam or abrasion-peel them to detect blackspot bruises. A federal or state inspector is often employed, with the approval of the producers, to make impartial judgments about the extent of bruise damage in the delivered potatoes.

Timing the Harvest

The timing of the harvest can significantly affect tuber health throughout storage and marketing. In northern areas, the harvest should begin early enough to be completed before a hard frost is likely. Potatoes intended for long-term storage should not be harvested until the vines have been dead for at least 10–14 days, to allow for skin set. Immature tubers easily skin or "feather" during harvest and handling and do not store well.

Once harvesting has begun, soil moisture and temperature must be monitored closely. Optimal harvest conditions are 60–65% of available soil water and tuber pulp temperatures of 50–65°F (Fig. 4.2). Potatoes harvested from cold, wet soil are more susceptible to bruising, more difficult to cure, and more prone to breakdown in storage.

The amount of tuber hydration closely parallels soil moisture. Overhydrated tubers harvested from wet soil are highly sensitive to shatter bruise, especially when the pulp temperature is below 45°F. Slightly dehydrated tubers taken from dry soil are less sensitive to shatter bruise but are highly sensitive to blackspot (Chapter 10). Intermediate levels of tuber hydration are the best compromise to minimize overall bruise

Fig. 6.3. Good coordination between the harvester operator and the bulk truck operator is necessary to avoid dropping tubers into the truck from excessive heights or allowing the harvester's loading boom to plow into the pile of tubers on the truck. (Courtesy A. R. Mosley)

Box 6.2

Equipment Modifications for a Low-Bruise Harvest

Considerable research has been done to identify the areas in harvest and handling equipment where the most bruise damage to tubers occurs during the harvest operation. The modifications described here can be made to existing equipment to reduce bruising and promote the goals of a low-bruise harvest. When new equipment is being purchased, it is wise to look for these features as part of the original design.

Harvester

The harvester is the major source of mechanical damage to tubers (Fig. 6.2). Several modifications can be made that together reduce damage to tubers as they flow through the machine.

The digging blade on the harvester should be matched to the soil texture and be positioned so that the flow of soil and tubers is delivered up onto the digger chain, rather than bumping into the front of it. Hinged metal plates can be installed at the back of the digger blade to bridge the gap and rise from the blade to the primary chain bed.

With hooked chain on the primary conveyor, all links in the chain should be down links if bruise damage there is mainly due to pinching of tubers. If, however, bruise damage on the primary results mainly from an inability to separate soil from tubers without excessive shaking or rollback (mostly a problem with round tubers), a configuration with one straight link and three or four down links provides positive tuber movement and increased soil separation.

Ideally, all hooked chain on the harvester should be replaced with belted chain, which virtually eliminates pinching of tubers. Other improvements that should be considered are hydraulically activated shakers on the primary bed, to improve operator control of soil separation, and full-width belted primary chain, particularly if windrowers are used with the harvester. When potatoes that have been windrowed into the furrow between rows are being picked up by the harvester, considerable damage to tubers is inflicted by the lag hooks of the twin-bed harvester chain. A full-span belted primary chain with accompanying full-span lifting blade delivers windrowed potatoes onto the harvester with a minimum of bruising. Belting or rubberized deflectors should be installed along the sides of the conveyors to deflect tubers away from the gap between these areas and the edge of the chain.

The secondary conveyor on the harvester should operate in conjunction with the overriding deviner chain, if one is present. The deviner is frequently a major source of tuber damage on both harvesters and windrowers. If the first one or two sets of deviner chain rollers are removed, the chain runs flat on the secondary conveyor for the first few inches following the drop from the primary conveyor. Before this is done, the secondary chain speed and the deviner chain speed must be measured and adjusted so that they are the same. This rather inexpensive modification can result in a significant reduction in bruise damage on many harvesters.

It is important to minimize the drop from one conveyor system to another, as these can be major sources of bruise damage. The drop from the secondary chain to the rear cross conveyor is the largest one on most harvesters. The 90° change in direction of the potato flow, in addition to the drop, increases the potential for damage at this point. The best padded chains available should be installed on the rear cross conveyor to help reduce bruise damage. In addition, the upper end of the secondary chain should be modified to minimize the drop, by installation of a dogleg drive sprocket, which can decrease this drop to 6 inches or less. This modification is most easily achieved if belted chain is used on the secondary bed.

Modifications at both ends of the rear cross elevator may significantly reduce bruise damage. A split secondary chain can be used, with the inside of the secondary extended over the rear cross elevator; the extension should be about one-third of the width of the rear cross. Similarly, the rear cross conveyor can be extended over the side elevator, just enough to avoid damage at the inside corner, where the end of the rear cross meets the inside of the side elevator conveyor. Additional padding and chain edge deflectors can also be installed in the side elevator conveyor to reduce bruising.

Bruising due to rollback is a serious problem on the side elevator, because the angle of flow is rather steep. Rollback can be reduced by operating the chain at a speed that allows it to remain full of material. If this cannot be done, rollback can be reduced by installing a plastisol flight link every eight lengths of the side elevator chain. The plastisol material is stiffer at the wing ends of the flight and thus reduces rollback along the elevator edges. Another way to reduce rollback is to install a hugger belt on the side elevator conveyor.

The drop from the side elevator to the front cross conveyor is also a key site for bruising, especially if many stones are present. This drop should be minimized as much as possible. Deflector belting is essential on the sorting table, to cover hooked or belted chain edges, where bruise damage often occurs. Exposed chain edges at the sorting table are also a safety hazard, as they are places where harvest personnel might catch their fingers.

All areas of potato flow on the harvester should be examined carefully, and padding devices should be installed wherever possible, to reduce the tuber buffeting that causes mechanical damage.

Harvester Chain Speed Calibration

An important low-bruise principle is that all chains on the harvester should be filled to capacity at all times during operation, to prevent bouncing, buffeting, and rollback of tubers. To accomplish this, the chain speed and the forward ground speed must be coordinated, so that the volume of material handled on each chain is equal to its capacity. Chain speed can be calculated from the chain's length and its number of revolutions per unit of time.

First, measure the circumference of the chain with a flexible tape. Next, mark the chain with spray paint, and then time it as it makes one full revolution. The chain speed (in feet per second) is equal to the chain length (in feet) divided by the time taken for one revolution (in seconds).

To express the speed in miles per hour, multiply the number of feet per second by 0.68. The desired speed of various harvester chains in relation to ground speed has been established for most areas and can be obtained from local advisors. Adjustments to chain speed should be based on these recommendations.

Details of harvester modifications and chain adjustment to minimize bruising have been outlined in several bulletins and in three videos prepared by the National Potato Anti-Bruise Committee in cooperation with the University of Idaho and Washington State University (see Sources of Additional Information, at the back of this book). Local advisors or potato specialists with the Cooperative Extension Service should be consulted to obtain these and other sources of more detailed information.

Bulk Trucks

There is considerable potential for damage to tubers during handling between the harvest operation and the warehouse (Fig. 6.2). Bulk truck bodies should be inspected, and any rough areas that could cause injury during handling should be repaired or padded to protect the crop. Unloading chains or belts should be repaired or modified to minimize damage during unloading. Bulk trucks should be equipped with tarps or mechanical covers to protect potatoes from wind, rain, or sunburn during transit. A self-tarping mechanism can be installed to avoid any need for walking on the potatoes when the truck is being covered (see the photograph below).

Bin Piler

The bin piler is another significant source of bruise damage as the crop is moved into storage (Fig. 6.2). All rough or abrasive surfaces should be padded with protective foam or rubber cushioning. The piler should be modified to limit all drops to 6 inches or less. If necessary, the stinger end of the piler should be modified so that it can be raised up under the bulk truck's unloading belt sufficiently to minimize the drop of tubers into the hopper. All switches and control levers on a bin piler should be located conveniently for the operator, to ensure operation with minimal damage to the crop. The chain speed of the bin piler and the rate of unloading of all bulk trucks should be adjusted so that the bin piler conveyors remain filled to capacity at all times. To accommodate different unloading rates, a variable speed control can be installed on the conveyor system.

When purchasing a new bin piler, look for features that will reduce bruising. Select a unit with a wide, shallow, well-padded hopper with sufficient capacity to prevent spill-out and with fingertip-adjustable height to minimize the drop from the truck. Rubberized draper chain or belted chain on the unloading conveyor is desirable, as it allows any remaining soil to sift out before the potatoes flow into the bin. The length of the boom conveyor should be about double the planned depth of the pile. To avoid rollback, the boom conveyor should never be operated at an angle greater than 45° from the floor. Hugger belts installed on the piler also minimize rollback (see the photograph below). Additional features, such as a sorting table, a sizing chain area, a telescoping boom, variable conveyor speed, and multiple stingers, may make bin piling more efficient and may significantly reduce tuber damage during operation.

Bulk truck with self-tarping mechanism. (Used by permission of Spudman magazine)

Bin-loading conveyor with hugger-belt system, which prevents tuber rollback. (Used by permission of Spudman magazine)

damage (Fig. 6.4). Soil moisture at harvest also has other effects. Dry, cloddy soil may result in more bruising, and wet soil is difficult to separate from tubers. Tubers from wet soil may also become oxygen-starved and have enlarged lenticels (Fig. 10.1), conditions that increase their susceptibility to decay.

Proper pulp temperature at harvest is critical. Harvest operations should not begin until tuber pulp temperatures are at least 45° F, and preferably 50° F. Tubers become much more sensitive to bruising at pulp temperatures below 50° F (Fig. 6.5). If the soil is frosty or the air temperature is near or below freezing, it is best to begin harvest later in the morning, when temperatures have risen, and then work into the evening. Soil temperatures are usually highest from 11 A.M. to 11 P.M. (Fig. 6.6). Tuber pulp temperatures can also be too high—harvest should be delayed if they are above 65° F. Tubers harvested with pulp temperatures above 70° F are very susceptible to breakdown in storage due to bacterial soft rot or Pythium leak (Chapter 17). Thus, in warm weather, the early morning hours may be the best time for harvest.

Harvest scheduling is often unpredictable, with weather

Box 6.3

Chemical Tests for Bruise Detection

Fresh Breaks in the Skin

An easy test for detecting any fresh bruises that break the skin, such as shatter bruises or skinning, is to soak tubers in a solution of catechol. This chemical reacts with an enzyme present in exposed tuber tissues, and thus it detects only fresh bruises. It does not detect internal blackspot. The procedure for the catechol test is as follows:

1. Mix 1 ounce of catechol in 1 gallon of clean tap water. Add a teaspoon of liquid detergent as a wetting agent.

2. Wash the tubers to be tested.

3. Immerse the washed tubers for 5 minutes in a bucket containing the catechol solution.

4. Remove the tubers, drain them, and set them aside for about 10 minutes, to allow the reaction to proceed. Bruised and skinned areas gradually turn dark red to purplish black (see the photograph).

Catechol stains tubers dark red to purplish black, revealing fresh bruises that break the skin. (Courtesy R. W. Chase)

5. To evaluate bruise severity, use a vegetable peeler to remove successive layers of tissue from the damaged area. If the tuber is simply skinned, one stroke of the peeler usually removes all visible coloration. If slight bruising has occurred, two strokes are usually required. Where three or more strokes are required, a severe bruise has occurred—generally, a deep shatter bruise.

6. Dispose of the treated tubers in a way that will ensure they will not be consumed by humans or animals.

Use caution in handling the catechol solution. Avoid spilling it on the skin or clothing or getting into the eyes. Use rubber gloves throughout the test. Remove and thoroughly wash any soiled clothes immediately. Do not use the containers in this test for any other purpose. Do not discard any remaining catechol solution where it might enter a water source.

Internal Blackspot

A quick and simple chemical stain test using a solution of triphenyltetrazolium chloride allows the detection of blackspot bruises within 40 minutes. The procedure for the test is as follows:

1. Prepare a 1% solution of triphenyltetrazolium chloride in clean tap water.

2. Wash and thinly peel the tubers selected for testing.

3. Immerse the peeled tubers for about 40 minutes in a bucket containing the tetrazolium solution.

4. Bruises appear as light to dark pink areas on the peeled tuber surface. The color reaction may occur in as little as 10 minutes in some tubers. The reaction and intensity of the stain may be improved by conducting the test with warm water (70° F) and in bright sunlight. Experience is needed to detect blackspot bruises consistently with this test.

5. Dispose of the treated tubers in a way that will ensure they will not be consumed by humans or animals.

Because the chemical agent used in this test is toxic to humans, the same precautions apply here as in the catechol test.

always a significant factor. Fall rains and early frosts often hamper operations. Good managers base their harvest decisions on soil and crop conditions, weather forecasts, and their own experience. In spite of best intentions, however, optimal harvest conditions are not always present, and compromises sometimes must be made. Keep in mind that the more closely

Harvest operations should not begin until tuber pulp temperatures are at least 45°F, and preferably 50°F.

harvest operations can be made to coincide with favorable environmental conditions, the healthier the crop delivered to storage will be.

Operating the Harvester

The most important principle in minimizing bruise damage during digging is that the volume of soil, tubers, and other material moving through the harvester should be held at capacity at all points in the machine. Operating the harvester with the chains filled below capacity causes tubers to bounce and roll excessively and greatly increases the amount of bruise damage. Operating with the chains overfilled also results in increased bruising, due to excessive rollback.

The digger blade must be set deep enough to lift the maximum amount of tubers with minimal damage. If it is set too deep, the machine becomes overloaded with soil, and the result is poor separation of tubers. For each inch the blade is set too deep, the harvester handles about 1 ton of extra soil per minute for each row. If the blade runs too shallow, however, it cuts many tubers, and insufficient soil is carried up the primary chain. It is important to carry a layer of soil one-half to two-thirds of the way up the primary chain to cushion the tubers. Operators should closely monitor supplemental agitation of the primary chain and reduce it if tubers are bouncing. Chain agitation should be stopped if an appropriate cushion of soil cannot be maintained up the primary, which is often the case with dry, sandy soil.

To keep the machine filled to capacity with soil and tubers, forward speed and chain agitation must be adjusted as conditions change within a field. Some harvesters are equipped with a variable chain speed, allowing an additional adjustment. The harvester operator should visually judge changing conditions and adjust the forward speed or the blade depth to maintain the desired amount of soil on the primary bed.

Windrowers are used routinely in some production areas. Two or more rows are dug with a windrower, and the tubers are placed on the ground between adjacent undug rows (Fig. 6.7). A harvester then follows and digs these adjacent rows, picking up the windrowed tubers at the same time. This not only increases the efficiency of the harvester but also helps lower overall bruising, by increasing the volume of tubers going through the machine, thus making it easier to keep the chains filled to capacity at all times.

Weather governs the management of windrowing operations. If tubers dug by the windrower are damp, they can be allowed to dry on the ground for 30–45 minutes before being harvested. Dry tubers, however, should be picked up immediately, to avoid dehydration. If pulp temperatures are near 50°F and the air temperature is below that, windrowed tubers should be picked up immediately, to avoid further cooling. If pulp temperatures are closer to 65°F and the air temperature is above that, they should also be harvested immediately, to avoid further warming. Windrowed potatoes should not be left lying on warm, moist soil, because these conditions favor rapid development of Pythium leak after the tubers are in storage. Any windrowed potatoes exposed to rain should be kept separate and marketed immediately, as they may not store well.

One of the most serious errors is to harvest potatoes from low, poorly drained areas of a field where water may have stood. These tubers are much more susceptible to bacterial

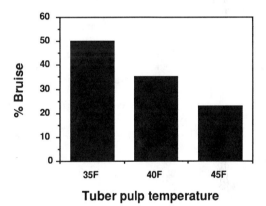

Fig. 6.5. Average bruise damage to tubers during handling at various pulp temperatures. (Adapted from G. D. Kleinschmidt and M. K. Thornton, 1991, Bruise-Free Potatoes: Our Goal, Bulletin 725, University of Idaho Cooperative Extension System, Moscow)

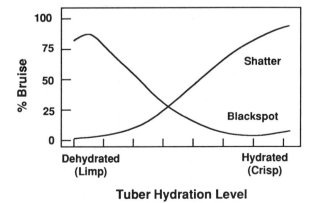

Fig. 6.4. Effect of tuber hydration level on blackspot and shatter bruise injury during harvest. (Reprinted, by permission, from R. E. Thornton and H. Timm, 1990, Influence of fertilizer and irrigation management on tuber bruising, American Potato Journal 67:45-54)

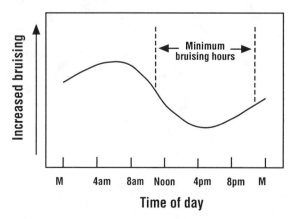

Fig. 6.6. Effect of the timing of harvest operations on injury to tubers during harvest as a result of daily changes in soil temperature. (Adapted from G. D. Kleinschmidt and M. K. Thornton, 1991, Bruise-Free Potatoes: Our Goal, Bulletin 725, University of Idaho Cooperative Extension System, Moscow)

soft rot, Pythium leak, and pink rot. If dug and mixed with healthy tubers in storage bins, they can be a major source of breakdown during storage. It may be best to leave tubers from such areas unharvested, but if they are dug, they should be kept separate and marketed immediately.

In areas where potatoes are grown in stony soils, some harvesters are equipped with air-vacuum devices to assist in separating tubers from stones as they pass by on the conveyor. The air-vac system takes advantage of the lower density of potatoes (a potato may weigh half as much as a stone of the same size) to lift them from among the stones and place them onto the sorting or boom conveyor. With ideal soil moisture, harvesters equipped with air-vacs are 95–98% effective in separating potatoes from stones. In Maine, machines equipped with air-vacs have caused less bruise damage under these conditions than some conventionally equipped harvesters. Harvester operation must be monitored closely. The volume of stones plus tubers must be considered in order to determine the appropriate forward speed to chain ratio needed to minimize tuber damage. After stones have been removed by an air-vac, the appropriate chain speed is related only to the volume of tubers.

Because stony soils compound the potential for bruise damage during harvest, growers who produce potatoes on such soils should develop a management plan for removing stones from the field. Stone removal should be a standard practice either before or after each potato crop. The harvester can be equipped with a stone-receiving hopper, and the separated stones should be placed in windrows in the field, to be removed after harvest by special stone-picking equipment.

Placing the Crop in Storage

Transporting potatoes in open trucks in cold weather is very risky. Low temperatures affect exposed potatoes in an open truck much as human skin is affected by windchill. Chilling injury predisposes potatoes to breakdown in storage. Exposure to hot sun during transport may warm tubers excessively. Even mild sunburn interferes with wound healing in storage and may promote the development of Pythium leak or Fusarium dry rot. To avoid these problems, bulk trucks should be covered with a tarp after loading. It is especially important to protect harvested tubers from rain.

Since storage facilities are often located some distance from harvest sites, crews are usually rushed to get the trucks unloaded and back to the field. Rushing the unloading operation, however, often leads to additional bruising. To ensure tuber health in storage, unloading must be managed as carefully as harvesting. Assign one person to operate the bin piler who is properly trained in low-bruise operation of this machinery. Be certain that personnel do not walk on the potatoes during unloading. Feed the potatoes out of the truck at an even rate, and keep the unloading conveyor tight up under the back of the truck. A rubber spout is useful for buffering the drop of the tubers onto the conveyor. As always, the drop should not exceed 6 inches. Bin-loading conveyors, just like harvesters, must be operated fully loaded to prevent bouncing and rollback. To accomplish this, the conveyor speeds must be matched to the rate of unloading the truck, and the speed of each successive conveyor must be matched to the delivery capacity of the preceding one. Hugger belts installed on bin-loading conveyors also help reduce bouncing and rollback (Box 6.2). When a truck has been unloaded, shut off all conveyors. When shut off, they should be left full, rather than being emptied and refilled with the next truck.

If any significant amount of disease or frost damage is evident, or if excessive amounts of stones or debris are present, the tubers should be graded to remove culls, stones, and debris before being placed in storage (Fig. 6.8). Never wash potatoes before placing them in storage—washed potatoes do not store well. Crops containing over 1–2% blighted or soft-rotted tubers should be isolated from lots of healthy tubers and marketed quickly, as long-term storage of such crops is usually unsuccessful (Chapter 16).

To control Fusarium dry rot, the fungicide thiabendazole (TBZ) is often applied to tubers as they are placed in storage (Chapter 17). TBZ is applied as a fine mist from an applicator mounted on the bin piler at a point where most of the free soil has been removed from the tubers. Complete coverage of all tuber surfaces is necessary. Follow the directions on the label carefully. A very low application rate should be maintained, to avoid wetting the tubers before putting them into storage.

In bin piling, a progressive or stepped piling procedure minimizes rollback on the pile face (Fig. 6.9). An even flow of potatoes should be maintained on the bin piler, which should be kept as full as possible, to avoid rollback. Avoid high

Fig. 6.7. A windrower digs two or more rows and places the tubers on the ground between adjacent undug rows. A harvester then follows and digs these adjacent rows, picking up the windrowed tubers at the same time. (Used by permission of Spudman magazine)

Fig. 6.8. Potatoes are graded before being placed in storage, to remove diseased or frost-damaged tubers along with excessive amounts of stones or debris. (Courtesy R. C. Rowe)

conveyor speeds that fling potatoes against the ceiling, bulkheads, or walls. Keep the boom close to the top of the pile, to minimize the drop. Short, frequent movements of the piler limit the height of the drop and evenly distribute any soil or debris carried onto the face of the pile. Any pockets of soil within the pile prevent uniform airflow and may promote bacterial soft rot. In-floor air duct slots located under conveyors and bin pilers should be covered during the piling operation, to prevent them from being filled with soil, which would interfere with air distribution after the pile is formed. Tubers should not be piled more than 10–12 feet deep, to avoid excessive pressure bruise.

Maintaining Tuber Health Through the Storage Cycle

An important principle for the potato health manager to keep in mind is that even the best storage can only maintain the quality of the tubers put into it. Tuber health never improves in storage. The potato tuber is a living organism, even though it is dormant during most of the storage period. Stored tubers utilize oxygen and produce heat, moisture, and carbon dioxide. A proper storage environment is essential for controlling respiration, water loss, and sprouting. It is also the key factor in maintaining tuber health during storage by promoting wound healing and preventing disease, pressure bruise, and excessive accumulation of reducing sugars in the tissues.

> ### Even the best storage can only maintain the quality of the tubers put into it. Tuber health never improves in storage.

Tubers undergo several distinct physiological stages during the storage cycle: 1) a curing or "sweat" period, during which harvest wounds heal, 2) a cooling period, when the pulp temperature is lowered as appropriate for the intended use of the tubers, and 3) a holding period, during which the tubers are dormant at first and respiration is low, and then dormancy is broken, respiration increases rapidly, and sprouting may occur. Modern storages are designed to facilitate the precise management of temperature, humidity, and air movement needed at each of these stages to hold tubers in ideal market condition (Table 6.1). Minimizing losses in tuber weight and quality during storage is critical to profitability. Preventing weight loss is also necessary to slow the physiological aging of seed potatoes.

The Curing Period

Despite precautions taken during harvest and handling, some injury to tuber surfaces will occur. A curing or sweat period must be provided to promote suberization of wounds prior to long-term storage. Proper suberization is the key to minimizing losses in storage. Weight loss, which occurs most rapidly during the first month of storage, can be slowed dramatically with proper suberization. In addition, rapid wound healing minimizes infection by disease organisms present on tuber surfaces at harvest and greatly improves the ability of tubers to resist infection throughout the storage period. Details of the suberization process are discussed in Chapter 4 under the topic of seed cutting.

Although suberization can be completed in a few weeks under ideal conditions, most storage bins are filled over a period of several weeks. The curing period for a given storage should be considered to begin when the first potatoes are placed in the bin and end when suberization is complete for the last potatoes placed there—usually a total of 6–8 weeks. Crop management during this time sets the stage for the entire storage season.

Suberization is greatly affected by temperature, oxygen and carbon dioxide levels, and humidity. Although the process occurs most rapidly at about 70° F, compromises must be made to prevent tuber decay. Most pathogens decline in activity at lower temperatures. If the crop is generally healthy, the curing temperature can safely be maintained at 57–60° F. However, if any significant amount of tuber disease is present, a curing temperature nearer to 50° F is preferable. Tuber pulp temperatures should be continually monitored with a pulp thermometer (Fig. 4.2) or with thermocouples placed in tubers within the pile. The temperature of the return air supply should also be monitored, since it indicates conditions at the top of the pile.

> ### Free water on tuber surfaces inhibits the exchange of oxygen and carbon dioxide and promotes bacterial soft rot.

Air movement within the pile is essential during the curing period. Evenly distributed airflow is necessary for controlling temperature, providing oxygen, and removing carbon dioxide and excess moisture. The airflow should be sufficient for cooling without causing tuber desiccation. To prevent weight loss and promote rapid suberization, the relative humidity of the supply air must be kept above 95%. It is, however, very important that condensation not develop on the tubers. Always remember that free water on tuber surfaces inhibits the exchange of oxygen and carbon dioxide and promotes bacterial soft rot.

Since relative humidity and air temperature are interrelated, differences between the supply air temperature and the tuber pulp temperature must be monitored closely. If saturated air much colder than the tubers is forced through the pile, it will be warmed by the tubers, and the relative humidity will drop considerably. This may result in tuber dehydration and increased pressure bruising. Conversely, if saturated air warmer than the tubers is introduced, condensation will occur on cold tuber surfaces, and this favors the development of bacterial soft rot. The best practice is to monitor the tuber pulp temperature carefully and keep the supply air just a few degrees cooler until the pile is cooled to the desired curing temperature. After that, the supply air should be kept at the same temperature as the tubers.

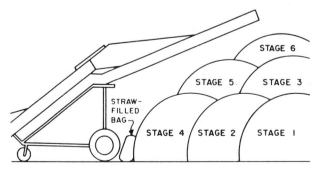

Fig. 6.9. A progressive or stepped bin-piling procedure minimizes the rollback of tubers on the pile face. (Reprinted, by permission, from G. D. Kleinschmidt and M. K. Thornton, 1991, *Bruise-Free Potatoes: Our Goal*, Bulletin 725, University of Idaho Cooperative Extension System, Moscow)

Table 6.1. Environmental management for tuber health in storage

	Curing period	Cooling period	Holding period	Marketing period
Temperature	Maintain tuber pulp temperature at 57–60°F if tubers are healthy 50°F if some tuber decay is present	Rapidly cool seed and fresh-market tubers to the appropriate holding temperature Slowly cool processing tubers, lowering tuber pulp temperature by 2–3°F per week	Maintain tuber pulp temperature at 38–40°F for seed and fresh-market tubers 45°F for french fry processing tubers 50–55°F for chip processing tubers	Warm slowly to 50–55°F over several weeks
Relative humidity	Maintain at 95–99%	Maintain at 95–99%	Maintain at 90–95%	Maintain at 90–95%

The storage manager must be aware of the amount of disease in lots of tubers coming into storage in order to properly manage the curing period. Storage of tubers with a substantial amount of disease is difficult. If more than 1–2% of the tubers have symptoms of bacterial soft rot, late blight, pink rot, or Pythium leak, or if a similar proportion are frost-damaged, they should be cooled to below 50°F immediately after being placed in storage. The problems of weight loss and subsequent pressure bruise must be considered secondary to potential losses from decay. In this situation, the use of humidifiers should be avoided, and fans should be operated continuously to prevent the buildup of free moisture in the pile. In warm weather, no attempt should be made to store a heavily diseased crop unless pulp temperatures throughout the pile can be brought down and maintained below 50°F. If tubers at the top of the pile cannot be cooled properly, decay will start there, and the entire pile may "melt down" and be lost. It is preferable either to grade tubers in this condition carefully and market them straight from the field or to delay harvest until the weather permits rapid cooling in storage.

The Cooling Period

After wound healing is complete, cooling should be initiated (Table 6.1). Potatoes to be sold as seed or for fresh consumption should be cooled to 38–40°F. The activity of fungal and bacterial soft rot organisms is greatly reduced at these temperatures. Seed or fresh-market potatoes may be cooled relatively rapidly by careful introduction of outside air or by refrigeration. Care must be taken to maintain high relative humidity in the cooling air to prevent desiccation. Precautions regarding temperature differences and condensation during the curing period apply here as well.

Potatoes to be used for processing must be cooled more slowly, preferably by no more than 2–3° per week. The supply air temperature should never be more than 5–8° lower than the tuber pulp temperature. The final holding temperature is determined by the intended use. Potatoes stored for french fry manufacture generally may be cooled to 45°F, although individual processors may have specific requirements. Potatoes for chip processing must be stored at a slightly higher temperature to avoid the accumulation of reducing sugars, which form rapidly within tubers below 45°F. In order to produce acceptable chip fry color, the reducing sugars glucose and fructose must not be allowed to accumulate during storage. Generally, healthy chip potatoes harvested at soil temperatures of 55–70°F may be stored at 48–50°F with minimal concern about reducing sugars. Chipping potatoes harvested during cooler weather may require long-term holding at 50–55°F to ensure acceptable fry color. Chipping cultivars have been developed that recondition well after storage at lower temperatures; however, the prevailing temperature and rainfall during production and soil temperature at harvest may affect the chipping performance of potatoes removed from storage.

The Holding Period: Dormancy Present

After the appropriate long-term storage temperature has been reached, the frequency of ventilation may be reduced if desired. During the holding period it is necessary to provide enough air movement through the pile to supply oxygen for tuber respiration, remove carbon dioxide and excess heat, and maintain a constant temperature. The temperature should be maintained within 2° of the desired holding temperature, and the variation within the pile should not exceed 2–3° from top to bottom. The relative humidity should be kept at 90–95% throughout the holding period, to minimize weight loss and pressure bruising.

Condensation is a problem in some storages. Excess moisture dripping from the ceiling onto the top of the pile creates wet areas, which are ideal sites for tuber rot to begin developing. Adequate insulation is the key to minimizing condensation. An insufficiently insulated storage will sweat even when the outside air is only moderately cool. Ceiling condensation can be reduced by a constant flow of air between the top of the pile and the ceiling, maintained by small circulating fans. Outside air warmer than the potatoes in the pile should never be introduced into the storage, as this can result in condensation directly on the tubers.

During the holding period most cultivars enter a dormant state, characterized by very low respiration and the production of only minimal heat and water vapor. The length of dormancy is a cultivar characteristic. Generally, early-maturing cultivars (such as Norland and Superior) have a very short dormancy period, whereas late-maturing cultivars (such as Russet Burbank) have a longer dormancy period.

Chemical sprout inhibitors can be used to lengthen the dormancy period when potatoes are to be held for many months. If maleic hydrazide has not been applied during growth as a sprout inhibitor, some producers apply CIPC (isopropyl N-chlorophenylcarbamate) to tubers in storage to prevent sprouting. The proper timing of this treatment is critical to tuber health, as CIPC may interfere with suberization and wound healing if applied too early in the storage cycle. Tubers must have completed the curing process before it is applied. In northern areas, the treatment is normally delayed until early December.

CIPC is applied by a contract custom applicator franchised by the manufacturer. The material is injected as an aerosol into the storage ventilation system and is distributed with the ventilation air throughout the bins. Well-balanced and evenly distributed airflow is necessary during application. Any tuber buds not adequately covered by the CIPC aerosol may enlarge and produce appressed, rosette-type sprout clusters, which may grow inward to produce ingrown or internal sprouts. Since thorough distribution of the material is so essential, a prestorage inspection of the ventilation and duct system by the custom applicator is advisable. Measures taken to ensure uniform airflow through the pile before the storage is filled will prevent serious problems later.

No sprout inhibitors of any kind should be used on seed potatoes. Bins treated with CIPC should not be used the following spring to store incoming seed potatoes (Chapter 4).

The Holding Period: Dormancy Broken

During the latter part of the holding period, potatoes in storage begin to break dormancy. The time when this begins is determined by the dormancy characteristics of the particular cultivar, the storage temperature, and whether a sprout inhibitor has been applied. As a tuber breaks dormancy, its respiration rate increases, and internal changes lead to rapid cell division in growing points, resulting in sprouting. The rise in metabolic activity results in increased oxygen demand, generation of heat, and emission of water vapor.

Proper storage management becomes critical after dormancy is broken, because tuber health may easily be jeopardized. Maintaining a uniform low temperature throughout the storage can significantly extend dormancy in most cultivars. Refrigerated storages are most valuable at this time. For potatoes not treated with a sprout inhibitor, especially seed potatoes, careful management to avoid sprouting is critical when bins are frequently opened to market tubers. Premature sprouting advances the physiological age of seed tubers, which may result in significant loss of vigor affecting the health of the new crop.

Throughout the holding period the storage manager should monitor the pile closely for wet spots, sunken areas, objectionable odors, or the presence of fruit flies. All these are signs of tuber decay within the pile. Most modern storages feature adjustable airflow dampers at duct entrances to allow extra ventilation air to be delivered to trouble spots in the storage bin. Generally, once a pocket of breakdown occurs in a bin, the prospects for continuing long-term storage are greatly reduced. If decay is detected, the storage humidity should be lowered, the pile opened, and potatoes graded and marketed promptly.

Maintaining Tuber Health During Post-Storage Handling

To minimize mechanical damage to tubers while they are being removed from storage for marketing, it is essential to raise the pulp temperature gradually to above 50°F over a period of several weeks. This can be accomplished by restricting ventilation and allowing the heat of respiration to increase the temperature of the pile. Handling potatoes when they are cold results in a high incidence of shatter bruise or internal blackspot. Rough handling may cause chipping potatoes to accumulate significant quantities of reducing sugars within a few hours, resulting in unacceptable fry color. Fresh-market potatoes may develop internal blackspot, after-cooking darkening, or other surface defects that lead to excessive waste during peeling. French fry processors often reject roughly handled loads or impose heavy penalties for accepting them.

Once desired tuber pulp temperatures have been reached and removal from storage begins, the manager must concentrate on bruise control, applying the same principles of low-bruise handling used when loading the storage. Careful operation of bulk unloading equipment is essential. Dumping heights into hoppers and trucks should be held to 6 inches or less. If a bin loader is used to move potatoes into trucks, load through the back to minimize the drop as loading is begun, and then continually adjust the loader as loading progresses. As in filling the storage, bruising is minimized by maintaining the flow of potatoes at capacity on all conveyors and padding sharp and rough surfaces on all equipment.

All equipment should be cleaned and sanitized to prevent the spread of bacterial pathogens. If a fluming system is used to transport tubers in water, it must be cleaned and sanitized frequently, and the flume water must be changed often. During fluming, tubers should not be submerged more than an inch or two, because the water pressure may force some bacteria into lenticels. Clean water should be used for washing fresh-market potatoes on the packing line, and the wash water should not be recirculated. It is very important that washed tubers be well dried before packaging, as a film of moisture left on them may lead to the development of bacterial soft rot in the bag, later in the marketing chain. Ventilated bags help to ensure complete drying.

> **Under no circumstances should cull potatoes be dumped outside in piles. Cull piles are notorious sources of spores of the late blight fungus, which form in the spring on sprouts from surviving tubers.**

Removing seed tubers from storage requires intense precaution to maintain seed quality. In some production areas, seed tubers may be treated with the fungicide TBZ as they are removed from storage, to reduce the development of Fusarium dry rot (Chapter 17). If off-farm trucks are used to transport bulk or bagged seed, they must be thoroughly cleaned and properly sanitized before loading.

After packaging, bagged seed or fresh-market potatoes are damaged mainly at the time of loading and unloading. Bagged potatoes are likely to suffer severe shatter bruising when dropped onto a hard surface from a height greater than 30 inches. When potatoes are being shipped, the outside temperature should be watched carefully. If it is below freezing, precautions must be taken to prevent frost damage during transit.

Proper disposal of waste potatoes is an important management practice to ensure the health of future potato crops. A plan for proper disposal must be in place before cull potatoes are generated in the packing-out operation. Under no circumstances should cull potatoes be dumped outside in piles. Cull piles are notorious sources of spores of the late blight fungus, which form in the spring on sprouts from surviving tubers. They also serve as reservoirs of some viruses. Acceptable waste disposal methods include using culls as livestock feed, composting them, and spreading them in the winter to freeze on land not intended for potato production the following season. An expensive and less desirable method is to bury cull potatoes at least 6 feet deep. Groundwater contamination may result from this, however, if proper precautions are not taken.

Mechanical damage continues to be a major factor in potato health management, not only because of the direct results of injury, but also because of the introduction of disease organisms. Healthy seed tubers are critical to the potato industry—they are the vital link from one season to the next. Repeat orders at the processing plant and in the fresh-market chain depend on tuber health. The potato grower, along with employees, field advisors, and creditors, must maintain vigilance to ensure that a tuber health management program is followed through harvest, storage, and marketing. Continued profitability in potato farming depends on the ability of the potato health manager to accomplish this objective.

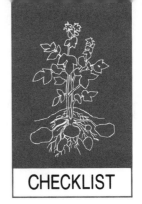

CHECKLIST

Checklist of Activities

A Holistic Plan for Potato Health Management

☑ The Year Prior to Growing Potatoes

☐ Select cultivars appropriate for intended markets and production conditions. Identify reputable seed potato growers and visit farms to examine seed lots and certification records. Arrange for delivery of high-quality, certified seed potatoes.

☐ Establish an appropriate long-term crop rotation, with potatoes grown no more often than every third year. Use a rotation that suppresses diseases and insect and nematode pests, and implement rotation-wide weed control strategies. Destroy volunteer potatoes and weeds that may harbor diseases or insect pests.

☐ Manage potato production fields to avoid soil compaction, herbicide carryover, and poor drainage. Monitor fields for soilborne pests and disease organisms, and apply pesticides or fumigants if necessary and feasible. Apply appropriate soil amendments as needed to adjust the pH to an acceptable level.

☑ Preplant

☐ Collect and analyze soil samples for fertility, pH, and other pertinent factors. Apply preplant fertilizers and soil amendments as indicated by the results of soil analysis. Establish permanent records of fertility, rotation, cultural management, and pesticide use for each field.

☐ Perform tillage operations necessary to manage weeds and crop residues, minimize erosion, and provide tilth for planting. In irrigated production, establish sufficient soil moisture in the root zone to provide adequate available water until the potato plants are fully emerged.

☐ Properly dispose of waste potatoes left from previous crops—never in cull piles.

☐ Clean and sanitize storage facilities and seed-handling equipment prior to receiving seed potatoes.

☐ Examine seed tubers for diseases and defects upon delivery. Handle and store seed properly to maintain tuber health. Do not hold seed in storage areas that have been treated with a sprout inhibitor and may still be contaminated.

☑ Planting

☐ Manage seed-cutting and healing operations carefully to ensure healthy, uniform, properly sized seed pieces. Sanitize cutting equipment at least daily and before cutting each seed lot. Apply a seed piece fungicide treatment as needed. Provide conditions for cut seed to suberize properly, or plant immediately after cutting, when soil conditions permit.

☐ Delay planting until soil temperatures are above 50° F. As much as possible, schedule planting operations to coincide with favorable soil conditions and weather. Operate the planter so that the seed pieces are planted at the intended spacing and at a depth that will ensure rapid emergence. Apply fertilizers and pesticides as appropriate.

☑ Growth Stage I: Preemergence

☐ Perform operations for preemergence weed control and any practices that reduce soil crusting and promote rapid emergence.

☐ In irrigated production, do not water prior to emergence unless the soil becomes excessively dry at the depth of the seed pieces.

☑ Growth Stage II: Vegetative Growth

☐ In irrigated production, provide uniform soil moisture and avoid especially wet or dry soil.

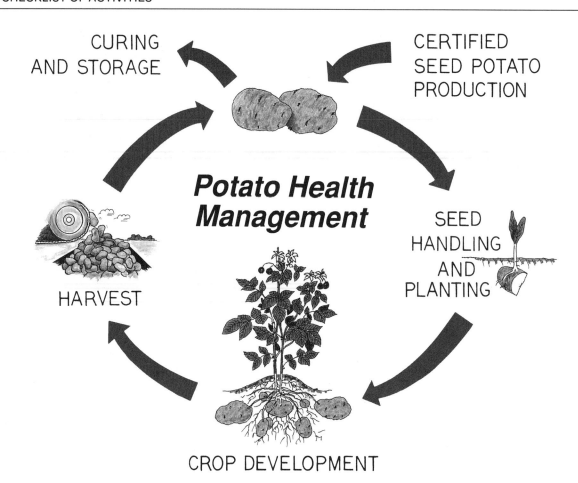

Potato Health Management

CURING AND STORAGE

CERTIFIED SEED POTATO PRODUCTION

SEED HANDLING AND PLANTING

HARVEST

CROP DEVELOPMENT

☐ Apply postemergence herbicides as appropriate. Complete hilling–cultivating operations well before row closure, and avoid root pruning during tillage. Apply fertilizer side-dressings prior to the last hilling.

☐ Begin insect scouting and disease monitoring. Delay the first insecticide or fungicide application until the action threshold for the target pest or disease has been reached.

☑ Growth Stage III: Tuber Initiation

☐ Avoid especially wet or dry soil, to minimize the development of common scab and tuber disorders.

☐ Begin petiole analysis for nutritional management, if appropriate.

☐ Continue insect scouting and disease monitoring, and apply pesticides as needed.

☑ Growth Stage IV: Tuber Bulking

☐ In irrigated production, maintain uniform adequate soil moisture. Avoid overwatering, to minimize disease development and nitrate leaching. Apply nutrients through sprinklers, if appropriate.

☐ Continue insect scouting and disease monitoring, and apply pesticides as needed.

☐ If desired, apply a sprout inhibitor to plants when most tubers are at least 2 inches in diameter.

☑ Growth Stage V: Tuber Maturation

☐ Reduce irrigation to promote tuber skin set, minimize tuber disease, and manage late-season weed growth.

☐ Cease applications of nitrogen in irrigation water 4–6 weeks before vine killing. Schedule vine-killing operations to allow complete desiccation of the vines before harvest. Continue foliar applications of fungicide and insecticide, if appropriate, until the vines are completely dead.

☐ Inspect, repair, and sanitize storage facilities and harvest equipment. Make necessary modifications to harvest equipment to minimize bruising.

☑ Harvest

☐ Train personnel for a safe, low-bruise harvest. Conduct all harvesting, transportation, and bin-loading operations with bruise management as a primary goal. Ensure that tubers are not dropped from heights of more than 6 inches.

☐ Begin harvesting after the vines are completely dead, early enough in the season to avoid frost damage. Coordinate harvest operations with current and expected weather conditions, so that tubers are dug when conditions are as close as possible to optimal (60–65% of available soil water and tuber pulp temperatures of 50–65° F.)

☐ Remove as much soil and debris as possible from tubers during harvest.

☐ Tarp loads in the field to protect harvested tubers from rain, direct sun, and adverse temperatures. Isolate damaged or diseased lots in separate bins for immediate grading and marketing.

☑ Storage

☐ Manage the curing period carefully to provide appropriate conditions for wound healing (50–60° F, relative humidity 95–99%, and good air movement).

☐ Monitor air movement, humidity, and temperature throughout the pile, and maintain the environmental conditions appropriate for each stage of the storage cycle. Avoid condensation on the walls and ceiling of the storage and on tubers. Continually monitor the pile for any signs of decay, and take appropriate action if decay develops.

☐ If appropriate, have a chemical sprout inhibitor applied by a custom applicator after the curing process has been completed.

☐ Before removing tubers for marketing, warm the storage to raise pulp temperatures above 50° F. Manage bin-unloading operations to minimize bruising, following the same principles applied at harvest.

☐ Ensure that washed or flumed potatoes are well dried before packing. Use ventilated bags.

☐ Dispose of waste potatoes properly—never in cull piles.

Part Two

Managing Factors That Affect Potato Health

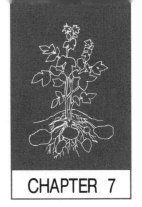

Steven A. Slack
Department of Plant Pathology
Cornell University, Ithaca, New York

CHAPTER 7

Seed Certification and Seed Improvement Programs

The use of certified seed potatoes is the foundation of any management program designed to maintain a healthy potato crop. Potatoes are vegetatively propagated, and the use of tubers rather than true seed for crop production causes unique problems in the control of disease. Many disease organisms that would be eliminated or minimized by the use of true seed are carried on or within tubers. Seed potato certification programs have been established to reduce the incidence of tuber-borne pathogens and to provide seed stocks of clones of improved cultivars free of cultivar mixtures. Anyone involved in commercial potato production must have a good understanding of the rationale and procedures involved in modern seed potato certification and seed improvement programs, because of their pivotal role in all potato health management strategies.

Seed Potato Certification Programs

History of Seed Potato Certification

Prior to 1900, it was widely believed that the propagation of potatoes by tubers was responsible for the degeneration of cultivars and decreased yields, which were invariably observed over a period of years. It was assumed that the initial vitality of a cultivar that had become unproductive, or "run out," could be restored only by propagation from true seed. We now know that what the use of true seed did was to eliminate many tuber-borne pathogens, especially viruses, which had accumulated in seed stocks of the cultivar over several years of field propagation. The plants produced from true seed, however, were not true to type of the original cultivar clones.

By 1900, Dutch and German agriculturists found that certain symptoms of degeneration, such as leaf curling, rolling, crinkling, and blotching, could be transmitted from plant to plant and persisted from one crop to another. Careful observation taught them that removing plants with these symptoms from seed fields was helpful in controlling these problems. A few U.S. scientists traveled to Europe in the early 1900s to study potato diseases and observe the systems for inspection and production of potato seed stocks used in Germany. It became evident to them that pests and disease organisms were being distributed with seed stocks, which were being allowed to move freely throughout the world. This situation was officially recognized by the U.S. government by the passage of the National Plant Quarantine Act of 1912. This law prohibited the introduction of potatoes with black wart, a disease caused by the fungus *Synchytrium endobioticum*. Two years later, a similar embargo was placed on potatoes with powdery scab, caused by the fungus *Spongospora subterranea*.

These events set the stage for the establishment of seed potato certification programs. In 1914, scientists from the U.S. Department of Agriculture presented a proposal for certification at the first annual meeting of the Potato Association of America and at the first official Potato Seed Certification Conference. Seed potato certification programs were initiated between 1913 and 1915 in the Canadian provinces of New Brunswick and Prince Edward Island and in the United States in Idaho, Maine, Maryland, Vermont, and Wisconsin. By 1922, programs were in place in 22 states, covering about 24,500 acres of seed potatoes.

Today, seed potato production in North America is concentrated in the northern United States and in Canada, where pressure from virus-carrying insects is lower. Sixteen states and 10 provinces annually certify nearly 270,000 acres of seed potatoes (Table 7.1). Over 100 cultivars are certified, but over 80% of the acreage is used to produce only 10 cultivars (Table 7.2).

Certification Procedures

Certification is a voluntary program in which commercial growers of seed potatoes agree to participate. In the United States, the authorized certification agency in each state develops and publishes its own standards covering eligibility of seed lots, fees paid by participating growers, disease tolerances, cultivar purity, cultural conditions, grade requirements, identification of specific seed lots, and rules governing sale as certified seed. Although the relationship between the grower and the certification agency is voluntary, each agency has official legal status, and the certification program is protected against fraudulent use of the term *certified seed potatoes*.

In Canada, national guidelines regulate seed potato certification in all provinces. Each seed grower is provided with application forms, on which the seed source, history, acreage, cultivars, and location of fields are listed. Such information determines eligibility for inspection.

During the growing season, each field entered for certification is inspected at least twice, at times when conditions are most satisfactory for visual detection of diseases and cultivar mixtures. At the end of the season, tubers are again inspected, at harvest or in the bin. To pass inspections, seed lots must be found not to exceed a prescribed maximum allowable incidence of disease or mixture of cultivars. Seed lots that pass these inspections are assigned a seed class (in the United States) or a seed grade (in Canada) (Table 7.3).

Final tolerances for individual virus diseases, such as leafroll or mosaic, vary among programs but are generally about 1% for certified seed. Tolerances are usually higher at the first inspection (1.5–2%) than at the second. This enables seed growers to remove symptomatic plants from fields that were marginal on the first inspection, in order to try to meet the

Table 7.1. Seed potato acreage passing certification by U.S. states and Canadian provinces in 1990[a]

State	Acres certified	Percentage of total	Province	Acres certified	Percentage of total
Idaho	47,738	27.0	Prince Edward Isl.	57,705	63.0
North Dakota	33,713	19.1	New Brunswick	16,771	18.3
Maine	24,618	13.9	Manitoba	5,024	5.5
Minnesota	21,871	12.4	Alberta	4,786	5.2
Wisconsin	10,128	5.7	Quebec	3,781	4.1
Colorado	9,111	5.2	British Columbia	1,720	1.9
Montana	8,570	4.9	Ontario	1,129	1.2
Nebraska	6,637	3.8	Saskatchewan	366	0.4
Oregon	3,751	2.1	Nova Scotia	264	0.3
Michigan	2,739	1.6	Newfoundland	62	0.1
Washington	2,085	1.2	Total	91,608	
South Dakota	1,749	1.0			
New York	1,735	1.0			
California	1,280	0.7			
Utah	730	0.4			
Pennsylvania	246	0.1			
Total	176,701				

[a] U.S. data from National Potato Council, Englewood, Colorado. Canadian data from National Seed Potato Bureau, Ottawa, Ontario.

Table 7.2. Acreage of the 20 leading potato cultivars passing seed certification requirements in the United States and Canada in 1990[a]

	U.S. acreage	Canadian acreage	Total acreage	Percentage of total[b]
Russet Burbank	62,238	33,092	95,330	35.5
Superior	8,085	12,488	20,573	7.7
Norchip	17,581	1,948	19,529	7.3
Atlantic	13,041	5,016	18,057	6.7
Kennebec	4,507	11,853	16,360	6.1
Shepody	4,594	10,795	15,389	5.7
Russet Norkotah	12,997	2,152	15,149	5.6
Sebago	5,318	3,272	8,590	3.2
Norland	7,190[c]	904	8,094	3.0
Red Pontiac	2,339	1,718	4,057	1.5
Monona	2,920	420	3,340	1.2
Centennial Russet	3,314	…	3,314	1.2
Red LaSoda	2,891	60	2,951	1.1
Yukon Gold	415	2,219	2,634	1.0
Katahdin	2,089	271	2,360	0.9
Norwis	2,344	…	2,344	0.9
Chieftain	320	1,960	2,280	0.8
Russet Nugget	1,973	…	1,973	0.7
Frontier Russet	1,948	…	1,948	0.7
Ontario	1,599	…	1,599	0.6
Total	157,703	88,168	245,871	91.4

[a] U.S. data from National Potato Council, Englewood, Colorado. Canadian data from National Seed Potato Bureau, Ottawa, Ontario.
[b] Percentages of a total of 268,319 acres. This total includes 111 cultivars grown on 176,701 acres in the United States and 83 cultivars grown on 91,608 acres in Canada.
[c] The following lines and acreages are included: Norland (1,030), Norland Dark Red (3,573), Norland Red (2,575), and Norland Super Red (12).

final tolerance on the second inspection. Removing undesirable plants from seed fields is called roguing. Tolerances for cultivar mixtures are also usually higher at the first inspection, with a final tolerance of 0–0.25%. Throughout North America, there is zero tolerance for bacterial ring rot (Chapter 15). Therefore, a single infected plant or tuber detected at inspection is cause for the entire seed lot to be rejected for certification. This regulation was implemented because ring rot bacteria can be easily spread within a seed stock, especially during seed cutting.

The agency may refuse certification not only because of failure to meet prescribed standards but also because of undesirable amounts of other diseases or pests (such as vascular wilts, blackleg, or nematodes), poor stand or cultural conditions, lack of isolation, any condition that interferes with visual inspection (such as herbicide damage or excess weeds), or any other condition that may impair seed quality. The inspector completes a written report on each field, and copies are left with the grower. These certification inspection records are an important source of information regarding each seed lot.

Most states also require a winter test for seed stocks, and a few agencies have made this test compulsory for all seed classes. Winter tests are essential for predicting disease incidence in a seed lot and its performance when planted the following season (Fig. 7.1). Samples of 300–800 tubers per seed lot are planted, generally in California or Florida, where winter growing conditions favor expression of virus symptoms. These tests facilitate evaluation of the incidence of virus infection, cultivar mixtures, and other factors affecting seed productivity, such as herbicide exposure, which may influence the growth of the following crop.

Evaluation for virus incidence is particularly important, because late-season flights of green peach aphids can be responsible for spreading potato leafroll virus, whose diagnostic symptoms are not expressed until the next crop is grown from the harvested seed tubers. As a general guideline, the incidence of leafroll, mosaic, and spindle tuber cannot exceed a total of 0.5% in stocks of early-generation or Foundation classes and 5% in stocks of Certified class. These tolerances are higher than those in summer field inspections because the

Table 7.3. Generalized seed class terminology

U.S. seed class[a]	Canadian seed grade	Description
Pre-Nuclear	Pre-Nuclear	Stocks maintained in tissue cultures with test history for specific pathogens; this designation may also be used for tubers from greenhouses or other protected production environments
Nuclear	Pre-Elite	Tubers from first field year (in Canada and 10 states); this designation may also be used for tubers from greenhouses or other protected production environments
Generation 1	Elite I	Tubers from second field year
Generation 2	Elite II	Tubers from third field year
Generation 3	Elite III	Tubers from fourth field year
Generation 4	Elite IV	Tubers from fifth field year
Generation 5	Foundation	Tubers from sixth field year
Generation 6	Certified	Tubers from seventh field year

[a] Generation 1 through Generation 6 may be designated Foundation or Certified class seed in some states, depending on disease incidence and year in field. In some states, Generation 1 denotes tubers harvested from the first field year.

winter tests use a smaller sample and therefore have a greater margin of sampling error.

In most states, a final federal or state shipping-point inspection is required to verify tuber size and quality factors that determine seed grade. A shipping-point inspection and properly tagged carriers are considered to be the final step in official certification.

Most states use a blue tag to indicate the top seed grade and follow the U.S. No. 1 Seed Grade criteria. To meet this grade, tubers must not show any signs of freezing or low-temperature injury, blackheart, late blight, bacterial ring rot, or bacterial soft rot, including wet breakdown of any kind. Additionally, they must be free of damage caused by dirt, second growth, growth cracks, air cracks, cuts, shriveling, sprouting, scab, Fusarium dry rot, or *Rhizoctonia* and must not be seriously damaged by sunburn, hollow heart, or internal necrosis. Most states permit minimum and maximum tuber sizes to be specified in contracts; a 10- or 12-ounce maximum and a 1½-inch minimum size is normal.

A second grade, indicated by a yellow tag, has higher tolerances for defects that do not affect productivity, such as greening, tuber type, and well-healed mechanical damage.

Seed is packed in new, clean bags or containers, with a tag listing the cultivar, crop year, and grower's name and address attached in such a way that the container cannot be opened without destroying the seal. Some agencies prefer to number each tag rather than give the grower's name.

Seed potatoes are commonly shipped in bulk, to reduce hauling and packing costs. Trucks and other carriers moving bulk seed are required to be cleaned and sanitized before use. A certified seed tag containing the same information required for bags must be attached to the carrier with a metal seal. Some states that do not have seed potato certification programs have regulations that define the quality and labeling procedures required for seed potatoes brought into the state for planting commercial acreages.

Fees are charged by each agency to cover the cost of services. A fee is paid when application is made for inspection, and most agencies require an additional acreage fee before certification is final. A tag fee may also be charged, and a final shipping-point inspection fee is charged on each bag or container of seed being shipped.

Following field inspections, each agency prepares a list of all growers whose fields have passed inspections. Names of cultivars and acreages are given along with the name and address of the grower. These seed potato directories are distributed widely for promotion, sales, and informational purposes.

Seed Potato Improvement Programs

Seed potato improvement programs deal with the selection and production of the basic seed stocks used to plant various classes or generations of seed grown prior to the production of certified seed. Requirements for basic seed stocks are necessarily more rigid than those for certified seed. Field tolerances for certain diseases are about 0.25–0.5% for early-generation seed stocks, compared to 1% for certified stocks. Growers of early-generation seed often must enter their entire acreage for inspection and must follow strict sanitary practices and use greater care and precision in handling and storing the crop. Production practices are usually modified to permit accurate selection of desirable clones for increase. Other special practices include isolation of cultivars in separate fields, tuber-unit planting, the use of systemic and other insecticides to control insects that may carry viruses, and the use of herbicides for weed control rather than repeated cultivation.

Limited-Generation Programs

Most seed potato improvement programs organize their production of basic stocks into strict limited-generation schemes designed to "flush out" seed stocks within a prescribed number of years (Table 7.3). In the limited-generation concept, seed stocks are automatically reduced to the next lower class after each year of field production. If an early-generation stock is found to exceed a prescribed tolerance, it is reduced by more than one class or rejected completely and made ineligible for further certification.

The rationale for limited-generation programs is that the probability of contamination of a seed lot with one or more tuber-borne pathogens increases with each generation of field production. Thus, if stocks are continually flushed out of the system, there is less chance that pathogens will build up in early-generation stocks.

Limited-generation programs begin with individual tubers or plants selected for the initial production cycle. These stocks, called Pre-Nuclear class seed, are generally increased for one generation in a greenhouse or screenhouse. The harvested tubers are classified as Pre-Nuclear or Nuclear in the United States and as Pre-Elite in Canada. In several states and provinces, government- or university-operated farms in geographically isolated areas are devoted exclusively to the production of these basic seed stocks (Fig. 7.2). In other states and prov-

Fig. 7.1. Winter test plot for seed potatoes near Homestead, Florida. Samples of seed tubers were treated to break dormancy before planting. The sample with poor emergence was not treated.

Fig. 7.2. The Cornell–Uihlein Foundation Seed Potato Farm (317 acres, including 150 tillable acres), where early-generation seed stocks are produced for growers of New York certified seed potatoes. Pre-Nuclear stocks are generated in the Henry Uihlein II Laboratory and grown in greenhouses.

inces, the certifying agency works closely with a few selected private seed growers to increase Nuclear class stocks. Nuclear seed stocks are also provided by private companies in some situations.

During the 1980s, most states and provinces initiated limited-generation programs based on tissue culture, in which *in vitro* plantlets are established from selected plants or tubers. These are grown in glass test tubes or other containers under closely controlled laboratory conditions (Fig. 7.3). The plantlets produced in these tissue cultures are screened to ascertain their freedom from spindle tuber viroid and specific viruses, bacteria, and fungi. Since it is now possible to remove systemic viruses from tissue-cultured plantlets, stocks of important established cultivars that are free of recognized pathogens have become a practical reality.

Sophisticated laboratory tests to monitor freedom from pathogens, not just freedom from disease, in Pre-Nuclear and other selected stocks have been incorporated into elaborate virus-tested seed-increase programs. *Virus-tested* means that the plants or a sample of the plants in a lot have been tested and found to be free of potato viruses A, M, S, X, and Y and potato leafroll virus. Other terms, such as *virus-free* and *X-free*, have been used to refer to stocks tested for the presence of potato virus X (PVX) or other viruses. Since these terms are somewhat misleading, *virus-tested* is the preferred general term.

The enzyme-linked immunosorbent assay (ELISA) has had a profound impact on seed stock indexing. This is an extremely sensitive serological technique capable of detecting minute amounts of virus. Since ELISA can detect all potato viruses in crude tissue extracts and can detect some viruses in a single infected plant in a composite sample (for example, one PVX-infected leaf in a 100- to 1,000-leaf sample), it is an excellent test for mass indexing programs. Recently, several techniques of modern molecular biology have been adapted as screening tools and have been successfully used to identify spindle tuber viroid in seed stocks.

Several field generations (usually five to seven) follow the greenhouse or screenhouse propagation in a limited-generation program (Table 7.3). In the United States, the tubers harvested from the first field generation are classified as Nuclear (in most states), and subsequent increases are numbered by generations—Generation 1 (G-1), Generation 2 (G-2), and so forth. In some states, G-4 is known as Foundation class, and G-5 or G-6 is Certified class. In others, G-1 through G-6 may be designated Foundation or Certified class seed, depending on disease incidence and year in field. The terminology is not completely standardized in the United States because each state regulates its own seed industry. In Canada, a uniform nomenclature is used: the first field generation is designated Pre-Elite, and subsequent generations are Elite I, Elite II, Elite III, Elite IV, Foundation, and Certified.

Early-generation stocks are often increased by tuber-unit planting, in which each seed tuber is cut into four equal parts, about 1.5–2 ounces each, which are planted consecutively. In order to clearly identify tuber units, extra space is left between each unit of four seed pieces and the next (Fig. 7.4). Tuber-unit planting facilitates the removal of all plants that originated from the same seed tuber if any one is later found to be diseased or offtype.

Winter field tests in Florida or California are important parts of most limited-generation programs.

Limitations on Seed Potato Quality

Since the initiation of seed improvement programs, knowledge of the factors affecting seed productivity has continually expanded. As the application of this knowledge has increased productivity, expectations have risen in both the potato industry and consumers. Although the objectives of seed improvement programs are being met, it must be recognized that there are inherent limitations that preclude a perfect system in which the detection and exclusion of all defects are ensured.

Two major limitations on seed potato quality are that inspections are based on visual examinations of samples of plants, rather than all plants, and that infected plants may be symptomless or exhibit indistinct symptoms when inspected. In spite of these limitations, certification programs have a good record for meeting the quality needs of the industry and the consumer. Certifying agencies minimize these limitations by training inspectors in proper procedures for field inspection and by timing inspections to coincide with the optimal expression of disease symptoms. Inspectors also benefit from their personal knowledge of each individual seed grower's farm operation and the history of that grower's seed stocks.

The quality of potato seed stocks has continually improved. During the formative years of 1919–1929, there were high rejection rates (25–65%) and fairly lenient disease tolerances. As certification programs and seed sources stabilized, rejection rates were generally lower (8–10%), and stricter disease tolerances were applied. During the period 1968–1972, the leading reasons for rejection from certification and the percentage of acreage rejected were bacterial ring rot (5.6%), leafroll (0.8%),

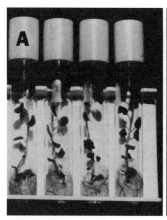

Fig. 7.3. Tissue-cultured potato plantlets are produced in test tubes (**A**) or in larger containers (**B**) in a limited-generation seed program. The plantlets are tested to ensure their freedom from viroids, viruses, bacteria, and fungi.

Fig. 7.4. Tuber-unit planting of early-generation seed potatoes. Each seed tuber is cut into four pieces, which are planted consecutively, with extra space left between each unit of four seed pieces and the next. Seed lots are separated by a space of one or more rows. If any plant is later found to be diseased or offtype, it and the other plants from the same tuber are removed.

cultivar mixture (0.7%), and mosaic (0.5%). More recently, the establishment of tissue-cultured, pathogen-tested Pre-Nuclear seed stocks has enabled the seed industry to initiate cycles of seed stock increase with the highest quality ever.

In spite of these improvements, it should be recognized that the genetic susceptibility or resistance of potato cultivars to diseases has not been changed by this technology. Therefore, recontamination of seed stocks with pathogens can and does occur.

The development and modernization of seed improvement programs have ensured a steady supply of high-quality, certi-fied seed stocks for commercial growers. It is inevitable, however, that the seed potato industry will continue to change as technological advances become applicable to potato production systems and as market demands insist on specific improvements in quality. Because potato growers will always need productive seed stocks that meet expectations for cultivar performance and purity, and because disease organisms carried in seed tubers will likely continue to be major limitations on production, it appears that effective seed certification programs will remain the foundation of all potato health management systems.

CHAPTER 8

David Curwen
Department of Horticulture
University of Wisconsin, Madison

Water Management

Profitable potato production depends on an adequate supply of water available to the roots throughout the growing season. Water is a major constituent of potato plants, making up 90–95% of green tissues and 75–85% of tubers. It is important in many physiological processes necessary for plant growth and development and is a source of carbon, hydrogen, and oxygen. One third (by weight) of the carbohydrate and protein in plant tissues is derived from chemically combined water.

A growing potato crop uses a lot of water. Under optimal growing conditions, well-watered potato plants transpiring at an average rate will replace their entire water content about four times a day. If water was withheld from the roots at noon on a clear day, these plants would wilt in about 12 minutes. Such extreme conditions are not often found in commercial production, but depletion of soil moisture without replenishment can have serious effects on tuber yield and quality. When managing water resources, the potato health manager should keep in mind that the plant always balances precariously between too much and too little water.

Water Stress and Potato Health

Water stress, whether from too little or too much water, can significantly affect the health of a potato crop. Excess soil moisture following planting can delay emergence and promote bacterial seed piece decay. Excess water from rainfall or irrigation leaches nitrate nitrogen from the soil and carries it below the root zone, thus reducing the amount of available nitrogen and resulting in nitrogen-deficient plants. Flooding of the soil for more than 8–12 hours can cause root death due to oxygen deprivation, and this may lead to irreversible wilting and death of plants.

Although excess water can be a problem in poorly drained soils in rain-fed production areas or in any field with excessive or improperly timed irrigation, the more common water management problem is a plant water deficit resulting from too little water. When the rate of transpiration is high and soil moisture is low, the water content of the plant decreases rapidly. If the water content decreases by 10%, growth is slowed and may even cease. If it decreases by 20%, the plant wilts, and most physiological processes slow or cease; and if it decreases by 40%, the plant usually dies.

Most plant water deficits occur when water stored in the soil is depleted below some critical level. Soil water storage is commonly expressed as a percentage of available soil water, also referred to as available soil moisture, available water (or moisture), or available water-holding (or moisture-holding) capacity. In this book, the term *available soil water* will be

> **The moisture status of the soil becomes critical when the percentage of available soil water drops below 60–65%.**

used. This term is defined more completely later in this chapter (see Water Management Strategies). For potatoes, the moisture status of the soil becomes critical when the percentage of available soil water drops below 60–65%. Thus when 35–40% of available soil water has been used, a water deficit develops in potato plants in most soils.

Effects of Plant Water Deficit on Tuber Yield

The potato plant is sensitive to relatively small changes in soil moisture. This sensitivity is likely due to its rather shallow root system and its physiological responses to moderate plant water deficits. The first of these responses is closure of the leaf stomata, the small pores on the leaf surface that control gas exchange. As a plant water deficit develops, the stomata close as a defense against further water loss, and the leaves become darker green. Prolonged stress causes wilting due to loss of turgor pressure (the internal water pressure in plant cells) in the leaves. While stomatal closure reduces water loss through the leaves, it also reduces carbon dioxide uptake by the plant. This slows photosynthesis, lowering the production of photosynthetic products by the plant and restricting their transport from leaves to tubers.

The yield of a potato crop depends on the accumulation of these products of photosynthesis in the tubers. When the plant makes more of these products than is needed for respiration and continued growth, the excess is stored in the tubers. In a plant water deficit, the rate of photosynthesis slows, as do root and stem development and the rate of increase in

Table 8.1. Potato health problems associated with deficient or excess soil moisture

	Deficient soil moisture	Excess soil moisture
Growth stage I: from planting to emergence	Prevents proper healing of seed pieces, thus favoring seed piece decay	Increases clod formation during planting Promotes seed piece decay
Growth stage II: vegetative growth	Inhibits plant development and response to fertilizer May cause foliar tipburn	Increases soil compaction and clod formation during tillage May favor infection by *Verticillium*
Growth stage III: tuber initiation	Favors development of common scab and some tuber disorders (translucent end, irregular shape)	Favors development of some tuber disorders (brown center, stem-end hollow heart)
Growth stage IV: tuber bulking	Favors development of common scab May initiate premature senescence and lead to increased early blight and early dying Intermittent dry conditions favor some tuber disorders (internal brown spot, growth cracks, irregular shape)	Promotes nitrate leaching, which may lead to increased early blight Promotes lush canopy, which may favor early blight, late blight, aerial stem rot, and Sclerotinia stalk rot May favor development of bud-end hollow heart
Growth stage V: tuber maturation	Dehydrates tubers May cause stem-end vascular discoloration	Leads to enlargement of lenticels, which allows entry of bacteria causing tuber soft rot Favors development of Pythium leak, pink rot, and late blight tuber rot May delay senescence and tuber skin set
Harvest	Increases tuber susceptibility to blackspot bruising Favors formation of dry soil clods, which bruise tubers during harvest	Increases tuber susceptibility to shatter bruise and thumbnail cracking Causes soil to cling to harvested tubers, which makes separation of tubers from soil more difficult and may favor tuber rot in storage

leaf area. The lack of vine expansion limits total photosynthetic capacity, while the lack of root development limits the plant's ability to take up water and nutrients. The combined effect is a reduced potential to form and accumulate the products of photosynthesis.

Tuber yield is a result of both the number and the size of tubers. Accumulation of photosynthetic products during the period of stolon development (growth stages II and III) is needed to promote tuberization. A plant water deficit at these stages of growth limits yield largely by reducing the number of tubers that are set. During tuber bulking (growth stage IV), excess photosynthetic products are translocated to the rapidly developing tubers. A plant water deficit at the bulking stage limits yield by reducing the production of photosynthetic compounds and thus limiting the size of tubers. Because of the length of growth stage IV, the potential for yield restrictions resulting from plant water deficits is greatest during this period.

Effects of Soil Moisture on Tuber Quality

Several tuber disorders that reduce the marketability of the crop are associated with excess, deficient, or fluctuating soil moisture. The relationships between these disorders and various soil moisture conditions are not always clear. The occurrence of a particular disorder may be affected by the water status of the plant together with some other growth factor, most notably temperature. Tuber disorders and what is known of their causes are discussed in detail in Chapter 10. Only those in which water management plays a role are briefly mentioned here and in Table 8.1.

Lenticels on tubers become enlarged (Fig. 10.1) when soil moisture is excessive, particularly during growth stages IV and V. Enlarged lenticels can be significant entry sites for soft rot bacteria and thus may affect the storability of the crop after harvest.

Fluctuations in soil moisture often interrupt tuber growth, leading to the development of disorders when normal growth resumes. Growth cracks (Plate 4) form after a plant water deficit when the resumption of normal growth causes a rapid increase in the volume of internal tissues. Malformations referred to as bottleneck, dumbbell, and pointed end (Plate 2) and second growth resulting in knobby tubers similarly occur after plant water deficits, depending on the stage of development of the tubers when growth is interrupted (Chapter 10).

Certain internal tuber disorders have also been associated with either low or high soil moisture. The direct relationships between these disorders and the water status of the plant, however, remain unclear. Translucent end (Plates 8 and 9) often develops following a plant water deficit and usually occurs in tubers with second growth and pointed stem ends. The translucent areas often break down readily and may then serve as entrance sites for decay organisms. Brown center and hollow heart (Plate 5), considered different phases of the same disorder, seem to be associated with rapid tuber growth and high soil moisture, although the exact relationship with plant water status is unclear. Internal brown spot (Plate 7) has been linked to low or fluctuating soil moisture. Discoloration of the tuber vascular ring at the stem end may develop following vine kill if soil moisture is low (below 50% of available soil water), especially if the vines die rapidly.

Soil moisture status is also a significant factor in the amount and type of mechanical damage that tubers sustain during harvest operations. Tubers are more susceptible to blackspot bruising (Plate 10) if they are dehydrated and more susceptible to shatter bruise during harvest if they are turgid (Fig. 6.4), especially at low temperatures.

Interactions Between Water Management and Other Cultural Practices

Water management affects and is affected by other cultural practices, with either positive or negative consequences for potato health (Table 8.1). Some of these interactions may significantly limit crop productivity or have detrimental effects on the environment. In developing and implementing water management strategies that are appropriate to a holistic health management plan, growers must consider not only the crop's need for water but also potential interactions with other cultural practices and possible consequences for the environment.

Tillage

Tillage practices greatly influence water infiltration and surface runoff from production fields. Excessive tillage, especially of wet soil, usually leads to soil compaction (Fig. 2.4), which can affect the water infiltration rate and also the rooting depth and root distribution. The result may be a shallow-rooted crop, a reduction in the water-holding capacity of the soil, and a decrease in the amount of soil water available to the plants. Soil drainage may also be altered, which may result in poor aeration of roots and seed pieces when excess water is present. Tillage of fine-textured soils when they are wet leads to excessive clod formation, which increases tuber bruising at harvest.

Surface runoff results in poor use of water resources, loss of topsoil through erosion, and contamination of surface waters with plant nutrients and pesticides. Runoff can be minimized by techniques such as contour farming (Fig. 2.2), minimum tillage or no-till (Fig. 2.6), or reservoir tillage (Fig. 2.1).

Hilling of potato plants (Fig. 5.3) significantly affects water infiltration patterns, particularly in sandy and loamy sand soils. In these soils, effective irrigation management is needed to replenish moisture but avoid leaching nitrate nitrogen and pesticides and thereby contaminating groundwater. The effect of hilling on water infiltration is illustrated in Plate 1. The infiltration pattern in Plate 1A, defined by the red dye, resulted from irrigation water applied to a level soil surface. The pattern in Plate 1B, formed after a similar irrigation, shows the effect of hilling—deeper infiltration in the furrow area, largely due to water directed down the sides of the hill. Some water also runs off the canopy edges and into the furrow, and some runs down the plant stem into the hill. Plate 1C shows the result of applying irrigation water in excess of the water-holding capacity of the soil—significantly deeper infiltration in the furrow area.

The significance of this effect is that it limits water uptake by the plant. Because potatoes are shallow-rooted, with a rooting depth of 12–18 inches, and the majority of the roots are concentrated directly under the hill, the potential for water uptake from the furrow area is considerably less. Aside from limiting water uptake by the plant, excessive water infiltration in the furrow area may leach nitrates out of the root zone.

Fertility Management

The productive potential of any fertilizer management program can be realized only if water is not limiting. Thus

> ## The productive potential of any fertilizer management program can be realized only if water is not limiting.

the amount of fertilizer applied should be matched with the available water. This is particularly important for nitrogen, because the response of the plant to nitrogen is directly related to the availability of water. Plants severely stressed because of inadequate water show little response to added nitrogen. Excess water is also detrimental, because nitrate nitrogen is easily leached (Chapter 9). Thus water supplied in excess of the water-holding capacity of the soil carries nitrates away

from the root zone. Continued leaching can cause nitrogen deficiency in the plants, thus limiting crop productivity.

In areas with sandy soil and a shallow water table, there is a high potential for contamination of groundwater by nitrates leached from the root zone. As discussed above, nitrate leaching is enhanced by hilling. Because of the risk of groundwater contamination, it may be unwise in such situations to apply nitrogen through sprinkler irrigation systems or to use irrigation to incorporate broadcast nitrogen. However, if irrigation is used for these purposes, only small amounts of water (0.1–0.2 inches per acre) should be applied at any one time (Box 9.2).

Disease Management

Water management is closely linked to disease, because of the effects of water on the life cycles of disease-causing organisms. Wet soil is conducive to most tuber-rotting pathogens. Excessive soil moisture following planting can promote seed piece decay. Lenticels on tubers in wet soil become swollen and serve as entry sites for soft rot bacteria. Pink rot and Pythium leak are also problems in wet soil, and tubers near the soil surface can become infected by spores of the late blight fungus washed down from the leaves. Dry soil, especially during the early stages of tuber development, favors common scab. Maintaining 80–90% of available soil water during tuberization and early bulking is a useful scab management technique.

> ## Potential effects on disease should always be considered when a water management program is being developed and implemented.

Rainfall and irrigation affect the epidemiology of foliar diseases by altering the microenvironment within the crop canopy. Most pathogens require free water in order to reproduce and infect plants. The length of time during which leaves are wet with dew, rain, or irrigation water is a major factor affecting the ability of pathogenic fungi to form spores and the ability of these spores to germinate and cause infections. Irrigation programs that permit vines to remain wet for long periods create a microenvironment conducive to early blight, late blight, Sclerotinia stalk rot, and aerial stem rot (Chapters 15–17). Rainfall and irrigation also spread fungal spores or pathogenic bacteria by washing and splashing them from infected leaves to uninfected sites. Watering also lowers the temperature within the crop canopy, which favors some diseases. For example, at temperatures between 70 and 79°F each spore of the late blight fungus germinates only once, but at temperatures below 65°F a spore releases six to eight smaller, swimming spores, each of which can cause an infection (Box 16.1).

Early blight provides an example of the complexity of interactions between water management, nitrogen management, and tillage in their effect on disease development. Plant stress due to low soil moisture can initiate premature senescence. This favors earlier infection by the early blight fungus, because this pathogen develops first on physiologically older leaves. However, excess water can also accelerate the development of the disease. Excessive irrigation or rainfall leaches nitrates away from the root zone and thus can cause nitrogen deficiency, which may also lead to premature senescence and increased early blight. Tillage practices that promote nitrate leaching, such as hilling, can aggravate this situation.

Potential effects on disease should always be considered when a water management program is being developed and implemented. Soil management practices that avoid compaction and provide optimal drainage help minimize disease problems associated with wet soils. Irrigation should be timed carefully, so that water is applied only when the crop needs it. If possible, it is best to schedule irrigation so that the vines are not wet for a long period and have a chance to dry before nightfall.

Water Management Strategies

The goal of water management is to maintain adequate soil moisture throughout the growth of the crop, while avoiding extremes and excessive fluctuations.

In production areas that depend on rainfall to maintain soil moisture, water management options may be limited to

> **The goal of water management is to maintain adequate soil moisture throughout the growth of the crop, while avoiding extremes and excessive fluctuations.**

using appropriate water conservation techniques, such as not planting potatoes on steep slopes, implementing conservation tillage practices, using soil preparation techniques that enhance water infiltration, and forming ridges in furrows to slow the movement of surface water (reservoir tillage). Details of these techniques are discussed in Chapter 2. In areas where excessive rainfall is often a problem, selecting well-drained sites,

Fig. 8.1. Center-pivot overhead sprinkler irrigating a potato field. (Used by permission of Spudman magazine)

providing proper drainage, and avoiding soil compaction may be the most effective water management strategies.

Irrigation is the major strategy for maintaining adequate soil moisture in many potato production areas. Various methods of irrigation are described below.

Methods of Irrigation

Methods of irrigation used in potato production include overhead sprinkler irrigation, furrow irrigation, subirrigation, and drip (trickle) irrigation. Each offers certain advantages and has some disadvantages.

Overhead Sprinkler Irrigation. The most common method used in potato production is irrigation by overhead sprinklers, which apply water over the crop, thus simulating rain (Fig. 8.1). Several types are used: periodic-move (moved by hand or on wheels), continuous-move (center-pivot, linear-move, and traveling-gun systems), and solid-set (with lines left in place for the entire season). Overhead sprinklers offer efficiency and considerable flexibility.

The advantages of sprinkler systems are uniformity of water distribution (periodic-move and continuous-move types are good and solid-set types are excellent in this respect); moderate to good water-use efficiency (periodic-move types are the least and solid-set types the most efficient sprinklers); and good control of the amount of water applied and the frequency of application (continuous-move and solid-set types provide better control than periodic-move types). The application rate can be matched to soil infiltration conditions by adjusting sprinkler and nozzle sizes and spacings, pump pressure, and travel speed of the system. Other advantages are that sprinklers can be used to irrigate fields with slopes as high as 10–15%; the application of water overhead cools the crop and the soil somewhat; and the system can be used effectively to apply some fertilizers and pesticides, thus maximizing equipment use and avoiding additional trips across the field. Details of fertilizer application through overhead sprinklers are discussed in Chapter 9.

A major disadvantage of sprinkler irrigation is high energy use, because of the pressure required to distribute water through the system. This can be reduced by means of "low-pressure" nozzles. In center-pivot and linear systems, the towers are moved sequentially to reduce effective overlap and achieve a uniform distribution of water. Various equipment options for sprinkler irrigation involve trade-offs of capital costs for labor. Continuous-move systems require a high initial investment but have relatively low labor costs. Periodic-move systems, on the other hand, have high labor costs, but the initial investment is much lower. Solid-set systems are intermediate in initial investment and labor costs.

Furrow Irrigation. In this form of surface irrigation, water flowing under the force of gravity is carried across the field in furrows running parallel to the slope of the field. Furrow irrigation is still practiced in some areas but has largely been replaced by sprinkler irrigation.

The advantages of furrow irrigation are uniformity of water distribution when the system is adjusted for variations in the rate of infiltration, a low energy requirement (because the system operates by gravity flow), and a relatively low equipment cost. Good water-use efficiency can be achieved if the excess water running off the low end of the field is reused.

The major disadvantages of furrow irrigation are relatively high labor costs (except in automated systems) and difficulty in managing the system in fields with substantial variations in infiltration rate. Furrow irrigation is not adapted to coarse-textured soils, because of their high infiltration rates, and it can be practiced only in fields with slopes of less than 3%.

Subirrigation. This method supplies water to the root zone by raising and lowering the water table. Subirrigation is adapted only to low-lying production areas where the water table is close to the soil surface and can be manipulated—primarily muck soils in drained wetlands.

Subirrigation has several advantages: it places water directly in the root zone and provides very uniform distribution with high water-use efficiency.

The major disadvantages of subirrigation are that it is not adapted to most production areas and is costly because of the need to build and maintain structures (dams and ditches) for controlling the water table.

Drip (Trickle) Irrigation. In this method, special plastic tubes are laid in the field to place water at the base of the plants, on or just under the soil surface. It is used in potato production in a few areas where water is in short supply.

The advantages of drip irrigation are very high water-use efficiency and low total use of water, excellent uniformity of distribution, and the ability to irrigate fields with any degree of slope. Its energy requirements are low, because the system operates at low pressure. Drip systems allow accuracy in both the volume and the frequency of application of water. They are also very accurate and efficient in applying fertilizers and some pesticides.

The major disadvantage of drip irrigation as it is practiced in potato production is a high annual capital and labor cost. It also requires that water be filtered, to prevent plugging of the drip outlets, which reduces the uniformity of water distribution.

Available Soil Water and Allowable Depletion

Regardless of the type of system used, an irrigation-scheduling program is needed in order to determine the correct frequency of application and amounts of water to be applied. Plant water stress occurs when soil moisture has been depleted below some critical level, expressed as a percentage of available soil water. For a particular soil, *available soil water* is the difference between its field capacity (the amount of water retained in the total soil pore space after saturated soil has drained) and the permanent wilting point (the point at which plants can no longer obtain water from the soil and thus wilt and die) (Fig. 8.2). Because losses of yield and quality occur in potatoes before the permanent wilting point is reached, there

is a critical amount of available soil water that can be depleted without inducing plant stress. This critical depletion amount is the *allowable depletion.*

The amount of available soil water for potatoes in a particular soil largely depends on its texture (the proportion of sand, silt, and clay particles) (Table 8.2) and the effective rooting depth of potatoes in that soil (usually 12–18 inches). In general, the amount of available soil water increases with increasing clay content of the soil (Fig. 8.3).

Data on the capacity of specific soils to store available water can be obtained from local offices of the U.S. Soil Conservation Service. This information can be used to calculate the available soil water within the rooting depth of potatoes in a particular soil. Because most fields are not uniform in soil texture, an average value must be determined for each field, based on the capacity of each major soil type present. Once the available soil water in a particular field has been determined, the allowable depletion can be calculated (Box 8.1).

The relationship between allowable depletion and available soil water is shown in Figure 8.2. Most soils must be maintained above 60–65% of available soil water to avoid plant stress. During crop growth, however, it is preferable to maintain the soil above 70–75% of available soil water, to avoid any limitations on yield and tuber quality. Box 8.2 describes percentages of available soil water needed by potatoes at each growth stage.

Table 8.2. Available soil water and infiltration rates in soils of various textures

Soil texture[a]	Available soil water (in./ft)	Infiltration rate (in./hr)
Coarse sand	0.4–0.7	0.5–1.0
Fine sand	0.7–0.9	0.5–1.0
Loamy sand	0.9–1.3	0.5–1.0
Sandy loam	1.2–1.9	0.5–1.0
Loam	1.8–2.6	0.3–0.5
Silt loam	2.0–3.0	0.3–0.5
Clay loam	2.0–2.6	0.1–0.3
Clay	1.8–2.4	0.1–0.3

[a] Soil textures are defined in Figure 2.3.

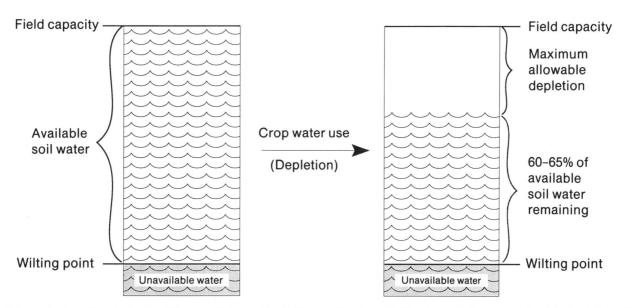

Fig. 8.2. Available soil water is the difference between the field capacity of a soil (the amount of water retained in the total soil pore space after saturated soil has drained) and the permanent wilting point (the point at which plants can no longer obtain water from the soil and thus wilt and die). Allowable depletion is the point to which available soil water can be depleted without inducing plant stress. For potatoes, the soil must always be maintained above 60–65% of available soil water.

Measurement of
Percent Available Soil Water

To determine when allowable depletion has been reached in a field, the percentage of available soil water must be monitored. In some irrigation-scheduling programs, available soil water is measured directly. This is done simply by judging the feel and appearance of soil in the hand or by using simple monitoring instruments (tensiometers or electrical conductivity sensors) or a sophisticated instrument, the neutron probe. With experience these methods can be effectively used to schedule irrigation, but direct measurement of the percentage of available soil water can be rather time-consuming, because of the number of locations that must be checked per field.

Judging the feel and appearance of soil is the least accurate method, but with experience the percentage of available soil water can be estimated to within 10–15%. Table 8.3 describes

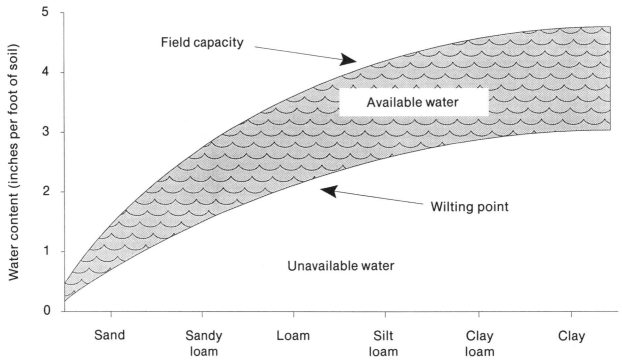

Fig. 8.3. Available soil water in soils of different textures. In general, the available soil water increases with increasing clay content of the soil.

Box 8.1

Calculation of Available Soil Water and Allowable Depletion

The following example illustrates the calculation of available soil water and allowable depletion for a specific soil type, Richford Loamy Sand. Local data indicate that the effective rooting depth of potatoes in this soil is 15 inches. Information from the U.S. Soil Conservation Service indicates that the capacity of this soil to store available water is 0.12 inches per inch of depth in the 0- to 7-inch profile and 0.11 inches per inch of depth below that.

Available soil water at a rooting depth of 15 inches is calculated as follows:

$$7 \times 0.12 = 0.84 \text{ inches in the first 7 inches of soil}$$
$$+ 8 \times 0.11 = 0.88 \text{ inches in the next 8 inches of soil}$$
$$\overline{ 1.72 \text{ inches in the 15-inch rooting depth}}$$

The allowable depletion can now be calculated by multiplying the available soil water by the maximum percentage of depletion allowed at each growth stage of potatoes (see Box 8.2). Since the soil should be maintained above 70% of available soil water, the allowable depletion will not exceed 30%. In this case, it is calculated as follows:

$$1.72 \text{ inches} \times 30\% = 0.52 \text{ inches}$$

It is important to remember that the calculated available soil water is only an estimate of the soil's capacity for storing available water. Thus the calculated allowable depletion value may have to be modified according to personal experience. If several soil types are present in a field, an average of individual values may be more appropriate.

Once the allowable depletion has been determined for a particular field, this figure along with data on rates of water infiltration into the soils in the field (Table 8.2) can be used to determine amounts of irrigation water to be applied and rates of application.

the appearance and feel of soils of various textures containing different percentages of available soil water.

A tensiometer consists of a long plastic tube with a vacuum-measuring gauge at one end and a hollow, porous ceramic tip at the other end, which is placed in the soil at the desired depth. The porous tip allows water to pass through it but is impermeable to air and soil particles. Tensiometers are usually installed in a field and left in place for the entire season. Readings on the gauge do not directly measure the amount of water in the soil but rather measure soil suction, which represents the energy a plant must exert to extract water from the soil. Tensiometers require a great deal of experience to use, as a special calibration curve is needed for each soil to convert measurements of soil suction into percent available soil water. Once this is established, however, an experienced manager knows immediately after reading the gauge whether irrigation is needed. Tensiometers are more useful in coarse-textured soils, because they are not accurate at all levels of soil suction, especially at the higher tensions that occur in fine-textured soils. It is also time-consuming to read and service the instruments several times per week.

An electrical conductivity sensor consists of electrodes mounted in a block of plaster of paris, gypsum, or some other porous substance, which is buried in the soil at the desired depth. It operates on the principle that electrical conductivity across the electrodes varies with the percentage of available soil water. This is measured by a resistance meter connected by wires to the porous block. Electrical conductivity sensors give fairly good results if properly calibrated before use. Like tensiometers, they require considerable experience for accurate use, and the manufacturer's instructions must be followed carefully. Each block must be calibrated in the soil with the meter to be used. When the blocks are installed, the replaced soil must be packed to the same density as the rest of the profile, and good contact between the block and the soil must be ensured to obtain accurate readings.

The neutron probe is an expensive device and is used in only a few production situations. This instrument contains a radioactive source emitting neutrons from a probe placed in the soil at the desired depth. The instrument detects the velocity of neutrons bouncing back to the probe, which is a measure of the water content of the soil at that depth. A separate calibration curve must be developed for each soil at each depth to convert readings to percent available soil water. The system is very expensive and time-consuming, but it is highly accurate.

Crop Water Use: Evapotranspiration

Because of the difficulty and expense of direct measurement of percent available soil water, most irrigation-scheduling programs are based on an indirect measure. In this case, irrigation is scheduled according to a water budget, in which the water used by the crop is balanced against irrigation and precipitation. To do this, some estimate is needed of how much water the crop uses on any given day. Crop water use is usually expressed as *evapotranspiration*. This is the sum of two forms of water loss—evaporation from the soil surface and transpiration from the plants. Evapotranspiration is affected by several climatic factors and plant characteristics. It increases as solar radiation, temperature, and wind velocity increase and as the size of the plant canopy (leaf area) increases. It decreases as relative humidity increases and as stomata on the leaves close in response to water stress.

Box 8.2

Guidelines for Water Management in Irrigated Production of Potatoes

Growth Stage I: Sprout Development

Avoid planting in excessively wet or dry soil. The soil profile should contain a moderate amount of moisture (70–80% of available soil water). This provides good planting conditions and adequate water for sprout development. If the soil is excessively dry, it should be irrigated before planting. Postplant irrigations prior to crop emergence are not advisable, because of the risk of inducing seed piece decay.

Growth Stage II: Vegetative Growth

As plants emerge and grow, most soils can be maintained at 75–85% of available soil water. In sandy soils in areas with high rainfall, the percentage should be slightly lower, to provide a water storage buffer. This reduces the potential for nitrate leaching as a result of heavy rainfall before the root system of the plant has developed sufficiently to take up applied nitrogen.

Growth Stage III: Tuber Initiation

The soil should be maintained at 80–90% of available soil water during tuber initiation. This provides the moisture required for optimal tuber set and reduces the development of common scab on newly formed tubers. If problems with brown center and hollow heart are anticipated, the soil should be kept drier (70–80% of available soil water), especially during cool weather.

Growth Stage IV: Tuber Bulking

The potato crop's highest demand for water occurs during tuber bulking: 80–90% of available soil water should be maintained at this stage. Water stress during bulking can significantly affect tuber yield and quality and the development of disease in the crop. However, excessive irrigation (in which the soil is held near saturation and vines are kept wet for long periods) should be avoided, to minimize the development of early blight, late blight, aerial stem rot, and Sclerotinia stalk rot.

Growth Stage V: Maturation

Demand for water is reduced as the plants begin natural senescence. Soil moisture can be allowed to decline to 60–65% of available soil water to promote skin set (the development of tuber periderm). High soil moisture (above 65% of available soil water) should be avoided during maturation, to minimize problems with pink rot and Pythium leak of tubers and the development of enlarged lenticels, which can increase the potential for bacterial soft rot in storage. Excessively dry soil at harvest (below 60% of available soil water) can hinder effective harvesting, increase tuber bruising caused by soil clods, and favor blackspot bruising.

Various methods have been developed for estimating daily evapotranspiration. The least accurate method is a simple bookkeeping approach in which estimates are based on data tabulated according to daily weather conditions, as in Table 8.4. Locally developed guides to crop water use are available in some production areas and may provide more accurate estimates.

In some areas, the Cooperative Extension Service or local agencies estimate evapotranspiration from current climatic data, and this information is provided to growers by telephone, radio, or newspapers. This may also be available as an on-line service through regional computer networks, such as the AgriMet network in the Pacific Northwest. The estimates are generally calculated for a well-watered potato crop or reference crop at full cover. The irrigation manager then uses a correction factor to adjust this value to the current growth stage of a specific potato crop. Local irrigation specialists or Cooperative Extension Service personnel should have information about evapotranspiration estimates available for specific production areas.

Irrigation Scheduling

Irrigation-scheduling programs are usually tailored to specific production areas, because of variation in soils and climatic conditions, requirements of different cultivars, and the availability of irrigation water. Daily depletions of available soil water are calculated from data on soil moisture measured directly in the field or, in the case of the water budget approach, from estimates of evapotranspiration. When these calculations show that the allowable depletion has been reached, irrigation is applied in amounts sufficient to replace the depleted water, thus restoring the appropriate percentage of available soil water.

Irrigation-scheduling programs based on a water budget approach not only are more convenient but also are readily computerized. In several major potato-producing regions, scheduling programs are available for on-farm computers. For instance, in the Wisconsin Irrigation Scheduling Program (WISP), estimates of daily evapotranspiration are used to determine the current percentage of available soil water, the frequency of irrigation, and the amount of water to be applied.

Table 8.3. Guidelines for estimating percent available soil water from the appearance and feel of soil in the hand[a]

Percent available soil water	Test[b]	Soil texture	
		Loam, silt loam, clay loam	Sand, loamy sand
50	B	Readily forms a ball that holds its shape. No moist feeling on the hand. Soil fragments do not cling to the palm. The ball breaks easily and crumbles into small particles.	Forms a very weak ball or several balls with fingerprint outline barely visible. Soil grains stick to the palm.
	R	Too crumbly to form a ribbon.	Does not form a ribbon, but a patchy layer may stick to the thumb.
	P	Crumbles readily into individual particles.	. . .
60–65	B	Forms a firm ball with visible finger marks imprinted. The hand feels damp but not moist. Soil fragments do not cling to the palm. The ball is pliable but, when broken, shatters or breaks into medium-sized fragments.	Forms a weak, brittle ball with indistinct fingerprint outline. Soil particles stick to the palm in patches.
	R	Ribbons out ¼ inch or barely forms a ribbon.	Does not form a ribbon, but a patchy layer may stick to the thumb.
	P	Breaks into granules and continues to crumble until a tiny round ball remains.	. . .
70–80	B	Soil feels damp, heavy, and slightly sticky. Forms a tight, plastic ball that shatters with a burst into large particles when squeezed. The hand feels moist.	Forms a weak ball with distinct fingerprint outline. Soil particles stick to the palm.
	R	Ribbons out ½ inch. Moist soil particles are left on the thumb.	Does not form a ribbon, but soil particles stick to the thumb in a distinct layer.
	P	Can be rolled into a round, somewhat plastic ball that does not readily shatter.	. . .
100	B	Soil feels wet, sticky, doughy, and slick. Forms a very plastic ball that handles like modeling clay. The ball changes shape when squeezed and cracks before it breaks. Water remains on the hand.	Forms a somewhat sticky ball with sharp fingerprint outline. When the ball is squeezed, no water appears, but a wet outline of the ball is left on the palm.
	R	Ribbons out readily if not too wet.	Does not form a ribbon, but soil particles form a smooth layer on the thumb.
	P	Forms a tight ball that can be rolled into a long, pencil-like shape.	. . .

[a] Adapted from Anonymous, 1976, Soil Moisture Scheduling Procedure, Miscellaneous Series, No. 39, University of Idaho Cooperative Extension System, Moscow.
[b] B = ball test; R = ribbon test; P = open-palm test. The *ball test* evaluates the effects of squeezing soil hard in the fist to form a ball and then breaking the ball with the thumb and forefinger. The *ribbon test* evaluates the ability of the soil to form a ribbon when rolled out between the thumb and forefinger, held ⅛ inch apart. The *open-palm test* evaluates the effects of rolling soil gently between the palms of the hands.

Table 8.4. Daily evapotranspiration estimates based on weather conditions

Weather	Evapotranspiration (in./day)				
	May	June	July	Aug.	Sept.
Dull, cloudy	0.12	0.15	0.15	0.12	0.09
Partly sunny	0.15	0.20	0.20	0.15	0.12
Bright, hot	0.20	0.25	0.25	0.20	0.15

The irrigation manager using WISP enters the following data:

- Allowable depletion (AD) value determined for the field

- Initial AD balance—the portion of AD that is present at crop emergence, when irrigation scheduling begins

- Amount of rain and irrigation water added to the field

- Daily evapotranspiration (ET) estimate based on calculations done by the manager or obtained from local sources

- Percent canopy cover (or other coefficient) to adjust the ET estimate when the crop is at less than full cover

The WISP program then gives the following information:

- ET estimate adjusted for the crop at less than full cover

- Current AD balance—the portion of AD present in the field

- Projected AD balance for the next 24 and 48 hours

Using the current and projected AD balances from WISP, the manager can make decisions regarding irrigation frequency and amounts of water to be applied. The goal is to keep the AD balance from dropping to zero, at which point potato plants begin to experience stress.

Regardless of the irrigation-scheduling method, two general guidelines always apply in irrigated production of potatoes:

1. The soil must always be maintained above 60–65% of available soil water throughout the growing season.

2. Wide fluctuations in soil moisture should be avoided whenever possible, especially those that lead to extremely wet or dry soil.

Irrigation scheduling can be fine-tuned to make allowances for the potato plant's changing water needs at various growth stages. Guidelines for this take into account not only the crop's need for water but also interactions between water management and other cultural practices (Box 8.2). Effective water management strategies are key components of any holistic potato health management plan. Good water management promotes optimum plant health, profitable tuber yield and quality, and environmental integrity.

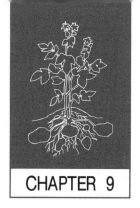

CHAPTER 9

D. T. Westermann
U.S. Department of Agriculture
Agricultural Research Service, Kimberly, Idaho

Fertility Management

A comprehensive strategy for potato health management requires that all essential plant nutrients be available in amounts needed for optimal potato growth and development. Essential nutrients are those required for a normal life cycle and for which no other nutrient can be substituted. Sixteen nutrients are known to be essential for higher plants. These function as major constituents of plant cells or are used in metabolic processes within the plant. Carbon, hydrogen, and oxygen are supplied in water and in the atmosphere. The remaining essential nutrients must be taken up by the roots of the plant from the soil solution or absorbed by the leaves from foliar sprays.

Nutritional Needs of the Potato Plant

The nutritional requirements of the potato plant change at various stages of crop development. Appropriate fertility management strategies for potato production are based on the different nutritional needs of the crop at each growth stage.

Changes in Nutritional Needs As the Crop Develops

The distribution of dry matter within a potato plant changes at each stage of growth and development (Fig. 9.1). During growth stage I (sprout development), the seed piece is the sole source of energy for growth, because photosynthesis has not yet begun. Soil nutrients are not available to the plant until roots develop.

Photosynthesis begins during growth stage II (vegetative growth) and provides energy for the growth and development of vegetative parts of the plant. Roots actively absorb plant nutrients from the soil during this stage.

The onset of growth stage III (tuber initiation) is controlled by growth-regulating hormones produced in the plant. Before tuber initiation can begin, photosynthesis must supply more carbohydrate (in the form of sucrose) than is needed for the growth of leaves, stems, and roots. Soil moisture and temperature, nitrogen nutrition, and plant hormones all affect tuber initiation.

During growth stage IV (tuber bulking), development proceeds in a nearly linear fashion if no growth factor becomes limiting. Tubers become the dominant sink for carbohydrates and mobile inorganic nutrients. Carbohydrates in the form of sucrose are transported into tubers and converted to starch, which increases the ratio of dry matter to water in the tubers. Environmental and other factors may reduce the plant's ability to supply carbohydrates or inorganic nutrients at sufficient rates for tuber growth. If this occurs, these materials are solubilized in the vegetative parts of the plant and transported to developing tubers, which eventually causes premature senescence of the vines. Plants in this condition may be more susceptible to certain diseases, such as early blight and early dying. Late-maturing cultivars may continue some vegetative growth during tuber bulking, but at a slower rate than in growth stage III. Most of the nutrients used by the plant are taken up during growth stage IV, and uptake is nearly complete by the end of this stage.

During growth stage V (maturation), the dry matter content of the tubers reaches a maximum. Nutrients in the tops and roots are solubilized and moved into the tubers, which may accumulate an additional 10–15% of their dry weight during this stage. The portion of nutrients absorbed by the plant that ends up in the tubers at harvest depends upon the mobility of each nutrient within the plant. In the case of highly mobile

> ## Most of the nutrients used by the plant are taken up during growth stage IV.

nutrients, such as nitrogen, 90% or more of the total amount taken up by the plant may end up in the tubers at maturity. In the case of relatively immobile nutrients, such as calcium, however, the portion is only 10–20% of the total uptake.

Nutritional Disorders

Nutritional disorders can result from deficiencies, excesses (toxicities), and antagonisms between nutrients in the soil or as they are taken up by the plant. Soil pH plays a major role in nutrient availability (Fig. 9.2). At pH 5 and below, problems may be encountered with calcium, magnesium, and molybdenum deficiencies; phosphorus fixation; ammonium, manganese, and aluminum toxicities; and increased leaching of some elements, such as magnesium. At pH 7.5 and above, deficiencies of boron, copper, iron, manganese, and zinc may occur, and phosphorus may be less available, because of the

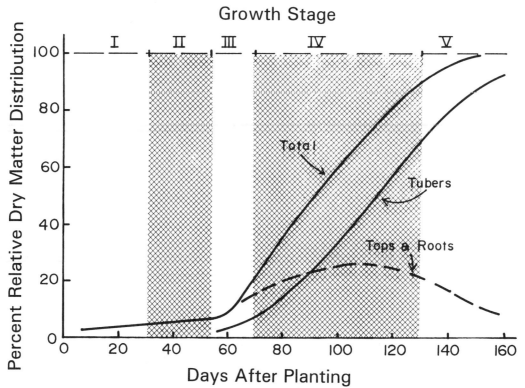

Fig. 9.1. Dry matter distribution in Russet Burbank, a late-maturing cultivar. Early-maturing cultivars have similar distributions, with their growth stages beginning earlier. Local growing conditions affect the actual timing of growth stages. The growth stages are defined in Figure 1.3.

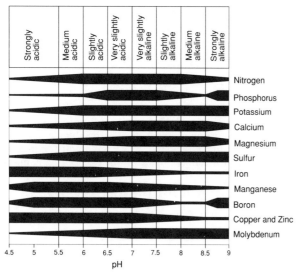

Fig. 9.2. Availability of nutrients to plants in relation to soil pH. The widest parts of the bars indicate maximum availability. (Reprinted, by permission, from R. J. Cook and R. J. Veseth, 1991, Wheat Health Management, American Phytopathological Society, St. Paul, MN, as redrawn from C. J. Pratt, 1965, Chemical fertilizers, Scientific American 212 [June]: 62-72)

precipitation of calcium phosphates.

Nutrient deficiencies in potato plants can sometimes be identified from visible symptoms (Box 9.1), but visual diagnoses can be misleading, and diagnosis can be complicated by nonnutritional factors or multiple deficiencies. Symptoms may not be readily apparent as nutritional problems develop, and by the time they are visible it is often too late to make corrections to avoid a loss of tuber yield or quality. Another

problem with visual diagnosis is that symptoms of nutrient disorders are sometimes masked by those due to infection by pathogenic microorganisms, and some disease symptoms resemble those of certain nutrient disorders. More precise and timely identification of nutrient disorders can be obtained from a chemical analysis of plant tissues (see Nutritional Management Tools, below).

Factors Affecting Nutritional Needs

Potential Tuber Yield

As long as pests and diseases are not limiting factors, adequate nutrition will maximize tuber yield potential within the genetic limitations of the cultivar and the climate in which it is grown. Rates of nitrogen, phosphorus, and potassium uptake for tuber bulking (growth stage IV) in selected cultivars are shown in Table 9.1. These may be adequate for early-maturing cultivars if the plants are large enough to meet the demand for products of photosynthesis. In late-maturing cultivars, such as Russet Burbank, nutrient uptake rates during growth stage IV must be slightly greater than that needed for tuber growth. This is necessary to allow for some new vegetative growth to offset the effects of leaf aging and maintain maximum production of dry matter. Low nutrient concentrations may reduce the rate of photosynthesis and ultimately result in lower tuber yield if insufficient quantities of the products of photosynthesis are generated during growth stage IV.

Potential tuber yield and appropriate fertilization strategies are affected by the maturity class of the cultivar grown and the length of the growing season. Early-maturing cultivars generally have a shorter growing cycle from planting until the start of maturation. They generally have higher rates of nutrient uptake during growth stages II and III and hence need adequate preplant fertilization. Late-maturing cultivars may have a greater maximum leaf area and may produce more total dry matter, and their potential tuber yield may thus be greater if healthy leaves remain active long enough.

The potential tuber yield of a late-maturing cultivar also increases as the length of the growing season increases, provided other factors are not limiting. In a 130-day frost-free growing season, growth stage IV may last about 70 days; in a 180-day growing season, it may last 100 days or longer. If the average daily tuber growth rate is 700 pounds per acre, the potential tuber yields in these two growing seasons would be 490 and 700 cwt per acre, respectively. Approximately 70 more pounds of nitrogen per acre would be required for tuber growth in the longer growing season. Proportionally more of the other nutrients would also be needed.

Nutrient Interactions

The plant's response to the application of a specific nutrient depends on the availability of other nutrients. The response to one nutrient is limited if any other nutrient is insufficiently available. This situation can be corrected by identifying the nutrient or nutrients that are limiting and applying the amounts needed to attain the potential yield of the cultivar in the production area where it is grown.

For example, chloride applications suppress the concentration of nitrate in the petiole. Potassium suppresses magnesium uptake, and vice versa. High amounts of ammonium suppress potassium uptake. Excessive iron induces manganese deficiency. Heavy applications of phosphorus induce zinc deficiency in soils low in available zinc. Nitrogen and sulfur are related within the plant, because they are essential components of protein, in a ratio of about 15:1.

These problems can be offset somewhat by the capacity of the plant to make use of nutrients over a wide range of availability in the soil if individual elements are not at deficient or toxic concentrations. In addition, fertile soils have some buffering capacity to supply needed nutrients regardless of what is applied as fertilizer.

Environmental Factors

Soil and air temperatures have a major effect on the early-season growth of potatoes. Low soil temperatures during growth stages I and II reduce rates of root growth and nutrient uptake, especially phosphorus uptake. It is possible to partially compensate for low soil temperatures by using starter fer-

Table 9.1. Tuber growth rates and nutrient use by selected potato cultivars during growth stage IV

Cultivar[a]	Average daily growth rate of tubers (lb/acre)	Daily nutrient use (lb/acre)		
		Nitrogen	Phosphorus	Potassium
Russet Burbank	850	2.5–3.6	0.37–0.54	2.8–3.6
Lemhi Russet	890	2.2–3.9	0.39–0.56	2.9–3.7
Centennial Russet	800	2.5–3.6	0.35–0.50	2.6–3.4
Norgold Russet	1,070	2.7–4.0	0.47–0.67	3.5–4.5
Pioneer	1,200	3.1–4.9	0.53–0.76	3.9–5.0
Norchip	700	1.8–2.8	0.31–0.44	2.3–2.9
Kennebec	1,300	3.3–5.2	0.57–0.82	4.2–5.5
Red McClure	1,000	3.4	0.50	3.3
Oromonte	1,000	3.0	0.40	3.4
White Rose	860	2.9	0.35	4.5
Four unspecified cultivars (avg.)	800	2.8	0.28	4.2

[a] Russet Burbank, Lemhi Russet, Centennial Russet, Norgold Russet, Pioneer, Norchip, and Kennebec from Kimberly, Idaho; Red McClure and Oromonte from Colorado; White Rose from California; and four unspecified cultivars from Maine.

Box 9.1

Nutrient Deficiency Symptoms of Potato Foliage

Nitrogen	Entire plants may turn light green. Young leaves remain green; older leaves turn yellow to light brown and become senescent.
Phosphorus	Plants are stunted. Leaves are dark green, and their margins roll upward. Some purpling occurs in pigmented leaves. The severity of leafroll increases as the deficiency increases.
Potassium	Plants may be stunted. Young leaves develop a crinkly surface, and their margins roll downward. Leaves have slightly black pigmentation. Marginal scorching with necrotic spots may occur on older leaves.
Calcium	The youngest mature leaves roll upward and become chlorotic with brown spotting. Growing buds may die. In tubers, a brown discoloration develops within the vascular ring before symptoms appear on vegetation.
Magnesium	Young mature leaves are affected with interveinal chlorosis and brown spotting, which develop into interveinal scorching and necrosis. Leaves near growing buds remain green.
Sulfur	The symptoms are similar to those of nitrogen deficiency, except that chlorosis develops first in young leaves. Affected leaves turn uniformly yellow.
Boron	Growing buds die. Plants appear bushy, having shorter internodes. Leaves thicken and roll upward. Leaf tissue darkens and collapses.
Zinc	Young leaves are chlorotic, narrow, and upward-cupped and develop tipburn. Other leaf symptoms are green veining, necrotic spotting, blotching, and erect appearance.
Iron	Young leaves are yellow to nearly white but not necrotic. Leaf tips and edges remain green the longest. Green veining occurs in leaves.
Manganese	Young leaves are affected with interveinal chlorosis and then gray and black flecking and leaf cupping. The flecks eventually develop into small dead patches.
Copper	Young leaves develop a pronounced rolling, and then leaf tips wilt and die. Leaves remain green and are of normal size.
Molybdenum	Leaves turn yellow or greenish yellow. The symptoms are similar to those of nitrogen deficiency.
Chloride	Young leaves are light green, turn purplish bronze, and may curl upward or appear pebbled.

tilizers, by banding fertilizers at planting, or by using higher fertilizer application rates. The objective is to provide nutrients sufficient to promote early development of leaf area for optimal light interception and photosynthesis, but not enough to stimulate excessive vegetative growth. This is important for both maturity types, but particularly for late-maturing cultivars, as relatively high concentrations of available nitrogen during growth stages II and III tend to delay the onset of linear tuber growth rates in these types.

High soil temperatures can accelerate early plant development and thus hasten senescence, particularly in early-maturing cultivars. Premature senescence can also result from physiological stresses on the plant, caused by high ambient temperatures, air pollutants, or low soil moisture. Abnormally high temperatures coinciding with high nitrogen status in the plant during growth stage IV can stimulate excessive vegetative growth in late-maturing cultivars. This may limit the growth of tubers or cause problems with tuber quality.

The specific effects of adverse temperatures are difficult to predict, because of the many relationships between various factors affecting plant growth. In general, high nutrient concentrations in the plant do not relieve plant stresses caused by climatic abnormalities and may intensify their effects.

Soil moisture also has important effects on plant growth and affects some fertility relationships (Chapter 8).

Diseases and Tuber Disorders

The severity of many potato diseases often increases if the plants are also stressed by heat, insufficient amounts of nutrients or water, or other adverse environmental factors. Good management of soil fertility and plant nutrition can help to suppress many diseases and minimize their effects on yield. Appropriate applications of nitrogen, phosphorus, and potassium, based on analyses of soil and leaf tissue, will help suppress symptoms of potato early dying (Chapter 17) and early blight (Chapter 16). Heavy applications of nitrogen can stimulate excessive vegetative growth, resulting in an extensive plant canopy. The moist microclimate maintained underneath such a canopy promotes the development of aerial stem rot (Chapter 15), Sclerotinia stalk rot (Chapter 17), and tuber diseases associated with wet soils, such as pink rot (Chapter 17).

> **The severity of many potato diseases often increases if the plants are also stressed by heat, insufficient amounts of nutrients or water, or other adverse environmental factors.**

A nutrition program that allows tubers to reach full maturity before harvest generally helps to minimize losses resulting from tuber disorders and diseases. The specific gravity of tuber tissues is lower in relatively immature tubers harvested because of premature senescence or because normal maturation was prevented. Nutrient deficiencies can cause premature senescence, whereas high rates of nitrogen fertilization tend to delay normal maturation, particularly in late-maturing cultivars. Tubers that attain high specific gravity with good fertility management practices also tend to have lower concentrations of reducing sugars, good chip and fry colors, and fewer problems with blackspot bruise and decay. Adequate calcium concentrations in tubers may also help reduce bacterial soft rot in storage. Additional calcium applied to soils in which calcium is limiting may also reduce internal tuber disorders, such as internal brown spot, brown center, and hollow heart.

Good fertilization and nutrient management practices will maximize tuber quality (Chapter 10).

Nutritional Management Tools

Fertility management is an important part of any holistic potato health management program. The goal in managing crop nutrition is to promote uniform and continuous growth of plants and tubers throughout all growth stages. Soil testing and plant tissue testing for nutrient analysis should be used routinely by managers to guide nutritional programs.

Soil Analysis

The relative availability of nutrients in the soil before planting can be measured by soil testing. Soil test data can be used in selecting fertilizers and application rates that are appropriate for the specific needs at a particular planting site. Soil testing can also identify production areas where additional

> **The goal in managing crop nutrition is to promote uniform and continuous growth of plants and tubers throughout all growth stages.**

fertilizers are not needed, enabling growers to cut expenses and avoid overfertilization and potential environmental pollution. Different soil-testing laboratories may use different chemical procedures and may vary in their interpretations of the results and their subsequent recommendations. Laboratories using procedures developed and calibrated for a specific growing region generally give the best results in that area.

Soil samples submitted for analysis must be representative of the sampled area. It is essential that each field be sampled in such a way that variations within the field are accurately represented. In general, fields should be divided into areas of uniform soil color or texture, cropping history, and fertilization or manuring history. One sample should represent no more than 20 acres, even if the soil is uniform. Usually, 10–20 soil cores (0.75 inch in diameter) are randomly taken in a zigzag pattern across the sampled area and then combined to make up a single sample. A sampling depth of 12 inches is adequate for most nutrients, but for analysis of residual nitrogen a second sample should be taken from the 12- to 24-inch profile. Extensive precipitation that causes considerable leaching following soil sampling can nullify the analysis of residual nitrogen. Managers are encouraged to seek professional help in determining correct sampling procedures for their particular fields. It cannot be overemphasized that an appropriate preplant fertilization program depends on thorough and accurate soil sampling for nutrient analysis in each field.

Fertilizer recommendations are based on soil test results, the potential yield of the chosen cultivar at a particular site, the intended market for the crop, the efficiency of various application methods, the soil texture, and the amount of plant nutrients available from other sources, such as manure or irrigation water. All these variables must be integrated into a single recommendation to fit a particular situation. Individual growers, assisted by professional advice, must ultimately determine their own fertilizer programs.

Plant Tissue Analysis

Chemical analysis of plant tissues is widely used as a diagnostic tool to determine nutrient status during crop growth.

This method is based on known relationships between nutrient concentrations in plant tissues and the growth rate or yield of the plant at different growth stages. The growth rate is low at low nutrient concentrations but increases considerably at slightly higher concentrations and continues to increase with nutrient concentration until nutrition no longer limits growth (Fig. 9.3). Further increases in nutrient concentrations do not increase the growth rate and may actually reduce it if they reach toxic levels. An appropriate nutrient management program is one that maintains nutrient concentrations in the "sufficient" range during all stages of plant growth, but not in the deficient or the toxic range.

Particular tissues are usually selected for chemical analysis because their nutrient concentrations relate well to the nutritional status of the whole plant and are sensitive to changes in the availability of nutrients. In potatoes, the petiole of the fourth leaf from the top of the plant is generally used for chemical analysis (Fig. 9.4). The leaflets are stripped off the petiole and discarded immediately after sampling. Sometimes the entire leaf is used, rather than just the petiole.

Plant samples for tissue analysis must be representative of the sampled field. Approximately 40–50 petioles should be collected from the sampled area, in a pattern similar to that used in collecting soil samples. Areas with different soil types or different cropping and fertilization histories should be sampled separately. Tissue samples should be dried immediately at 150°F or kept cool until submitted, because nutrient concentrations may change in moist samples that are stored warm. They should be placed in clean bags or containers in which they cannot be contaminated with any nutrient element. Details on sampling procedures and guidelines for handling tissue samples should be obtained from the plant analysis laboratory where they will be submitted.

Problems encountered in using tissue analysis to monitor nutritional status include selection of the correct leaf for sampling, changes in nutrient concentrations with plant age, recent fertilizer applications, and differences between cultivars.

It is very important that tissue samples be taken only from the fourth leaf from the top of the plant. Analysis of samples consistently taken from younger or older leaves gives significantly different results, which do not represent the actual nutritional status of the plant.

Nutrient concentrations in plant tissues change with the age of the plant. Most nutrients are at their peak concentration in vegetative tissues during tuber initiation (growth stage III), and the concentration usually declines until late maturation (growth stage V) unless additional amounts are applied during the growth of the crop. Thus, a nutrient concentration that is adequate during growth stage III is generally more than sufficient for growth during growth stage IV. Nitrogen, phosphorus, potassium, copper, zinc, and sulfur decrease in concentration in foliage with increasing plant age, if no additional nutrients are applied, while calcium, magnesium, boron, iron, chloride, and manganese increase in concentration.

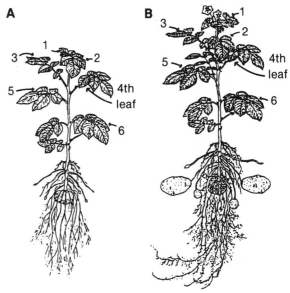

Fig. 9.4. Vegetative shoot (**A**) and shoot with a floral spike (**B**). The fourth leaf from the top of the plant is used in tissue analyses to determine the nutrient status of the plant during growth.

Table 9.2. Suggested ranges of nutrient concentrations in the fourth leaf from the top of the potato plant during growth stage IV

	Low	Marginal	Sufficient
Petiole without leaflets[a]			
Nitrate nitrogen,[b] ppm	< 10,000	10,000–15,000	> 15,000
Phosphate phosphorus,[b] ppm	< 700	700–1,000	> 1,000
Phosphorus, %	< 0.17	0.17–0.22	> 0.22
Potassium, %	< 7.0	7.0–8.0	> 8.0
Calcium, %	< 0.4	0.4–0.6	> 0.6
Magnesium, %	< 0.15	0.15–0.3	> 0.3
Sulfur, %	< 0.15	0.15–0.2	> 0.2
Sulfate sulfur,[b] ppm	< 200	200–500	> 500
Zinc, ppm	< 10	10–20	> 20
Boron, ppm	< 10	10–20	> 20
Manganese, ppm	< 20	20–30	> 30
Iron, ppm	< 20	20–50	> 50
Copper, ppm	< 2	2–4	> 4
Molybdenum, ppm	...[c]	...[c]	...[c]
Entire leaf (petiole plus leaflets)[a]			
Nitrogen, %	< 2.5	2.5–3.5	> 3.5
Phosphorus, %	< 0.15	0.15–0.25	> 0.25
Potassium, %	< 2.25	2.25–3.50	> 3.50
Calcium, %	< 0.30	0.30–0.60	> 0.60
Magnesium, %	< 0.15	0.15–0.25	> 0.25
Sulfur, %	< 0.12	0.12–0.20	> 0.20
Zinc, ppm	< 15	15–20	> 20
Boron, ppm	< 10	10–20	> 20
Manganese, ppm	< 10	10–20	> 20
Iron, ppm	< 11	11–30	> 30
Copper, ppm	< 2.0	2.0–5.0	> 5.0
Molybdenum, ppm	...[c]	...[c]	> 1.0

[a] Values for petiole concentrations are for Russet Burbank; those for the entire leaf are suitable for many cultivars.
[b] Concentration of soluble nutrient (ppm = parts per million).
[c] Concentration unknown.

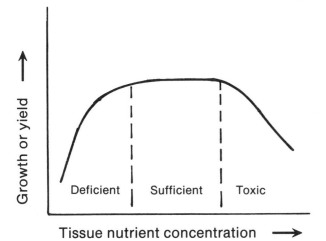

Fig. 9.3. Growth or yield of potato plants in relation to the nutrient concentration in plant tissues.

Differences in nutrient concentrations in various tissues and changes in these concentrations with the age of the plant reflect differences in the mobility of nutrients within the plant and the balance between the rate of supply and the use of nutrients in various tissues. Thus the nutrient concentrations that are considered sufficient vary from one growth stage to another.

Nutrient concentrations in plant samples taken soon after a fertilizer application are probably not indicative of the true nutritional status of the plant. Within the first few days after a nitrogen application, the petiole nitrate concentration usually reflects a buildup of nitrate within the plant, because the conversion to protein has not yet occurred. The petiole nitrate concentration may also not respond quickly to an application of ammonium if soil nitrification is inhibited by cool, wet soil or a nitrification inhibitor. A high chloride concentration or a heavy application of chloride suppresses the petiole nitrate concentration but not the leaf protein nitrogen concentration.

Table 9.3. Nutrient concentrations in petioles of three potato cultivars relative to the concentration in Russet Burbank (the latter set at 1.00 for each nutrient)[a]

Nutrient	Norgold Russet	Norchip	Kennebec
Nitrate nitrogen	0.88	0.99	0.96
Phosphorus	1.25	0.98	1.32
Potassium	0.98	0.94	1.05
Calcium	0.89	1.19	0.77
Magnesium	0.90	1.43	0.78
Zinc	1.04	0.98	1.19
Manganese	0.85	1.47	1.01
Copper	1.26	1.24	1.25

[a] Suggested ranges of petiole nutrient concentrations in Russet Burbank are given in Table 9.2.

Table 9.4. Fertilizer materials suitable for application as foliar sprays to correct nutrient deficiencies in potato plants

Nutrient	Source	Comments[a]
Phosphorus	Monoammonium phosphate Orthophosphate materials	May cause leaf damage at high soluble rates; benefits are very short-lived
Boron	Sodium borates Solubor Boric acid	Apply at growth stage II or III; repeated applications may be necessary; soil applications are preferable
Copper	Copper sulfates Copper chelates	Apply at growth stage II or III; one application may be sufficient
Iron	Iron sulfate Iron chelates	Repeated applications are necessary to correct most deficiencies
Magnesium	Magnesium sulfate	One application may be sufficient
Manganese	Manganese sulfate Manganese chelates	Effective method for correcting deficiencies; two or three applications may be necessary
Molybdenum	Sodium molybdate Ammonium molybdate	Effective method for correcting deficiencies; very low rates are sufficient
Zinc	Zinc sulfates Zinc chelates	Apply at growth stage II or III; one application may be sufficient

[a] Foliar sprays are generally not recommended for treatment of nitrogen, phosphorus, potassium, calcium, or sulfur deficiencies. Consult a local fertilizer or crop advisor for correct application rates before applying any of these materials.

Nutrient concentrations determined soon after foliar sprays have been applied (including some pesticides that contain nutrients) are likely to include external nutrients not yet absorbed by the plant tissues.

Nutrient concentrations in the petiole without leaflets and in the entire leaf (petiole and leaflets) are divided into low, marginal, and sufficient ranges (Table 9.2). These ranges vary for different cultivars (Table 9.3). Deficiency symptoms (Box 9.1) are generally visible or soon develop when concentrations are in the low range. Symptoms are probably not visible when concentrations are in the marginal range, but additional nutrient applications may be needed if a significant portion of the growing season remains. Concentrations in the sufficient range are generally adequate for plant and tuber growth at the time of sampling. Nutritional problems may still develop before the end of the growing season, but these can be detected by later tissue samplings.

Fertilizer Nutrients and Application Strategies

Crop managers should adopt fertilization practices that effectively utilize their available resources, allow flexibility, and satisfy the nutritional requirements of the crop. The availability of equipment and materials, characteristics of the site, relative costs, personal preference, and convenience are also important factors.

Application Methods

Fertilizer application methods include 1) preplant broadcasting followed by incorporation, 2) banding before or at planting, 3) side-dressing after planting, 4) spraying the foliage during crop growth, and 5) injection into irrigation water. Each method has inherent advantages and disadvantages.

Broadcasting before planting is satisfactory if soil fertility is generally high and no appreciable soil fixation is expected. Soil fixation occurs when nutrients become chemically bound in the soil and unavailable to the plants. Surface-broadcast fertilizers need to be incorporated into the moist layers of the seedbed where roots will be active, but not deeper than 12–18 inches. Preplant application can largely eliminate the need for additional fertilizer during planting, freeing more time for management of the planting operation.

Banding during planting is a common fertilization practice. An efficient and safe band placement is about 2 inches to the side and 2 inches below the seed piece. Sometimes fertilizers are banded preplant during marking-out operations. The bands should be placed close enough to the seed pieces to provide benefits for early growth, but they must not be in direct contact with the seed pieces, or else injury may result.

Side-dressing is used mostly for applying nitrogen during growth stage II, up to 60 days after planting. The later the application, the greater the risk of root pruning during the operation. Side-dressing is generally not recommended for other fertilizer materials, particularly nutrients that stimulate early growth, such as phosphorus.

Spraying liquid nutrients directly onto foliage often brings forth a quicker response from plants than soil applications, and foliar sprays are effective for treating some existing nutrient deficiencies (Table 9.4). This method is also advantageous for elements that are less effective in soil applications because of soil fixation. A surfactant tank-mixed with the nutrient solution usually improves absorption through the leaf surface. The amount of any nutrient that can be applied in a single spray is limited, because concentrated sprays can cause leaf damage.

Water-soluble fertilizers (Table 9.5) are commonly applied by injection into irrigation water in some production areas.

This method has the advantage of providing nutrients according to the needs of the crop and moving them partially into the root zone. Careful irrigation management is essential in this method. The uniformity of the fertilizer application is no better than that of the water while the fertilizer is being injected. In addition, irrigation that supplies more water than is lost to evapotranspiration may cause leaching or runoff of applied nutrients, leading to environmental pollution. This technique should only be used on fields where the potential for runoff is low. The irrigation system must be equipped with check valves to prevent contamination of water sources due to back-draining. The compatibility of the fertilizer materials with the irrigation water should be checked, as materials that remain soluble are the most effective. Many liquid fertilizer materials are compatible with each other, but further information about compatibility should be obtained from suppliers or local advisors before any fertilizers are mixed. A strong acid, such as phosphoric or sulfuric acid, should not be combined with a strong base, such as potassium carbonate. When application rates are calculated for specific nutrients, the portion of the crop's nutritional requirements supplied by soluble nutrients already present in the irrigation water itself must be taken into account.

Response to Applied Fertilizer

Many factors can alter the expected response of a potato crop to fertilizer applications. Soil fumigants greatly change the populations of microorganisms in the soil, many of which play roles in nutrient cycling. Some fumigants may retard the biological conversion of ammonium to nitrate or the mineralization of nutrients from organic forms in the soil. Tillage practices affect soil compaction and rooting depth, which may influence the response to applied fertilizers. Overirrigation may cause nitrate leaching in sandy soils (Plate 1C), whereas the availability of nutrients is reduced if low soil moisture limits growth. A large weed population reduces tuber yield by competing for nutrients and water, and plants with significant insect

Table 9.5. Liquid fertilizer materials suitable for application in irrigation water

Nutrient	Analysis	Source[a]
Nitrogen	20–0–0	Aqua ammonia[b]
	82–0–0	Anhydrous ammonia[b]
	32–0–0	Urea and ammonium nitrate
	28–0–0	Urea and ammonium nitrate
	20–0–0	Ammonium nitrate
	17–0–0	Calcium ammonium nitrate
Phosphorus	8–24–0	Ammonium orthophosphate
	9–30–0	Ammonium orthophosphate
	10–34–0	Ammonium orthophosphate and polyphosphates
	Phosphoric acid	Phosphoric and polyphosphoric acids
	11–44–0	Urea phosphoric acid
Potassium	0–0–30	Potassium carbonate
	8–8–8	Blends of ammonia, nitrogen
	8–16–8	solutions, phosphoric acids,
	4–8–12	urea ortho- and poly-
	7–21–7	phosphates, and potassium chloride or potassium hydroxide
Sulfur	0–0–0–32	Sulfuric acid
	12–0–0–26	Ammonium thiosulfate
	20–0–0–(40–45)	Ammonium polysulfides
	8–0–0–17	Ammonium bisulfite

[a] Check the compatibility of the fertilizer with the irrigation water before any application is made.
[b] For surface irrigation only.

damage or disease are generally not able to use applied fertilizers as efficiently as healthy plants.

Nitrogen. Most soils need nitrogen applications to produce a profitable yield of potatoes. The common forms of fertilizer nitrogen are nitrate, urea, and ammonium. Plants can use either nitrate or ammonium nitrogen.

> **Soil fumigants greatly change the populations of microorganisms in the soil, many of which play roles in nutrient cycling.**

Nitrogen fertilizers are most efficiently used in split applications, with one-third to two-thirds of the total requirement side-dressed after plant emergence or applied by irrigation in several smaller applications. Dry nitrogen fertilizers may also be successfully top-dressed by aircraft during plant growth if the application is followed by either rainfall or sprinkler irrigation. Ammonia may volatilize from urea under some conditions if the material is not watered in soon after application.

Potato crops intended for early harvest require less nitrogen. The entire nitrogen requirement for early-maturing cultivars can be applied preplant if losses due to leaching are expected to remain low during growth stages I and II. For late-maturing cultivars, application of the total nitrogen requirement at planting is not recommended, because it tends to delay early tuber development.

Several precautions should be taken in planning nitrogen applications. High rates of banded urea or diammonium phosphate can cause ammonia toxicity, particularly in calcareous alkaline soils. If these materials are placed with the seed pieces at planting, not more than 150 pounds per acre should be used. A much higher rate can be used if these fertilizers are banded at least 2 inches from the seed pieces. The total salt index of the fertilizer mix should also be considered. Nitrogen applications 1.5–2 times higher than recommended rates can stimulate excessive foliar growth, leading to delayed tuber maturity, lower specific gravity, and increased problems with tuber quality (Chapter 10). Nitrate forms of nitrogen are subject to leaching before plant uptake, particularly in coarse-textured soils (Chapter 8 and Box 9.2).

> **Nitrogen fertilizers are most efficiently used in split applications, with one-third to two-thirds of the total requirement applied after plant emergence.**

Nitrogen is particularly suitable for application by sprinkler irrigation. Several liquid nitrogen fertilizers can be applied by this method (Table 9.5), and nitrogen is also a component of most other liquid fertilizers containing phosphorus, potassium, and sulfur that are applied by sprinklers. This method increases the total efficiency of the fertilizer while maintaining or even increasing tuber yield and quality. Sprinkler application of nitrogen should not begin before the end of growth stage III. Until then the root system is generally not sufficiently developed to capture most nitrogen applied by this method, and thus the nutrients may be leached below the root zone.

In sprinkler irrigation, 20–40 pounds of nitrogen per acre is commonly applied every 10–14 days during tuber bulking (growth stage IV). This maintains the petiole nitrate concentration in the desired range (Fig. 9.5). Repeated application of more than 40 pounds per acre is not recommended, because it stimulates excessive vegetative growth. An average Russet Burbank crop requires about 3 pounds of nitrogen per acre every day to maintain a daily growth rate of 700 pounds of tubers per acre. An application of 40 pounds per acre is sufficient for only about 10 days if the nitrogen uptake efficiency of the plant is 75%. The number of applications needed depends upon the length of growth stage IV.

It may be necessary to apply nitrogen with every irrigation in areas where the crop must be irrigated quite often, such as fields with coarse-textured soils or environments with high evapotranspiration. A drawback of this practice is that it tends to stimulate more vegetative growth than needed, which may aggravate some diseases, particularly if the petiole nitrate concentration is kept above 20,000 parts per million. To reduce this problem, only enough nitrogen should be applied to replace that taken up by the crop since the last application.

To enhance tuber maturity at harvest, the petiole nitrate concentration should be allowed to drop below 10,000 parts per million by the end of growth stage IV. Nitrogen should not be applied within 4–6 weeks of vine killing. Applications late in growth stage IV and in growth stage V do not increase tuber yield and may reduce tuber quality, skin maturity, and the storability of the crop (Chapter 6).

Anhydrous ammonia and aqua ammonia should not be applied by sprinkler irrigation because of potentially high losses due to volatilization. Volatilization is also a problem in applying these materials by surface irrigation if the pH of the water is high. These materials may also cause calcium to precipitate and increase the sodium hazard in some irrigation water. The addition of acidic materials, such as sulfuric acid, generally corrects this problem.

Most other liquid nitrogen materials may be successfully applied by surface irrigation if precautions are taken to avoid runoff. In general, injection of the fertilizer into the irrigation system should be started after the water is partway across the field and should be completed by the time it begins to leave the field.

Ammonium forms of nitrogen may not be immediately available for plant uptake, because they are held by the soil in the irrigation furrow until they are converted to nitrate. As an alternative, growers using surface irrigation could consider banding the entire nitrogen requirement at planting or side-dressing it later.

Phosphorus. Phosphorus fertilization is needed in many soils for a profitable yield of potatoes. This nutrient contributes to early crop development and tuberization and enhances tuber maturation. It is not readily leached, but phosphorus fertilizer should always be incorporated into the soil to prevent loss in runoff water, especially if soil erosion is likely to occur.

The total phosphorus fertilizer requirement may be broadcast in the fall or in the spring before planting. It may also be banded at planting, to the side of and slightly below the seed piece. Banding gives the highest efficiency in phosphorus-fixing soils. The fertilization rate may generally be reduced by as much as 30% by banding, compared with broadcasting, if soil tests show low phosphorus concentrations. The availability and uptake of phosphorus may be increased by banding with fertilizers containing ammonium.

Liquid and dry sources of phosphorus are equally effective for potato production. A phosphorus starter fertilizer low in ammonium (such as monoammonium phosphate, 11–48–0) may be beneficial, particularly if it is placed about 1 inch above the seed pieces at planting and applied at a rate of up to 100 pounds per acre.

Potatoes respond to phosphorus applied through sprinkler irrigation if the fertilizer materials (Table 9.5) are compatible with the irrigation water and the plants have enough roots near the soil surface. Phosphorus applied by sprinklers penetrates only about 2 inches into the soil. Maximum penetration

---

Box 9.2

A Checklist of Practices for Avoiding Nitrate Leaching

Nitrate nitrogen is readily leached by rainfall or irrigation, especially in coarse-textured soils. Leaching decreases the efficiency of nitrogen fertilizer applications, increases fertilizer expenses, and may lead to contamination of surface waters and groundwater. To avoid applying nitrogen in excess of the plant's needs and to avoid the loss of nitrates due to leaching, the following practices should be part of any nitrogen management program:

- Conduct soil tests to determine preplant fertilization rates.

- Make split applications of nitrogen.

- Make fertilizer applications as close as possible to the actual time of plant demand for nitrogen.

- Conduct petiole tissue analysis for nitrate nitrogen to evaluate the need for applications during crop growth.

- Allow the petiole nitrate nitrogen concentration to drop below 10,000 parts per million by the end of growth stage IV.

- Schedule irrigations according to crop water use and soil characteristics. *Do not overirrigate.*

- Plant a winter cover crop after the potato harvest to capture residual nitrogen in the soil.

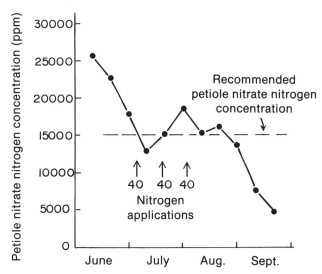

Fig. 9.5. Petiole nitrate concentration in Russet Burbank. Arrows represent points during the growing season when nitrogen was applied (at the rate of 40 pounds per acre) through a sprinkler irrigation system.

occurs when the soil surface is wet before the application. The concentration of phosphorus in petioles usually increases within 10–14 days after application.

Conditions necessary for successful application of phosphorus with irrigation water include 1) an active root system in the upper 2 inches of soil under a full plant canopy, identified by small white roots visible on or immediately below the soil surface under the canopy, 2) a fertilizer material that is compatible with the irrigation water (Box 9.3), and 3) applying the fertilizer before a phosphorus deficiency develops. Normally this practice is not recommended unless plant analysis shows that phosphorus will become limiting before the end of growth stage IV. If the irrigation water is not compatible or if surface irrigation is being used, supplemental phosphorus must be applied in foliar sprays (Table 9.4).

Potassium. Potassium fertilizer requirements for potatoes vary considerably in different soils. This nutrient influences both yield and tuber quality, including specific gravity, susceptibility to blackspot bruise, after-cooking darkening, reducing sugar content, chip fry color, and storage quality. Potassium chloride, particularly at high rates of application, usually results in lower tuber specific gravity than potassium sulfate. This problem is reduced as the interval between application and planting is increased.

Banding increases the effectiveness of potassium fertilizers in soils where significant fixation occurs. Because of potential problems with salt toxicity, however, potassium fertilizer should not be banded at planting at rates exceeding 300 pounds of K_2O_5 per acre. High rates should be split between broadcast and banded applications. Fall broadcast applications can be effective but are not recommended on sandy soils in areas with winter rainfall, because of potential leaching. In irrigated production, the potassium content of the irrigation water should be considered when fertilization requirements are calculated.

Several liquid potassium fertilizers are available for application by sprinkler irrigation (Table 9.5). In general, however, potassium should only be applied during crop growth if a deficiency is likely to occur before the end of growth stage IV. It is immobile in soil and can only be absorbed by active, healthy roots near the soil surface. It is also required in relatively large amounts, with uptake rates similar to those for nitrogen (Table 9.1). In addition, potassium fertilizers have relatively low analyses. All these factors tend to reduce the effectiveness of irrigation systems in supplying the potassium required during tuber growth.

Calcium and Magnesium. Supplemental applications of calcium and magnesium are needed for potato production in some acid soils, to provide needed calcium and raise the soil pH (Chapter 2). The increase in soil pH may also improve phosphorus uptake by the plant. If the magnesium content of the soil is low, dolomitic lime should be used. Soils in which common scab is a problem, however, should be held below pH 5.5 (Chapter 17). Calcium sulfate or magnesium sulfate can be used without raising the soil pH. Calcium nitrate can be applied if both nitrogen and calcium are needed.

Most calcium and magnesium fertilizers should be applied before or at planting. Magnesium sulfate may be applied as a foliar spray or added to fertilizer mixes. Calcium applied to foliage is not translocated to developing tubers. The immobility of calcium in soil and within the plant and potential problems with its compatibility with irrigation water limit the effectiveness of sprinkler-applied calcium.

Sulfur. Application of sulfur is usually needed for potatoes where the soil or irrigation water is naturally low in this nutrient or where it has not accumulated from previous applications. Many pesticides and some fertilizers (ammonium sulfate and potassium sulfate) contain significant amounts of sulfur.

Sulfur is applied as a sulfate or as elemental sulfur. The sulfate form is readily available for plant uptake, while elemental sulfur must be oxidized to sulfate before being taken up by the plant. The soil pH may be lowered by the oxidation of elemental sulfur. Sulfates are susceptible to leaching from soil.

Supplemental sulfur can be applied with irrigation water (Table 9.5). Sulfate sources induce a quick response in the plant, whereas the response to elemental sulfur is slower.

Box 9.3

Compatibility of Phosphorus Fertilizer with Irrigation Water

The compatibility of phosphorus fertilizer with irrigation water should always be determined before application by sprinkler irrigation is attempted. The effectiveness of this method is reduced if a precipitate forms before the water reaches the soil surface. Deposits may also form around and on sprinkler heads and nozzles, reducing their effectiveness or plugging them.

Compatibility can be tested by adding the appropriate amount of fertilizer solution to a gallon of fresh irrigation water. For hand lines, wheel lines, or solid-set irrigation, the amount of fertilizer solution (in teaspoons) to add to 1 gallon of water is calculated as follows:

$$x = \frac{0.0283 \times F}{W \times t \times P}$$

where

x = amount of fertilizer solution (tsp) per gallon of irrigation water
F = fertilizer application rate (P_2O_5, lb/acre)
W = water application rate (in./hr)
t = period of time during which the fertilizer is injected (hr)
P = fertilizer concentration (P_2O_5, lb/gal)

For center-pivot irrigation systems, the calculation is

$$x = \frac{0.0283 \times F}{D \times P}$$

where D = depth of water applied (in./acre).

If a fine white precipitate forms after the solution is thoroughly mixed, a smaller amount of fertilizer should be applied, or the injection time should be lengthened. In either case, the compatibility should be retested.

Irrigation water having a high pH or high calcium and magnesium content may be partially acidified to increase its compatibility with phosphorus fertilizer. The final pH should be kept above 5.0 to prevent corrosion damage to the irrigation system. The pH may be lowered by the use of an acidic liquid fertilizer, such as urea phosphoric acid or phosphoric acid, as a phosphorus source.

Several problems are associated with injecting sulfuric acid into irrigation water because of the difficulty in handling this material and the resulting excessively low pH of the water.

Micronutrients. Certain micronutrients must be supplied for potato production in some soils. Zinc and manganese may be needed in calcareous alkaline soils. Banding fertilizers containing ammonium may help correct some micronutrient deficiencies in calcareous soils. Some fungicides contain significant amounts of certain micronutrients and can be significant sources of these if the micronutrients are absorbed by the plant. For example, mancozeb is a source of zinc, and copper fungicides supply that element.

Copper may be needed in peat and muck soils but is usually sufficient in mineral soils. Boron may be needed where soils or irrigation waters are naturally low in that element. Most soils do not require an application of iron for potatoes. Chloride and molybdenum are generally not deficient in soils used for potato production.

The most effective application method depends upon the micronutrient needed, local soil conditions, and the point in the growing season at which a deficiency is recognized. Generally, zinc, copper, manganese, and boron can be broadcast and incorporated into the seedbed. On calcareous alkaline soils, however, manganese should be banded or applied as a foliar spray. Foliar applications are effective for zinc, copper, and manganese. Boron can be applied as a foliar spray, but it is not translocated from the foliage to the tubers. Repeated foliar applications are necessary to correct an iron deficiency. Sources of micronutrients suitable for foliar application are outlined in Table 9.4. Application of any micronutrient at rates higher than required by the plant may cause toxicity or deleterious interactions affecting the uptake of other nutrients. For this reason, micronutrients should only be applied in response to recommendations based on results from soil tests or foliar analyses.

Color Plates

1. Influence of hilling on water infiltration patterns (defined by red dye) in sandy or sandy loam soil. **A,** Level soil surface after nonexcessive irrigation. **B,** Hilled surface after nonexcessive irrigation, with deeper infiltration in the furrow area. **C,** Hilled surface after excessive irrigation, with significantly deeper infiltration in the furrow area.

2. Tubers with bottleneck, dumbbell, and pointed-end malformations.

3. Little tuber, a form of second growth—small daughter tubers are formed directly from the seed piece. (Courtesy R. C. Rowe)

4. Severe growth crack. (Courtesy R. C. Rowe)

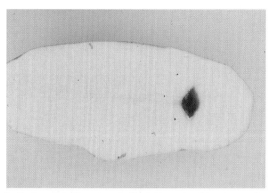

6. Bud-end hollow heart. Brown center is not usually associated with this type of hollow heart.

5. Brown center and stem-end hollow heart (usually associated with the prior development of brown center) in tubers of different sizes.

7. Internal brown spot. In the tuber on the far left and the one at the top, the brown tissue appears to be more closely associated with the vascular ring; symptoms in this location are often confused with those of heat necrosis.

8. Translucent end affecting the stem end of a tuber. This disorder is usually associated with second growth and pointed stem end. (Courtesy R. C. Rowe)

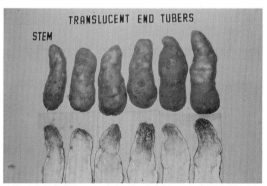

9. Tubers with translucent end. The darker fry color at the stem end (bottom) results from an accumulation of reducing sugars in affected areas.

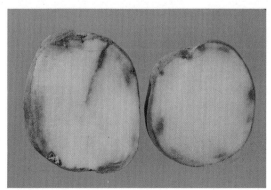

10. Blackspot in tissues below the skin of bruised areas. (Courtesy R. C. Rowe)

11. Tipburn, a climate-induced disorder, on actively growing leaves. (Courtesy R. C. Rowe)

12. Annual broadleaf weeds at the one- and two-true-leaf stages, when control measures should be implemented. **A,** Redroot pigweed (*Amaranthus retroflexus*). **B,** Common lambsquarters (*Chenopodium album*). **C,** Black nightshade (*Solanum nigrum*) (left) and hairy nightshade (*S. sarrachoides*) (right).

13. Annual grass weeds at the one-leaf to the three-leaf stage, when control measures should be implemented. **A,** Large crabgrass (*Digitaria sanguinalis*). **B,** Witchgrass (*Panicum capillare*). **C,** Fall panicum (*P. dichotomiflorum*).

A **B**

14. Perennial weeds in early growth stages, when control measures should be implemented. **A,** Quackgrass (*Elytrigia repens*). **B,** Yellow nutsedge (*Cyperus esculentus*).

15. Adult Colorado potato beetle (*Leptinotarsa decemlineata*) feeding on an emerging potato plant.

16. Adult, larva, and egg mass of Colorado potato beetle. (Courtesy C. W. Hoy)

17. Colorado potato beetle larvae actively feeding on a potato leaf.

18. Colorado potato beetle larvae just hatching from an egg mass. (Courtesy C. W. Hoy)

19. *Lebia grandis*, a predator of Colorado potato beetle eggs.

20. Adult of a *Myiopharus* species, a parasite of Colorado potato beetle larvae.

21. Tenspotted ladybird beetle (*Coleomegilla maculata*), a predator of Colorado potato beetle eggs.

22. Potato tuberworm moth (*Phthorimaea operculella*). (Used by permission of the Regents of the University of California)

23. Potato tuberworm larva. (Used by permission of the Regents of the University of California)

24. Entry point of a European corn borer larva (*Ostrinia nubilalis*) on a potato stem, with characteristic frass deposits.

25. European corn borer moth.

26. Potato stem cut longitudinally to reveal a European corn borer larva tunneling inside. (Courtesy C. W. Hoy)

27. Pheromone trap for European corn borer moths.

28. Psyllid yellows, caused by potato psyllid nymphs (*Paratrioza cockerelli*) feeding on potato leaves. (Courtesy W. S. Cranshaw)

29. Potato psyllid damage to tubers. (Courtesy W. S. Cranshaw)

30. Potato psyllid adult. (Courtesy W. S. Cranshaw)

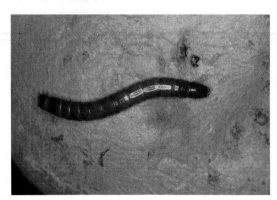

31. Wireworm larva.

32. Green peach aphid (*Myzus persicae*). (Courtesy D. N. Ferro)

33. Potato aphid (*Macrosiphum euphorbiae*). (Courtesy D. N. Ferro)

34. Potato leafhopper adult (*Empoasca fabae*). (Courtesy D. N. Ferro)

35. Potato leafhopper adult (left) and nymph (right). (Courtesy A. Al-Dawood)

36. Symptoms of plants grown from potato leafroll virus–infected tubers include rolled and leathery leaves (right) and chlorotic plants (left) that are usually stunted and more upright than healthy plants.

37. Symptoms of infection by potato virus Y strain O (PVY^O) in potato. **A,** Mosaic. **B,** Bunchy top and clinging necrotic leaves.

38. Aster leafhopper (*Macrosteles quadrilineatus*), the vector of aster yellows mycoplasmalike organism.

39. Symptoms of purple top of potato, caused by infection with aster yellows mycoplasmalike organism.

40. Aerial tuber on a potato plant infected with aster yellows mycoplasmalike organism.

41. Inky black decay of stem bases due to post-emergence blackleg.

42. Black stem base and foliar wilt symptoms of postemergence black-leg. (Courtesy R. C. Rowe)

43. Aerial stem rot lesion developing from infection through a leaf scar. (Courtesy R. C. Rowe)

44. Typical aerial stem rot lesion on a main vine. (Courtesy R. C. Rowe)

45. Soft rot of internal tuber tissues.

46. Foliar wilt symptoms of ring rot, with interveinal chlorosis and marginal leaf necrosis.

47. Internal and external tuber symptoms characteristic of ring rot. (Courtesy R. C. Rowe)

48. Advanced decay of the vascular ring due to ring rot, with cheesy rot exuding where the tuber is being squeezed with the thumb.

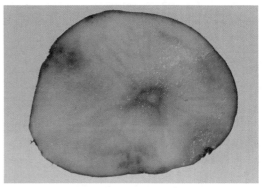

49. Mild internal tuber symptoms of ring rot, with only slight visible discoloration of the vascular ring.

50. Potato leaf with early blight lesions. (Courtesy R. C. Rowe)

51. Target spot or bull's-eye lesions, symptoms characteristic of early blight. (Courtesy R. C. Rowe)

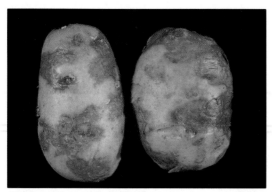

52. Early blight lesions on tubers.

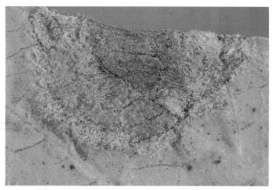

53. Cottony white growth of *Phytophthora infestans* associated with a late blight lesion on the underside of an infected leaf under moist conditions. Spores of the late blight fungus are formed in this growth. (Courtesy R. C. Rowe)

54. Late blight lesions on potato leaves that have turned brown and desiccated under dry conditions.

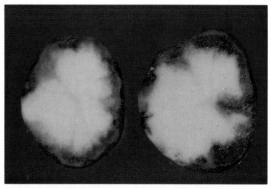

55. Coppery brown dry rot of internal tissues, typical of tubers with late blight. (Courtesy R. C. Rowe)

56. Leaf with uneven chlorosis and wilt often associated with potato early dying.

57. Foliar symptoms of potato early dying.

58. Stem lesions of Sclerotinia stalk rot.

59. White mold growth of *Sclerotinia*, associated with stem lesions of Sclerotinia stalk rot under moist conditions.

60. Black sclerotia of *Sclerotinia* forming inside stems with Sclerotinia stalk rot.

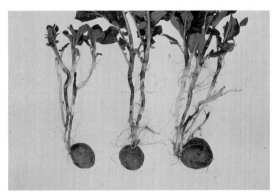

61. Brownish black, sunken stem lesions typical of Rhizoctonia canker.

63. Masses of sclerotia of *Rhizoctonia* on a potato tuber—"the dirt that won't wash off."

62. White, powdery mold growth of *Rhizoctonia* on potato stems just above the soil line.

64. External and internal symptoms of tubers with pink rot.

65. Common scab lesions on a tuber. (Courtesy G. A. Secor)

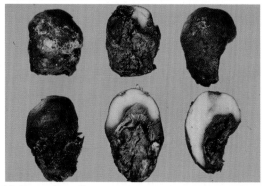

66. External and internal dry rot and associated white mold characteristic of Fusarium dry rot.

67. Fusarium dry rot, with white mold visible in decayed cavities within a cut tuber.

68. Effects of nematode feeding on the growth of potato plants. **A,** Stunting of plants caused by the golden (cyst) nematode on roots; the damage is typically patchy within a field due to uneven distribution of the nematodes. **B,** Stunting caused by sting and root-knot nematodes (right), alleviated by application of a nematicide (left). (A, courtesy B. B. Brodie; B, courtesy D. P. Weingartner)

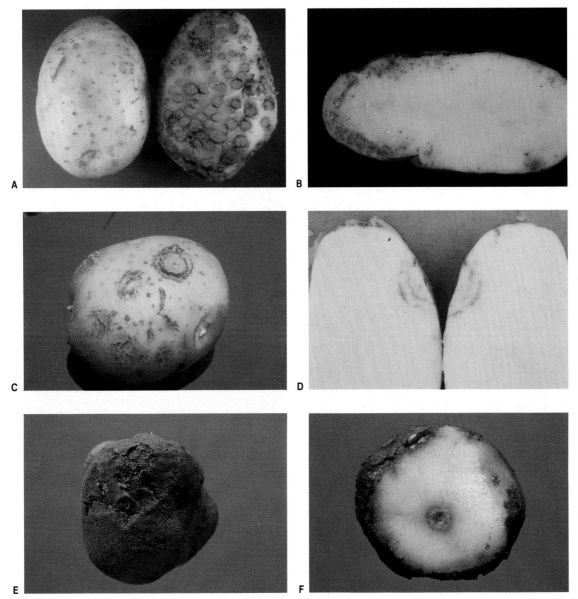

69. Damage to potato tubers due to nematode feeding. **A,** Bumpy tuber, caused by root-knot nematodes, with a healthy tuber on the left. **B,** Internal browning caused by root-knot nematodes. **C and D,** External and internal symptoms of corky ring spot, caused by tobacco rattle virus, which is vectored by stubby-root nematodes. **E and F,** Surface cracks and internal dry rot caused by the potato rot nematode. (A, reprinted, by permission, from D. W. Dickson and D. P. Weingartner, Nematode Control on Potatoes, Circular 380, Florida Agricultural Experiment Station, Gainesville; B, courtesy G. S. Santo; C, reprinted, by permission, from D. P. Weingartner, J. R. Shumaker, and G. C. Smart, Jr., 1983, Why soil fumigation fails to control potato corky ringspot disease in Florida, Plant Disease 67:130-134; D, courtesy D. P. Weingartner)

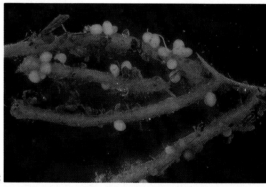

70. Symptoms of nematode feeding on potato roots. **A,** Root galls caused by root-knot nematodes. **B,** Swollen root tips caused by sting nematode feeding. **C,** Females (cysts) of the golden nematode on potato roots; the females appear white when alive but turn yellow as the cysts mature. (A, reprinted, by permission, from D. W. Dickson and D. P. Weingartner, Nematode Control on Potatoes, Circular 380, Florida Agricultural Experiment Station, Gainesville; B, courtesy D. P. Weingartner; C, courtesy B. B. Brodie)

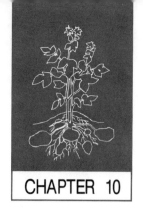

CHAPTER 10

Larry K. Hiller
Department of Horticulture and Landscape Architecture
Washington State University, Pullman

Robert E. Thornton
Department of Horticulture and Landscape Architecture
Washington State University, Pullman

Management of Physiological Disorders

Potato plants, and particularly tubers, are susceptible to a large number of noninfectious physiological disorders, which cause pronounced and often detrimental changes in their shape, function, and appearance. Tuber defects include external and internal blemishes, changes in shape and size, and alterations in the color of the skin and flesh. Most physiological disorders do not cause any significant change in the nutritional value of affected tubers. However, because of the detrimental effect of these disorders on appearance and culinary uses, growers can incur large economic losses as a result of lowered grade and yield of marketable tubers.

Physiological disorders are important whether the potato crop is intended for the fresh market or for processing, but greater economic losses are usually incurred when tubers do not meet fresh-market grade standards. Tubers not acceptable for the fresh market are often acceptable for processing, although the use of low-quality tubers results in increased sorting and trimming waste and overall processing costs. Disposal of processing wastes is also a concern. Severely affected tubers are usually used to make dehydrated potato products or starch or are used for livestock feed—alternatives that bring minimal returns to the grower. In extreme cases, tubers must be discarded completely. Because of the economic losses associated with physiological disorders, cultural practices that minimize their occurrence play an extremely important role in any holistic potato health management plan.

Causes of Physiological Disorders. Physiological disorders are often referred to as abiotic, nonpathogenic, nonparasitic, or noninfectious diseases. The significant characteristic of all physiological disorders, however, is that they are *not caused by pathogenic microorganisms* and thus should not be confused with or referred to as diseases. Physiological disorders result from internal imbalances that alter or disrupt the normal growth and development of plants and tubers. Some of these disorders may be brought on or accentuated by environmental factors or disease.

Most tuber physiological disorders develop rather slowly, and symptoms may be observable only late in the crop growth cycle. In many cases, however, the damage is already done by the time symptoms are observed. This often makes it difficult to correctly identify the cause of a specific disorder and to determine when the problem began. Disorders that affect plants directly, such as those resulting from hail, lightning, and freezing temperatures, are associated with easily identified causal factors. Others, however, such as hollow heart, are caused by a complex interaction of environmental and cultural factors. To complicate matters even more, many of these disorders occur erratically from year to year and location to location.

Tuber Physiological Disorders

Tuber physiological disorders are classed as external disorders, internal disorders, and bruises. External disorders are visible on the exterior of affected tubers and are easily observed. Internal disorders, however, can be detected only by cutting into tubers and examining internal tissues. Bruises caused by impacts that do not result in abrasions of the tuber surface also may be visible only after cutting or peeling.

External Tuber Disorders

Tuber Malformation

Tuber malformation includes deformities known as knobby, bottleneck, dumbbell, and pointed-end tubers (Plate 2). Affected tubers are also referred to as misshapen or rough tubers.

Knobby tubers result from secondary lateral growth in one or more eyes following a cessation or inhibition of normal tuber growth. Knobs of various sizes and shapes are formed, depending on the stage of tuber development in which the disorder begins. The plant and the interior of the tuber usually have no symptoms.

Bottleneck, dumbbell, and pointed-end tubers result from irregular longitudinal growth, characterized by a constriction along the long axis of the tuber. Bottleneck tubers are smaller at the stem end than at the bud end, but many variations exist. Dumbbell tubers have a constriction in the middle. Pointed-end tubers have a definite constriction at either the stem end or (more commonly) the bud end. They often have higher amounts of reducing sugars in the pointed end and may also develop translucent end.

Large differences have been reported in cultivar susceptibility to tuber malformation, but no cultivar appears to be completely resistant. Cultivars that have long tubers, such as Russet Burbank, tend to be more susceptible than those with round or blocky tubers.

The particular shape and severity of the deformity is

influenced by the stage of tuber development in which growth is interrupted, the size of the tuber, and the severity of associated stress factors. An interruption in growth during the early phases of tuber development may result in bottleneck or pointed–stem end tubers. An interruption during midseason results in dumbbell-shaped tubers. An interruption in the later phases of development results in pointed–bud end tubers.

Tuber malformation is often associated with periods of moisture or temperature stress that retard or stop tuber growth. Stress periods are usually followed by more favorable growing conditions and consequently a resumption of rapid tuber growth. Sudden or severe stress generally leads to a higher incidence of malformation, compared with gradually increasing or continuous stress. Stress caused by inadequate soil moisture is apparently not the only factor resulting in malformation, since this disorder has been reported to occur under optimal irrigation regimes. High temperatures induce malformation by causing a temporary reduction in the tuber growth rate, an increase in plant and tuber respiration rates, a decrease in cell division, a deviation in normal plant hormone levels, and a temporary reduction in the supply of carbohydrates to the tuber. When conditions more favorable for tuber growth return, growth and starch synthesis resume only in certain areas of the tuber, commonly next to buds, where cell division is more active.

Other factors contributing to the occurrence and severity of tuber malformation include the number of stems per plant (single-stem plants have fewer tubers per hill), poor plant stands, low tuber set per hill due to *Rhizoctonia* infection, the size and physiological age of seed pieces, improper soil fertility, and excessive vine growth. Certain management practices that result in rapid growth of foliage and tubers, such as heavy irrigation and nitrogen fertilization, following a stress period, may increase the amount of tuber malformation.

To limit the incidence and severity of tuber malformation, establish a uniform stand of multiple-stem plants, and follow management practices that provide balanced irrigation and fertility.

Second Growth

Three distinct types of second growth occur in potatoes: heat sprouts (also called aerial sprouts or heat runners), tuber chaining (also called chain tuberization or gemmation), and little tuber (also called little potato, kinder tuber, or sprout tuber). Heat sprouts are produced from stolons or tubers and grow as new sprouts or become leafy aboveground stems. Tuber chaining is characterized by the formation of a series of small tubers on a single stolon. Little tuber is the simultaneous development of small daughter tubers and development of sprouts. The daughter tubers are formed on extremely short sprouts or directly on the seed piece (Plate 3).

Heat sprouts and tuber chaining result from renewed growth following periods of interrupted or irregular development during normal tuber growth. These disorders can be initiated by soil temperatures above 75° F. Further second growth can occur at lower temperatures, but the extent of these disorders depends on the length of exposure to temperatures above 75° F. Low soil moisture alone does not initiate these disorders. During the growing season, however, high temperatures are often accompanied by moisture stress, and these two factors can interact to limit the tuber growth rate.

Little tuber is commonly associated with physiologically old seed tubers. This disorder can develop in storage, in the field before plant emergence (generally with seed held in warm storage and then planted when the soil temperature is low), or when very limited top growth has occurred.

The incidence of second growth is related to an alteration in the apical dominance of the primary tuber, a temporary deviation in the tuberization process, changes in the amounts and proportions of various growth hormones, and elevated concentrations of carbon dioxide and ethylene in the tuber zone.

Cultural practices that promote uniform growth of plants and tubers throughout the season help minimize second growth. Seed potatoes should be stored at 38–40° F until they are warmed for handling and planting. Physiologically old tubers, from long-term or high-temperature storage, should not be used for seed. If seed that has been aged must be used, it should not be planted in cold, dry soil. To minimize the occurrence of these disorders, ensure uniform spacing and a plant population of the desired size, apply fertilizer in the correct amount and with the correct placement, and maintain uniform soil moisture sufficient to meet the water requirements of the crop.

Tuber Cracking

There are three distinct kinds of physiological tuber cracking: growth cracks, thumbnail cracks, and air checks.

Growth cracks are shallow to moderately deep fissures in the surface tissues of tubers (Plate 4). They occur more frequently on the bud end and usually extend lengthwise in long tubers. Growth cracks are usually associated with uneven availability of soil moisture and rapid water uptake resulting in large changes in tuber turgidity and growth rate. These conditions occur after rain or irrigation following a period of dryness or high-temperature stress. Other contributing factors include plant spacing; fertilizer rate and placement and the timing of application; and an inadequate amount of boron in the soil.

Growth cracks may also develop when plants are infected with certain pathogens (potato yellow dwarf virus, potato mop top virus, or spindle tuber viroid) or damaged by exposure to certain herbicides. Growth cracks that result from disease or herbicide damage are quite difficult to distinguish from those due to physiological factors, and identification of their causes requires observation of foliar symptoms and sometimes laboratory diagnosis.

Cultural practices that maintain constant plant and tuber growth during the entire growing season are required in order to minimize physiological growth cracking. These practices include maintaining the desired plant population and uniform plant spacing, maintaining an adequate number of stems per hill, providing uniform irrigation for even distribution of soil moisture, and applying fertilizer at the correct rate and with the correct placement and timing.

Thumbnail cracking and air checks are shallow, random breaks in the skin of extremely turgid tubers that have been exposed to drying conditions. Shallow, irregular splits in the tuber surface may occur from physical impact during harvest and are often related to high tuber hydration and low temperatures. This surface splitting should not be confused with shatter bruise, which is a bruise injury. These surface cracks usually heal slowly, especially in a low-humidity atmosphere, and thus affected tubers are subject to dehydration and a greater incidence of tuber rot. Similar-appearing cracks that are not related to physical impact may develop in storage.

Greening

Exposure of tubers to sunlight, indirect daylight, or artificial light enhances chlorophyll development and results in a green color beneath the skin. Even light of relatively low intensity induces greening. The higher the light intensity and the longer the exposure, the more intense the color. Greening occurs more rapidly at temperatures above 55° F. All cultivars are prone to greening, but white-skinned cultivars and tubers with poorly developed skin are somewhat more susceptible.

Greening occurs in the field in tubers that develop near

the soil surface and are exposed to light. Parts of tubers may become exposed if seed pieces have been planted too shallow or because of improper hilling or erosion of hills. Some cultivars naturally set tubers near the soil surface, which increases the possibility of exposure to sunlight. Greening may become a problem late in the season prior to harvest, when the vines die and no longer cover the hills. It can also result from exposure of tubers to light following harvest.

Greening can be controlled by planting the seed pieces at a sufficient depth and forming hills of the proper shape and size to keep the tubers covered with soil.

Sunscald

Sunscald is caused by frequent or prolonged exposure of tubers to intense sunlight and high temperatures. The tuber surface takes on a blistered, metallic appearance. The underlying tissues may become watery and turn brown. Affected areas may dry out or be invaded by secondary bacteria.

Sunscald can be reduced or prevented by the practices recommended for preventing greening. In addition, tubers should be covered during transport, to avoid exposure to sunlight and wind.

Skinning

Immature tubers have a thin, delicate skin, which can easily be torn or frayed during harvest and grading. Skinning—often referred to as feathering—can also occur in mature tubers if they are roughly handled. Early-harvested potatoes are especially susceptible, particularly if the vines have not died or been killed sufficiently prior to harvest for the skins to set properly. The bud end of tubers is more prone to skinning than the stem end. Wound healing of skinned areas proceeds quickly under conditions favorable to suberization, and the new tissue is similar to the original skin in its resistance to water loss and invasion by microorganisms. However, if tubers are subjected to high temperatures, low humidity, and drying air (conditions such as those imposed during transport following harvest), skinned tissues dehydrate and may sunscald easily.

Unless tubers will be marketed immediately following harvest, they should not be dug and handled until the skin has set. Fertilizer rates and the timing of applications should be adjusted according to the growing season and the anticipated harvest date to achieve skin set by harvest time. If vine desiccation or removal is necessary, allow sufficient time between treatment and harvest (usually 1–3 weeks) for the skin to toughen. During harvest and handling, operate equipment with chain speeds adjusted to minimize bruising (Chapter 6). Cover tubers in the field and during transport to protect them from heat, sunlight, and air movement. See Chapter 6 for details of proper harvest procedures.

Enlarged Lenticels

Lenticels are small, inconspicuous pores on the tuber surface. If tubers have an insufficient supply of oxygen, as in excessively wet, waterlogged soil or in very compacted dry soil, lenticels become enlarged and prominent (Fig. 10.1). Enlarged lenticels may resemble scab lesions but are smaller and lighter in color. They detract from the appearance of tubers and provide entrance sites for bacterial pathogens. Freshly harvested tubers held wet can be deprived of sufficient oxygen and may develop enlarged lenticels and tuber soft rot (Chapter 15).

Several practices minimize the development of enlarged lenticels. Provide good field drainage, especially in low areas that may remain wetter. Avoid overwatering during the growing season. When tubers are being placed in storage, remove free surface moisture by providing adequate ventilation, and prevent condensation of free moisture on tuber surfaces. Do not harvest areas of fields where tubers show a significant amount of enlarged lenticels, or keep these tubers separate and market them immediately.

Freezing and Chilling Injury

Chilling damage to tubers may occur at temperatures below 38° F. The symptoms are somewhat variable, depending on the temperature, the exposure time, and the cultivar. The surface of damaged tubers may appear wrinkled and flabby. Internal tissues may turn bluish gray to black, or diffuse smoky gray areas may develop in them. Blackening of the vascular ring may also occur, and this may closely resemble net necrosis, caused by potato leafroll virus (Fig. 14.1). Tubers that have been frozen at temperatures below 29° F become soft and watery. Frozen tissues tend to disintegrate and eventually dry out.

Tubers for commercial and seed use should be protected from temperatures below 38° F both in storage and during shipping. Harvesting operations should not proceed if tuber pulp temperatures are below 45° F.

Internal Tuber Disorders

Brown Center and Hollow Heart

Brown center (also called incipient hollow heart, brown heart, or sugar center) and hollow heart are considered two different phases of the same internal disorder. They are believed to be initiated by the same conditions. Even though they are related, the two disorders often occur separately. Tubers that have brown center do not always develop hollow heart, and hollow heart may occur without being preceded by brown center. Brown center is initiated when tubers are very small, the most susceptible period being from tuber initiation (late growth stage III) to the time when tubers weigh about 2 ounces (early growth stage IV). Hollow heart also occurs in tubers this small.

The first symptom of brown center is light brown pith tissue near the center of the tuber. The brown area can vary in size and intensity of color. Severe changes occur in the tissues that turn brown, eventually resulting in rupture and death of affected cells. If the tuber grows slowly and uniformly after the discoloration develops, the dead cells may be spread apart by the growth of living cells interspersed among them, and the brown color may dissipate by the end of the growing season.

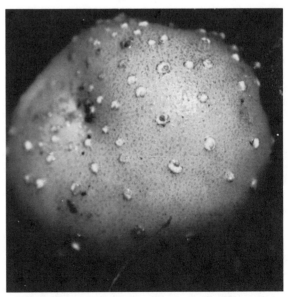

Fig. 10.1. Enlarged lenticels on a tuber, resulting from exposure to excessively wet soil. (Courtesy M. L. Powelson)

If, on the other hand, the tuber grows rapidly, the affected tissue may split apart and form an internal cavity, and thus the disorder develops into hollow heart.

Hollow heart is characterized by a longitudinal or transverse irregularly shaped cavity in the flesh of the tuber. Cavities can range from tiny openings to pockets nearly the size of the entire pith tissue. They form in the center or near the stem end or the bud end of the tuber, depending on when the disorder is initiated. Those occurring closer to the stem end are invariably preceded by brown center and develop early in the season. This form of the disorder is called stem-end hollow heart (Plate 5) and is common in the cultivar Russet Burbank. Cavities occurring closer to the apical end form later in the growing season and usually are not preceded by brown center. This late-season disorder is called bud-end hollow heart (Plate 6). The cultivars Norgold Russet, Lemhi Russet, and Atlantic are noted for this form of the disorder. Bud-end hollow heart can also develop in Russet Burbank but is not as common as the stem-end disorder in that cultivar.

The exact causes of brown center and hollow heart are not known, but important factors in the initiation and development of these disorders are air and soil temperatures, soil moisture, and tuber size and growth rate. Other factors that may influence the incidence of hollow heart are soil fertility, the fertilizer application method and timing, plant density and uniformity, the planting date, the number of stems per seed piece, seed piece size, and seed quality, including physiological age.

One theory to explain the development of hollow heart is that stresses during or shortly after tuber initiation cause potato plants to take water, minerals, and carbohydrates from the young, growing tubers, resulting in the death of some cells. When the stresses are relieved, the return of favorable growing conditions results in rapid tuber enlargement, causing the injured cells to separate, thus forming the hollow-heart cavity. A second theory suggests that hollow heart results from rapid tuber enlargement without any associated stresses. In either case, fast-growing tubers are more likely to develop this disorder.

Temperature is a factor in the initiation of brown center in Russet Burbank. A period of cool weather resulting in soil temperatures below 55° F for 5–7 days during tuber initiation and early bulking is sufficient to incite this disorder.

A second factor is the amount of soil moisture during tuber initiation. Maintaining more than 80–85% of available soil water (Chapter 8) may increase both brown center and stem-end hollow heart. The increase may be due to the slow warming of wet soils, which increases the chance of exposing newly developed tubers to temperatures below 55° F. Maintaining 70–80% of available soil water during cool periods when tuber initiation is occurring may decrease the incidence of brown center and hollow heart, but it does not entirely eliminate these disorders. Allowing fields to dry down to below 65% of available soil water is not recommended, as this may cause sufficient stress to induce second growth or tuber cracking. Excessively dry soil during tuber initiation limits total yield and results in lower tuber specific gravity. In the fall when the crop is nearing maturity, very wet soil may increase the incidence of bud-end hollow heart. If possible, uniform soil moisture should be maintained throughout the growing season. If a soil water deficit does occur, a gradual return to a more favorable percentage of available soil water is preferable to a large, sudden addition of water.

A late planting date generally results in a lower incidence of brown center, since soils tend to warm as the season progresses. Late planting may also result in lower yield, but this can be offset by increased tuber quality. Any effect of the planting date, however, is closely associated with weather patterns in a given year. Planting seed tubers with brown center or hollow heart does not affect the incidence of these disorders

in the subsequent crop. Uniformly close spacing of seed pieces, with few skips, and planting large seed pieces to produce multistemmed plants are also associated with lower incidence of hollow heart.

Fertility also can influence the incidence of these disorders. Nitrogen applied preplant or in small amounts periodically throughout the growing season usually results in a lowered incidence of hollow heart. Nitrogen applied at or shortly after tuber initiation may stimulate the tuber growth rate and thus enhance the development of brown center and hollow heart. The role of other nutrients in these disorders is not well understood. Maintaining a balance of nutrients so as to avoid stresses seems to be important.

Potato cultivars differ widely in their susceptibility to brown center and hollow heart. Norgold Russet, Lemhi Russet, Atlantic, and NorKing Russet are more susceptible than Russet Burbank. Butte and related advanced breeding lines are more resistant to hollow heart than Russet Burbank.

A management program to limit brown center and hollow heart starts with cultivars that are less susceptible to these disorders. Cultural practices that ensure good plant stands with several stems per hill and adequate plant competition are also helpful. If possible, choose a planting date to ensure that tuber initiation does not occur during a period of low soil temperature. Maintain uniform soil moisture and fertility, and strive to achieve uniform plant and tuber growth rates throughout the season.

Internal Brown Spot and Heat Necrosis

Many different names have been used to describe symptoms of internal necrosis in tubers. The two most common are internal brown spot and heat necrosis. The physiology of these two disorders is not completely known, but they differ in being associated with different tissues and in producing symptoms at different locations within the tuber. Symptoms of both disorders can be confused with those of the virus disease corky ring spot (Fig. 14.2). The latter can be distinguished from physiological disorders by means of laboratory diagnostic techniques.

Internal brown spot is characterized by small, round or irregularly shaped, light tan, reddish brown, or rust-colored spots or blotches scattered throughout the tuber flesh (Plate 7). The lesions can occur at any place within the tuber but are generally more common in tissues inside the vascular ring, and predominantly those toward the bud end. Tubers affected with internal brown spot normally do not show external symptoms, although some reports have associated this disorder with malformed or large tubers or those with a thickening or abnormal russeting of the skin.

Internal brown spot may occur at various times throughout the growing season. It may develop soon after tuber initiation or during bulking in periods of rapid or uneven tuber growth. The symptoms tend to increase in severity during the growing season and can continue to intensify in storage. Immature tubers and those stored at temperatures above 60° F generally have a higher incidence of the disorder.

The cause of internal brown spot is poorly understood. It has been suggested that the primary cause may be reabsorption of water or other tuber constituents to support vegetative development. The disorder has been associated with coarse-textured soils and with several climatic conditions, including hot, dry weather, high soil temperatures, and low or fluctuating soil moisture.

Calcium deficiency has also been suspected as a cause of internal brown spot, because calcium concentrations have been reported to be lower in tubers with this disorder than in unaffected tubers. Internal brown spot lesions do not always develop in tubers with low levels of calcium, however. Deficiencies of other nutrients can also result in necrosis of cells in tuber flesh, but this may be due to their influence on the availability of calcium to affected tissues. Internal brown spot has not been consistently controlled by field applications of calcium, but the lack of success may be due to poor uptake and movement of calcium to the tubers, especially during the stress periods thought to induce the disorder.

It is difficult to develop a management program to minimize the incidence of internal brown spot, since the disorder and the factors associated with it are not well understood. Delayed planting has resulted in decreased incidence of internal brown spot, perhaps by reducing the proportion of large tubers and by shifting the critical developmental stage to a later part of the growing season. Irrigation and fertilization practices that promote even growth without periods of stress on the plants and tubers are helpful in lowering the incidence of the disorder.

Heat necrosis lesions are principally confined to the vascular ring tissue near the bud end, but they may form anywhere in the tuber. This disorder has been associated with external tuber deformations and with depressions in the skin and related cracking or rough areas. It is most common in tubers growing near the soil surface, where they are exposed to higher temperatures, especially after the vines begin to die. To lessen the chances that these conditions will occur, time the harvest so as to prevent exposure of tubers to high soil temperatures, follow harvest procedures that protect them from exposure, and keep the harvested tubers under optimal storage conditions.

Translucent End

Translucent end (also called sugar end, incipient jelly end, or jelly end rot) affects the stem end of tubers (Plate 8). The affected tissue has a lower dry matter content and a higher reducing sugar content than unaffected areas of the same tuber (Plate 9). Cultivars with long tubers, such as Russet Burbank, are prone to this disorder. It is often associated with tubers having second growth and pointed stem ends.

The stem end of Russet Burbank tubers normally has a higher starch content than the bud end, but seasonal variations and growing conditions can influence the relative amounts of both starch and reducing sugars. Different theories have been proposed to explain the lower dry matter content in the stem end of tubers with translucent end: 1) carbohydrates move out of the stem-end tissues and into the plant for renewed vegetative growth following a period of stress, 2) carbohydrates move from the stem end to the bud end for development and maturation of the bud end following a period of stress, 3) starch in the tissues that become translucent is converted to sugars as a result of stress, 4) the carbohydrates produced during photosynthesis do not move to the stem end of affected tubers, and 5) sugars produced by photosynthesis, when moved to the tubers, are not converted to starch.

Translucent end is most often associated with a water deficit in the plant. This may result from low soil moisture, high air temperature, drying winds, or a high ratio of tops to tubers. It was once thought that translucent end occurred only near harvest. More recently, however, it has been shown that water stress during tuber initiation can result in an increase in the incidence of this disorder.

Cultural practices to minimize the occurrence of translucent end should promote good stands and maintain constant, uniform soil moisture and fertility, to ensure uniform growing conditions and minimize moisture stress during periods of high temperature.

Vascular Discoloration

Discoloration of varying intensity may develop in the vascular system at the stem end of tubers. This discoloration is generally confined to the area within ½ inch of the point of stolon attachment, but it may extend throughout the entire vascular ring to the bud end in very severe cases.

Vascular discoloration appears as speckled, light tan to reddish brown or even dark chocolate-colored streaks. Although immature tubers are susceptible, this disorder occurs more frequently when tubers are near full maturity. The discoloration can be present in the field, or tubers that have been exposed to the causal factors in the field may develop symptoms during the first 1–2 months in storage. This physiological vascular discoloration is sometimes confused with vascular net necrosis, caused by potato leafroll virus (Fig. 14.1), or with vascular discoloration related to *Verticillium* infection.

Physiological vascular discoloration is generally associated with low soil moisture and rapid death of green vines due to chemicals, frost, or mechanical removal. High-temperature stress at the time of vine killing generally increases the severity of the discoloration. Irrigation prior to vine killing decreases the amount of stem-end discoloration, regardless of the method of vine killing.

Blackheart

Internal blackheart occurs as the result of a deficiency of oxygen available to the tuber for respiration. It is relatively easy to diagnose, as the center of affected tubers is black to blue-black in an irregular pattern, and the discolored area usually has a very distinct border. Sometimes a cavity forms in the center of the tuber. The darkened areas are usually fairly firm, in contrast to those affected by Pythium leak, which are spongy and watery (Chapter 17). There is no odor associated with blackheart.

Blackheart develops when tubers are held in a low-oxygen environment, such as a poorly aerated storage, truck, or railcar, or when gas diffusion through the tubers is slowed because of very low or very high temperatures. This condition can also develop in the field when the soil is flooded. Proper soil drainage and good aeration in storage and transit prevent this problem.

Bruise Damage

Three different types of bruise damage to potato tubers are distinguishable: blackspot, shatter bruise, and pressure bruise. Blackspot and shatter bruise both result from a bruising force or impact. Pressure bruise occurs during storage as a result of the pressure of tubers being forced against each other or against storage structures.

Blackspot is an internal discoloration that begins to develop just under the skin 6–8 hours after bruising has occurred. It is visible only if the outer layer of skin is removed from the tuber. Bruised areas are bluish gray to black, variable in size and shape, and rarely deeper than the vascular ring (Plate 10). The stem end of the tuber is usually more susceptible to internal bruise damage than the bud end. A bruising force sufficient to rupture cells is required, and thus blackspot can occur any time tubers are handled.

Shatter bruise is characterized by cracking of the outer surface of the tuber. The cracks often extend into the tuber flesh, presenting an appearance of small multiple fissures or splits. Shatter bruises do not discolor, although the damaged cells around the margins of the fissures may discolor and make them appear similar to blackspot bruises. Unlike blackspot, shatter bruises may penetrate deeply into the tuber flesh. They may not be readily observed at the time of damage without special diagnostic techniques (Box 6.3), but they usually become evident after the affected tissue becomes slightly dehydrated and some shrinking occurs.

Pressure bruises are flattened or slightly sunken areas that develop in storage at points of contact between tubers or at points where they are pressed against the storage structure or equipment. The bruise results from dehydration of the affected area due to the external pressure causing a shift in the distribution of water within the tuber. Pressure bruises vary in size and shape, depending on the extent of the contact and the amount of pressure. The problem increases if the relative humidity in the storage is allowed to drop below 90%. Slight bruises tend to disappear, but severe ones persist, and severely bruised tubers may be more susceptible to blackspot when handled.

In order for blackspot or shatter bruise to occur, the tubers must be in a physiologically susceptible condition, and a bruising force sufficient to rupture cells must be applied. Tuber turgidity (amount of hydration) and pulp temperature are two very important factors in the susceptibility of tubers to bruising. In general, susceptibility to shatter bruise increases as tuber hydration increases, and susceptibility to blackspot increases as tuber hydration decreases (Fig. 6.4). If tubers are extremely dehydrated, however, they become less susceptible to blackspot. As tuber pulp temperature decreases, total bruise damage (blackspot plus shatter bruise) increases, especially below 45°F (Fig. 6.5). Shatter bruise is especially common in cold, crisp tubers. The optimal tuber hydration for minimal total bruise damage shifts somewhat with pulp temperature (Fig. 10.2). Other factors that influence susceptibility to blackspot and shatter bruise include tuber maturity, planting date, soil moisture, potassium fertilization, and vine condition just prior to harvest, all of which are related in some way to tuber hydration. In addition, cultivars differ in susceptibility to these disorders.

Reduction of total bruise damage is a critical step in potato health management in order for producers to maintain high tuber quality. Bruise reduction requires an integrated management program beginning at planting and continuing until the potatoes reach the consumer or processor. Since cultivars vary in susceptibility to bruise, selection of a less susceptible cultivar is desirable, provided it is acceptable to the intended market. It is also important to provide ample fertility, especially potassium, and provide soil moisture and pest control favoring the development of healthy vines and good root growth until harvest. Close attention must be paid to soil moisture, tuber hydration, and pulp temperatures at harvest. Careful management of all handling procedures during harvest, storage, and post-storage operations is critical to minimizing bruising (Chapter 6).

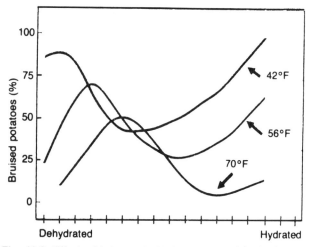

Fig. 10.2. Effect of tuber pulp temperature and hydration on susceptibility to blackspot and shatter bruise. (Reprinted, by permission, from G. D. Kleinschmidt and M. K. Thornton, 1991, Bruise-Free Potatoes: Our Goal, Bulletin 725, University of Idaho Cooperative Extension System, Moscow)

Plant Physiological Disorders

Various physiological disorders affect the appearance and function of potato foliage. These include hail damage, lightning damage, leaf tipburn, air pollution damage, chemical damage, water damage, and nutritional imbalances. Damage to foliage influences photosynthetic and respiratory activity, water relations, and other physiological processes vital to healthy plant growth and development. Because the growth of foliage is inherently related to the growth of tubers, foliar disorders and tuber disorders are often interconnected. Competition between foliage and tubers for water and nutrients can influence the occurrence and severity of many of the tuber disorders discussed in the preceding section.

Hail Damage

Hail damage to potato plants during summer storms can range from partial defoliation to complete mutilation of leaves and stems. Losses are related to the amount of damage sustained, the growth stage of the crop when the damage occurs, the cultivar, and the cultural practices imposed and the weather following the damage.

Slight leaf damage at any stage of growth will not affect yield, but the loss of more than 25% of the foliage will result in lower total yield and marketable yield. Increasing amounts of foliar damage will result in lower yields of marketable tubers, higher numbers of small and malformed tubers, and lower tuber specific gravity. Moderate hail damage sustained during growth stage II generally has little effect on yield or tuber grade. Stem damage deep enough to cut vascular tissues can limit yield, especially if it occurs before, during, or just following bloom (growth stage III). The greatest losses are inflicted when hail damage occurs early in growth stage IV, during the 2- to 4-week period following bloom. Besides limiting yield, damage during this period results in lower tuber starch content, proportional to the amount of foliage removed. Potato plants have a remarkable capacity for recovery from both leaf and stem damage, but partial loss of foliage at any stage may result in delayed maturity of the crop, a factor that must be considered in planning for harvest.

Weather and soil fertility influence the degree to which plants will recover from hail damage. If the damage is moderate, favorable growing conditions following the hailstorm and management to provide appropriate soil moisture and fertility will allow quick recovery, without any major effect on normal growth. Damaged tissues normally heal quickly, which reduces the development of diseases associated with hail damage, such as soft rot.

Lightning Damage

Symptoms resulting from a lightning strike in a potato field normally appear within 2–24 hours as a well-defined circular or elliptical area of injured or dead plants. The damage is relatively uniform within the affected area, although it may diminish near the margins. Occasionally, scattered individual plants or small groups of plants with injury symptoms are intermingled with less severely affected or unaffected plants. Areas of damage often follow water drainage patterns within the field and frequently occur in the lowest spots. Variations in the amount of soil moisture and differences in the intensity of electrical discharge influence the injury pattern and distribution within a field. Because the affected area is highly visible and so localized, inexperienced observers may assume that some disease has begun and is spreading from a point source.

Stems of lightning-damaged plants are soft, water-soaked, and discolored brown to black. They often collapse at the top and generally wilt irreversibly. Damaged tissues dry quickly and turn brown to tan, with surface layers appearing light tan to almost white. A characteristic sign of lightning damage is that stem pith tissues collapse and form horizontal plates, appearing crosshatched or ladderlike. This can be observed by longitudinally slicing the stems of affected plants.

Tubers may initially appear unaffected, but dark brown to black necrotic spots soon form, with some skin cracking. Severely injured tubers appear cooked, with an extensive collapse of the central pith and less damage to the outer cortical tissues. Breakdown and decay of the pith generally continue, often leaving a hole through the tuber. Damaged tubers are extremely susceptible to secondary pathogens and generally decay prior to harvest.

Tipburn

The tips and margins of potato leaves and leaflets may turn yellow and then gradually die, roll upward, turn brown or black, and become brittle (Plate 11). Tipburn is a weather-induced disorder, caused by excessive moisture loss from leaves under hot, dry, windy conditions following a period of cool, moist weather. Under these conditions, the amount of water transpired by the leaves exceeds that taken up by the roots.

This disorder can be confused with potato leafroll virus infection or foliar blights. Tipburn is often mistaken for late blight (Chapter 16), but tipburn lesions are uniformly brown and have very abrupt margins, rather than grading from brownish black to yellow to green, which is typical of late blight lesions. Furthermore, late blight lesions are located on the sides or centers of leaves as well as the tips (Plate 54).

Sucking insects, such as leafhoppers and aphids, may accentuate tipburn. Root pruning during cultivation is commonly a contributing factor.

Measures that conserve soil moisture, irrigation during hot, dry periods, and care in cultivation to avoid root damage are helpful practices in reducing tipburn.

Air Pollution Damage

Potato foliage can be damaged by exposure to one or more atmospheric pollutants, such as the photochemical oxidants ozone and peroxyacetyl nitrate (PAN). This often occurs during temperature inversions, when warm, stagnant air is held close to the ground for several days. Oxides of sulfur may contribute to the problem in areas downwind from a power plant or smelter. The symptoms vary, depending upon the concentration of pollutants in the air and the duration of exposure. The reported tolerance and sensitivity of cultivars vary from one geographic area to another.

Ozone damage usually causes a condition known as speckle leaf, expressed as chlorotic or necrotic speckling of the upper leaf surface. Severe symptoms include more pronounced chlorosis, bronzing, and necrosis of leaves, resulting in early maturity of affected plants. PAN produces a silvering or glazing of the lower surfaces of affected leaves, with the most severe symptoms on young, fully expanded leaves. Damage to tubers has not been reported to result from exposure to air pollutants, except for lower yields associated with premature senescence.

The only control for air pollution damage is to avoid growing potatoes in areas heavily polluted with ozone, PAN, or sulfur oxides. In marginally polluted areas where some damage regularly occurs, only tolerant cultivars should be planted.

Chemical Damage

Considerable damage can be caused by accidental or improper application of a wide range of agricultural chemicals. The symptoms and the severity of the damage vary considerably, depending upon the type of chemical involved, dosage, application method, growth stage, cultivar, and environmental factors. Various aberrations, distortions, chlorosis, and necrosis of foliage and external and internal symptoms, deformations, and stunting of tubers may result. The symptoms

are usually more severe in a plant water deficit.

Growth-regulating chemicals, such as herbicides, can cause leaf distortions and chlorosis, which may be confused with symptoms of virus infections or other diseases. Tuber deformations, changes in skin color, and surface disfigurations may also occur. Chemical damage can be caused by herbicides applied directly to the potato crop or by residues carried over from those used on preceding rotational crops. Stem-end vascular discoloration of tubers may develop following application of preharvest vine defoliants, particularly if the plants are stressed (see Internal Tuber Disorders). Improper fertilizer application to foliage can cause leaf burn. Fertilizer damage to seed pieces can cause shoot and root burn, followed by seed piece decay. This may lead to poor stands and low plant vigor.

Proper diagnosis of chemically induced disorders is difficult, generally requires much experience, and is beyond the scope of this book. Considerable caution must be exercised in evaluating these problems. Observe and record the condition of not only the potato plants but also nearby weeds or other crops that may have been exposed. Gather all pertinent information on agrochemicals applied in current and previous crops, rates, application methods, and prevailing weather conditions. Consultation with an experienced diagnostician is usually necessary to determine the causes of chemical damage.

Water Damage

Potato plants and tubers may be damaged by excessively wet conditions or flooding that lasts for more than a few days. The damage occurs primarily as a consequence of oxygen deprivation in the root system. Enlarged lenticels normally develop in tubers under excessively wet conditions (Fig. 10.1). Relations between soil and plant water and potato health are discussed in Chapter 8.

Nutritional Disorders

Many nutritional disorders can affect both potato plants and tubers. Severe nutrient imbalances may result in visible foliar symptoms (Box 9.1), but proper diagnosis of nutrient disorders is best done before these symptoms develop, by submitting leaf samples to a tissue analysis laboratory. Nutrient imbalances are influenced by many factors, including the concentrations of mineral elements in the soil and in the plant, the availability and chemical form of the nutrients, their balance with other nutrients, soil pH, soluble salts in the soil, ion-exchange levels, the general health of the plant, and a wide range of environmental conditions. The causes and management of nutritional disorders are discussed in more detail in Chapter 9.

Management of Physiological Disorders

The development of physiological disorders in potato plants and tubers is influenced by unfavorable environmental factors (air and soil temperatures, rainfall, humidity, and wind), improper cultural practices, and inadequate or excessive soil moisture and fertility. Because climatic conditions cannot be manipulated by the grower, control of physiological disorders depends on the careful management of factors over which the grower does have control. These include cultivar selection; seed quality, size, and placement; planting date; fertility; cultivation; irrigation; and pest management. Although the exact causes of most physiological disorders are not known, the basic management objective for minimizing these disorders is to provide the best possible conditions for uniform growth of the crop throughout the growing season.

Cultivars differ greatly in susceptibility to these various

disorders. Growers should be aware of the limitations of the cultivars being grown and implement appropriate management plans. If possible, cultivars highly susceptible to certain physiological disorders should be avoided. Planting should be timed to allow rapid emergence and avoid periods of low soil temperature during tuberization. It is important to keep seed potatoes cool in storage, to avoid long storage periods, and not to plant physiologically old seed pieces in cold, dry soil. The size and physiological age of seed pieces have a significant

> **The basic management objective for minimizing physiological disorders is to provide the best possible conditions for uniform growth of the crop throughout the growing season.**

influence on the number of stems and on tuber set. The goal is to establish a uniform stand of multiple-stem plants throughout the field. Uniform spacing of seed pieces is important to ensure adequate plant competition and control tuber size and growth rate. Different cultivars require different plant spacings, and local recommendations should be obtained. The desired planting depth for seed pieces also varies with the cultivar, the soil texture, and the climate. Seed pieces must be planted shallow enough to allow quick emergence, but deep enough that tubers are not set too shallow. This is important in order to avoid greening and sunscald and to protect the tubers from infection by the early and late blight pathogens.

During the growing season, management practices should promote *uniform and continuous plant and tuber growth*. As much as possible, soil moisture should be managed so that the soil is not excessively wet or dry at any time. If irrigation is available, a strict irrigation management plan should be followed to accomplish this goal (Chapter 8). In rain-fed production, proper drainage should be provided, and planting should be timed to minimize problems associated with excess water. Careful management of fertility is critical and is often closely tied to water management. The goals are to avoid nutrient deficiencies at any growth stage, by providing for the continuous nutritional needs of the crop, and to avoid growth spurts resulting from excess applications of fertilizer, especially during tuberization or after periods of environmental stress.

As tubers develop, they must be protected from environmental stresses as much as possible. Adequate hilling before row closure is important in minimizing greening and sunscald later. Vine-killing procedures and timing should be chosen so as to minimize the development of vascular discoloration and allow tuber skins to set properly prior to harvest. The reduction of harvest damage requires careful management to maintain tuber quality and marketability (Chapter 6). To minimize bruising, harvest and handling equipment must be used properly, and harvested tubers must be protected from exposure to high or low temperature, sunlight, and excess moisture. Timely movement of the crop to properly managed storages is essential to maintaining the quality of the harvested tubers.

Minimizing the development of physiological disorders is an essential part of an overall potato health management plan. Although there is still much to learn about the causes of these disorders and the effects of environmental and cultural variables, these problems can be minimized by providing the best possible growing conditions for the crop.

Robert H. Callihan
Department of Plant and Soil Science
University of Idaho, Moscow

Robin R. Bellinder
Department of Fruit and Vegetable Science
Cornell University, Ithaca, New York

CHAPTER 11

Management of Weeds

All fields in which potatoes are grown contain billions of weed seeds. Weed seeds already in the soil, called the soil seed bank, are the primary source of weeds with which the potato grower must contend. Because of the great quantity of seeds produced by most weed species and the longevity of these seeds in the soil, appropriate weed management strategies must be incorporated into all potato health management programs.

Weeds directly limit crop yields by shading crop plants and by competing with them for resources such as space, water, and nutrients. Dense weed infestations restrict the growth of potato plants, which results in undersized tubers. Weeds can also affect crop quality by direct injury (for example, by piercing tubers with sharp rhizomes). Water stress due to weed competition can result in tuber physiological disorders and in lowered dry matter content.

In addition to direct effects, weeds may have several indirect effects on potato production. Insects such as psyllids, aphids, and leafhoppers may multiply in the spring on weeds before entering potato fields. Some viruses can survive in weeds, although they are not major sources of potato viruses. Weed species may affect the survival of some nematodes. Excessive weed growth can stress the crop, which may lead to early senescence and increased susceptibility to diseases such as early blight and early dying. Weed growth can also interfere with the drying of foliage during the day, thus lengthening periods of leaf wetness and increasing the chances of infection by pathogens causing foliar blights.

Heavy weed growth can interfere with the proper operation of harvesting equipment. Weed species that do not naturally senesce to a dry state by harvest or do not dry after vine-killing operations or freezing weather are especially difficult in this regard. Even species that dry by harvest may cause difficulty in harvesting, because of their root masses. Vine beaters, cutters, or other mechanical devices may be necessary to manage such weeds where potatoes are harvested by diggers and handpicking.

Commercial potato production is not feasible without special operations to control weeds. Fields with poor weed control can yield 20–40% less than their full productive potential. Cultivating the crop for weed control can lower yields by more than 5% and, in addition, may cause some loss of tuber quality. Misuse of herbicides can cause injury to the potato crop or to subsequent crops grown in rotation. Even with an adequate weed control program, uncontrolled weeds and the adverse effects of normal control practices generally limit yields by as much as 7%, compared with those theoretically possible in the absence of weeds. Improved control practices can minimize the effects of weeds but can never eliminate their effects completely. Potato health will always be limited to some extent by weeds, either by the weeds themselves or by the practices used to control them.

Types of Weeds and General Management Strategies

Weeds are generally classed as annual or perennial and as broadleaf or grass species. Annual species live only a single year and reproduce by seed. They die naturally at the end of the season—after they have produced their seed crop. Perennial species live several years and reproduce by various types of vegetative structures in addition to seed. They can regenerate shoots each year using food reserves stored in vegetative structures in the soil, and thus they are not dependent on seed germination for their survival. They can also resprout when their top growth has been removed mechanically or by other means, as long as the underground storage organ is intact.

Annual Weed Species

Most annual broadleaf weeds that affect potato production are species common to any arable land. Examples include various species of pigweed (*Amaranthus* species) (Plate 12A), common lambsquarters (*Chenopodium album*) (Plate 12B), mustards (Cruciferae), purslanes (*Portulaca* species), mallow (*Malva* species), wild buckwheat (*Polygonum convolvulus*), knotweed (*Polygonum aviculare*), smartweeds (*Polygonum* species), and kochia (*Kochia scoparia*). Annual broadleaf species are generally controllable by appropriate cultivation together with suitable herbicides. The diversity of these species, however, is sufficient to require well-planned weed control programs.

Annual broadleaf seedlings are generally very susceptible to uprooting and burial by cultivation. They are also very susceptible to minimal doses of specific foliage-applied herbicides during the period from the cotyledon stage through the second-true-leaf stage (Fig. 11.1A). This period generally spans from 7 to 14 days after emergence. By the time the plants have formed six true leaves, they are well established and able to recover from substantial injury, and they can survive a day or more after being uprooted in soil. This increases the likelihood of rerooting and recovery following cultivation. Although the seedling vigor of these species is vastly inferior to that of potato sprouts, broadleaf weeds germinate in the warmer surface soil and have the potential to compete effectively with potatoes after establishment.

Sunflower (*Helianthus annuus*) and cocklebur (*Xanthium strumarium*) are large-seeded, warm-season broadleaf species that appear after potato emergence in some production areas. These weeds are difficult to control effectively in potato crops by either cultivation or herbicides, although they are susceptible to postemergence applications of the triazinone herbicide metribuzin. A crop rotation that includes cereals allows the use of herbicides effective against these species in a rotation-wide management strategy.

Annual nightshades (*Solanum* species) (Plate 12C) are especially troublesome in potato crops, since they survive well below the canopy of potato plants and often develop at the same growth rate. In addition, since they are in the same plant family as potato, most herbicides that control nightshade are harmful to potatoes. Nightshades can be suppressed by a combination of cultivation and application of acetanilide herbicides (such as metolachlor) or urea herbicides (such as linuron). Acceptable control of nightshade in potatoes must involve a rotation-wide management strategy. Including corn in the rotation, for example, allows herbicides that control nightshade to be used while that crop is in the field.

Dodders (*Cuscuta* species) are yellow, vining annual weeds that may cause severe losses in potato crops. They germinate on the soil surface and later detach from the soil to survive parasitically on other plants. Fields known to be thoroughly infested with dodder should be avoided for potato production. If infestations are confined to small areas, all dodder plant parts and all affected potatoes should be removed in bags and burned, or the areas should be treated with an herbicide that completely destroys both dodder and potatoes.

Volunteer grain can sometimes become a weed problem in potato crops. Seed of winter or spring cereals, including wheat (*Triticum aestivum*), barley (*Hordeum vulgare*), rye (*Secale cereale*), and corn (*Zea mays*), often remain from a previous crop. Grain seedlings may be effectively controlled by allowing time for or promoting germination and growth prior to normal tillage for potato seedbed preparation. Postharvest irrigation can promote germination if temperatures are high enough and if a long postharvest period is not required before seed dormancy has passed. Tillage for potato seedbed preparation, drag-off, and hilling normally dispose of volunteer small grains, and these plants are also susceptible to most preemergence herbicides used for weed control in potatoes. Since corn usually germinates after potato plants emerge, these tillage operations are seldom adequate to control volunteer corn. However, postemergence herbicides are available for controlling corn in potato crops.

Warm-season annual grasses are the most troublesome group of annual grass weeds. Barnyard grass (*Echinochloa crus-galli*), crabgrass (*Digitaria* species) (Plate 13A), green foxtail (*Setaria viridis*), yellow foxtail (*S. glauca*), sandbur (*Cenchrus* species), wild proso millet (*Panicum miliaceum*), witchgrass (*P. capillare*) (Plate 13B), fall panicum (*P. dichotomiflorum*) (Plate 13C), and other warm-season grasses normally germinate at soil temperatures well above those required for potatoes and consequently appear well after potatoes have emerged.

Cool-season annual grasses are seldom problems in potato production. Wild oat (*Avena fatua*) is an exception, often becoming a serious weed in potato crops. This species is sometimes controlled by vigorous drag-off tillage with weighted flex-tine harrows, followed by hilling tillages. It is also susceptible to certain herbicides, including EPTC, metribuzin, and sethoxydim.

Perennial Weed Species

Perennial weeds limit yields more than annual weeds, because perennials grow more vigorously and generally are not controlled as well in potato crops. Potato yields have been reduced by as much as 70% by Canada thistle (*Cirsium arvense*) (Fig. 11.2), 16% by field bindweed (*Convolvulus arvensis*), and 32% by Russian knapweed (*Centaurea repens*). Quackgrass (*Elytrigia repens*) (Plate 14A) and yellow nutsedge (*Cyperus esculentus*) (Plate 14B) not only greatly limit yield but also lower quality by causing deformation of tubers and penetrating them with rhizomes.

Cultivation suppresses many perennial weeds, but since the buds from their creeping roots and rhizomes continue to emerge until most of their shoots are flowering, cultivation simply delays their growth. Covering their emerging shoots with soil does not kill them as it does annual weeds. Most perennials

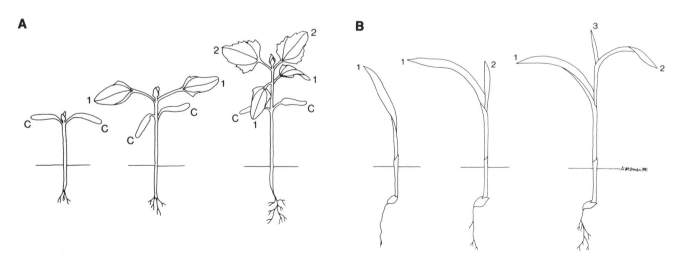

Fig. 11.1. Annual weed seedlings in early growth stages, when control measures should be implemented. C = cotyledon; 1 = first true leaf; 2 = second true leaf; 3 = third true leaf. **A,** Annual broadleaf weed: common lambsquarters (*Chenopodium album*) in cotyledon, first-true-leaf, and second-true-leaf stages. **B,** Annual grass weed: giant foxtail (*Setaria faberii*) in one-, two-, and three-leaf stages. (Drawing by Anne Westman)

tolerate herbicides used on potatoes. Fields heavily infested with perennials such as Canada thistle, field bindweed, quackgrass, or Russian knapweed should be avoided for potato production, because control of these species is generally unsatisfactory in potato crops.

Serious perennial weed problems require persistent management programs targeting individual species and implemented over several rotational cropping cycles. The best control program for perennial weeds is to plan rotations and the time of planting so that infested areas are crop-free during late summer and early fall. A choice of suitable herbicides is available, and these weeds are fairly susceptible to herbicide treatment at this time. As the days shorten, perennials move food reserves from leaves and stems downward into the overwintering storage organs, in preparation for growth the following spring. Herbicides applied to perennials late in the growing season are moved into underground buds and thus limit the reproductive ability of the weeds. For this strategy to be successful, green leaves must be present at the time of application. If possible, fields should be disked 7–12 days after the initial treatment. Perennial weed infestations often require two or more seasons of treatment to achieve adequate control.

> **Serious perennial weed problems require persistent management programs targeting individual species and implemented over several rotational cropping cycles.**

Hormone-type herbicides (such as 2,4-D) and the substituted amino acid herbicide glyphosate are particularly effective in controlling broadleaf perennials. Combinations of these herbicides, which allow the use of lower rates of each, often achieve more effective control than either one alone. Product labels should be consulted for specific information regarding this use.

Combining herbicide applications with tillage offers the most efficient control of quackgrass and yellow nutsedge. Both weeds can be suppressed early in the season with the thiocarbamate herbicide EPTC, but potato production will still be hampered by surviving or late-germinating plants. Quackgrass can be suppressed in a growing potato crop by postemergence treatment with sethoxydim, but it is most effectively controlled by the nonselective herbicide glyphosate applied in the fall. Fall-applied glyphosate is translocated with carbohydrates into underground vegetative rhizome buds, effectively reducing the number of buds that emerge the following season. Drying quackgrass roots by spring-tooth tillage of dry soil two or more times in midsummer or late summer following harvest of a small grain crop can also be effective in controlling this weed. This practice, however, is not recommended in areas with coarse-textured, highly erodible soils. In these areas glyphosate treatment is preferable, to minimize soil erosion.

Yellow nutsedge reproduces predominately by means of underground tubers that sprout after the soil has warmed. In many areas, it emerges 2–3 weeks later than annual weeds such as common lambsquarters, pigweeds, mustards, and quackgrass. Nutsedge grows vegetatively until midsummer and then begins tuber formation as the days begin to shorten slightly. Early-season control with cultivation or herbicides reduces both competition from the vegetative nutsedge plants and the number of these plants that live to produce new tubers. Late-season control is also critical, because that is when these plants form tubers—even very small plants. Early-maturing

potato cultivars should be planted in fields known to be heavily infested. Because nutsedge does not compete well in heavy shade, planting a potato cultivar that quickly emerges and rapidly develops a dense canopy helps suppress this weed. Glyphosate can be used to control nutsedge during the non-cropping season, and the acetanilide herbicide metolachlor selectively suppresses it in a potato crop.

Cultural Practices Important to Weed Management

Appropriate cultural practices are the foundation of any sound weed management program. Steps should be taken to minimize the introduction of troublesome weed species that are not yet present. Only clean, tested, certified seed should be used to plant other crops in the rotation. Seed certification is an important protection against the introduction of new weed species, although it is not a guarantee. Inspect seed lots before purchase, and check the tag for weed seed tolerance. By law all certified seed sold through commercial channels must be labeled.

Vehicles, equipment, and livestock can spread weed seeds and thus contaminate fields with new species. Mud generally contains weed seeds and should be washed from vehicles, equipment, and livestock before they are permitted access to potato production areas. Controlling weeds in uncultivated areas, fencerows, roadsides, field borders, and ditch banks is an important potato health management practice. Weedy areas can harbor insect pests and some viruses, and the weeds themselves may spread into fields. Rather than relying on soil sterilants for weed control in these areas, plant a good grass cover for biological control, and then keep it weed-free and healthy. Install screens at headgates and pumps to exclude weed seeds from irrigation water.

If an unknown or new weed species is noticed, samples should be taken to an expert for identification. Do not neglect new weeds. If practical, it is wise to remove and burn them. Although seeds of many species can survive in the soil for

Fig. 11.2. A severe infestation of perennial weeds such as Canada thistle can adversely affect the yield and quality of a potato crop. (Courtesy R. C. Rowe)

many years, only a fraction actually do, so it always helps to keep the numbers down. Even among weed species that have long-lived seed, most seeds germinate or die in the first 2–5 years.

A good crop rotation is an important part of any weed management program. Certain weeds naturally become associated with certain crops because of similar life cycles, similar growth requirements, or similar herbicide tolerances. If any one crop is grown continuously, weeds associated with that crop (such as annual nightshade in potatoes) tend to dominate and proliferate year after year. A diverse crop rotation discourages domination by any one set of weed species and provides the opportunity to control troublesome species during various portions of the rotation.

> **A good crop rotation discourages domination by any one set of weed species and provides the opportunity to control troublesome species during various portions of the rotation.**

Rotation-wide management plans often lead to the best overall weed control, and they are the only effective strategy against some species. When herbicides are selected for use in rotational crops, compatibility with the potato crop must always be considered. Some problems have arisen with imidazolinone and sulfonylurea herbicides used in small grains. These are effective, long-lasting herbicides, but some carryover has occurred, and potatoes are highly susceptible to even small residual amounts of them in the soil. Current labels for these products explicitly describe this problem, and crop rotation restrictions should be followed closely.

In irrigated areas, applying irrigation in late summer or early fall following harvest of a rotational crop encourages germination of weed seeds, so that the seedlings can be destroyed by herbicide applied in late fall or spring, by tillage, or by winter freezing. Full-season potato growth is necessary for full-season weed control. Implementation of optimal management strategies to maintain the health of the potato crop will lead to vigorous, competitive potato plants that emerge early, close the rows rapidly, and remain healthy until vine kill, leaving less space and resources available for developing weeds. Management of late-season weeds is accomplished mainly by maintaining sufficient crop cover. If possible, late-season weeds that develop as the crop matures should be killed before they form seed. Chemical or mechanical vine-killing procedures should be targeted to kill all weeds along with potato vines, to prevent a buildup of weed seeds in the soil. This is not effective, however, if weeds have already formed seed prior to the application of vine killer.

Weed Control Procedures

Direct control of weeds growing within a crop must be done by hand weeding, cultivation, or the application of herbicides. Hand weeding, although useful in a few situations, is generally far too labor-intensive to be a viable alternative to other methods. Moreover, for weeds to be pulled by hand they must be allowed to grow so large that they damage the crop through competition. Hand weeding also damages the crop by causing soil disturbance due to pulling or hoeing, and further by causing

compaction due to foot traffic. In potato production, most growers use a combination of cultivation and herbicides in an integrated weed management program. In designing an appropriate weed management plan, managers should be aware of the advantages and disadvantages of both systems.

Cultivation

Cultivation is the economical alternative to hand weeding where herbicides cannot be used, as in organic farming or in areas where they are prohibited. It is effective against all annual weed species if it is done while they are still very young. Annual broadleaf species should be cultivated when they are at the two-true-leaf stage or smaller (Fig. 11.1A), and annual grasses before they have more than three leaves (Fig. 11.1B). Cultivation is only partially effective against perennial weeds.

Compared with herbicide application, cultivation requires less technical competence on the part of operators, and it is not complicated by governmental regulations. The operation is not restricted by windy weather or herbicide-sensitive crops in adjacent fields. Cultivation also introduces no chemical residues into the potato crop, whereas herbicide residues may remain to threaten next year's crop or run off to pollute surface water or groundwater.

The major disadvantage of cultivation is that it causes more damage to the crop than the use of herbicides does. Cultivation causes direct damage to potato roots and tops and indirect damage due to increased soil compaction. Potatoes require continuous high soil moisture, and soils containing sufficient

> **The major disadvantage of cultivation is that it causes more damage to the crop than the use of herbicides does.**

moisture are wet enough that they easily become compacted. When a four-row cultivator is used, 25% of the field is covered with wheel tracks, and every row of potatoes is adjacent to and affected by compacted soil. With a six-row cultivator, four out of every six rows are adjacent to and affected by compacted soil. Compaction reduces soil aeration, which in turn reduces potato growth (Chapter 2). It also leads to the formation of clods, which bruise the crop at harvest (Chapter 6).

Herbicide sprayer swaths are two to five times wider than those of cultivators, and soil compaction is proportionally less. In Idaho, side-by-side comparisons with appropriate herbicides have shown that growers who followed normal cultivation practices lost 12–20% of total yield potential with only two cultivations. In evaluating options for weed control, potato health managers must balance the potential losses due to cultivation against the costs of and potential losses due to alternative practices or leaving the weeds uncontrolled.

Cultivation has several other disadvantages. It is not effective on wet soils, in which weeds can readily reroot. It is slower than herbicide application and requires repeated operations, resulting in increased labor and fuel costs. Herbicides generally provide more uniform weed control and better control of perennial species. Cultivation provides less control of weeds growing within rows than of weeds between rows, because covering those within rows is not as effective in killing them as cutting or uprooting those between rows. Weeds that germinate after potato row closure cannot be controlled by cultivation. The process also promotes soil erosion on sloping land. Some potato viruses (PVX, PVS, and PVY) and the potato spindle tuber viroid can be transmitted by cultivators that brush against foliage along a row of potato plants (Chapter 14). The risk of transmission of these disease agents is especially undesirable in seed potato production.

In spite of these disadvantages, cultivation can play a key role in weed management programs as long as it is done properly (Box 11.1) and in a timely manner.

Principles of Effective Cultivation

Successful cultivation programs are based on the application of several principles. Newly emerged weeds should be killed when they are very small: cultivate before annual broadleaf species get past the two-true-leaf stage or before annual grasses have more than three leaves (Fig. 11.1). If allowed to grow larger, these weeds can reroot, and those on hills can reemerge through soil thrown up to cover them. The longer annual weeds are allowed to compete with potato plants, the more effect they will have on potato yield.

If annual weeds reach the proper stage for cultivation before the potato sprouts are within 2 inches of the soil surface, a drag-off operation with a flex-tine or spike-tooth harrow will kill weeds without injuring the sprouts. Check the depth of harrowing to avoid injuring the sprouts, and make sure that all weeds are being uprooted. If not, add a second gang of harrows behind the first. It is helpful to pull a ripper shank behind the tractor wheels while harrowing. This reduces compaction and helps guide the tractor more precisely for the next operation, which should not be needed until the potatoes are well emerged.

Planting techniques vary in different production areas and have a direct effect on cultivation practices. In some areas, potatoes are planted 4–5 inches deep and covered with only a slight hill. In others, seed pieces are planted at or near the

> ## Newly emerged weeds should be killed when they are very small: cultivate before annual broadleaf species get past the two-true-leaf stage or before annual grasses have more than three leaves.

soil surface and covered with a 10- to 12-inch hill. There are also many intermediate practices. In planting systems in which a large hill is formed early, fewer cultivations and hillings are generally recommended, and they are done primarily to prevent frost damage and tuber greening. More frequent tillage is necessary where hill-building begins slowly and is done to reduce soil crusting, increase soil aeration, and control weeds. Thus, the number of postplant tillage operations can vary from one or two to as many as four or five, depending on the planting technique.

Box 11.1

Common Errors in Potato Cultivation

Failure to monitor the cultivation operation carefully

Close attention must be paid to the cultivation operation to avoid injury to potato plants and uneven weed control. Rolling cultivator gangs may fill up with vegetation or soil and lose their effectiveness or even stop rolling and start pushing soil. Shovels may shift because of loose bolts, and loose hookups may affect tracking.

Waiting too long after the emergence of annual weeds to begin cultivation

To effectively kill annual weeds, broadleaf species should be cultivated before they are past the two-true-leaf stage of growth, and grass species before they have more than three leaves (Fig. 11.1).

Trying to cultivate unmatched sets of rows

A cultivator should never cover more than one planter width or straddle rows belonging to adjacent planter passes. The planting operation is not accurate enough to maintain constant, precise spacing. Planter marks should be followed as cultivator tractor guides. Ripper marks are even more reliable as guides, especially with tractors having single-rib front tires.

Trying to realign hills with planted rows of potatoes

If the hills are crooked because of misaligned planter hilling or bad cultivation, they should be left that way.

Attempts to straighten the rows only make the alignment worse, usually make it impossible to cultivate effectively, and cause more injury to potato plants and more tuber greening.

Cultivating too deep

Cultivate only deep enough to kill weeds. Cultivating too deep increases fuel use, disturbs crop roots, and slows the entire operation.

Cultivating wet soil

Avoid cultivating wet soil. Cultivated weeds readily reroot in wet soil, and the operation may cause serious soil compaction.

Covering potato plants with soil during cultivation

Covering potato plants with soil can seriously delay crop growth. The longer the plants have been emerged, the more serious the delay due to covering them completely.

Irrigating too soon after cultivation

The timing of irrigation after cultivation is critical. Effective weed killing generally requires that cultivated weeds lie for at least one full day in warm, dry surface soil. Irrigating too soon may result in excessive rerooting of cultivated weeds. Failure to irrigate as soon as the weeds are dead, however, may result in excessive crop stress.

If the field is left flat after planting, hill formation should be started only after weeds have emerged. Hilling and cultivation are then combined in one operation. This allows maximum opportunity to cover weeds in the row. Avoid covering the potato plants completely. The first cultivation after the potatoes have emerged should be done with equipment adjusted to throw soil around the base of the plants, covering small weeds without covering many potato leaves. If annual weeds reach the two-true-leaf stage before the potato plants are large enough that the cultivator can avoid covering them, then a second, "blind" cultivation can be done with a flex-tine harrow. Potatoes that have just emerged are normally strong enough to survive flex-tine harrowing with no more than about 5% shoot breakage. The forward speed of the tractor is critical during this operation—too high a speed results in excessive damage to the potato plants. Plants with broken shoots are set back as much as they would be from a freeze. However, a small amount of shoot breakage is preferable to covering all the potato plants in a hilling operation.

It is important to plan the hill-building process. In all cultivations except the last one, throw only enough soil with the cultivator to cover the entire hill with 1–2 inches of soil. This should kill the weeds within the row, which the cultivator cannot uproot. Less soil does not cover uniformly to kill all weeds throughout the field. Coverage with more than 2 inches of soil builds the hill too quickly, so that later cultivation cannot add enough to cover and kill young weeds.

Cultivation should be done in the driest part of the field first, so that weeds will be killed by drying prior to scheduled irrigation or expected rainfall. This is effective because cultivated weeds die most readily in the driest soil. Lying uprooted in warm, dry soil for at least 1 day kills most annual weeds in the two-true-leaf stage or smaller. Cultivating on drier soil also minimizes soil compaction and its effects on yield and clod formation. When irrigation is being scheduled, the need for relatively dry soil for optimal response to cultivation should be considered, although irrigated fields should never be allowed to fall below 70% of available soil water in the upper 6 inches during growth stages I and II (Chapter 8).

The last hilling cultivation, often called lay-by, must form the final hill and should throw enough soil around the base of the potato plants to kill any small weeds beginning to grow there. To avoid damaging the crop, this operation should be performed well before row closure—that is, before leaves from adjacent hills touch each other across the furrow. This is important because midseason stress can lead to early maturity

of the crop, malformed tubers, and other quality losses. Where row closure is expected 60–80 days after planting, potato plants usually grow rapidly enough that lay-by cultivation should be done when there is still 12 inches of space between plants across the rows. At that time, an 18-inch tire can pass without significant crop damage, and root pruning is minimized. Within 5 days, the rows will grow too close to avoid damage. Within 7–10 days, the rows will be completely closed, and a vigorous crop canopy will then prevent most weed development.

Some weed seeds may germinate and seedlings may emerge after row closure, but the growth of these weeds is generally suppressed by the crop. Exceptions are perennial weeds, such as Canada thistle, and shade-tolerant annual weeds, such as nightshade. Nightshade survives under the crop canopy but is not released from competition until the potato vines begin to die from frost or late-season disease. If a late-spring or early-summer frost or hail reopens the vines after lay-by, weeds are then released from competition with the potato plants and can develop into a severe problem. In this case, postemergence selective herbicides may be needed.

Herbicides

Herbicides can be very effective components of a weed management program. When herbicide applications are effectively integrated with timely cultivation, the two can complement one another and overcome some of the disadvantages of using either alone. The first step in devising an appropriate herbicide treatment plan is to properly identify the weed species that require management in each field. Are they annuals that develop from seeds or perennials that grow from rhizomes or other underground structures surviving from year to year? Are they susceptible to herbicides registered for use on potatoes? Herbicides are selective and, like medicines, are not cure-alls, and they must be chosen to fit both the "problem" (the weeds) and the "patient" (the potato crop).

To avoid possible complications, plan herbicide treatments carefully—well in advance of actual use. Choose an herbicide or combination of herbicides that, together with cultivation and other practices, will control all weed species that are likely to be a problem. Special programs may have to be devised for troublesome species, especially some perennial weeds. A single surviving weed species can pose as much competition as would occur if other weeds were not controlled.

Read the current labels of all herbicides being considered for use. Products listed in published recommendations were approved for use at the time of publication, but registrations may change at any time. *Review the labels thoroughly.* Find out whether the herbicides under consideration are currently registered for use on potatoes. The label is a government document approving the product for specific uses and *must be followed precisely.* Pay special attention to sections relating to potatoes, including restrictions that may apply to certain cultivars. If necessary, seek additional information from qualified specialists.

In order to obtain the best weed control possible, it is important to plan in detail how herbicide management procedures will fit into the overall potato health management program. Determine exactly how and when herbicides are to be applied and whether multiple applications are necessary. As in the case of cultivation, weeds should be treated with herbicides when they are very young (Fig. 11.1), because less herbicide is required and treatments are more effective when weeds are in their early growth stages. Choose an effective application rate, but do not exceed the labeled dosage for existing soil and weed conditions. Excessive doses could cause crop injury, leave residues in tubers, or even injure the next crop in the rotation (Fig. 11.3). Study the label to determine

Fig. 11.3. Damage to a potato crop resulting from carryover of the herbicide atrazine applied to a rotational crop the previous year. (Used by permission of American Vegetable Grower magazine)

whether the use of the herbicide affects other cultural operations, and anticipate any changes in customary procedures that may be needed.

Before applying herbicides, become completely familiar with the application equipment that will be used and any adjustments that may be required and special techniques or skills that must be learned. Check the label directions to see whether cultivation or operation of other equipment in the field after treatment will jeopardize successful weed control. If so, final hilling or other necessary surface conditioning must be done before herbicide application. Determine whether soil moisture is critical to the effectiveness of the treatment. For example, metolachlor, in a preemergence application under dry conditions, requires either incorporation or irrigation in order to be activated.

> **When herbicide applications are effectively integrated with timely cultivation, the two can complement one another and overcome some of the disadvantages of using either alone.**

To avoid problems with herbicide carryover, find out if the products considered for use are compatible with the rotational crops planned for the field, especially those that follow potatoes. Are special efforts, such as deep plowing, needed to protect the next crop from traces of undecomposed herbicides, or must different rotational crops be selected? Carryover must also be considered in choosing herbicides for use in crops preceding potatoes (Fig. 11.3).

Carryover can be especially troublesome following a dry winter. Some herbicides (imidazolinones and sulfonylureas) applied to cereal crops at labeled rates can remain in the soil the following year at concentrations high enough to limit potato yield and affect quality. To minimize this problem, follow the label directions for the time needed between application of these herbicides and planting a sensitive crop, keep complete and accurate records of pesticide use on all cropland, and apply these herbicides only at labeled rates.

Principles of Herbicide Use

Herbicide selectivity—the ability of herbicides to kill some plants without appreciably injuring others—is the result of complex interactions between physiological, chemical, environmental, and physical factors. Selectivity is a basic principle in using herbicides in crop production. It is almost always relative and dose-related. The degree to which a plant is capable of responding to an applied herbicide is a measure of its susceptibility to that chemical under specific environmental conditions. If a plant is tolerant of an herbicide at high doses, this is physiological selectivity. If an herbicide can be used in such a way that contact between it and the crop can be prevented or minimized, this is placement selectivity. For example, if the roots of the crop plants develop below the depth at which weeds germinate, herbicides that do not move downward in the soil will not injure the crop if placed in the weed germination zone.

The selectivity of specific herbicides is dependent on their mode of action, placement in the soil, and application timing. Rapid-acting herbicides, or those that kill on contact, have an acute effect that is often useful in controlling annual weeds. Slow-acting herbicides, or those that are translocated within the plant, have a chronic effect. These types are more useful in controlling perennial weeds, which have underground vegetative reproductive structures.

Herbicides are applied as preplant-incorporated treatments or are applied on the soil surface in either preemergence or postemergence treatments. These terms can cause confusion over whether they refer to the crop or the weeds. *Preplant-incorporated* means applied before the crop is planted. *Preemergence* and *postemergence* usually refer to the emergence of the weeds.

Herbicides are incorporated into the soil for three reasons: 1) to reduce herbicide loss through photodegradation and volatility, which lower the efficacy of treatments and can result in injury to susceptible nontarget crops in adjacent fields, 2) to activate herbicides by placing them in the moist soil of the subsurface environment, and 3) to place them in the germination zone of weed seeds. Herbicides that do not volatilize or photodegrade are frequently applied to the soil surface after planting and before either potatoes or weeds have emerged. Weeds are thus killed as they grow through the layer of treated soil. These herbicides require moisture for activation and movement into the weed seed zone. When the soil is dry, they may fail, as surface moisture will be inadequate to activate them by placing them in solution for absorption by weed seedlings.

Preemergence herbicides are generally absorbed through the early-developing roots and shoots of weed seedlings and halt basic plant processes, resulting in death below or just above the soil surface. At the time of this writing, the chemical families of herbicides registered for preemergence (both incorporated and surface-applied) grass weed control in potatoes are the thiocarbamates (including EPTC), dinitroanilines (including trifluralin and pendimethalin), and acetanilides (including metolachlor). These herbicides also control a number of broadleaf and sedge weeds. Most of them are applied and incorporated 7–14 days after planting, or as late as after the final or lay-by hilling operation. Herbicide families that control predominantly broadleaf weeds in potatoes are the ureas (including linuron) and triazinones (metribuzin).

Postemergence applications are made at various times following weed emergence. Certain contact herbicides (paraquat and glyphosate) may be applied to emerged weeds prior to crop emergence. Following potato emergence, metribuzin and sethoxydim can be used for control of many broadleaf and grass weeds, respectively. Through the use of these two herbicides, it is now possible to control many weeds in potatoes on an as-needed basis, after crop emergence.

Deep cultivation or hilling operations following a preemergence application tend to dilute the herbicide by mixing it with the soil, usually resulting in decreased weed control. It is important, therefore, to plan the timing of cultivation and herbicide applications to obtain the greatest benefit from both operations. Timely cultivations or hilling operations during the first 35–40 days after planting, coupled with an herbicide application at lay-by, provide season-long weed control in many regions. Split applications—application of a preemergence product after planting and a postemergence product at lay-by—may also provide effective weed control.

Because pesticide labels are constantly changing, the current labels of any herbicides mentioned in this book should be checked for registration of use on potatoes before any are applied.

Application of Herbicides

Herbicides can be applied with ground-operated boom sprayers, by aircraft, or through sprinkler irrigation systems. Each method has advantages over the others as well as inherent drawbacks, depending upon the individual situation.

Ground Sprayers. Under the right conditions, ground sprayers are the most precise application system with the least off-target drift. The use of ground rigs, however, is limited by their slowness in completing the job, by wind resulting in drift, and by soil physical conditions, especially soil moisture. They also cause soil compaction and may inflict mechanical injury if the crop is near row closure at the time of application.

Proper sprayer operation is essential for successful results. The pumps, screens, agitation system, connections and fittings, pressure regulator, gauges, and nozzle tips should be checked thoroughly before use. Each tip should be inspected to ensure that all are the same size. Replace tips and other components where needed. Be sure that the nozzle spacing on the boom and the boom height are both correct. Each nozzle tip must be calibrated individually and should deliver within 10% of the rated amount specified in the manufacturer's manual. Use the amount of water per acre specified on the herbicide label. Check the tractor speedometer or tachometer for accuracy under actual field conditions. Do not just assume it is correct! Calibration of the sprayer system is essential to achieving correct herbicide placement and rate of application.

In preparation for spraying a soil-incorporated herbicide after planting and before potatoes emerge, all incorporation implements should be checked before use. It is essential that the teeth of the implement are set for the proper row spacing so as to thoroughly mix the upper 2–4 inches of each prebedded potato hill. The entire tractor-drawn assembly should be field-tested before the herbicide is applied. The tractor must be able to maintain a precise, constant speed in the field to deliver the right amount of herbicide. This is especially important in sloping or contoured fields, as changing gears or engine speed can cause serious variations in the application rate.

Aerial Application. Application of herbicides by aircraft has several advantages over spraying by ground equipment. Soil compaction and mechanical injury to the crop are completely eliminated. Fields can be treated very rapidly, and applications can be made when field conditions prevent the use of ground sprayers. This facilitates treatment of weed seedlings at the proper growth stage, when herbicides are most effective. Another advantage is the convenience—custom aerial application services can provide relief to the crop manager during a busy farming schedule.

The major disadvantage of aerial application is that off-target drift occurs more readily from aircraft than with other methods, because of the greater height of the equipment, air turbulence, and other aerodynamic factors, such as winds and low-level inversions. Swath spacing and boundaries are also less precise in aerial application than in spraying with ground equipment, although field markers can help eliminate skips.

Sprinkler Application. Application of herbicides through sprinkler irrigation equipment is becoming more common in some production areas. This method has several advantages. Soil compaction and mechanical injury to the crop are not factors, because heavy equipment is not used in the field. Uniformity of application is excellent in properly designed and maintained irrigation systems, and the large volume of water applied is an effective way to move herbicides into the upper layer of soil, where it is needed. The rinsing effect of the large volume of water reduces the amount of herbicide retained on the leaves of crop plants. There is also less pattern displacement by light winds, because of repeated sprinkling. Wind is an especially severe deterrent to the use of ground sprayers in years when springtime winds continue from daybreak until dark for several weeks during the critical times when herbicide application is needed. Since irrigation equipment can run unattended, herbicides can be applied during the calmer nighttime hours.

Continuously moving lines, either linear-move or center-pivot systems, provide more uniform application than fixed-set systems, such as wheel-move, hand-line, or solid-set types. Continuous-move systems can cover a field in a shorter time and are less subject to leaks and failures due to frequent disconnection, disassembly, reconnection, and restarting. Fixed-set systems, on the other hand, allow more control over the way in which the herbicide is moved into the soil, and therefore some herbicides can be used more effectively in these systems. Herbicide applied during the last portion of an irrigation set may be lost from the soil surface or may be ineffective, whereas herbicide applied earlier in the irrigation set is moved deeper into the zone of germinating weeds, where effectiveness is maximized.

There are some limitations to application of herbicides through sprinklers. Only a few products are registered for this use. These are all soil-applied herbicides, because the large volume of irrigation water moves most of the herbicide through the foliage to the soil. Other limitations are related to the irrigation process itself. Irrigation may not be appropriate at the time when herbicide is needed, because of spring rains, the need for early-season weed control, or irrigation-scheduling requirements. Some short-distance, off-target drift from sprinklers can occur during air inversions or in light winds. Also, sprinklers often place some water well outside the field boundaries. Strict state and federal requirements also specify fail-safe devices and procedures to prevent back-siphoning of pesticides into wells or points where surface water or groundwater could be contaminated.

An effective weed management strategy is an essential component of any holistic potato health management program. Identification of weed species that require management is the first step. Cultural practices that minimize weed problems must be integrated into the total crop management system. Appropriate cultivation can then be combined with herbicide applications as needed to keep weed development below economic loss levels (Fig. 1.5). Effective management of weeds allows the potato plants maximum use of all the resources made available by the crop management plan and will result in vigorous plants better able to respond fully to other management strategies aimed at disease and insect pests.

CHAPTER 12

David N. Ferro
Department of Entomology
University of Massachusetts, Amherst

Gilles Boiteau
Agriculture Canada
Fredericton, New Brunswick

Management of Insect Pests

Potatoes are grown throughout North America under a wide range of environmental conditions, which greatly affect the distribution, abundance, and importance of specific insect pests. The significance of various insects to potato production differs from region to region, as do economically allowable levels of damage and appropriate management strategies. Generally, early-maturing cultivars, such as Superior, are more sensitive to midseason defoliation by insects than later-maturing cultivars, such as Russet Burbank. This difference appears to be due to the greater ability of later-maturing cultivars to grow new leaves to replace those eaten by insects, even after tuberization has begun.

> **To manage insect pests successfully, fields must be checked regularly—at least weekly throughout the growing season.**

To manage insect pests successfully, fields must be checked regularly—at least weekly throughout the growing season (Fig. 12.1). Foliage should be examined for Colorado potato beetles, aphids, leafhoppers, potato psyllids (in some regions), and flea beetles. It is also advisable to sample fields at the end of each growing season and at the beginning of the next for over-wintering stages of soil-dwelling insects. Where potatoes follow alfalfa, cereals, or pasture, soil samples should be taken to determine the presence and density of wireworms. Pheromone traps can be used to monitor for European corn borers and potato tuberworms.

Decisions on when and how to control insect pests of potato require accurate estimates of the population of each pest in a field and should be timed according to the appropriate action threshold for each pest—the point at which action should be taken to prevent an economic loss. This chapter contains basic information on the biology and management of six key insect pests. These management strategies should be integrated into a holistic potato health management plan appropriate to the individual production situation, as discussed in Part One of this book.

Colorado Potato Beetle

The Colorado potato beetle (*Leptinotarsa decemlineata*) is the major defoliating insect pest of potato in North America. Its biology and response to environmental conditions vary from one area to another, as does its importance as a pest.

It is thought that the Colorado potato beetle originated in southern Mexico and gradually moved north. Prior to the introduction of the potato into the midwestern United States, this insect survived on wild host plants, mainly silverleaf nightshade (*Solanum elaeagnifolium*) and buffalobur (*S. rostratum*). It was well distributed throughout Colorado and as far east as Iowa and Nebraska before potatoes were grown there. It entered Canada in 1870, and by the 1880s it had become well established throughout most potato production areas of North America. The Colorado potato beetle is now found throughout

Fig. 12.1. Scouting fields regularly is a necessary part of any successful insect management program. (Courtesy R. C. Rowe)

most of the United States and in the Maritime provinces (except Newfoundland) and southern portions of Canada (Fig. 12.2).

If uncontrolled, the Colorado potato beetle can completely defoliate all potato plants in a field by midseason. Although well established in western production areas of North America, except for California, it is not presently a major pest in these areas, because it is controlled by insecticides applied to control aphids. In areas of the northeastern United States where it has historically been a serious pest because of its resistance to insecticides, growers sometimes use up to 12 insecticide applications per season to keep its populations below economic loss levels.

It is not necessary to keep plants completely free of the Colorado potato beetle. The potato plant can tolerate considerable defoliation before and after flowering, and up to 20% during flowering, with no reduction in yield (the ability to tolerate defoliation varies somewhat with growing conditions). Thus there is no need to control this pest when it is first observed. To effectively manage the Colorado potato beetle, it is important to have a thorough understanding of its biology.

Identification and Biology

Adult Colorado potato beetles are stout, oval, strongly convex beetles, about 3/8 inch long, with black and yellow stripes running lengthwise along the wing covers (Plates 15 and 16). They are often referred to as hard-shells. The orange, bullet-shaped eggs are laid mostly on leaves, in masses of about 30 (Plate 16). The orange to reddish brown larvae are often referred to as grubs or slugs (Plates 16 and 17).

Colorado potato beetles overwinter as adults in their field of origin, in uncultivated areas adjacent to the field, and in wooded areas away from it. A study in the northeastern United States showed that 95% of the adult beetles colonizing a potato field in the spring originated in that same field. Within a few

days of colonizing a field, the beetles feed and begin to deposit egg masses composed of 25–40 eggs. Each colonizing female can produce about 450 eggs, which hatch in 3–10 days, depending on temperature. The small first-instar larvae emerge from the eggs, feed on the egg cases, and then disperse from the egg mass within 1–2 days (Plate 18). The first and second instars cause little feeding damage, and the third only slightly more. Approximately two-thirds of all larval feeding is by the fourth-instar larvae, each of which consumes about 4 square inches of foliage before dropping to the ground to pupate. First-generation adults emerge from the soil 5–7 days later and begin to lay eggs within 7–10 days. Under optimal conditions, the cycle from egg to adult can take as little as 3 weeks.

The Colorado potato beetle can go through three complete generations per year in some areas. Little growth occurs below 50° F in any of its life stages, and extremely high temperatures also limit development. Growth slows as the temperature approaches 85° F, and many individuals are killed if it exceeds 90° F. Even when air temperatures are this high, many larvae and adults can survive by moving to shaded parts of the plant. In the north, cool summers and long winters restrict the number of generations to one per year, while the moderate, modulated temperatures of the Maritime provinces and southern Ontario and Quebec allow up to two generations. In most other areas farther south, there are two or occasionally three generations per year. In some western states, such as Colorado, Utah, and Idaho, only two generations per year are produced, because the days are too hot and the nights too cold for optimal growth and development.

In northern production areas, the beetles respond to a shortening of the day length by physiologically preparing for cold winter weather and entering diapause (a type of hibernation). In Massachusetts, 90% of adult beetles that emerge before August 1 develop flight muscles and a reproductive

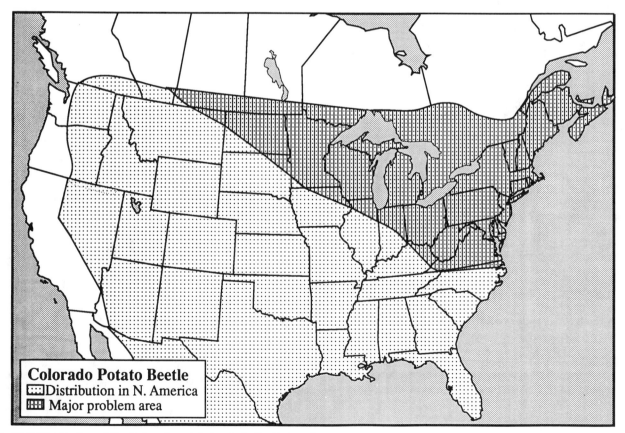

Fig. 12.2. Distribution of the Colorado potato beetle in North America.

system, whereas less than 10% of those that emerge the following week develop flight muscles or lay eggs. Beetles that do not develop flight muscles or lay eggs do not produce a larval population until the following year. They cause little current-season damage and thus need not be controlled.

Besides feeding on potato, eggplant, and tomato, the Colorado potato beetle survives on a number of wild host plants. In the Pacific Northwest, it lives on hairy nightshade (*Solanum sarrachoides*), a weed commonly found in disturbed habitats in agricultural production areas. From central Canada south to Mexico, it is found on horsenettle (*S. carolinense*), silverleaf nightshade, and buffalobur. Horsenettle is typically present in potato fields in the eastern United States and appears to be the primary wild host there. The Colorado potato beetle is also found on both horsenettle and climbing nightshade (*S. dulcamara*) in the northeastern states, but it is never abundant on these plants. Other host plants include solanaceous weeds (*S. triquetrum* and *S. angustifolium*) and groundcherries (*Physalis* species).

Population Monitoring and Action Thresholds

Management decisions for control of the Colorado potato beetle must be based on an accurate estimate of the population density at each stage of crop development. The whole plant is the appropriate sampling unit for the first generation of this insect. In regions with more than one generation, the appropriate sampling unit for the second and third generations is the main stem, excluding lateral vines. A proper sample is composed of about 50 plants (or main stems) randomly selected along a V-shaped sampling path extending into the field at least 100 yards and intersecting 50–100 rows. Early in the season, when beetles are colonizing fields, it is advisable to take samples from throughout the field and also from along its edges to detect any hot spots, where beetles are colonizing the edges first. This is particularly important in potato fields adjacent to those in which potatoes were grown during the previous year. All plants should be checked carefully, especially for the small larvae (Plate 18), because they are easy to miss.

The life stages of the Colorado potato beetle that should be recorded from the sample depend on the control method selected or available. If synthetic pyrethroid insecticides are to be used, application decisions should be based on the number of early (first- and second-instar) and late (third- and fourth-instar) larvae present. If BT (*Bacillus thuringiensis*) insecticides are used, the number of egg masses and the number of early-instar larvae should be recorded, because BT is most effective against early instars.

Appropriate action thresholds for the Colorado potato beetle vary with the production region, time of year, and insecticide used. It is advisable to consult with Cooperative Extension Service specialists or local advisors for thresholds adapted to specific areas. The thresholds in Table 12.1 are used by several integrated pest management programs in New England during midseason, when potato plants are most vulnerable to attack by this pest.

Management

No single management technique can successfully control the Colorado potato beetle, and thus several practices must be integrated into a logical management program.

Crop Rotation. Crop rotation is the single most effective tactic available to combat the Colorado potato beetle and should be a part of every management program. Only a small proportion of any population of Colorado potato beetles leaves its field of origin by flying. If potatoes are grown in a field that was not planted with potatoes the previous year and is isolated by several hundred yards from any overwintering sites (such as adjacent fields that were in potatoes the previous

year), colonization of the field can be delayed by 2–3 weeks. Isolated fields without overwintering beetles are colonized only by beetles flying in from overwintering sites or from other potato fields. After the beetles emerge in the spring, they need 1–2 weeks to regenerate their flight muscles. In addition, many of these late colonizers will have already fed and laid eggs in other potato fields.

In nonrotated fields and those adjacent to fields in which potatoes were grown during the previous year, overwintering adults emerge in close proximity to current-season potato plants or colonize fields by walking from adjacent areas. In heavily infested areas, this often occurs even before the potato

> **Crop rotation is the single most effective tactic available to combat the Colorado potato beetle and should be a part of every management program.**

plants have emerged. Where potatoes are grown in relatively narrow strips alternating with wheat or another rotational crop, as they often are on hill contours in some areas (Fig. 2.2), Colorado potato beetles can readily colonize strips planted with potatoes, because of the maximum edge effect created by this cropping pattern.

The number of colonizing beetles decreases as the distance from the nearest overwintering site increases. Because the density of the first larval generation in rotated fields is much lower than in nonrotated fields, the first insecticide application can usually be delayed by 2–3 weeks. The first generation of larvae also pupates later, and in more northern areas many of the second-generation adults emerge in late summer but never lay eggs until the following year, thus leaving only one larval generation to control. If short-season or midseason cultivars are grown in this situation, it may be possible, depending upon market conditions, to plant later in the season and thus delay emergence and colonization by the beetle. This would not be feasible, however, in areas where this insect goes through three complete generations each year.

Insecticides. Application of insecticides is a necessary part of most management programs for controlling the Colorado potato beetle. The effectiveness of specific insecticides, however, varies throughout North America. Label restrictions on certain systemic insecticides may limit their usefulness. Some insecticides are effective against this pest only when it is in certain life stages. Potato health managers must have a thorough understanding of how various insecticides work and the conditions under which they are most effective.

Table 12.1. Action thresholds for Colorado potato beetle in New England

Life stage	Number of larvae or beetles per 50 plants or main stems[a]	
	Low-density threshold	High-density threshold
Larva		
First and second instars	75 or fewer	200 or more
Third and fourth instars	30 or fewer	75 or more
Adult beetle	15 or fewer	25 or more

[a] If a broad-spectrum insecticide, such as a pyrethroid, is to be applied, the high-density threshold should be used for the first and second instars, and the low-density threshold for the third and fourth instars. If a BT (*Bacillus thuringiensis*) insecticide is to be applied, the low-density threshold for early instars is appropriate.

Synthetic pyrethroid insecticides are less effective at high temperatures. By restricting their use to the early season, when day temperatures are below 80° F, managers can achieve better control and reduce the chances that resistance to these compounds will develop in local populations of the insect. It is best to apply these materials when the foliage is dry. Other

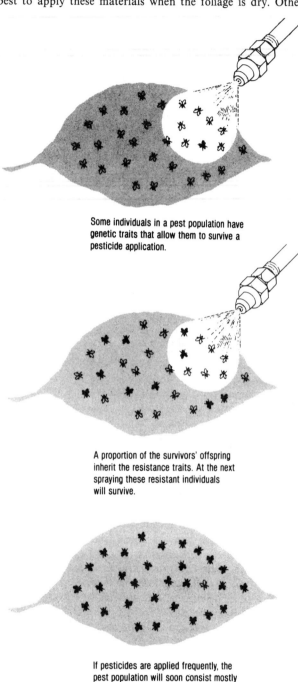

Some individuals in a pest population have genetic traits that allow them to survive a pesticide application.

A proportion of the survivors' offspring inherit the resistance traits. At the next spraying these resistant individuals will survive.

If pesticides are applied frequently, the pest population will soon consist mostly of resistant individuals.

𝕏 susceptible individual   𝕏 resistant individual

Fig. 12.3. Intensive use of insecticides places a tremendous selective pressure on insect populations, favoring the survival of individuals that are able to tolerate the toxin and eventually resulting in a population composed predominantly of insecticide-resistant individuals. (Reprinted, by permission, from Western Regional IPM Project, 1986, Integrated Pest Management for Potatoes in the Western United States, Publication 3316, Division of Agriculture and Natural Resources, University of California, Oakland)

recommended types of insecticides, including carbamates (such as oxamyl and carbofuran) and organophosphates (such as azinphosmethyl), can be used throughout the season. However, to reduce the development of resistance to these materials in local populations of the insect, it may be best to save them for later in the season and then use them alternately. Ideally, products from any group of insecticides (pyrethroids, carbamates, organophosphates, etc.) should be applied no more than once per season, or at most once per Colorado potato beetle generation.

BT insecticides, based on toxins of new strains of the bacterium *Bacillus thuringiensis*, are highly effective against the first and second instars but kill only about half of the older larvae. These materials are very safe for both applicators and beneficial insects. BT insecticides can easily be included in an integrated pest management program in which predators and parasites of the Colorado potato beetle play an important role. The timing of applications of BT insecticides is extremely important. The first application should go on soon after egg hatch but before the second-instar larvae molt. Treated foliage must be ingested for the BT toxin to be effective, and thus the more foliage ingested, the more toxin taken into the insect gut. The toxin affects the insect's midgut, ultimately resulting in death by starvation. For this reason, BT insecticides are more effective during the warmer parts of the season, when the larvae are actively feeding. Thorough coverage of the foliage is necessary for best results, and plants should be sprayed at midmorning, because the larvae feed most actively during the warmer part of the day.

Optimal coverage of plants with insecticidal sprays is generally best achieved by means of a boom sprayer applying 50–60 gallons of tank mix per acre at a pressure of about 80 pounds per square inch (psi). High-pressure sprayers (200–300 psi) produce very small spray droplets, which do not adhere well to foliage, whereas low-pressure sprayers (30–40 psi) produce overly large spray droplets, which have too much mass and tend to roll off the plant. Application by aircraft allows treatment of large blocks of a field at one time, and in some cases it may be the only feasible way of applying insecticides in a timely manner. To monitor coverage of an aerial application, water-sensitive cards can be placed in the center of the plant canopy and along the edge and in the center of the field prior to treatment. Application of insecticides with ground sprayers usually results in much better coverage of plant surfaces than aerial application, however.

When using insecticides, managers must always remember that few insects have shown the potential to develop resistance to as broad a range of insecticides as the Colorado potato beetle has. In one locality or another, it has developed resistance to the arsenicals, organochlorines, organophosphates, carbamates, and synthetic pyrethroids. The beetle has a great capacity to tolerate exposure to insecticides, because of its natural biochemical ability to detoxify them and isolate toxins within its body away from physiologically active sites. This ability is related to its natural survival on native host plants that contain high levels of toxins such as alkaloids and glycoalkaloids. Since there is no reason to believe that the Colorado potato beetle will not be able to develop resistance to new insecticides as they become available, new products must be managed wisely.

Intensive use of insecticides to control the Colorado potato beetle places tremendous selective pressure on beetle populations, favoring the survival of individuals that are able to tolerate the toxin (Fig. 12.3). In most areas, there are usually too few individuals that escape exposure to insecticides and too few susceptible individuals that migrate into commercial potato fields to affect the overall genetic makeup of treated populations. In some areas of the Pacific Northwest, however, Colorado potato beetle populations living on wild host plants may be large enough to provide a constant influx of insecticide-susceptible individuals, so that the development of resistant populations is delayed.

The highest levels of insecticide resistance develop in areas with 1) daily summer temperatures that range between 65 and 90° F, with a mean of about 80° F, allowing the maximum number of Colorado potato beetle generations per year, 2) sandy soils that allow overwintering adults to burrow deep enough for maximum winter survival, 3) production systems in which potatoes are not rotated with other crops, and 4) excessive amounts of insecticides applied on a fixed schedule, causing a maximum selective pressure on the beetle population. Although environmental factors that favor the development of insecticide resistance cannot be controlled, the use of proper crop rotations, the selection of insecticides, and the timing of applications are management options. The development of resistance can be greatly retarded by rotating potato fields each year, to delay the initial colonization of fields by emerging adults in the spring, and by delaying insecticide applications until population densities reach appropriate action thresholds.

To minimize the development of resistance, insecticides from the same chemical group should be applied no more than once per Colorado potato beetle generation. Once resistance to a specific insecticide has been detected in a field, there is little value in continuing to use it in rotation with other insecticides, because genes for resistance to this chemical are already at a high frequency in the population. For this reason, if an insecticide belonging to a new chemical group becomes available, it should be used judiciously, so that it, too, is not lost to resistance. Too often a material that works well is continually used until it is no longer effective.

Biological Control with Natural Enemies. Only a few native natural enemies of the Colorado potato beetle are at all useful in biological control of this pest. Their presence in commercial potato fields varies regionally and is greatly affected by heavy use of pesticides. These organisms include the fungi *Beauveria bassiana* and *Paecilomyces farinosus*; the predaceous stinkbugs *Podisus maculiventris* and *Perillus bioculatus*; the predaceous beetles *Lebia grandis* and *Coleomegilla maculata* (tenspotted ladybird beetle); and the parasitic flies *Myiopharus aberrans* and *M. doryphorae*.

B. bassiana is capable of causing high levels of mortality in Colorado potato beetle populations, especially in emerging adults. However, the fungicides chlorothalonil and mancozeb, commonly used to control early blight and late blight, also kill this fungus. The fungicide metalaxyl is nontoxic to *B. bassiana*. Minimizing fungicide applications and delaying the initial application whenever possible may allow the population of this fungus to increase and become a more important natural mortality factor for the Colorado potato beetle.

The predatory stinkbugs are voracious and can kill a large number of Colorado potato beetle larvae in a short time. However, they are rarely present in numbers great enough to be of much practical value.

Recent studies with the carabid beetle *L. grandis* (Plate 19) have shown this predator to cause high levels of mortality in Colorado potato beetle eggs. Larvae of *L. grandis* seem to feed exclusively on Colorado potato beetle larvae. This beneficial insect, however, is very sensitive to most herbicides commonly used in potato fields and therefore may be of little value in commercial fields.

The parasitic *Myiopharus* flies (Plate 20) can cause up to 80% mortality in the prepupal stage of the Colorado potato beetle, especially in the second generation of this pest. The flies lay larvae in the second-, third-, and fourth-instar larvae of the Colorado potato beetle, and the fly larvae remain dormant until the fourth-instar Colorado potato beetle larvae burrow into the soil to pupate. This beneficial insect is a strong flier and appears able to rapidly colonize new potato fields at the same time as Colorado potato beetle adults, which makes it a good candidate for integration into a crop rotation scheme.

The tenspotted ladybird beetle (Plate 21) is a generalist predator. It can cause as much as 35% mortality in first-generation Colorado potato beetles and up to 60% in the second generation. Both larvae and adult ladybird beetles also feed on aphids and corn pollen. Field corn appears to provide an excellent food source for this predator, and large populations develop in cornfields. Adult ladybird beetles overwinter in undisturbed habitats around the edges of cornfields. Where potatoes are rotated with corn, large numbers of these beetles often move into potato fields and feed on eggs of first-generation Colorado potato beetles. By the time eggs of the second generation of Colorado potato beetles have been deposited, aphids have colonized the potato fields and are also fed upon by ladybird beetles. Populations of ladybird beetles do not build up in potato fields in which there is little food for their larvae. In areas where suitable overwintering habitats are not available, such as the Pacific Northwest, or where these predators do not have a good food source, the role of ladybird beetles in Colorado potato beetle control is often variable and unpredictable.

Although the use of natural enemies for biological control of the Colorado potato beetle is appealing as an alternative to extensive use of insecticides, this method cannot stand alone and is successful only when combined with other strategies in an integrated management plan. Constraints associated with biological control of the Colorado potato beetle include 1) the inability of natural enemies to control high populations of this insect, 2) the timing of the life cycles of natural enemies with the potato growth stages in which the crop needs protection from this pest, 3) the cost of raising and releasing large numbers of natural enemies, and 4) insufficient knowledge of which natural enemies are most effective in Colorado potato beetle management. Considerable research is needed before biological control will significantly replace the use of insecticides in the control of this pest.

> **Because potato plants can withstand some defoliation with no reduction in yield, it is important to postpone any insecticide application until Colorado potato beetle populations reach the appropriate action threshold.**

Host Plant Resistance. Commercial potato cultivars that are presently available are not resistant to feeding by the Colorado potato beetle. Research is under way to breed resistant cultivars, but these will probably not be commercially available until the late 1990s. Recently, however, genes for production of the *B. thuringiensis* endotoxin have been transferred into certain commercial cultivars by genetic engineering techniques. This has resulted in potato plants that are capable of producing the BT toxin internally and are totally resistant to feeding by the Colorado potato beetle. When or if these lines will become commercially available is presently unknown. More importantly, it is likely that widespread use of transgenic plants producing high amounts of BT toxin will select for Colorado potato beetle populations that are highly resistant to this toxin. If this occurs, it will compromise not only these genetically engineered plants but the use of BT insecticides as well.

Integrated Control Strategies. Combining several of these practices into an integrated management strategy is the key to controlling the Colorado potato beetle. A good crop rotation is the foundation of all successful management programs for this pest. Applications of insecticides to control this pest, if they are delayed until absolutely necessary, may be reduced to one or two per year in an appropriate crop rotation that allows populations of natural enemies to build up. Because potato plants can withstand some defoliation with no reduction in yield, it is important to postpone any insecticide application until Colorado potato beetle populations reach the appropriate action threshold. Natural enemies of this pest will not be effective if synthetic insecticides, fungicides, and herbicides are used indiscriminately. However, if pesticide applications are made when insect enemies are not actively foraging in the field, such as at the end of the first Colorado potato beetle generation and prior to egg laying by second-generation adults, then these tactics may be compatible.

Potato Tuberworm

The potato tuberworm (*Phthorimaea operculella*) is a pest of potato in warm climates worldwide. In the United States, it is a potato pest on the East Coast from Virginia south to northern Florida; it is an occasional pest of potato in the southwestern states; and it routinely infests potatoes grown in central and southern California (Fig. 12.4). On the East Coast it damages mostly stored tubers, but in California it attacks tubers both in the field and in storage. Potatoes grown under furrow irrigation sustain infestations up to 50 times greater than those grown under sprinkler irrigation. Although the larvae do some feeding on potato foliage and stems, the economic importance of this pest is in the damage it causes to tubers.

In the field, the potato tuberworm can damage up to 25% of the tubers, but in storage it can damage 100% of the tubers. The larvae tunnel through tubers, filling the tunnels with frass and webbing and allowing the entry of pathogens such as *Fusarium* fungi and *Erwinia* bacteria. Infested potatoes are unmarketable for either fresh-market or processing purposes. Most damage in the field occurs just prior to harvest, especially when vines dying naturally or from vine killers are left over the rows. As the vines die and dry out, the tuberworm larvae leave the vines, and if the soil is dry and cracked they move down the cracks and infest tubers. Tuberworm moths lay eggs directly on tubers left uncovered in the field, recently harvested, or in storage.

Identification and Biology

The adult potato tuberworm is a small gray moth with a wingspan of about $1/2$ inch (Plate 22). The wings are narrow, fringed with hairs, and mottled with black and brown spots. The larvae are slender caterpillars with dark heads and tan bodies that are sometimes tinged with pink or green (Plate 23).

Tuberworm moths are active throughout the year in warm areas but are most active from late April to early August. Besides potato, tuberworms feed on other solanaceous plants, including tomato, eggplant, pepper, tobacco, horsenettle, black nightshade (*Solanum nigrum*), silverleaf nightshade, and jimsonweed (*Datura stramonium*). Most infestations originate from volunteer potato plants or tubers and from cull piles.

Adult females lay eggs on foliage, soil, plant debris, or exposed tubers. The moths crawl through cracks in the soil or burrow short distances through loose soil to reach tubers. Generally, this pest does little feeding on foliage. Larvae often move from foliage to feed on exposed tubers, or they gain entry to tubers by crawling down cracks in the soil. They do not bore into tubers via the stems.

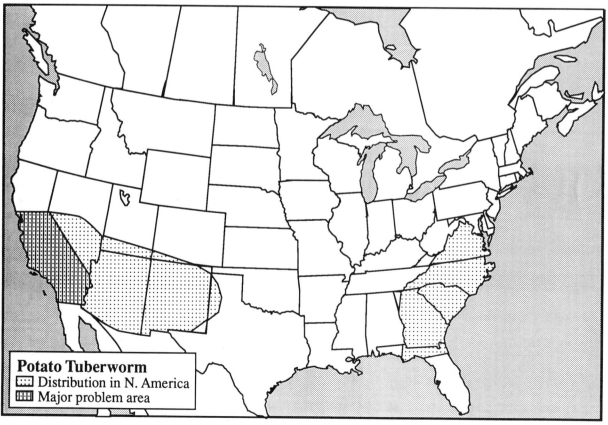

Fig. 12.4. Distribution of the potato tuberworm in North America.

When ready to pupate, the larvae spin cocoons on the soil surface or on debris under plants. They rarely pupate in tubers. Larvae that have fed on potatoes in storage can crawl considerable distances to find protected sites for pupation, such as crevices in walls, floors, and crates. Adults mate soon after emergence from their cocoons. The female moths release into the air a chemical (pheromone) that attracts males for mating. This pheromone has been synthesized for use in traps for monitoring the moth population. The moths are active at dusk and throughout the night.

During the summer, the potato tuberworm can complete a generation in about 3 weeks. Larval growth and development slow down at cooler temperatures but continue as long as temperatures are above 52°F. During the winter, the tuberworm may take as long as 7 months to complete a generation.

Population Monitoring and Action Thresholds

Sampling for potato tuberworm larvae or larval damage is extremely time-consuming, and by the time larvae are found it may be too late to prevent damage to tubers. In areas where the tuberworm is a problem, it is best to use pheromone traps and to base control decisions on moth catches and the growth stage of the crop.

Monitoring traps can be made from pans about 8 inches in diameter, filled with water to a depth of at least 3 inches. The pheromone lure is placed beneath a piece of sheet metal bent to form a tent-shaped cover over the pan. The lure should be suspended 1–2 inches above the water surface, so that male moths attracted to it fall into the water. A few drops of soap are added to the water to break the surface tension and prevent the moths from escaping. Alternatively, the delta trap, a three-sided cardboard shelter with a sticky inner surface, can also be used to catch moths. Pan traps are generally better than delta traps for monitoring tuberworms, because they are easily cleaned and refilled each time they are checked, and they are not disturbed by sprinkler irrigation.

At least four pan traps should be used per field, with one or more in each quarter of the field. The traps should be placed between plants, on the tops of beds at least 14 rows, or 50 feet, in from the edge of the field. Every 3 or 4 days, count the moths in each trap and replenish the water. In hot weather, be sure to check often enough to prevent the water from evaporating between observations. For each field, record the average number of moths per trap per night (MTN) over the interval between collections.

Action thresholds vary according to the potato cultivar and field conditions, and local information should be obtained. Fields in which tubers are well protected by soil can tolerate more moths than those in which many tubers are exposed. As a general rule for fresh-market potatoes, treatment should be started when the number of trapped moths reaches 15–20 MTN at any one time the traps are checked, or when the average for the season exceeds 8 MTN. For chipping potatoes, the threshold is 40 MTN at any one time or 15–20 MTN for the seasonal average. If moth activity does not reach the action threshold value before vine kill, no treatment should be applied. Insecticides applied at vine kill are not effective in reducing tuberworm damage.

Management

Many cultural practices can limit the development of the potato tuberworm and minimize damage to tubers. Never plant seed tubers infested with tuberworm. When crop rotations are being planned, potato fields should be located as far as possible from previous potato plantings. Any volunteer potato plants growing in uncultivated areas and in fields rotated out of potato should be destroyed.

Any practice that reduces the exposure of tubers to egg-laying females will limit tuberworm damage. The moths cannot reach tubers covered with more than 2 inches of soil, unless it is deeply cracked. Potato cultivars that set tubers relatively deep in the soil are less susceptible to infestation than shallow-setting cultivars, such as Kennebec.

Furrow irrigation should be avoided in areas where the tuberworm is a problem. Soils tend to crack more under furrow irrigation than under sprinkler irrigation. Sprinkler irrigation helps to keep the soil surface sealed, especially in fine-textured soils, which tend to form deep cracks upon drying. If there is no alternative to furrow irrigation, fields should be properly graded, and furrows and hills well maintained, to prevent washouts and exposure of tubers.

It is extremely important to harvest tubers as soon as possible after they have matured. During harvest, avoid leaving tubers on the soil surface or in bulk trucks overnight. Never cover newly dug potatoes with green vines, because as they wilt, tuberworm larvae leave them and infest the tubers underneath. After harvest, make sure all unharvested or discarded tubers are deeply buried or destroyed. In areas that do not freeze, tubers left in the field are a food source for developing larvae throughout the winter months.

Stored potatoes should be protected from egg-laying females by screens placed over any potential entry points into storage facilities. All used sacks and storage bins should be thoroughly cleaned of plant residues and tuberworms in any life stage before use with newly harvested tubers. This is best accomplished by fumigating or steam cleaning. If at all possible, potatoes should be stored below 50°F to prevent egg hatch and larval feeding.

> **Insecticides for control of the potato tuberworm should be applied only if the moth catch in pheromone traps exceeds the appropriate action threshold.**

Insecticides for control of the potato tuberworm should be applied only if the moth catch in pheromone traps exceeds the appropriate action threshold. It is extremely important to control this pest prior to harvest. The application instructions on the label of the insecticide used should be carefully followed. Insecticide sprays are directed toward the newly hatched larvae, and for this reason it is especially important that sprayers are properly calibrated and the correct nozzles are used, to ensure coverage. As in the control of the Colorado potato beetle, sprays should be applied at about 80 psi, so that medium-sized spray droplets are formed, since these adhere well to foliage.

European Corn Borer

The European corn borer (*Ostrinia nubilalis*) is a native insect in Europe, where it survives on over 200 different host plants. It is thought to have been introduced into North America in infested broomcorn in the late 1800s. It is found from southern Canada to northern Florida and westward to Saskatchewan and Colorado, mostly in corn-producing areas (Fig. 12.5).

In localized areas of North America, the larvae can cause direct damage to potato vines by boring into the stems, causing severe wilting above the point of entry (Plate 24). Larval feeding in stems may also restrict the movement of plant nutrients and water, and entry wounds can serve as entrance sites for bacteria that cause aerial stem rot (Chapter 15).

Identification and Biology

European corn borer adults are buff-colored moths with dark brown, wavy bands across the wings and a wingspan of about 1 inch (Plate 25). The male moth is smaller and darker than the female. The white eggs are laid in a mass containing 15–35 eggs arranged in a scalelike pattern. The larvae are light tan, with dark brown heads, and about 1 inch long when mature (Plate 26).

The European corn borer completes one to four generations per year, depending on the latitude (Fig. 12.5). It produces three or four generations per year in North Carolina, two per year in southern Maine and southeastern Ontario, and only one per year in northern Maine and the rest of Canada. First flights generally occur in mid-April in North Carolina, early June in southern Maine, and late June in Canada. Mating occurs outside the field in nearby dense vegetation. The female moths release a pheromone into the air to attract mates. The pheromone has been synthesized and is now used in monitoring populations of this pest.

In the evening, female moths leave their mating sites to lay eggs on potato foliage. Eggs hatch in 4–9 days, depending on the temperature. The young larvae wander on the foliage and feed on immature leaves before boring into the stems. The larval stage lasts about 30 days, again depending on the temperature. The last larval instar pupates inside the stems, and adult moths emerge in about 14 days and soon mate. Each female lays about 400 eggs over a 14-day period. In North Carolina, this cycle is repeated several times on a sequence of host plants. Generally the second and third generations do not infest potato in North Carolina but are more of a pest on corn and pepper. The importance of this insect as a potato pest in the northern and central areas of its range is not well known. It is rarely considered a pest of economic importance in regions where it produces only one generation per year.

Population Monitoring and Action Thresholds

The European corn borer is not a pest in every field in a particular region or in every year on a specific farm. For this reason, monitoring for this pest should be done before beginning any control program. In regions where it is a potentially serious pest, monitoring sites should be established on each farm. A blacklight trap is highly effective in capturing moths, but much expertise is required to properly identify European corn borer adults among all the moths caught.

A simpler approach is to collect infested cornstalks from several sites in the immediate area of the farm, place them in a screened cage, and monitor the emergence of moths. This provides information on the timing and rate of emergence. This is a useful technique to assist in deciding when to apply an insecticide, if the European corn borer has historically been a pest in the area.

A more accurate and efficient way to monitor male moth activity is to use pheromone traps. These traps are relatively specific for individual moth species, which makes identification easier. Two biotypes of the European corn borer exist in North America, and if both occur in the same area, separate traps with appropriate pheromone blends must be used. The traps should be placed at least 50 feet apart in weedy areas around the edges of the field or within the field, depending on local experience. In North Carolina they are more effective within the field, but in Massachusetts they are more effective around the edges. The bottom of the trap should be suspended just above the weed or crop canopy. The most efficient design is the Scentry trap, which looks like a fish trap (Plate 27). Trap placement is extremely critical.

Managers familiar with the biology and habits of the European corn borer can walk through weedy areas, headlands, and ditches and observe moths flying in front of them. With experience, this can be a fairly efficient monitoring technique.

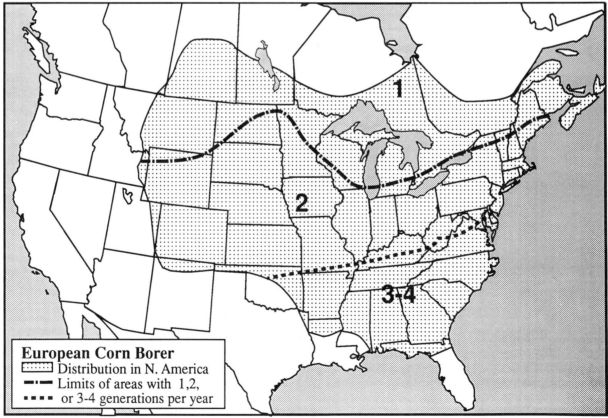

Fig. 12.5. Distribution of the European corn borer in North America.

Once it has been determined that the moths have emerged and are flying, fields should be checked, beginning 7–10 days after the first moths were observed. A total of 50 potato stems should be randomly selected from throughout the field and examined for feeding damage. Control measures should not be applied until 15% of the stems are infested with European corn borer larvae. Since the potato plant can withstand damage to as much as 20% of the stems with no effect on yield, there is no need to start spraying as soon as moths are caught or on a calendar basis.

Management

The European corn borer has many uncultivated hosts, but plantings of field corn and sweet corn are usually the sources of most moths. For this reason, it is useful to plow under corn stubble in the fall or early spring to destroy overwintering habitats. Where conservation tillage is being practiced and the stubble cannot be plowed under, it is best to plant potatoes as far away from such sites as possible. The last instars of the European corn borer do not overwinter in potato fields.

If potentially damaging populations of this pest are present and past experience indicates that economic damage may occur, insecticides are the only practical option for control. From the time when the action threshold is exceeded, insecticides should be applied to the foliage weekly until the moths stop flying, usually in about 3–4 weeks. The objective is to kill the larvae while they are feeding on the foliage but before they bore into the stems. Once larvae have bored into the stems, they are protected, and further insecticide applications will not be effective. In spraying for this pest, it is extremely important to get thorough coverage of the foliage—use at least 50 gallons of water per acre. Do not use nozzles designed for applying herbicides, as they produce too large a droplet.

Flea Beetles

Several species of flea beetles (*Epitrix* species) infest potato (Fig. 12.6). In the northeastern and north central United States and throughout southern Canada, except for British Columbia, the most important species is the potato flea beetle (*E. cucumeris*). The western potato flea beetle (*E. subcrinita*) is widely distributed throughout the western and Mountain states and into British Columbia and Alberta. The tuber flea beetle (*E. tuberis*) is prominent in Oregon, Washington, and British Columbia. The tobacco flea beetle (*E. hirtipennis*) is found in some southeastern and central states.

Adult flea beetles cause characteristic feeding damage to potato leaves, referred to as shotholes (Fig. 12.7). Generally, the greatest damage is done to newly emerged plants early in the season. Larvae of all flea beetle species feed on roots, stolons, and tubers, but only the tuber flea beetle causes extensive tunneling damage in tubers, making them unmarketable. Damaged tubers are often invaded by soft rot bacteria (Chapter 15) or Fusarium dry rot fungi (Chapter 17).

Identification and Biology

Adults of the various flea beetle species are about $3/16$ inch long. Some are entirely black; others are brown-black with faint lighter markings. When disturbed, they usually jump away rapidly—hence the name *flea beetle*. Their eggs and larvae are rarely observed.

All species of flea beetles overwinter as adults beneath crop debris and plant litter in cultivated fields or in surrounding uncultivated areas. When temperatures rise above 50° F in the spring, they become active and feed on various herbaceous plants until potatoes emerge. Each female lays about 100 eggs on the soil surface near potato plants. The eggs hatch in about

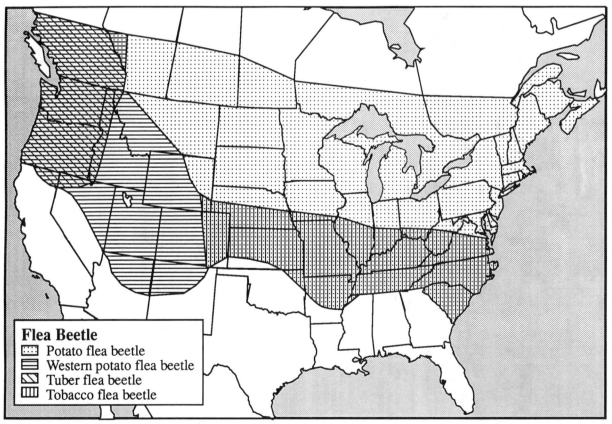

Flea Beetle
- Potato flea beetle
- Western potato flea beetle
- Tuber flea beetle
- Tobacco flea beetle

Fig. 12.6. Distribution of potato flea beetle species in North America.

10 days. The larvae feed on potato roots, stolons, and tubers and then pupate in the soil. Following pupation, adult beetles emerge, crawl to the surface, and feed on potato foliage. The life cycle typically requires 4–6 weeks, and one to three generations per year are produced, depending on the climate.

Population Monitoring and Action Thresholds

Because adult flea beetles are extremely active and are easily disturbed when approached, it is difficult to take direct samples of them. Sampling for larvae in the soil is time-consuming, and by the time larvae are observed, much damage may already have been done. The only feasible monitoring technique is to sample potato foliage for feeding damage by counting the number of shotholes per leaflet. Unfortunately, there does not appear to be a good relationship between the number of shotholes per leaflet and effects on yield. A conservative action threshold is 50 shotholes per leaflet. Thresholds may vary for different cultivars and at different times during the season. Early-maturing cultivars, such as Superior, are less tolerant to feeding injury late in the season than are later-maturing cultivars, such as Russet Burbank.

Management

There is rarely any need for control measures specifically for this pest, since insecticides applied to control Colorado potato beetles and aphids usually keep flea beetle populations in check. If damaging populations of flea beetles are present early in the season, however, most labeled insecticides are effective.

Fig. 12.7. Shothole damage to a potato leaf caused by flea beetle feeding. (Courtesy R. C. Rowe)

Potato Psyllid

The potato psyllid (*Paratrioza cockerelli*), although limited in its distribution, can cause severe damage to potato in areas where it is a pest. It is thought to be a native insect of the western United States, and its economic impact is felt mostly in the Mountain states, especially Colorado, Utah, and Wyoming (Fig. 12.8). It has been reported in western Canada but is not usually a problem there, because psyllids from the southern overwintering range must recolonize this region every spring. Psyllids are related to aphids and leafhoppers and feed in much the same way, by ingesting plant sap through sucking mouthparts.

Most of the damage is caused by nymphs, which inject a toxin while feeding. The toxin induces a condition known as psyllid yellows (Plate 28). Immature leaves on affected plants turn red or purple and are abnormally erect, with the basal portion cupped. Older leaves become unusually thick, roll upward, and turn yellow, and the internodes become shortened. The greatest effects on yield occur when plants become infested early in the season. Such plants are generally severely stunted or die prematurely, and they are much more susceptible to early blight. Affected plants produce excessive numbers of small, distorted tubers, which sprout without a dormant period (Plate 29). Small aerial tubers may also appear in leaf axils. Tubers produced in a heavily infested field are generally too small to be marketable and are not suitable as seed tubers.

Identification and Biology

The adult psyllid resembles a tiny cicada and is about 1/8 inch long (Plate 30). The membranous wings are held rooflike over the body when the insect is not in flight. The light yellow eggs are spindle-shaped and suspended on short stalks from leaves on which they are deposited. The nymphs are flattened, scalelike, and pale yellow-green.

The potato psyllid overwinters in southern California, Arizona, New Mexico, and Texas and into Mexico on a weed called matrimony vine (*Lycium* species), which grows along washes (Fig. 12.8). Psyllids are not a problem in potatoes every year, because they do not survive the winter in more temperate climates, and infestations that do develop must originate each year from winged migrants moving in from the overwintering area. Before migrants can move north to colonize potato fields, populations must build up on solanaceous weeds during the spring.

The colonizing adults lay eggs along leaf margins of host plants. There are five nymphal stages, and the life cycle is completed in about 4 weeks. The potato psyllid is very sensitive to temperature, which to a large extent determines its movement and distribution. Optimal temperatures for development are about 80° F, and development ceases above 90° F. Rising temperatures in the overwintering areas induce the production of migrants. Cool weather during late June and July is ideal for holding populations within an area, and outbreaks often follow cool periods in early summer.

Because the potato psyllid requires moderate temperatures for optimal development, larger plants that provide more shade are most likely to become heavily infested. The availability of suitable host plants when migrants move into an area is an important factor in maintaining populations in a region. For this reason, early-planted potatoes can be heavily damaged. Tomato crops and solanaceous weeds, such as matrimony vine, may also serve as early-season hosts.

The severity of damage caused by a psyllid infestation is determined by several factors, including the size of the colonizing population, the growth stage of the potato crop at the time of colonization, prevailing temperatures, and the presence and abundance of natural insect enemies. As few as three or four psyllids per plant can produce psyllid yellows on pre-bloom plants under favorable conditions, but it may take 15 or more per plant to cause damage to plants in bloom.

Population Monitoring and Action Thresholds

It is important to monitor for psyllids before initiating any control measures, since psyllid infestations are sporadic. Early scouting should concentrate on the lower leaves of early plantings of potatoes or on solanaceous weeds growing near potato fields. Yellow pan traps can be used for early detection, but there are no good correlations between trap catches and

> **It is important to monitor for psyllids before initiating any control measures, since psyllid infestations are sporadic.**

resultant damage. When a field is scouted, samples composed of 50 leaflets randomly selected throughout the field should be carefully examined. Treatment should commence if there is more than one nymph per 10 leaflets on young plants (prebloom) or three or four nymphs per leaflet on plants in full bloom or older. Feeding by adult psyllids has little or no effect on potato yields at any time.

Management

Because potato psyllid infestations are sporadic and are initiated by migrating adults, cultural practices such as crop rotation and the timing of planting have little effect as control measures. Several insects are natural enemies of the potato psyllid. These can affect psyllid population density and, if they are present in sufficient numbers, keep the population in check. Small parasitic wasps (*Tetrastichus* species) are the most important of these natural enemies. Larvae of the minute pirate bug, damsel bug, and lacewing also feed on psyllids.

If psyllid populations do reach action thresholds, insecticides provide the only consistent control measure. It is important to thoroughly cover the foliage and to penetrate the canopy with the spray, to control nymphs feeding on the undersides of leaves. Several soil-applied systemic insecticides provide effective control of early-season populations. However, this preventative approach should be taken only with fields where infestations are expected most years. Yearly applications of these materials can hasten the development of insecticide resistance by aphids and the Colorado potato beetle.

Wireworms

Many species of wireworms are of economic importance on potato in North America (Fig. 12.9). Because the biology and host preferences of these species vary, it is important to identify the species of wireworm causing damage and to know the cropping history of the field.

The most common species in western North America are the sugar beet wireworm (*Limonius californicus*), the Pacific Coast wireworm (*L. canus*), and the Great Basin wireworm (*Ctenicera pruinina*). The most troublesome species in the northeastern United States and eastern Canada is the eastern field wireworm (*L. agonus*). The main species in the north central United States and Canada are the wheat wireworm (*Agriotes mancus*) and the dusky wireworm (*A. obscurus*). The major wireworm pests of potato in the southeastern United States are the corn wireworm (*Melanotus communis*) and *Conoderus* species.

Wireworms are often a problem when potatoes follow cereal

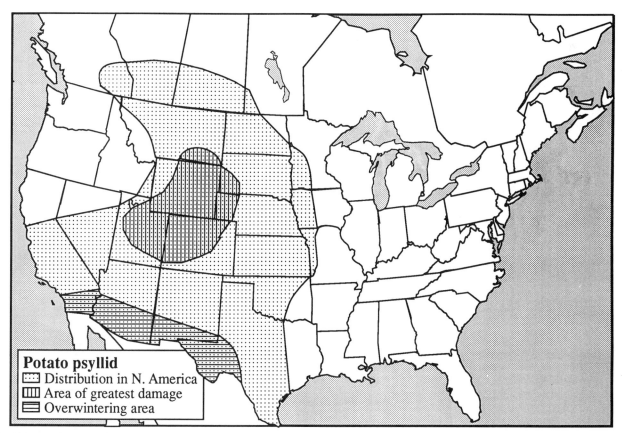

Fig. 12.8. Distribution of the potato psyllid in North America.

crops or are planted in fields taken out of sod, pasture, or a grass cover crop. They can be a problem in fields previously planted with alfalfa, but wireworms feed on weeds in the stand and not on the alfalfa itself.

Early in the growing season, wireworms may bore into potato seed pieces and developing shoots. These feeding sites often become infected with fungi or bacteria, which may result in weak shoots and thin stands. Later in the season, wireworms bore into tubers as they are bulking. Feeding holes in tubers may be shallow or deep, and damaged tubers are often misshapen, which lowers their quality and value.

Identification and Biology

The tan to black adult beetles of these species vary from $1/2$ to $3/4$ inch in length, depending on the species. The larvae, called wireworms, are slender, shiny, cylindrical, hard-bodied, wirelike, and yellow to brown (Plate 31).

Although the biology of different wireworm species is similar, their life cycle in the southeastern United States differs somewhat from that in temperate regions, because it is uninterrupted by cold winter temperatures. The life cycle takes from 1 to 5 years to complete, depending on species and soil temperature. This pest can overwinter in all life stages, and generally several different larval instars can be found at any one time during the summer. For this reason, the relative abundance of wireworms in different life stages may not be synchronous from one season to the next.

Because most of the life cycle is spent in the larval stages, it is the larvae that are predominant in a field. Wireworms feed on the roots of many crops and weeds and bore into stems and other plant tissues, including potato tubers. They move up and down in the soil profile in response to changes in temperature and moisture. In temperate areas, the larvae remain in the top few inches of soil during the growing season as long as temperatures remain below 80° F. They burrow down as deep as 2 feet when soil temperatures are above 80° F and to overwinter. In the spring, when soil temperatures reach about 50° F, they move back to the upper few inches of soil to resume feeding. Most damage to potato is caused by larvae in their second and third years of development.

Last-instar larvae form earthen pupal cells and either pupate immediately or overwinter in the cells as larvae and then pupate in the spring. Adult beetles that complete development in the fall may remain in the cells over the winter. In the spring and summer, the adults burrow to the surface, and if adequate host plants are not present, they fly to egg-laying sites. Female adults lay eggs in cracks or crevices or burrow into the soil to lay eggs near host plants. Young larvae feed on roots of cereal crops, pasture grasses, and weeds.

Population Monitoring and Action Thresholds

It is advisable to check for wireworms before planting potatoes in any field recently rotated from sod or pasture. This can be done in the fall before the first frost, when larvae move down into the soil profile, or in the spring after the soil has warmed to at least 45° F. Soil samples should be taken at random from as many sites in the field as may be reasonably examined. Each sample should represent an area of the same size as the others, so that the number of wireworms per square foot can be determined. In the spring and fall, soil should be sampled to a depth of about 6 inches, but in a hot summer it may be necessary to go down to 18 inches. If the soil is friable and easily sifted, $1/4$-inch hardware cloth can be used to sift the samples and extract the wireworms; otherwise, it may be necessary to sort through each sample by hand.

The presence of wireworms can also be monitored by using buried baits. Pieces of carrot can be buried about 3 inches deep at 10–20 marked sites throughout the field. In 2–3 days, the carrot pieces are retrieved and checked for wireworms.

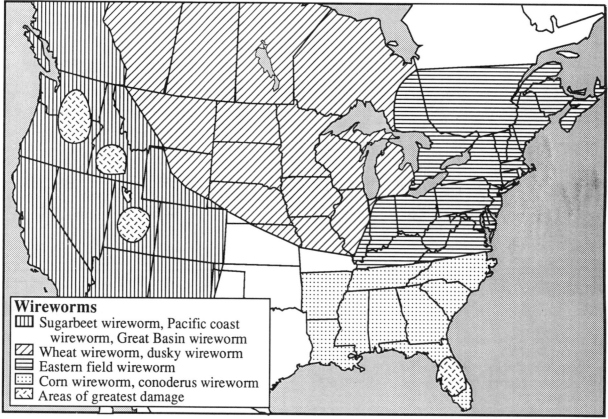

Fig. 12.9. Distribution of wireworm species in North America.

Another type of bait can be prepared by wrapping 2–3 tablespoons of coarse whole wheat flour, rolled oats, or oatmeal in a small piece of netting or nylon stocking and tying it shut. Baiting is an effective sampling method for wireworms, as long as there is not much plant debris in the field, and if the soil is not too cold, wet, or dry, since wireworms become inactive in the upper few inches of soil under these conditions.

If more than 0.4 wireworms per square foot are found by any of these methods, the field should either be treated before potatoes are planted or not be used for potato production. This action threshold may vary from one region to another, so local advisors or Cooperative Extension Service specialists should be consulted to determine an appropriate threshold for your area.

Management

If potentially damaging populations of wireworms are present in a field in which potatoes are to be planted, application of soil insecticides is the only viable management option. Insecticides for wireworm control can be banded or broadcast-incorporated before planting, or they can be side-dressed after potato shoots begin to emerge. For broadcast treatment, apply a labeled granular or tank-mixed product uniformly over the entire field, and mix the material into the soil immediately, to the depth specified on the label. For in-furrow applications, place a narrow band of granules 3–4 inches below the seed piece at planting.

To determine if a sidedress treatment is needed after planting, seed pieces should be dug at random throughout the field as soon as shoots begin to emerge, to be checked for wireworm injury. This is also an excellent way to determine the effectiveness of a preplant treatment. There is no well-established action threshold for this approach. If a second application is necessary, the insecticide applied should be different from that used in the preplant or preemergence treatment.

Once wireworm populations have been reduced in potato fields, they usually remain low, and treatment in subsequent years is not necessary. Populations will increase only if fields become weedy or are planted with a favorable host crop, such as a cereal or grass. Legume crops, such as alfalfa, are good rotational choices in fields prone to wireworm infestation, so long as they are kept weed-free. In southern Florida, sorghum-sudangrass cover crops are commonly planted following harvest of winter-grown potatoes during the period from February to May. Delaying the planting of this cover crop until July is a useful wireworm management technique for reducing damage to subsequent potato crops.

E. B. Radcliffe
Department of Entomology
University of Minnesota, St. Paul

D. W. Ragsdale
Department of Entomology
University of Minnesota, St. Paul

K. L. Flanders
Department of Entomology
University of Minnesota, St. Paul

CHAPTER 13

Management of Aphids and Leafhoppers

Aphids and leafhoppers are sucking insects that can affect the health of a potato crop directly by feeding damage and also indirectly by the transmission of viruses and viruslike pathogens that cause important diseases. As vectors (transmission agents) of these pathogens, aphids and leafhoppers are especially critical in the production of seed potatoes, because tuber-borne viruses can severely limit yields in subsequent crops.

Aphids

Aphids can injure a potato plant directly by sap feeding and are capable of transmitting several important potato viruses. High aphid populations can have substantial direct effects on yield, but such populations are uncommon in commercial potato production, because of insect control practices routinely used with the crop. The primary concern with aphids is usually their role as vectors in transmitting viruses.

Identification and Biology
Aphid species that colonize potato differ in the amount of feeding injury they cause and the particular viruses they spread. In North America, four species commonly colonize potato: the green peach aphid (*Myzus persicae*) (Plate 32), the potato aphid (*Macrosiphum euphorbiae*) (Plate 33), the buckthorn aphid (*Aphis nasturtii*), and the foxglove aphid (*Aulacorthum solani*). In the northeastern United States and Canada, the green peach, potato, and buckthorn aphids are the most common. In the Midwest, the green peach and potato aphids predominate, but the buckthorn aphid also can often be found. The foxglove aphid is generally the least common in both the Northeast and Midwest. In the western regions, over 95% of the aphids in potato fields are green peach aphids, and the remainder are mostly potato aphids.

Most aphid species have both winged body forms (alatae) and wingless forms (apterae). Wingless aphids are by far the predominant form on potato during most of the year. The wingless forms of the four important aphid species can easily be differentiated in the field by observing specimens with a 10× hand lens. The key in Box 13.1 can be used to distinguish these species by their overall body shape and color, the length of the legs and cornicles, and the shape of the head and cauda (see also Fig. 13.1).

In regions too cold for continuous outdoor reproduction, potato-colonizing aphids usually alternate between several host plant species. The summer or secondary host range of some aphid species includes many unrelated plants. Most aphids, however, overwinter as eggs on a very restricted number of primary host species, often woody plants.

In spring, wingless aphids called stem mothers hatch from eggs on the primary host (Fig. 13.2). They and all their descendants of the spring and summer reproduce without mating, giving birth to live young. This asexual reproductive pattern, coupled with quick turnover of generations (7–10 days), facilitates rapid population increases. Under favorable environmental conditions, an aphid population may double in less than 2 days. Offspring of stem mothers are generally all wingless.

Winged spring migrants are not produced until at least the second generation on the primary host, and peak production occurs in the third generation. Spring migrants leave the primary host in search of suitable secondary summer hosts, usually herbaceous plants. Shortly thereafter, the primary host usually becomes unsuitable for further aphid survival. In mild

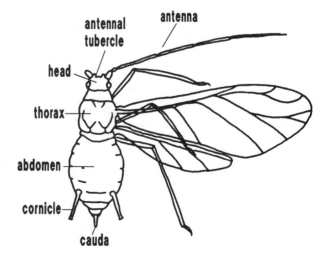

Fig. 13.1. External characteristics used to distinguish aphid species. The cornicles are tubelike structures protruding from the posterior of the abdomen. The cauda is the aphid's "tail." The antennae arise from protuberances, the antennal tubercles, on the front of the head.

117

climates, aphids may reproduce asexually all year on various weeds and crops.

Spring migrants are capable of traveling long distances. Green peach aphid migrants have been known to travel 1,000 miles and have been found in the atmosphere at altitudes of up to 10,000 feet. Winged aphids alight at random, since they cannot distinguish a host from a nonhost plant at a distance. To find a suitable host, winged aphids feed for short periods on sap from the epidermal tissues of plants on which they land. This is called sap sampling. Aphids remain on a secondary host plant only if they receive the proper feeding stimuli when sap sampling. They move from plant to plant until they locate a suitable secondary host. Sap sampling can result in the transmission of certain viruses, even by aphid species incapable of colonizing potato. The role of these transient feeders in the transmission of potato viruses is not completely understood.

Once an acceptable host is found, the spring migrants settle and reproduce. Their offspring are all wingless, but a small proportion of each succeeding generation is winged. As the quality of the host plants declines, more winged summer migrants are produced, which then fly to other secondary host plants. As the day length shortens, fall migrants are produced, both males and females. They return to the primary host plant, on which the females give birth asexually to wingless females, which then mate with the male fall migrants and lay fertilized, overwintering eggs. These overwintering eggs are usually deposited near buds of the primary host.

The buckthorn and potato aphids are typical aphids in that they alternate between primary and secondary host plants and produce sexual forms in the fall. The foxglove aphid has various seasonal cycles dependent upon the climate. The green peach aphid may go through the typical life cycle, or it may overwinter as wingless forms in greenhouses and sheltered areas where secondary host foliage remains green.

The life cycle of the green peach aphid varies between and within potato-growing regions. Spring migration in western states involves a mixture of migrants from primary hosts—peach (*Prunus persica*), apricot (*P. armeniaca*), and some other *Prunus* species—and migrants from secondary hosts. Peach trees and weeds on the orchard floor appear to be the most important sources of populations of true spring migrants

---

Box 13.1

Key to Wingless Forms of Four Aphid Species Commonly Found on Potato

1a Body outline egg- or teardrop-shaped; cauda short 2

1b Body outline elongate; antennal tubercles large and pointing outward; cauda long and pointed; cornicles longer than the distance between their bases; legs prominent; body green, yellow, or pink, sometimes with a darker dorsal stripe (Plate 33); aphids highly mobile .... **potato aphid**

2a Body thick; antennal tubercles prominent; antennae as long as or longer than body 3

2b Body flattened; no antennal tubercles; antennae shorter than body; cornicles almost as short as cauda; body opaque lemon yellow to green, turning black in autumn .... **buckthorn aphid**

3a Body pear-shaped, widest at base of cornicles; antennal tubercles prominent, with almost parallel sides; cornicles tapered, with dark tip and prominent flanges at the tip; body light yellow-green to dark green, with dark areas around base of cornicles; legs and antennae with dark joints .... **foxglove aphid**

3b Body egg-shaped, almost the same width from base of middle legs to base of cornicles; antennal tubercles prominent and pointing inward; cornicles unevenly swollen; body light green to almost translucent, pink, or peach; legs and cornicles the same color as body (Plate 32) .... **green peach aphid**

Information in this key is based on M. E. MacGillivray, 1979, Aphids Infesting Potatoes in Canada: Life Cycle and Field Key, Publication 1678, Agriculture Canada, Ottawa, Ontario.

Potato aphid

Elongate body form

Tubercles point outward

Long, pointed cauda

Long cornicles

Buckthorn aphid

Small, flat body form

No tubercles

Short cornicles

Foxglove aphid

Pear-shaped body form

Tubercles straight-sided

Cornicles tapered with dark tips

Green peach aphid

Egg-shaped body form

Tubercles point inward

Cornicles unevenly swollen

Identifying characteristics of four aphid species commonly found on potato. (Adapted from MacGillivray, 1979)

(second- or third-generation offspring of stem mothers). A single peach tree in someone's backyard may produce enough winged green peach aphids to cause economic infestations in 500 acres of potato! In regions with mild climates, such as the Pacific Northwest, winged migrants also develop from aphid populations that survive the winter as adults. These aphids may reproduce asexually on plants in sheltered areas, such as weeds in drainage ditches, or on winter cabbage (*Brassica oleracea* var. *oleracea*) and other brassica crops.

At high elevations and in areas with severe winters, greenhouse-grown bedding plants may be an important source of initial populations of green peach aphids in the spring. These aphids are not known to overwinter in the Red River Valley of Minnesota and North Dakota, and they rarely do so in New Brunswick. In these areas, spring migrants presumably originate on bedding plants or immigrate from distant locations. In parts of Maine, green peach aphid eggs overwinter on Canada plum (*Prunus nigra*), but bedding plants and long-distance migration may also be important sources of spring populations. Egg populations overwintering on peach in the Yakima Valley of Washington are much larger than those on Canada plum in Maine. Winged forms of the green peach aphid colonize over 100 species of secondary host plants, of which potato is only one.

The potato aphid appears to overwinter in the egg stage in all potato-growing areas. Its primary hosts are wild and cultivated roses (*Rosa* species), raspberry (*Rubus idaeus*), Canada plum, and other species of the family Rosaceae. Winged potato aphids are produced in June and colonize potato, tomato (*Lycopersicon esculentum*), groundcherry (*Physalis* species), and hairy nightshade (*Solanum sarrachoides*), among other species. When a large number of these aphids feed on the upper portion of a potato plant, they can cause a condition known as toproll in some cultivars.

In Maine, the foxglove aphid typically remains year-around on its primary hosts, hawkweed (*Hieracium* species) and foxglove (*Digitalis purpurea*). In the summer, a small portion of the population migrates to other hosts, including potato. In New Brunswick, this aphid alternates between primary and secondary hosts, but it survives the winter primarily as females reproducing asexually in greenhouses. In New Jersey, it exists year-around as asexually reproducing females that overwinter on both primary and secondary hosts. In all regions, potato is a secondary host, and few winged forms are ever produced. The foxglove aphid is found mainly on older leaves and in moist, shady areas, apparently requiring high relative humidity. It produces toxins while feeding, so it can cause economic injury at lower populations than other aphid species common on potato.

The buckthorn aphid generally overwinters as fertilized eggs on alder-leaved buckthorn (*Rhamnus alnifolia*) or common buckthorn (*R. cathartica*). Spring migrants move to potato in June or July. Summer migrants are typically few. Sexual migrants begin to appear in August.

The production of winged aphids is influenced by several environmental factors. For the green peach aphid, the most important factor is crowding, but the production of winged individuals is also promoted by unusually favorable or unfavorable host quality. High temperature generally inhibits the production of winged forms. Shortening day length triggers the production of fall migrants, but the photoperiod is not a factor in the production of summer migrants. Day length is the critical factor regulating the production of sexual forms, but temperature and the nutritional status of the host may also play a role. Winged aphids rarely give birth to winged progeny.

The length of time required for development varies for winged and wingless forms and is dependent upon temperature and food quality. At 70° F, the time from birth to first reproduction of wingless aphids ranges from 7 to 13 days, depending on the species. All aphids molt four times before becoming adults. Once the reproductive stage is reached, the mean number of offspring per wingless aphid ranges from 60 to 75. In all aphid species, the reproductive period is about twice as long as the maturation period, and peak reproduction generally occurs 5–10 days after maturation. Temperature is the major factor influencing the growth of green peach aphid populations, with optimum reproduction at 70° F.

Several other species of aphids are important on potato in certain regions. These include the melon aphid complex (*Aphis gossypii*, including *A. frangulae*), the black bean aphid (*A. fabae*), the mottled arum aphid (*Aulacorthum circumflexum*), the shallot aphid (*Myzus ascalonicus*), the bulb and

> ## Six of the viruses that cause potato diseases common in North America are transmitted by aphids.

potato aphid (*Rhopalosiphoninus latysiphon*), the rice root aphid (*Rhopalosiphum rufiabdominalis*), and *Smynthurodes betae*. All but the last two are potato virus vectors. The melon aphid is now a serious problem on Long Island and in Connecticut, Rhode Island, and the Canadian Maritime provinces. It is not controlled with insecticides used against the green peach and potato aphids.

Transmission of Viruses by Aphids

Successful potato production is dependent upon the ability of growers to plant healthy seed tubers. The development of seed stock in which virus infection levels are held below critical thresholds is one of the principal goals of modern seed certification and seed improvement programs, as outlined in Chapter 7.

Because of the critical role of aphids in the transmission of many important potato viruses, seed potato production is

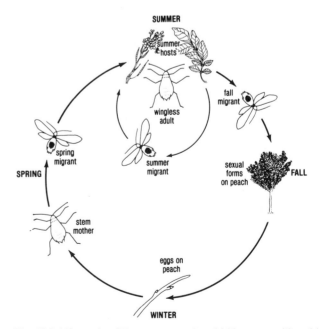

Fig. 13.2. Life cycle of the green peach aphid in areas with cold winters. (Reprinted, by permission, from Western Regional IPM Project, 1986, Integrated Pest Management for Potatoes in the Western United States, Publication 3316, Division of Agriculture and Natural Resources, University of California, Oakland)

concentrated in northern areas of the United States and in Canada, where aphid populations remain relatively low. Six of the viruses that cause potato diseases common in North America are transmitted by aphids: potato leafroll virus (PLRV), potato virus Y (PVY), potato virus A (PVA), potato virus S (PVS), potato virus M (PVM), and alfalfa mosaic virus (AMV), also known as potato calico virus. PLRV and PVY are the most important of these in limiting potato yield and quality (Chapter 14).

Both PLRV and PVY are transmitted by several aphid species, but the most important vector throughout North America is the green peach aphid. It is the most efficient vector of PLRV and also the most abundant species on potato. Both winged and wingless green peach aphids transmit viruses efficiently. The potato aphid is a poor vector of both PLRV and PVY. The buckthorn aphid is a relatively inefficient vector of PLRV, but it can be important in spreading PVY and PVA. The pea aphid (*Acyrthosiphon pisum*) transmits AMV from alfalfa. In addition to differences between aphid species, there are large differences within species in the efficiency of virus transmission.

Aphids transmit viruses in two basic ways, referred to as persistent and nonpersistent transmission (Table 14.1). These terms refer to how the virus particles move within the body of the aphid vector. PLRV is the only potato virus transmitted by aphids in a persistent manner. An aphid can acquire this virus only while feeding from the phloem cells in the conducting vessels of the host plant. After ingestion of PLRV-infested plant sap, virus particles pass through the aphid's gut wall and into the bloodstream. From there, the virus enters many insect tissues. When it enters the salivary glands, the aphid can transmit it to another plant while feeding. Aphids can acquire PLRV after feeding for only a few minutes, but it takes at least 12 hours for maximum transmission efficiency to develop. Once PLRV is acquired, an individual aphid generally retains the virus throughout its life, and hence the term *persistent*. Unlike other potato viruses, PLRV cannot be transmitted mechanically (by rubbing or by direct plant-to-plant contact) but depends entirely on aphids to move it from one plant to another.

In nonpersistent transmission, the virus particles do not pass through the gut wall or enter the blood and internal organs. Instead, they are confined to the mouthparts and the front of the gut. Aphids retain such viruses for only a few hours after feeding, and hence the term *nonpersistent*. An aphid can infect only a few plants before losing the ability to transmit a nonpersistent virus. Virus-free aphids that feed on an infected plant can acquire virus particles from epidermal tissues after sap sampling for only a few seconds, and they are then immediately able to transmit the virus to other plants.

Nonpersistent viruses, such as PVY, are concentrated in epidermal tissues, and any aphid that is sap sampling is a potential vector, regardless of whether it belongs to a species that colonizes the crop. PLRV is concentrated in the phloem tissues, and so in order to acquire the virus an aphid must accept the diseased plant as a host and feed in the phloem. Therefore, the number of aphid species capable of transmitting PLRV is less than the number of species that can spread PVY. A thorough discussion of virus diseases of potato and their management is given in Chapter 14.

Population Monitoring and Action Thresholds

The concept of economic action thresholds has not been widely applied to aphid management in potato production. An obvious reason is that the complex relationships between various aphid species, potato viruses, and cultivars, together with other factors causing crop stress and restrictions imposed by the intended uses of the crop, are difficult to quantify.

Nevertheless, tentative action thresholds have been proposed for aphid control in both fresh-market and seed tuber production in some areas.

In south central Idaho, economic losses from PLRV-induced net necrosis are predicted when the population density of wingless green peach aphids exceeds 10 per 50 leaves for two consecutive weeks. In southwestern Idaho, the corresponding threshold is 40 per 50 leaves. In Minnesota, North Dakota, and Wisconsin, the recommended action threshold for fresh-market production is 30 wingless aphids per 100 leaves. In California, sprays are recommended when 5% of the leaves are infested. In New Brunswick, controls are initiated when 10% of the plants are infested with 25 aphids per plant. In Pennsylvania, dynamic action thresholds have been developed, which increase with accumulating plant degree-days. A computerized pest management scheme that predicts green peach aphid population trends has been devised. This program, called GPA-CAST, runs on a microcomputer or a preprogrammed calculator.

Action thresholds for aphid control are more difficult to establish in seed potato production than in commercial potatoes. European seed producers have long relied on various systems of monitoring aphid flights to time insecticide applications or to recommend early harvest. Similar methods have been tried in North America. The most common means of monitoring aphids is to set yellow pan traps in the field—shallow pans painted bright yellow and filled with water. Migrating aphids are attracted by the color and then drown in the pans, where they can be counted later. These monitoring schemes have been of less benefit in North America. Apparently, large flights of summer migrants are more typical of aphids in Europe than those in the major production areas of this continent.

In New Brunswick, a vine-kill date is established after a cumulative total of five green peach aphids have been caught in any one yellow pan trap. This technique is ineffective, however, when pan captures exceed this threshold early in the season, prior to tuber initiation—a situation that occurs often in Minnesota. In the event of early-season flight activity, insecticide applications are the only recourse against the green peach aphid. In Idaho, pan captures correlate best with green peach aphid populations in adjacent fields, but they are of little value for predicting the risk of net necrosis. If the winged aphids that are trapped have come from virus-free plants, pan captures are of no significance except to indicate increasing numbers of aphids feeding on the crop. This information could be obtained more readily by counting aphids on sampled foliage.

Most European research suggests that the spread of a virus within a field and between fields correlates better with captures of incoming winged aphids than with counts of wingless aphids within the field. In North America, little research has been done in this area, but there is evidence that within-field spread often correlates better with the wingless aphid count. Studies in Minnesota have shown a high correlation between control of the within-field population of the green peach aphid and the spread of PLRV from individual infected plants. Research in New Brunswick has shown that PVY infections generally originate from infected seed and not from outside the field. Where the source of a virus infection is mainly or exclusively a few infected plants growing from infected seed pieces, prevention of a buildup of the aphid population on the crop is the most important consideration. This is true regardless of whether winged or wingless aphids are mainly responsible for transmitting the virus from diseased to healthy plants.

An action threshold of 10 wingless aphids per 100 leaves has been proposed for seed potatoes in the upper midwestern United States. Lower thresholds were found to result in excessive applications of insecticide with minimal overall gain in cumulative aphid control, while also increasing pressure for insecticide resistance and decimating natural enemies. Leaf counts are the simplest means of monitoring populations of wingless aphids within a field, to determine the need for treatment or to evaluate the success of previous control measures. Random sampling from the lower middle portion of the plant is most efficient for monitoring the green peach aphid. Sampling by sweep net is not a very useful technique for monitoring aphid populations, because few are collected, and these may be crushed and unrecognizable.

Management

There are three circumstances in which it is critical that control measures be directed specifically against aphids: 1) in seed tuber production, to eliminate virus vectors, 2) in the production of cultivars susceptible to net necrosis of the tubers (such as Russet Burbank), to prevent the spread of PLRV, and 3) in cases of aphid population outbreaks induced by previously applied insecticides. The appropriateness of different management tactics and strategies for dealing with aphids and aphid-borne viruses varies with the intended use of the

Control measures must be directed specifically against aphids in seed tuber production, in the production of cultivars susceptible to PLRV-induced net necrosis, and in cases of pesticide-induced aphid outbreaks.

crop, the cultivar, and the various possible combinations of aphid species and virus diseases that must be controlled. For example, control measures directed specifically against aphids are seldom necessary for fresh-market tubers, at least for cultivars whose tuber quality is not adversely affected by current-season infection with PLRV. In contrast, aphid control measures are essential in the production of basic seed potato stocks.

Even when virus spread is the critical consideration, control must be tailored to the specific situation, because each vector-virus relationship presents a somewhat different problem. For example, insecticides are much more likely to be effective in preventing the spread of PLRV than in preventing the spread of nonpersistent viruses. The continuous presence of insecticide residues sufficient to kill aphids may not preclude the transmission of nonpersistent viruses. In fact, the insecticide may agitate the aphids and cause them to increase their movements and sap sampling, thus resulting in increased spread of these viruses.

Cultural Control. In the Pacific Northwest, various cultural practices have been proposed for green peach aphid management. These are based on the observation that the most vulnerable period in the aphid life cycle is passed on the primary host. These strategies include the application of chemical defoliants to peach trees in the fall, to deny foliage to fall migrants; the use of tree bands to provide shelters for beneficial insects; and pruning trees to remove most overwintering eggs. When peach trees are pruned, the twigs that are removed must be destroyed, or else the eggs can still hatch, and the aphids then develop on various orchard weeds that can serve as spring hosts. In orchards where grass cover is not maintained, weeds can be important sources of aphid populations in the spring. In the Yakima Valley of Washington, wingless forms can

overwinter on weeds near irrigation ditches and warm-water springs.

Host Plant Resistance. Host resistance is not a useful control measure at present, because modern potato cultivars do not sufficiently differ in susceptibility to aphids. Some wild potato species are highly resistant to aphids. In some species, this resistance is associated with glandular, sticky hairs on the stems and leaves, which are effective barriers against a wide range of pests, including not only aphids but also leafhoppers, other small insects, and the Colorado potato beetle. Other wild potato species have different insect resistance mechanisms. In the future, host plant resistance may prove to be an important method of controlling aphids and the spread of aphid-borne viruses in potato.

Insecticides. Many insecticides registered for use on potato do not give satisfactory control of aphids. Insecticide resistance and insecticide-induced outbreaks in aphid populations, especially the green peach aphid, are common problems. The green peach aphid is one of the few insect species reported to be resistant to compounds in all of the major insecticide classes: organochlorines, organophosphates, carbamates, and pyrethroids. The potato aphid is also resistant to many insecticides. Usually, the season's first application of almost any foliar insecticide gives acceptable aphid control, but with subsequent applications, an aphid population can become virtually immune. With repeated applications, the population on treated potatoes may increase to a level many times greater than that on untreated potatoes.

It is important to recognize that many insecticides registered for use on potato, including carbaryl, azinphos-methyl, and esfenvalerate, can trigger outbreaks in aphid populations. Pyrethroid insecticides are generally not effective against aphids but are used extensively on potatoes because they have a broad spectrum of activity against other insect pests and are cost-competitive. Pyrethroids tend to be repellents to aphid feeding. The green peach aphid has shown resistance to both fenvalerate and permethrin, which may contribute to an increasing problem with PVY in some areas. Foliage-applied insecticides that are generally effective against aphids include endosulfan, methomyl, oxamyl, and methamidophos. The selective aphicide pirimicarb (available in Canada but no longer registered for use in the United States) is also very effective.

Insecticides applied for aphid control are of inconsistent benefit in protecting against the spread of potato viruses.

Insecticides applied for aphid control are of inconsistent benefit in protecting against the spread of potato viruses, even when they prevent the reproduction of aphids within the field. Many insecticides repel aphids but are not lethal to them and thus tend to promote plant-to-plant movement and increased flight activity, as does the movement of spray machinery through the field. This increased aphid activity may be less important with the fast-acting organophosphate and carbamate insecticides.

Several soil-applied systemic insecticides give good early-season control of aphids. They are effective in limiting the spread of PLRV but are much less useful in limiting the spread of nonpersistent viruses. Even when an effective residue is present, an insecticide may not kill quickly enough to prevent the transmission of viruses by winged aphids moving into the field. As an aphid becomes intoxicated, it may drop from the treated plant but then recover and move to another stem or plant, possibly several times, before finally succumbing.

This pattern could actually increase the spread of the virus. Nonpersistent viruses, such as PVY, can be transmitted within the first few seconds of sap sampling. Even PLRV can be transmitted before the vector has contacted enough insecticide to be killed. The principal benefit of aphid suppression in the control of nonpersistent viruses is the reduction of within-field spread. When the residue of a soil-applied systemic insecticide is no longer effective, it may be necessary to apply foliar sprays. Late-season aphid pressure is often more severe in potatoes treated with a soil systemic at planting than in untreated potatoes. Outbreaks in aphid populations may be a consequence of early-season control measures that prevent the establishment of natural enemies of the aphids. This is not a concern where foliar insecticides are applied following the use of a systemic, since natural enemies are not a significant factor in limiting aphid populations when these treatments are used.

The options for chemical control of the green peach aphid are limited by insecticide resistance. Both foliar sprays and soil systemics, applied in-furrow at planting or side-dressed following emergence, have been widely used on potatoes. In many regions aldicarb was formerly applied in-furrow at planting or side-dressed at plant emergence, followed by foliar sprays of methamidophos. Aldicarb was withdrawn from the

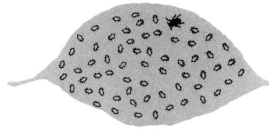

A pesticide applied to control pest A also kills natural enemies that are controlling pest B.

Released from the control exerted by natural enemies, pest B builds up to economically damaging levels

🪲 pest A　　◊ pest B　　🐜 natural enemy

Fig. 13.3. Outbreaks in an aphid population are often induced by repeated applications of an insecticide to which the species is resistant. These sprays kill natural enemies that may have been holding the aphid population in check. (Reprinted, by permission, from Western Regional IPM Project, 1986, Integrated Pest Management for Potatoes in the Western United States, Publication 3316, Division of Agriculture and Natural Resources, University of California, Oakland)

U.S. market in 1990, however, and the future status of this pesticide is uncertain at this time.

In New Brunswick, mineral oil sprays have been successful in reducing the transmission of nonpersistent viruses. Coverage is very important. Mineral oil interferes with the transmission of these viruses during aphid probing. This technique is not entirely effective, however, since some vectors (such as the potato aphid) prefer to land on and probe newly expanding leaves, which may not be protected. Application of 1–2% mineral oil in 100–125 gallons of water per acre is considered safe for the crop, but there is a risk of phytotoxicity if mineral oil is mixed with fungicides containing copper or zinc. Because of the cost and the need for weekly applications, this method is not widely used for aphid control.

Biological Control with Natural Enemies. Aphids on potato are typically low-density pests. When the crop is grown without the use of insecticides, aphids rarely become abundant enough to cause direct damage, since their populations are effectively regulated by their natural enemies. In Maine, aphid predators were shown to be typically more beneficial than aphid parasites. Of the predatory insects, ladybird beetles, lacewings, minute pirate bugs, hover flies, damsel bugs, and seed bugs are the most important. There are numerous species of parasites, mostly wasps, that attack aphids on potato, but these are seldom abundant, and apparently none are host-specific.

Several insect-pathogenic fungi, including *Pandora neoaphidis*, *Entomophthora planchoniana*, and *Conidiobolus obscurus*, attack aphids on potato. Mass infections by these fungi in large aphid populations can be spectacular, but the importance of infections in low aphid populations is less certain. Unfortunately, many fungicides and some insecticides commonly used on potato are highly detrimental to these fungi. Where the fungicide mancozeb is sprayed routinely, late-season populations of the green peach aphid can be more than 100 times greater than in control plots where fungicide was not applied. Other fungicide treatments may have less effect on aphid numbers, but all usually result in significantly lower rates of infection of aphids by insect-pathogenic fungi and significantly more aphids in treated than in untreated areas.

Because insecticides and fungicides are routinely applied in commercial potato production, current practices do not favor biological control. Nevertheless, naturally occurring biological control agents may still contribute to the regulation of aphid population densities. This may partially explain the tremendous outbreaks that can be induced when aphid populations are exposed to repeated applications of an insecticide to which the species is resistant (Fig. 13.3). Fungi offer possibilities for exploitation as microbial biocontrol products. *Conidiobolus obscurus* has been used for some years in Russia. Research to develop aphid pathogens for commercial use is in progress, but none are presently registered in the United States.

Selection of the most appropriate management techniques for aphids depends on the production locality, the cultivars grown, and the use for which the crop is intended. It is essential that potato health managers carefully analyze their needs for aphid control and the limitations of various control options. Consultation with local Cooperative Extension Service specialists or other advisors should be useful in devising a strategy that addresses regional needs for aphid control and can deal effectively with management limitations.

Leafhoppers

Leafhoppers are wedge-shaped insects, broadest in the head and thoracic regions and tapering along their wings. They are strong fliers and are much more mobile than aphids.

Unlike aphids, leafhoppers are important mainly because of the direct feeding damage they cause. The potato leafhopper

(*Empoasca fabae*) (Plates 34 and 35) is the most important species and has long been recognized as a major pest of potato in eastern North America. Its full importance was only appreciated with the introduction of DDT and parathion, the first truly effective insecticides used on potatoes. Between 1946 and 1950, average potato yields in the United States increased by more than 60%, most of the improvement being directly attributable to potato leafhopper control.

Unlike aphids, leafhoppers are important mainly because of the direct feeding damage they cause.

Prolonged feeding by the potato leafhopper causes a condition known as hopperburn. The first conspicuous symptom of injury is a brown, triangular lesion at the tip of the infested leaflet. As the symptoms develop, lesions spread backward and inward from the margin, eventually destroying the entire leaflet. Injury to potato plants, however, occurs even before the first symptoms of hopperburn are visible. A subtle curling of the leaflet and paling of the veins may signal the onset of injury, but these symptoms can easily pass undetected. Although some cultivars, such as Russet Burbank, may show little visible hopperburn, their yields may be severely limited. Commercial cultivars at present do not appreciably differ in their ability to withstand potato leafhopper infestation without an effect on yield. Both adults and nymphs are injurious, but late-instar nymphs can reduce yields more than twice as much as an equal number of adults.

Potato leafhoppers must feed in the conductive vessels of the plant. Damage from feeding is the result of disruption of the phloem—tissues responsible for transporting products of photosynthesis within the plant. It is not clear whether the disruption is due to a mechanical blockage, a toxin secreted during feeding, or a combination of both. Recent research in Missouri supports the idea that a chemical in the saliva of the potato leafhopper left behind after feeding probes induces swelling of the cells, which eventually crushes the phloem.

The damage caused by the potato leafhopper includes not only loss of leaf area to hopperburn but also reduced photosynthetic efficiency of the remaining leaf tissues. In addition, a large increase in respiration (energy consumption) occurs immediately in plants subjected to potato leafhopper feeding, depleting the plant's reserves, which would otherwise be available for growth and tuber development. When the leafhoppers are removed, the plant respiration rate soon returns to normal, but the reduction in photosynthetic efficiency is permanent.

Potato plants are susceptible to injury from the potato leafhopper at all growth stages, but infestations are most damaging during early tuber bulking (growth stage IV). Although the inverse relationship between the number of leafhoppers and yield (the higher the leafhopper population, the lower the yield) is not actually linear at all populations, it takes so few leafhoppers to cause economic injury in a potato crop that for all practical purposes the relationship can be considered linear.

Identification and Biology

The species of leafhoppers that commonly colonize potato vary among production regions. Damaging populations of the potato leafhopper are limited to east of the Rocky Mountains. This species occurs throughout most of the western United States but is of little importance there. In Canada, it is the most important insect pest of potato in western Ontario, but

it is rare or does not occur in the Maritime provinces and west of Manitoba. The southern garden leafhopper (*Empoasca solana*) is a minor pest of potato in the southern United States.

Other species of *Empoasca* occasionally limit potato yields in the western United States, but insecticides used to control other pests usually keep their populations low. These leafhopper species feed only on structural leaf tissues and typically cause small, white, stippled areas on the leaves. They cause much less damage than the potato leafhopper, which has a different feeding mechanism. The intermountain leafhopper (*E. filamenta*) is a potato pest in the high arid regions between the Rocky Mountains and the Sierra Nevada. The western potato leafhopper (*E. abrupta*) and the arid potato leafhopper (*E. arida*) are pests along the Pacific slope.

Three other species—the aster (sixspotted) leafhopper (*Macrosteles quadrilineatus*) (Plate 38), the beet leafhopper (*Circulifer tenellus*), and the clover leafhopper (*Aceratagallia sanguinolenta*)—are significant because they act as vectors of certain potato disease agents. None of these insects injure the crop directly. The aster and clover leafhoppers are present throughout most of North America. The beet leafhopper is primarily a desert species. It occurs in the largest numbers in the western United States and is of little importance east of the Rocky Mountains, although it has been found as far east as Kansas and in Illinois, Florida, and South Dakota.

All of these species have broad host ranges. The potato, aster, and beet leafhoppers each feed on over 100 species of plants, and the clover leafhopper on at least 38 plant species. The potato and clover leafhoppers are commonly found on legumes, the beet leafhopper most frequently on crucifers and plants in the family Chenopodiaceae (such as pigweed and lambsquarters), and the aster leafhopper most often on small grains. Each of these species maintains populations on a wide range of weeds, some of which are alternate hosts of certain potato pathogens. The intermountain leafhopper is found mainly on potato, beans, and sugar beet. The western potato leafhopper and the arid potato leafhopper are found on many truck crops in California. The western potato leafhopper prefers cucurbits, while the arid potato leafhopper favors potato and sugar beet.

Adults of the four leafhopper species commonly found on potato can readily be distinguished by close observation (Box 13.2): the potato leafhopper mainly by its color and size; the clover leafhopper by its robust body; the aster leafhopper by the distinctive pattern of spots on the top of its head, differentiating it from the beet leafhopper, which is highly variable in its color patterns.

Leafhoppers pass through three life stages: egg, nymph (in five instars), and adult. On potato, they usually complete several generations per year. The population density is dependent upon the date of arrival on the crop and the temperature. In northern states, the potato leafhopper can complete two to four generations per year on potato. On all hosts, the beet leafhopper may have three to five generations per year, and the clover leafhopper two or three. The aster leafhopper may produce as many as five generations per year, but unlike other potato-colonizing leafhoppers, this species does not reproduce on potato.

The leafhoppers that attack potato all overwinter as adults, often at great distances from potato production areas. The aster leafhopper can also overwinter as eggs. Overwintering eggs appear to contribute little to populations the following season in the North Central states, but they are the source of aster leafhopper populations in the Northeast.

Potato leafhopper adults overwinter only in a permanent breeding area along the Gulf Coast from southern Louisiana to northern Florida, especially in the Mississippi Delta region. In spring, the leafhopper population increases, and flying adults may be caught in updrafts and transported on upper-level airstreams to distant sites throughout the eastern two-thirds of the United States and southern Canada (Fig. 13.4). Wisconsin often receives the brunt of these long-distance invasions. Weather conditions that permit transport into Wisconsin are a high-pressure system over the East Coast, a low-pressure system over the Great Plains, a north–south front moving east, an east–west front over Wisconsin, and precipitation in the fallout area. Influxes of potato leafhoppers into Illinois have been associated with southerly winds, 36 hours or more in duration, and precipitation. Potato leafhoppers are carried to the eastern United States when weather conditions result in upper-level airflows extending from the Gulf Coast to the east. They often arrive in northern regions before potatoes have emerged. Often, it is the progeny of these migrants that make the first significant invasion of potato. There is evidence that potato leafhoppers move into potato after alfalfa is cut, but in Minnesota the largest increases in population density on potato are related to leafhopper maturation on undisturbed hosts.

In summer, potato leafhopper adults live 30–40 days, and some over 90 days, with the result that generations overlap. The females lay an average of two or three eggs per day and can lay as many as 200 over a lifetime. At summer temperatures, eggs hatch in about 10 days. The nymphs are yellowish green when young but closely resemble the adult leafhopper when older. They require about 12 days to develop into adults. New adults begin laying eggs when they are 6 days old.

The aster leafhopper's preferred hosts are grasses, and large populations of this species can build up in small grains, particularly oats and wheat. When weather conditions are right for long-distance transport, large influxes of aster leafhoppers can move into the Upper Midwest from maturing cereals in the South Central states (Fig. 13.4). There appears to be no reverse migration in the fall. In the North Central states, immigrating aster leafhoppers accumulate on small grains, mainly oats. Populations of immigrant origin can build up to damaging levels 5–6 weeks before damaging populations from locally overwintered leafhoppers can develop. As the cereals ripen, the aster leafhopper moves to other hosts, including potato. It feeds and lays eggs on potato, but those laid on potato fail to hatch. In the West, the aster leafhopper commonly overwinters in desert areas on Russian thistle (*Salsola iberica*). In California, it overwinters as adults on desert plants.

The clover leafhopper overwinters in northern areas as adults in and under residues of its host plants, such as alfalfa. In

---

Box 13.2

Key to Adults of Four Leafhopper Species Commonly Found on Potato

1a Body vivid lime green to yellow-green, with variable white markings on head and thorax; associated with marginal yellowing and necrosis (hopperburn) of host plant; 0.13–0.15 inch long (Plates 34 and 35); mainly found in low-altitude, humid regions east of the Rocky Mountains .... **potato leafhopper**

1b Body not vivid lime green but may be dull light green or some other color, without white markings 2

2a Body almost as wide as long; top of head between the eyes more than four times as wide as long; body brownish, with two black spots on top of head; 0.11–0.12 inch long; mainly found east of the Rocky Mountains (but not in Florida and the Gulf Coast), but also found in intermountain regions .... **clover leafhopper**

2b Body slender, less than one-fourth as wide as long; top of head between the eyes no more than four times as wide as long at the center 3

3a Body dull light green (may appear silvery gray when wings are folded at rest); six distinct spots on top of head; 0.08–0.22 inch long (Plate 38) .... **aster leafhopper**

3b Body yellow to pale orange to brown, with darker markings on darker-colored individuals; 0.12–0.14 inch long .... **beet leafhopper**

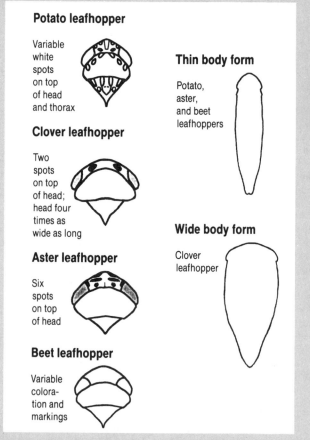

Potato leafhopper

Variable white spots on top of head and thorax

Thin body form

Potato, aster, and beet leafhoppers

Clover leafhopper

Two spots on top of head; head four times as wide as long

Wide body form

Clover leafhopper

Aster leafhopper

Six spots on top of head

Beet leafhopper

Variable coloration and markings

External characteristics of four leafhopper species commonly found on potato: top view of head and tail regions (left) and body forms (right).

central and southern areas, adults emerge on any warm day. They have been found in every month of the year in southern New York. Alfalfa, because of its predominance as a forage crop, is now the major source of clover leafhopper populations, but red clover (*Trifolium pratense*) and crimson clover (*T. incarnatum*) are the preferred hosts. On clovers, eggs of the clover leafhopper hatch after 5–12 days, and nymphs complete development in 25–30 days. The nymphs are creamy white with heavy dark spots and bands.

The beet leafhopper, in the western states, may either overwinter in the immediate area of their summer hosts or may have a seasonal migration. In localities where long-distance migration is characteristic, the leafhopper matures and leaves its summer hosts each fall, returning to permanent breeding sites. Seven such sites have been identified in the western deserts. The specific wild hosts used by breeding beet leafhoppers vary with the site, the season, and the amount of rainfall. Common wild hosts are Russian thistle in winter and wild mustards in spring and fall. On suitable host plants, the beet leafhopper inserts its eggs in rows of two to five, mainly in leaf veins. Each female is capable of laying 300–400 eggs, which hatch in about 5 days when temperatures average 100°F, but in over 40 days when they average 60°F. The nymphs are white when small, becoming spotted red and brown as they mature. The time required for nymphal development ranges from 13 days at 95°F to 75 days at 65°F. The length of the pre-egg-laying adult stage varies from 5 days at 90°F to 13 days at 68°F.

The intermountain leafhopper overwinters as adults in crop residues and plant debris along field margins. It produces a spring generation on various weed hosts and then moves to potato. It completes three or four generations per year. The eggs require an average of 12 days to hatch, and the nymphs develop in about 16 days.

Transmission of Viruses and Mycoplasmaslike Organisms by Leafhoppers

Some species of leafhopper are important to potato health not because of direct feeding but because of their role as vectors in the transmission of certain plant pathogens. The aster leafhopper is the most important in this regard. The clover and beet leafhoppers also transmit potato pathogens, but these are of only minor importance. No *Empoasca* species of leafhopper is known to transmit any potato pathogens.

The aster leafhopper is the principal vector of aster yellows mycoplasmalike organism (AY-MLO), which causes purple top in potato (Chapter 14). The leafhopper generally acquires the pathogen by feeding on an infected host plant during migration from ripening small grains to potato. More than 350 plant species have been identified as hosts of AY-MLO. The pathogen must incubate for several days within the leafhopper's body before the insect can transmit it. Moreover, it takes several hours of feeding by the leafhopper to successfully transmit the pathogen. These long incubation and feeding periods required for transmission of AY-MLO afford opportunities to reduce purple top by controlling the vector. Roguing plants with purple top is of no value in disease management, as the aster leafhopper cannot acquire AY-MLO from potato.

The clover leafhopper and the beet leafhopper are important in potato only because they are vectors of potato yellow dwarf virus (PYDV) and beet curly top virus (BCTV), respectively. The diseases caused by these viruses were at one time more prevalent but are now of minor importance in potato production. Red clover and crimson clover are hosts of PYDV and are preferred by the clover leafhopper. Alfalfa, which is far more abundant and is now the primary source of clover leafhopper populations, is immune to this virus. Although PYDV is present throughout the range of the clover leafhopper,

outbreaks of potato yellow dwarf have historically been confined mostly to the northeastern United States and Alberta. Circumstantial evidence suggests that the spread of PYDV is associated with drought that forces leafhoppers from clover to potato. Because the clover leafhopper harbors the virus within its body, it is able to transmit the pathogen throughout the winter. BCTV is of little importance in potato, because most potato production occurs outside the normal range of the beet leafhopper.

Population Monitoring and Action Thresholds

Potato leafhopper populations are relatively easy to monitor. Adults are best sampled by sweep net, and nymphs by examining randomly picked midplant leaves. The number of samples required to satisfactorily estimate the size of a population depends on the population density and the required degree of sampling precision. In Minnesota and Wisconsin, 25 sweeps across two rows with a net 15 inches in diameter or a sample of 35 picked leaves per location generally gives population estimates of sufficient accuracy for management decisions. In Minnesota, treatment is recommended when the population density exceeds 10 nymphs per 100 leaves.

In Wisconsin, potato is often subject to damaging populations of adult leafhoppers moving in rapidly, either as long-distance migrants or from alternate hosts. A dynamic model was developed for action thresholds there, in which insecticide treatment is recommended when the following condition is satisfied:

$$\frac{\text{Number of adults caught in 25 sweeps}}{25 - (\text{Number of nymphs observed on 25 leaves})} > 16$$

In practice, if there is a large immigration of adult leafhoppers, the recommendation in Wisconsin is to spray at the first appearance of nymphs. If the number of adults caught is less

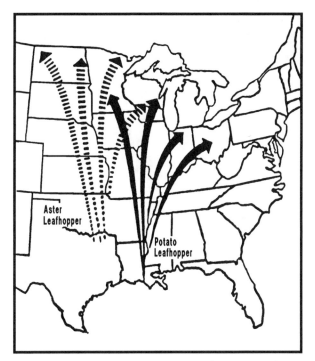

Fig. 13.4. Long-distance migration routes of the aster and potato leafhoppers. (Adapted from J. T. Medler, 1962, Long-range displacement of Homoptera in the central United States, pages 30-35 in: Proceedings, International Congress of Entomology, 11th)

than 1 per sweep, however, spraying can be delayed until the number of nymphs reaches 10 per 25 leaves. Local advice on appropriate threshold values for specific production regions should be obtained before any treatment is applied.

Management

The size of the population of potato leafhoppers required to cause economic damage varies with the cultivar, the stage of plant growth, and environmental circumstances. Early-maturing cultivars are generally assumed to be more susceptible to the potato leafhopper, but these cultivars bulk more rapidly, and their yield may actually be affected less. Another common assumption is that the potato crop is more susceptible to leafhopper injury if it is under stress and hence that it is more important to control leafhoppers under those conditions. Some

> **If leafhopper populations exceed locally accepted action thresholds, insecticides provide the only effective means of controlling these pests on potato.**

studies, however, have shown that the combined effects of potato leafhopper damage and water stress or certain diseases are less than additive.

If leafhopper populations exceed locally accepted action thresholds, insecticides provide the only effective means of controlling these pests on potato. Soil systemics applied in-furrow at planting or side-dressed at plant emergence give 6–8 weeks of control and can essentially prevent the transmission of leafhopper-borne pathogens. However, for reasons of cost, systemic insecticides are probably seldom used specifically for this purpose. The standard industry practice for leafhopper control on fresh-market potatoes is to apply foliar sprays.

Insecticide resistance is not a problem with the potato leafhopper, and almost any registered insecticide gives excellent control of this pest. Since both the insect and the initial stages of plant injury are inconspicuous, it is common practice in some production areas to spray on a routine schedule. This approach usually results in unnecessary insecticide applications, which may induce an outbreak in aphid populations (Fig. 13.3) and increases selective pressure for insecticide resistance in other pests (Fig. 12.3), such as the green peach aphid and the Colorado potato beetle. Growers in central Minnesota typically spray every 10 days, but equivalent potato leafhopper control can be achieved with as few as two applications for the season. As integrated pest management comes into more common usage in potato production, spray schedules should be based on appropriate action thresholds and actual leafhopper populations determined from field scouting.

Most leafhoppers seem to have few effective natural enemies. An insect-pathogenic fungus, *Erynia radicans* (synonyms *Entomophthora sphaerosperma* and *Zoophthora radicans*), infects the potato leafhopper in Wisconsin and Minnesota, but it is rarely found in Illinois. Temperatures may be limiting there, since the fungus does not germinate above 86°F. The beet leafhopper is susceptible to the same pathogen, but the aster leafhopper is not. This fungus appears to be very diverse and may actually comprise several species. *E. radicans* seems to be a pathogen new to North America, and it will be interesting to see whether it ultimately proves to be a valuable biological control agent. Most fungal pathogens operate under the limitation that they have strict temperature requirements, need high humidity for spore germination and infection, and are readily disseminated only when the host has a high population density. At the present time, biological control is not a viable management option for leafhoppers.

Ernest E. Banttari
Department of Plant Pathology
University of Minnesota, St. Paul

Peter J. Ellis
Agriculture Canada
Vancouver, British Columbia

S. M. Paul Khurana
Central Potato Research Institute
Simla, India

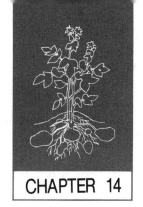

CHAPTER 14

Management of Diseases Caused by Viruses and Viruslike Pathogens

Viruses are protein-coated particles with nucleic acid cores and are visible only when viewed with an electron microscope. They cause systemic infections in susceptible hosts and can reproduce only within living cells. Viruses infecting potato are diverse in size and structure and in their effects on growth and yield. Most of them, including potato virus X (PVX) and potato virus Y (PVY), replicate in tissues throughout the plant, but a few, such as potato leafroll virus (PLRV), invade and replicate only in the phloem.

All potato viruses invade developing tubers and thus can be carried over from season to season in seed tubers. None of the potato viruses common in North America, however, are carried in true potato seed. Some viruses can be spread mechanically—by direct contact between sap from an infected plant and tissues exposed at the site of a tiny wound or cut surface. Mechanical transmission can occur during seed cutting, by leaf rubbing, or by contact between plants and farm equipment. PVX can remain infective on the surfaces of machinery, soil, or wood for several hours and thus can readily be spread from one tuber to another during seed cutting. Other viruses require a living organism (a vector), such as an aphid or a nematode, to move them from plant to plant. PLRV, for example, is spread only by aphids and cannot be transmitted by other means.

The effects of viruses on potato growth and yield vary with the virus and the virus strain, the genetic resistance of the potato cultivar, and the growth stage of the plant at the time of infection. For example, if tubers of a susceptible cultivar infected with a severe strain of PVY or PLRV are planted and the virus is then spread throughout the crop, plants can develop severe symptoms and yields may be reduced by up to 80%. Infection with PVX, however, may not result in any visible symptoms, even though yields may be reduced by as much as 10–30%. Strains of potato virus S (PVS) that are common in North America usually cause no visible symptoms and little or no effect on yield.

Two other types of viruslike pathogens, viroids and mycoplasmalike organisms (MLOs), cause important diseases in potato. Viroids are infectious nucleic acids (RNA) that lack the protein coat of viruses. Like viruses, they can reproduce only within living host cells. Potato spindle tuber viroid (PSTV) is the only viroid known to cause a significant disease in potato. It is mechanically transmitted and spreads quite readily in potato by vine contact, abrasion from farm equipment, and seed piece cutting. It is also transmitted in tubers from season to season and, unlike potato viruses common in North America, is carried in true potato seed.

MLOs are pathogens that are bounded by a membrane but lack a cell wall. They belong to belong to a group of organisms named Mollicutes. MLOs are not mechanically transmissible and are vectored by leafhoppers, planthoppers, and, in one case, a psyllid. Some survive and reproduce both in their plant hosts and in their insect vectors. During feeding, MLOs pass in salivary secretions from the vector into the phloem of the host plant, where they multiply and cause vascular plugging and other abnormalities. Temporary remission of the symptoms may be obtained by treating infected plants with tetracycline antibiotics. Two potato diseases in North America are caused by MLOs, purple top (aster yellows) and witches' broom. Epidemics of purple top develop sporadically. Witches' broom occurs much less frequently and is of minor importance.

Diseases caused by viruses and viruslike pathogens are a constant threat to potato production, particularly the production of seed stocks, even when the best health management practices are employed. Certain practices can minimize losses, while others may aggravate the spread and multiplication of potato viruses. Planting cultivars that do not show visible symptoms of normally severe viruses, such as PVY, makes detection and roguing of infected plants difficult and may be a major cause of virus spread. Excessive use of insecticides that are ineffective in controlling aphids but kill aphid predators increases the potential for the spread of PVY and PLRV. Picker planters increase the risk of spreading mechanically transmissible viruses as well as other tuber-borne pathogens. Potato health managers must be aware of the high potential for harm from viruses and viruslike pathogens and incorporate practices into holistic management programs that will control them or minimize their impact.

Symptoms and Epidemiology of Major Diseases

Potato Leafroll Virus

Potato leafroll, caused by potato leafroll virus (PLRV), is a major disease of potato in North America. PLRV can be introduced into a potato field either by planting infected seed tubers or by an aphid vector that brings the pathogen to the field from an outside source. Infections introduced by the latter means are referred to as current-season infections. The occurrence of this disease and severe outbreaks in major potato production areas are dependent upon the population of PLRV-carrying aphids, how well these vectors are controlled in affected fields, and also the success of certification programs in providing seed stocks virtually free of the virus.

Leafroll in plants grown from infected tubers may substantially reduce yield, but current-season infection with PLRV usually does not significantly affect yield unless it occurs very early in the season. However, in certain cultivars, such as Russet Burbank, Norgold Russet, Green Mountain, and Irish Cobbler, current-season infection causes net necrosis (Fig. 14.1) or stem-end browning in tubers, which are serious defects in quality. Net necrosis occasionally develops when leafroll originates from infected seed tubers but is less severe. Net necrosis may not be evident at harvest, but symptoms can develop during storage. Potatoes from severely affected fields are usually rejected by processors. Losses in marketable yield have been reported to be as high as 50–80%. In the western states, economic losses to PLRV-induced net necrosis can be extensive if appropriate management practices are not followed.

PLRV is transmitted in a persistent manner by several species of aphids (Table 14.1), mainly the green peach aphid (Chapter 13). Acquisition of the virus by the vector takes several minutes to several hours of feeding, but once infected, the aphid usually retains the virus for life. While feeding on potato, an aphid carrying PLRV deposits the virus into phloem tissues, where it then replicates. In susceptible cultivars this conductive tissue may become necrotic and lose its function.

The severity of symptoms depends on the virus strain, the susceptibility of the cultivar, the time of infection, and the environment. Current-season infections that develop late in the season may cause no visible symptoms, but some tubers may become infected. In early current-season infections, young leaves may become chlorotic (yellowed or slightly pinkish) and rolled and may stand upright. The lower leaves of plants grown from PLRV-infected seed tubers become rolled and leathery and may turn pinkish or yellow. Eventually the lower leaves begin to die, and chlorosis develops on the upper leaves. Infected plants are usually stunted and more upright than healthy plants (Plate 36).

PLRV is carried in infected seed tubers but is not transmitted mechanically by leaf contact or machinery. Infected seed stocks, cull potatoes, and volunteer potato plants are the most important sources of the virus. Until the development of sensitive immunoassays, such as the enzyme-linked immunosorbent assay (ELISA) (Chapter 7), identification of PLRV in certified potato seed stocks was difficult and relied principally on recognition of symptoms in seed fields, cumbersome transmission tests, and less precise laboratory assays. Control of aphid vectors and careful, repeated visual inspections of seed fields, coupled with winter test programs in Florida and California, have greatly reduced potato leafroll in seed potatoes. Visual inspection is now backed by ELISA testing in early-generation increases of seed potatoes to detect specific problems, such as strains of PLRV that may cause mild symptoms or symptomless infections in plants, which then serve as reservoirs of the virus. These assays have considerably strengthened the capability of potato certification agencies to detect and remove infected nuclear or limited-generation stocks from seed channels (Chapter 7).

Potato Virus Y

The other major aphid-borne virus of potato in North America is potato virus Y (PVY). Diseases caused by this pathogen are known as severe mosaic, leaf-drop streak, and potato veinbanding mosaic, and reported losses range from 10 to 80%. There are three principal strains of the virus. Strain O (PVY^O) occurs worldwide. Strain N (PVY^N), the tobacco veinal necrosis strain, was not reported in the United States or Canada until 1990, when it was found in eastern Canada. Strict quarantines were put in place in the affected areas to prevent the dissemination of infected seed stocks. At present, surveys for PVY^N are being made in production areas that might have received seed lots in the late 1980s from areas later found to be affected. Strain C (PVY^C) has not been found in North America.

PVY is transmitted worldwide by at least 30 species of aphids, of which the green peach aphid and the buckthorn aphid are the most important vectors. Recent evidence from New Brunswick suggests that other aphid species that may not normally colonize potatoes are also important in the spread of the virus there. Aphids landing on infected plants can acquire

Fig. 14.1. Russet Burbank tubers with net necrosis, caused by current-season infection with potato leafroll virus. (Courtesy A. R. Mosley)

Table 14.1. Methods of transmission of virus and viruslike pathogens of potato

Pathogen	Mechanical transmission	Vectors[a]
Potato leafroll virus	No	Aphids (P)
Potato virus Y	Yes	Aphids (N)
Potato virus A	Slight	Aphids (N)
Potato virus X	Yes	None
Potato virus S	Yes	Aphids (N)
Potato virus M	Yes	Aphids (N)
Tobacco rattle virus	Slight	Nematodes
Potato spindle tuber viroid	Yes	None
Aster yellows mycoplasmalike organism	No	Aster leafhopper

[a] P = persistent transmission; N = nonpersistent transmission.

PVY within a few seconds after beginning to feed, and they can transmit the virus immediately, in a nonpersistent manner. They usually retain the virus no more than an hour, but retention for up to 24 hours has been reported. Aphid transmission is the most important means of spread in the field, but all PVY strains are also mechanically transmissible by leaf contact and injury (Table 14.1), and they are carried in tubers.

PVY has a broad host range, including tomato, tobacco, and pepper, as well as many weed species, including nightshade and groundcherry. However, infected potato seed stocks and volunteers are the principal reservoirs of the virus.

Symptoms of current-season infection depend on the virus strain, the susceptibility of the cultivar, the age of the plants at the time of infection, and the environment. Mosaic or mottling (Plate 37A) may be masked when day temperatures are above 80°F.

The symptoms of infection by PVY^O may vary with the cultivar. In Russet Norkotah, visible symptoms do not become well developed, and in Shepody they may disappear after only a few days. In Norland, brown, angular lesions may develop in leaflets, along with veinal necrosis, whereas in Kennebec yellow mottling or mosaic may develop. Necrosis of petioles causes leaves to drop or cling to the stems, with the result that affected plants have bunchy tops and lower stems devoid of leaves or with clinging necrotic leaves (Plate 37B). Current-season infection that occurs late in the growing season may not cause foliar symptoms, although some tubers may become infected. Symptoms in plants originating from infected tubers include mosaic, mottle, and necrosis, but these are often less severe than the symptoms of early current-season infection. Infection with both PVY^O and PVX causes symptoms of severe rugose disease.

In contrast to PVY^O, PVY^N induces only a mild mottling of potato foliage in current-season infections and in plants grown from infected tubers. Although the foliar symptoms are mild, yields may be reduced by as much as 30%. Some cultivars may remain completely symptomless and thus are easily overlooked during roguing. Infected tubers are symptomless. PVY^N is quite destructive to tobacco, tomato, and pepper and can be a severe problem where these crops and potato are grown in the same area. Infection of tobacco by PVY^O together with PVX causes necrosis that is limited to leaf areas between the veins and does not spread to the veins.

PVY has become a major problem for potato producers in North America, because of its ability to be dispersed readily by many aphid species, by mechanical transmission, and in tubers, and because some cultivars that have been widely distributed do not express symptoms well. Fortunately, identification of PVY is now accomplished accurately and conveniently by ELISA, and this has greatly improved our capability to ensure that basic seed stocks are free of this virus.

Potato Virus A

Potato virus A (PVA) is serologically related to PVY and is also transmitted in a nonpersistent manner by aphids. At least seven species of aphids can transmit the virus, the green peach aphid and the potato aphid being the most important. PVA can also be mechanically transmitted, but the virus is unstable, and this is probably not an important means of spread in the field.

PVA causes a disease of potato known as mild mosaic. The virus is widely distributed in potato-growing areas of North America, and infection may reduce yields by as much as 40%. The symptoms usually appear milder than those caused by PVY. Mosaic or mottle occurs in leaves, with some areas appearing chlorotic and others darker green than normal. Leaf margins appear wavy, and leaves may be shiny and exhibit slight rugosity. The stems of infected plants tend to bend

Table 14.2. Retention of infectivity (in hours) by potato virus S (PVS) and potato virus X (PVX) on various materials

Material	PVS	PVX
Iron or aluminum foil	7	3
Unpainted wood	0	3
Painted wood	...	6
Burlap	120	6
Cotton	...	6
Soil	25	24
Rubber	25	3
Human skin	...	3
Expressed sap from potato foliage	120	...

slightly outward, giving the plants a somewhat open appearance. Infected tubers are generally symptomless. Symptoms may be masked when day temperatures are high, and the milder symptoms may be difficult to detect in bright sunlight. Convenient, accurate diagnosis of PVA in potato is now accomplished by ELISA.

Potato Virus X

Potato virus X (PVX) was widely distributed in North American seed potatoes until PVX-free seed stocks became available through certification programs. The disease caused by PVX is known as potato latent virus disease, potato mottle, or latent mosaic. After the first season's infection, the virus usually causes no symptoms in most cultivars and can be carried in seed stocks unnoticed. However, infection can reduce yields by 15% or more. Some strains, alone or in combination with PVY or PVA, may cause severe rugose mosaic. Certain strains alone can cause severe foliar and tuber necrosis and may kill infected plants. Symptoms of current-season infections are usually masked when temperatures are above 80°F.

PVX is readily transmitted mechanically and therefore may easily be spread by foliage or sprout contact, by seed piece cutters or picker planters, by cultivating or spray machinery, and possibly by insects with chewing mouthparts, such as grasshoppers. There are several systemic hosts among the solanaceous relatives of potato, including tomato and tobacco, but infected potato seed stocks are the principal source of PVX. The virus can survive up to 3 hours on iron surfaces, 6 hours on painted wood, and 24 hours in soil (Table 14.2), and it is readily transmitted from infected tubers to healthy tubers during cutting of seed pieces. PVX is detectable by several serological tests, including latex flocculation assay and ELISA.

Potato Virus S

Potato virus S (PVS) occurs widely in North American potato cultivars, but it can be eliminated from nuclear seed stocks by heat therapy and meristem culture. Infected plants are normally symptomless, but some strains cause bronzing of leaves, necrotic or greenish spots on senescent yellowing leaves, and a more open growth habit. In Russet Burbank, PVS together with PVX can cause greater damage than PVX alone. Although losses as high as 10–20% have been reported due to PVS alone, these findings have not been verified, and it is generally accepted that PVS alone does not usually cause significant economic loss.

Infected potato seed stocks are the most important source of PVS in field plantings. The virus is readily sap-transmissible and has been shown to remain infective for 7 hours on metal surfaces, 25 hours on rubber surfaces, and 120 hours on moist burlap (Table 14.2). It is easily transmitted from tuber to tuber during cutting, by foliage contact, and by mechanical injury to foliage during field operations. Some strains are spread by the green peach aphid and the buckthorn aphid. ELISA is most frequently used for accurate diagnosis.

Potato Virus M

Potato virus M (PVM) causes a potato disease named paracrinkle or potato leafrolling mosaic. This virus is probably of minor importance in North America, although the extent of its occurrence is unclear. It usually causes mild mosaic or mottle, crinkling and rolling of leaves, and stunting of the plant. Symptoms may not be apparent at temperatures above 75°F. PVM can occur along with PVS and PVX in potato plants.

PVM is readily transmitted mechanically and is tuber-borne. It is also transmitted in a nonpersistent manner by the green peach aphid and, less effectively, by the potato aphid and buckthorn aphid. The virus may remain infective for 2–4 days in plant juices rubbed on various surfaces. Diagnosis is readily accomplished with ELISA.

Tobacco Rattle Virus

Some strains of tobacco rattle virus (TRV) cause stem mottling in potato but no symptoms in tubers. Other strains cause a tuber disease called corky ring spot, tobacco ring spot, or spraing.

Stem mottle symptoms may occur as a result of current-season infections and in plants grown from infected seed tubers. Infected plants are stunted, and their leaves are small, mottled, and distorted. Patterns of yellow lines may form in the leaves.

Corky ring spot in tubers is characterized by concentric rings of alternating living and necrotic tissue, which may or may not extend to the tuber surface (Plate 69C and D and Fig. 14.2). Necrotic flecks or blotches may also form in tuber tissues. If the infection occurs early, tubers may become cracked and malformed. Producers can sustain large losses when fields of potatoes grown for processing are rejected for having this disease. Corky ring spot is reported in some western states, in Florida, and in western Canada. It generally occurs in plants growing in sandy soil infested with stubby-root nematodes, belonging to the genera *Paratrichodorus* and *Trichodorus* (Chapter 18).

TRV infects over 400 species of plants, both monocots and dicots, and is transmitted to potato mainly by nematodes feeding on tubers and roots. It is infrequently transmitted mechanically or in tubers, and therefore spread in seed stocks is not common. Movement of nematode-infested soils is probably the major means by which the virus is spread.

Nematode vectors are more prevalent in acidic, sandy soils with grass as a previous crop. Direct control of the pathogen or its nematode vectors in the soil is difficult (Chapter

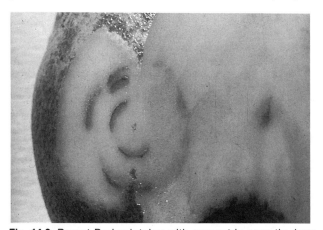

Fig. 14.2. Russet Burbank tuber with concentric necrotic rings caused by infection with tobacco rattle virus. (Courtesy R. Ingham)

18), but the risk of infection is reduced in a potato crop that follows certain other crops, such as alfalfa. Some cultivars are resistant to infection.

Potato Spindle Tuber Viroid

Potato spindle tuber disease, caused by potato spindle tuber viroid (PSTV), was once widely distributed but now occurs infrequently in most potato production areas of North America, because nuclear seed stocks are tested routinely. If infected stocks are replanted for several seasons, they rapidly degenerate, and tuber size diminishes. Infection with severe strains of PSTV may reduce yields by as much as 65–80%. Mild strains, which are more difficult to detect visually, occur more frequently than severe strains and cause losses in the 15–25% range.

Plants infected with severe strains of PSTV are stunted, and the foliage has a dull appearance. Leaves may develop rugosity and may be erect and slightly twisted. Infected tubers are elongated or pointed, and the eyes are more deeply indented and appear to have prominent eyebrows. Severely affected tubers may develop grooves, knobs, or swelling and internal necrosis.

PSTV is readily transmitted from infected to healthy tubers by cutting knives and in foliage by vine contact and abrasion by machinery. It is also tuber-borne and is spread by pollen and in true seed. These traits are especially important to potato breeders and necessitate thorough assays for the viroid in parental stocks. Reliable detection of PSTV in potato tissue is now possible through assays based on DNA hybridization techniques.

Aster Yellows MLO

Purple top, or aster yellows, caused by the aster yellows MLO (AY-MLO), occurs sporadically throughout North America. The disease has also been called bunchy top, purple-top wilt, and apical leafroll. Outbreaks of purple top depend on the abundance of the principal vector of AY-MLO, the aster leafhopper (Plate 38). These insects migrate into potato fields when adjacent susceptible crops such as barley or weed hosts mature and become unpalatable to them. Aster leafhoppers may also be moved several hundred miles by wind, to be deposited erratically in potato fields (Fig. 13.4).

The principal symptoms of purple top in potato are stunting, bunchiness and leaf roll of apical leaves, and yellowing, reddening, or purpling of leaves (Plate 39). Stems may become swollen, and aerial tubers may develop (Plate 40). Tubers at harvest usually appear normal, and depending on the time of infection, only some of the tubers on individual plants may be infected. Infected tubers stored beyond January and processed for chips often produce brown, discolored chips.

Leafhoppers cannot acquire AY-MLO from potato, but they can acquire it from over 350 species of weed and crop plants. The pathogen multiplies inside the insect vector, which is then able to transmit it to other plants about 10–20 days after feeding on an infected host plant. Once a leafhopper acquires AY-MLO, it can transmit the pathogen for life.

AY-MLO normally does not survive in potato tubers, and normal plants may emerge from tubers from infected plants. More frequently, infected tubers fail to sprout, or they produce thin, nonviable sprouts known as hair sprouts. In some cases, however, the pathogen survives in tubers and infects the plants that develop from them.

Disease Management

Certified Seed Tubers

The essential foundation of any management program for potato diseases caused by viruses and viruslike pathogens is the exclusive use of high-quality, pathogen-tested seed stocks, to avoid introducing these pathogens in infected seed tubers. This is especially important with pathogens that are mechanically transmitted (Table 14.1) and can be spread during seed cutting. However, planting only certified seed tubers also minimizes the number of infected plants that develop from infected tubers, which then provide a source of pathogens that can be spread by insect or nematode vectors.

> ## The essential foundation of any management program for potato diseases caused by viruses and viruslike pathogens is the exclusive use of high-quality, pathogen-tested seed stocks.

Several state-run seed potato certification and improvement programs in the United States and a federally administered program in Canada have been developed to provide commercial growers with such seed stocks (Chapter 7). Commercial growers should make the selection of quality seed stocks and seed growers one of their principal management priorities. Because planting certified, disease-tested seed stocks is such an essential potato health management practice, regulations mandating their use have been adopted in some states and Canadian provinces. Procedures for obtaining and handling healthy seed stocks are discussed in Chapters 3 and 4.

Cultural Practices

Since all of the major virus and viruslike pathogens of potato are tuber-borne and several are mechanically transmissible, an effective disease management program must emphasize proper procedures for storing and handling seed, field cultivation, and harvesting seed potatoes. Although many of these principles apply mainly to the seed potato grower, these concepts should also be integrated into commercial production practices.

Some viruses can remain infectious outside the host plant for several hours. Table 14.2 shows the retention of infectivity by PVS and PVX on various materials. Because of the ability of some viruses to survive outside the potato plant, it can be expected that some will survive in storage facilities and on potato-handling equipment, tractor tires, and machinery used for planting, tillage, and pesticide application. This contaminated equipment may transmit these viruses mechanically.

Equipment and storage buildings should be sanitized and inspected prior to harvest each growing season. Machinery and storage facilities on seed farms should be used only for the production of certified seed potatoes. High-pressure steam cleaning of machinery and storage areas is recommended. Several chemicals are somewhat effective in destroying viruses, including 3% trisodium phosphate, calcium hydroxide, quaternary ammonium compounds, chlorine dioxide, and sodium hypochlorite (household bleach, diluted to 1:50). Some of these are also good general disinfectants (Table 4.1). All surfaces to be treated must be cleaned first, as any disinfectant is much less effective on surfaces that are dirty or coated with potato starch or bacterial slime. Disinfectants are also discussed in Chapter 4.

Since potato tubers are a principal reservoir for all major viruses in the field, it is important that fields replanted with potatoes be free of cull tubers surviving from a previous crop and the resulting volunteer plants, which may harbor these viruses and serve as an important means of pathogen survival. In northern regions, winter freezing normally disposes of tubers left after harvest. If volunteer plants survive the winter, however, the most practical way to eliminate them is to conduct a program of summer fallow and cultivation or to plant rotational crops in the field and use an appropriate herbicide. For the same reasons no cull piles should be permitted in potato production areas. In areas where PVY^N is present, strict quarantines should be applied to prevent further dissemination of this strain.

A major consideration in the establishment of seed production farms and individual seed potato fields is that they should be isolated as much as possible from commercial potato production, other potential sources of viruses, and aphid flights. This is the usual practice in North America and accounts for the success of seed production programs in some northern states and Canada.

Planting whole B-size tubers ($1\frac{1}{2}$–$2\frac{1}{4}$ inches in diameter) rather than seed pieces cut from larger tubers reduces the spread of pathogens that are readily mechanically transmitted, such as PVS, PVX, PVY, and PSTV. They can spread rapidly when seed pieces are cut with machine cutters. Sanitation of this equipment is difficult, because of starch and slime buildups. Sanitation of hand knives used to cut small amounts of nuclear and foundation seed stocks can best be accomplished by dipping them in alcohol and then flaming them or by immersing them in a 3% solution of trisodium phosphate and then rinsing them in running water. Although the use of whole B-size seed tubers is an effective technique to limit the spread of these pathogens, the economics of the production and sale of whole seed has been a deterrent to its large-scale use in North America.

Planting potatoes for seed production with an assist-feed planter rather than a picker planter helps to limit the spread of PSTV, mechanically transmissible viruses, and other tuber-borne pathogens. Planting should be done as early as possible after soil temperatures are at least 50° F, to hasten early emergence, growth, and an early harvest. Drag-off cultivation (in which a drag is passed over the field to hasten the emergence of tubers planted in raised beds and to control early-season weeds) should be avoided in seed fields or, at least, should be done soon after planting, to prevent mechanical injury and the spread of viruses to developing sprouts.

> ## Monitoring and controlling aphids and leafhoppers is an important component of any management program for viruses.

To minimize mechanical transmission of PVS, PVX, PVY, and PSTV, cultivation, hilling, and other postemergence operations should be done when the plants are less than 6–8 inches tall, to prevent significant contact between the vines and tractor tires or machinery. In seed fields, weed control should be accomplished with herbicides whenever practical. Inspection of seed fields and roguing of offtype plants as well as those that exhibit symptoms of virus infection is a normal practice of seed producers. In nuclear and early-generation seed fields, tuber-unit planting (Fig. 7.4) is the accepted practice to facilitate roguing. If a plant with a virus infection is detected in a later-generation certified field that is solidly planted, the adjacent plants within the row and touching plants in adjacent rows should be removed from the field.

Insect Vectors

Monitoring and controlling aphids and leafhoppers is an important component of any management program for viruses

Table 14.3. North American potato cultivars with reported resistance to potato viruses and aster yellows mycoplasmalike organism

Pathogen	Cultivar	Resistance reaction[a]	Reference[b]	Pathogen	Cultivar	Resistance reaction[a]	Reference[b]
Potato virus Y	Abnaki			Potato virus A	Alamo	R	45:139
	BelRus				Belchip	I	57:61
	Canus				BelRus	I	58:111
	Cherokee				Canso	FR	28:697
	Chippewa	R	24:413		Cherokee	R	31:53
	Donna	MR	65:509		Chieftain	FR	45:293
	Golden Chipper				Chippewa	R	17:217
	Jemseg				Delta Gold	I	57:429
	Katahdin				DeSota	R	25:89
	Kennebec				Donna	MR	65:509
	Menominee				Early Epicure	FI	
	Monona				Houma	R	17:217
	Nipigon				Hunter	FI	40:275
	Niska	MR	68:143		Katahdin	FR	
	Norchief				Kennebec	FR	
	Norchip				LaSalle	R	25:89
	Nordak	FR	34:774		Lenape	R	45:142
	Norgleam	FR	34:774		Mohawk	R	20:71
	Norwiss	FR	67:371		Onaway	FR	38:353
	Onaway				Pennchip	I	41:54
	Ontario				Penobscot	I	41:140
	Oromonte	R	45:297		Redskin	FR	38:81
	Peconic				Rideau	MR	57:47
	Pennchip				Russette	I	61:77
	Red Gold	FR	65:49		Saco	FI	32:41
	Reliance				Sebago	R	17:217
	Sable				Seminole	FR	47:35
	Sebago				Simcoe	R	59:39
	Sequoia				Tawa	R	36:267
	Snowflake	FR	40:271		Wauseon	R	45:146
	Tawa				Yukon Gold	R	58:241
	Teton			Potato leafroll virus	Abnaki		
	Wauseon				Cascade		
	York	MR	47:201		Conestoga	MR	60:193
Potato virus X	Atlantic	I	38:353		Eramosa	FR	66:293
	Belchip	I	57:61		Houma	R	20:1
	Butte	R			Katahdin	MR	
	Crystal	R	59:131		Kennebec	MR	
	Donna	R	65:509		Niska	MR	68:143
	Early Epicure	FI			Norwiss	FR	67:371
	Hunter	FI	40:275		Ontario		
	Monona	R			Penobscot		
	Nampa	R	50:296		Red Gold	FR	65:49
	Nemarus	FI	66:703		Rideau	MR	57:47
	Norwiss	FR	67:371		Rosa	R	58:451
	Raritan	FR	47:264		Rose Gold	FR	65:325
	Reliance	I	40:406		Yampa	FR	26:35
	Rose Gold	FR	65:325		York		
	Saco	R	32:41		Yukon Gold	MR	58:241
	Sangre	MR		Potato yellow dwarf virus	Sebago	FR	20:277
	Saphir	R		Aster yellows mycoplasmalike organism	Early Gem	MR	40:406
	Sunrise	R	62:221				
	Targhee	R	50:293				
	Tawa	R	36:267				
	Yankee Chipper	R	60:295				
	Yankee Supreme	R	60:295				
	York	FI	47:201				

[a] Reported resistance reactions are I = immune, FI = field immune, R = resistant, MR = moderately resistant, and FR = field resistant.

[b] References are to volume and page numbers of reports in the American Potato Journal. Cultivars for which no reference is given were listed as resistant or field resistant by R. H. Bagnall and G. C. C. Tai, 1986, Field resistance to potato virus Y in potato assessed by cluster analysis, Plant Disease 70:301-304; R. H. Bagnall and G. C. C. Tai, 1986, Potato leafroll virus: Evaluation of resistance in potato cultivars, Plant Disease 70:621-623; and R. H. Bagnall, 1961, Hypersensitivity to viruses A and X in Canadian and American potato varieties, American Potato Journal 38:192-202. Early Epicure was listed as field immune to potato virus A and potato virus X by H. M. Darling, 1959, North American potato varieties, pages 19-39 in: Potato Association of America Handbook, PAA, New Brunswick, NJ. Butte, Monona, and Sangre were listed as resistant or moderately resistant to potato virus X by Western Regional IPM Project, 1986, Integrated Pest Management for Potatoes in the Western United States, Division of Agriculture and Natural Resources, University of California, Oakland. Saphir was listed as resistant to potato virus X by J. Munro, 1981, Potato virus X, pages 72-74 in: Compendium of Potato Diseases, W. J. Hooker, ed., American Phytopathological Society, St. Paul, MN.

and AY-MLO in both seed and commercial potato production. Vine killing and early harvest may be required in seed fields to limit late-season infection with aphid-transmitted viruses, particularly PVY and PLRV and possibly PVS. Insect vectors and their management are discussed in detail in Chapter 13.

Cultivar Resistance

Potato breeding for resistance to viruses began in North America in the 1920s, and various types of resistance to all the major potato viruses have been identified. Breeding for virus resistance has made a significant contribution to lessening the prevalence and severity of these diseases in potato when resistant cultivars are grown on significant acreages. Unfortunately, disease resistance has not always been a major criterion in the selection of potato cultivars for production. Horticultural adaptability, quality, and processing needs have promoted the continued production of Russet Burbank, a cultivar susceptible to nearly all the important potato viruses, over large acreages in North America. This is also true of several other popular cultivars.

The generalized resistance to PVY and PLRV of cultivars such as Kennebec and Katahdin has undoubtedly been an important factor in reducing the frequency and severity of diseases caused by these viruses in some North American production areas, particularly the Northeast. Moreover, Kennebec does not develop net necrosis, a severe problem affecting tuber quality, resulting from current-season PLRV infection of certain cultivars, such as Russet Burbank. Resistance to PLRV superior to that of Kennebec and Katahdin is available in Abnaki and Penobscot, but these cultivars are not widely grown. Since Katahdin also has high generalized resistance to PVA and has been chosen as a parent in many crosses,

many North American cultivars have some resistance to this virus. Table 14.3 lists North American potato cultivars with resistance to the major potato viruses and AY-MLO.

A few cultivars, such as Early Epicure, Saphir, and Saco, are immune to PVX. This resistance is conferred by the single dominant gene Rx and is effective against most strains of PVX in North America. In the future, genetic engineering may provide new sources of resistance to potato viruses, such as transgenic cultivars that express viral coat protein genes. Field tests are under way to test the effectiveness and horticultural traits of Russet Burbank lines that have been altered to express coat protein resistance to both PVX and PVY. Many laboratories are involved with genetic engineering of potato, and coat protein resistance to PVS and PLRV has been reported.

Cultivars with resistance to aphid vectors of viruses combined with resistance to the viruses themselves would appear to offer the ultimate control of aphid-vectored viruses in potato. Even if such cultivars were only moderately resistant to a particular virus, reduced feeding by insect vectors would diminish the amount of infection. *Solanum berthaultii*, a wild relative of potato, has glandular hairs exuding a sticky substance that traps aphids. Germ plasm from this species could be used to develop potato cultivars that might provide another type of control of certain aphid-vectored viruses, such as PLRV. Some studies suggest that plant resistance to a virus is more important than resistance to the vector alone. To our knowledge, no potato cultivars have yet been developed that combine aphid resistance with virus resistance. In order to realize the full potential of host resistance in managing virus diseases, considerable research is needed to develop virus-resistant cultivars with widespread acceptance by the potato industry.

Neil C. Gudmestad
Department of Plant Pathology
North Dakota State University, Fargo

Gary A. Secor
Department of Plant Pathology
North Dakota State University, Fargo

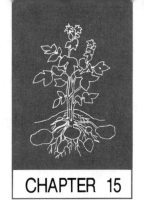

CHAPTER 15

Management of Soft Rot and Ring Rot

Several bacterial diseases are particularly important in potato production. These are soft rot (which includes blackleg, aerial stem rot, and tuber soft rot) and ring rot. Successful management of these diseases in seed stocks, during crop growth, and in harvested and stored tubers requires an integrated management approach. Control strategies for these diseases are focused on the disease management principles of exclusion, sanitation, and modification of the environment.

Blackleg, Aerial Stem Rot, and Tuber Soft Rot

Blackleg, aerial stem rot, and tuber soft rot are all soft rots of the fleshy parts of potatoes. The first two are diseases of the stem, whereas the third affects tubers. Both foliar and tuber symptoms are caused by bacteria called soft rot erwinias. Blackleg and tuber soft rot occur wherever potatoes are grown. Aerial stem rot is also widespread but is most severe in sprinkler-irrigated production.

Symptoms

Blackleg can occur in the field at any stage of plant development. The disease is initiated from contaminated seed pieces. In severe cases, entire seed pieces and developing sprouts rot prior to emergence, so that an uneven stand is produced. In postemergence blackleg, the stem bases of diseased plants typically exhibit an inky black to light brown decay (Plate 41). This decay originates in the seed piece and may extend up the stem for a distance of less than an inch to more than 2 feet. The leaves of infected plants tend to roll upward at the margins, become chlorotic, and wilt (Plate 42). The plants appear stiff and, if the disease occurs early in the season, are often stunted. They eventually wilt and die as the stems become girdled.

In contrast to blackleg, aerial stem rot (also called bacterial stem rot or aerial blackleg) is initiated by soft rot bacteria from sources external to the seed piece. Aboveground stems and petioles can become infected when the pathogen enters wounds caused by hail, windblown sand, insect feeding, or cultivation. The primary sites of stem infection, however, are natural openings, such as leaf scars (Plate 43). Diseased stems and petioles appear light brown to medium brown, and an inky black decay is not uncommon (Plate 44). The infection can girdle the stem, causing the plant to wilt and die.

Decayed tissues of soft-rotted tubers are very soft and watery and have a slightly granular consistency. The diseased tissue is cream-colored to tan, with a black border separating it from healthy areas (Plate 45). In the early stages, soft rot decay is generally odorless. A foul odor and a ropy or tacky consistency of decayed tissues usually develop as secondary decay organisms (commonly *Clostridium* bacteria) invade infected tissues. Soft rot may consume most internal tuber tissues, which causes the skin to collapse. Often a shell of skin remaining in the soil is the only indication that the disease has occurred.

Pathogens and Disease Development

Blackleg, aerial stem rot, and tuber soft rot are caused by two closely related bacteria: *Erwinia carotovora* subsp. *atroseptica* and *Erwinia carotovora* subsp. *carotovora*. Both bacteria are gram-negative, motile rods that can reproduce in the absence of oxygen. In culture, they form pits in media containing polypectate. The identification of subspecies requires additional biochemical and physiological tests. Serological techniques can be used to identify *E. c. atroseptica*, because it is serologically homogeneous, but are not as reliable for *E. c. carotovora*, because of the serological diversity of this subspecies.

E. c. carotovora occurs commonly worldwide and has an extensive host range, including most fleshy vegetables. It survives readily in many environments, including soil and surface waters, such as rivers, lakes, and even oceans. It is capable of multiplying and persisting in the root zones of many host and nonhost crop and weed species.

E. c. atroseptica, in contrast, is associated mostly with potatoes growing in temperate climates. It does not survive well in soil for more than 1 year but may survive longer in diseased tubers or other plant debris.

The bacteria that cause blackleg (usually *E. c. atroseptica*) are carried on contaminated seed tubers, mainly in the lenticels. Most seed lots are contaminated to some degree, but the bacteria are usually dormant and do not cause disease until environmental conditions are favorable. In contrast, the bacteria that cause aerial stem rot (generally *E. c. carotovora*) are introduced into the crop in irrigation water, in windblown aerosols, and by insects. Infested soil can also be an important source of these bacteria. The bacteria that cause tuber soft rot (which may be of either subspecies) usually come from decaying seed pieces, infested soil, and contaminated water sources and harvesting equipment.

Moisture and temperature are the two critical factors in the initiation and development of diseases caused by the soft rot *Erwinia* bacteria. High soil temperatures and bruising of seed tubers favor seed piece decay and preemergence blackleg. Cool, wet soils at planting followed by high temperatures after emergence favor postemergence blackleg. In addition, Fusarium seed piece decay (Chapter 17) may predispose developing plants to infection by the soft rot erwinias, resulting in increased soft rot of seed pieces and early-season blackleg. Dense plant canopies and long periods of leaf wetness favor infection of aerial plant parts.

> **Moisture and temperature are the two critical factors in the initiation and development of diseases caused by the soft rot *Erwinia* bacteria.**

Tuber soft rot can occur at any temperature above 50°F, but the optimum temperature range for disease development is 77–86°F. Soft rot caused by other bacterial pathogens—species of *Clostridium*, *Pseudomonas*, and *Bacillus*—is favored by temperatures exceeding 86°F. At high temperatures, these bacteria may actually take over tuber decay initiated by the soft rot erwinias.

Oxygen depletion in tubers also favors the development of soft rot. If seed pieces or tubers in soil or in storage become covered with a film of water, the tissues rapidly become depleted of oxygen. Oxygen depletion may also be induced by soil flooding, washing tubers, or spraying tubers with fungicides in water as they are placed in storage. Natural defense mechanisms in tuber tissues are inhibited by a lack of oxygen, while the soft rot erwinias are relatively unaffected.

Tuber soft rot can proceed rapidly in storage. "Wet" spots can form in the pile and flow to other areas, spreading the bacteria. Heat and moisture condensed on tuber surfaces can further adversely affect tubers in storage, resulting in accelerated "melt" of the pile.

Management

A thorough sanitation program and modification of the field and storage environments are necessary to minimize economic losses from blackleg, aerial stem rot, and tuber soft rot. Resistant cultivars and pesticides are not available for management of these diseases. Planting high-quality, certified seed stock is the foundation for management of many potato diseases, but it is of limited value in controlling these soft rot diseases, especially when the pathogen is *E. c. carotovora*.

In recent years, most seed potato certification agencies in the United States have dropped established disease tolerances based on field inspection for blackleg. This was done because environment plays such a prominent role in blackleg development. In addition, it is now recognized that little correlation exists between the amount of blackleg observed in a particular seed grower's field and the amount of disease that develops when that seed lot is planted in a commercial field the following year.

In spite of these limitations, there is still benefit in the use of "clean" seed stock in a blackleg management program. Because the soft rot erwinias are seedborne, clean seed minimizes the initial amount of contamination (especially by *E. c. atroseptica*) in the crop. In general, the fewer generations a seed lot is removed from pathogen-tested Nuclear stock, the cleaner the seed is. Contamination of seed tubers by the soft rot erwinias generally increases with each generation from the disease eradication process.

Planting seed lots in which a high percentage of the tubers are contaminated with soft rot bacteria does not necessarily result in a problem with bacterial seed piece decay or blackleg. The potential for these diseases to occur can be minimized by following certain procedures. Undamaged whole B-size seed tubers generally have the least problem with bacterial seed piece decay. When cut seed is used, all seed-cutting and handling equipment should be thoroughly cleaned between seed lots, to minimize the spread of bacteria between lots. Seed tubers should be warmed to about 55–60°F before they are planted. In early-season plantings, seed pieces should be treated with a fungicide. Although this treatment has no direct effect on soft rot bacteria, it does suppress infection by *Fusarium* and thus reduces seed piece decay and associated blackleg. Excessive bruising of seed tubers should be avoided both before and after cutting. Conveyors that load seed pieces onto trucks and planters should be lowered as much as possible to minimize the distance that the seed pieces drop, preferably no more than 6 inches. To promote rapid emergence and lessen the chances of the development of bacterial seed piece decay, seed pieces should be planted in well-drained soil when temperatures at the planting depth are at least 55°F. Cold seed pieces (below 50°F) may "sweat" when planted in warm, sandy soil (above 70°F), and severe decay may develop as a result. Planting under these conditions should be avoided. Unless absolutely necessary, the soil should not be irrigated following planting until the plants are well emerged.

None of these procedures prevent aerial stem rot, which often occurs from midseason to late in the season when the plant canopy is very dense. Dense canopies and long periods of leaf wetness created by overhead irrigation often lead to an increased incidence of this disease. Management of the plant

> **To promote rapid emergence and lessen the chances of bacterial seed piece decay, seed pieces should be planted in well-drained soil when temperatures at the planting depth are at least 55°F.**

canopy and manipulation of the environment within the canopy to reduce the duration of leaf wetness may limit the development of aerial symptoms. An integrated approach to managing aerial stem rot while maintaining high yields should include the following practices: avoiding cultivars that produce extensive vines and dense foliage, increasing the spacing between rows, controlling the timing and frequency of irrigation to avoid long periods of leaf wetness, and monitoring the nitrogen status of the plants to avoid excessive vegetative growth and the formation of a dense canopy.

Management of tuber soft rot is centered on the handling of the crop during harvest and storage. Irrigation should be closely monitored before harvest to avoid excessive soil moisture, which may favor increased infection of lenticels by soft rot bacteria. Only mature tubers should be harvested. Tubers left in the soil for 7–10 days after vine death have better skin set and are less subject to wounding. Those harvested from green vines are more susceptible to postharvest soft rot. If possible, tubers should be harvested when soil temperatures are between 50 and 65°F. Tubers harvested when pulp temperatures are above 70°F are very susceptible to breakdown in storage. Low spots in fields should be left unharvested if significant waterlogging has occurred. Procedures should be in place to minimize bruising and other mechanical damage during harvesting and handling (Chapter 6).

If a significant amount of soft rot is present at harvest, the tubers should be graded as they are moved into storage. Storage conditions should be managed to promote wound healing for 10–14 days, and then the storage temperature should be lowered to below 50° F as soon as feasible. Good ventilation should be maintained, to prevent the accumulation of CO_2 and avoid condensation. Tubers should never be washed before being placed in storage, as a moisture film left on them may promote the development of soft rot in the storage pile. Storage piles should be routinely monitored to check for wet spots, an indication of soft rot.

When tubers are removed from storage, they should be warmed before handling, to minimize bruising and prevent condensation on their surfaces. If they are washed before processing or packing for market, they should not be submerged in flumes or dump tanks. They should be washed with clean, chlorinated water and dried as rapidly as possible before being placed in well-ventilated bags or shipping containers. Details of storage and handling procedures are discussed in Chapter 6.

Bacterial Ring Rot

Bacterial ring rot is a potentially serious disease of potatoes and is one of the main reasons for the rejection of seed lots in potato certification programs in North America. The disease is feared by the seed grower because it may compromise a long-standing reputation for high-quality seed stock and result in severe economic losses when seed lots are rejected from certification. It is of concern to the commercial grower because it has the potential to spread throughout a production operation and may lead to severe disease losses if left unchecked. Ring rot was originally reported in Germany around 1900. The pathogen was introduced into Canada in 1931 and into the United States a year later. By 1940, the disease had been found in every North American potato production area.

Symptoms

Foliar symptoms of ring rot include wilting of leaves and stems along with chlorosis and necrosis of leaves (Plate 46). Initially, wilting may occur during hot periods of the day, with the plants recovering at night. The lower leaves usually wilt first, are slightly rolled at the margins, and appear paler green than healthy leaves. As wilting progresses, leaf tissues between veins turn yellow. In the later stages of disease development, the margins of the lower leaves become necrotic and brittle, and eventually entire stems senesce and die. If the stem of a plant with symptoms of advanced ring rot is cut at the base, near the roots, a milky exudate can usually be expelled from the vascular area by squeezing the stem. Frequently, only one or two stems per hill develop symptoms. Foliage of some cultivars, such as Russet Burbank, may develop a dwarf rosette symptom.

Ring rot derives its name from a characteristic breakdown of the vascular ring within the tuber, which can usually be observed in diseased tubers cut crosswise at the stem end (Plate 47). Occasionally, symptoms are absent in the stem end but present near the apical or bud end. A creamy yellow to light brown cheesy rot often develops in the vascular ring. In advanced stages of the disease, the vascular ring may separate from adjacent tissues, and a creamy or cheesy exudate can be expelled from it when the tuber is squeezed (Plate 48). Slightly sunken, dry, cracked areas may form on the outer surfaces of severely diseased tubers (Plate 47). Frequently, such tubers have been invaded by secondary decay organisms. Symptoms caused by these organisms may obscure those of

ring rot, and tubers originally infected by the ring rot pathogen may eventually disintegrate completely in the field as a result of these secondary infections.

Tuber symptoms are often not as obvious as those described above and may appear as only a broken dark line in the vascular ring or a continuous yellowish discoloration of the vascular tissue (Plate 47, lower left, and Plate 49). When tubers with mild symptoms are stored at temperatures exceeding 50° F, conditions that favor multiplication of the causal bacteria, the disease may progress and the characteristic symptoms of advanced ring rot may develop.

The Pathogen and Disease Development

Ring rot is caused by the bacterium *Corynebacterium sepedonicum* (synonyms include *Corynebacterium michiganense* subsp. *sepedonicum* and *Clavibacter michiganense* subsp. *sepedonicus*—there is disagreement about the proper name of this pathogen). It is a nonmotile bacterium with short-rod morphology. The rods are usually wedge-shaped or curved but may also appear straight. Single cells are usually evident in cultures from diseased plants, but V and Y configurations of bacterial cells may also be observed.

Ring rot bacteria overwinter mainly in infected seed tubers. They are also capable of surviving 2–5 years in dried slime on the surfaces of crates, bins, burlap sacks, and harvesting and grading machinery, even if exposed to temperatures well below freezing. They survive longest under cool, dry conditions. They do not survive in soil in the absence of potato debris but can survive from season to season in volunteer potato plants.

Wounds are necessary to enable ring rot bacteria to penetrate seed pieces. The pathogen is readily transmitted from diseased tubers to healthy seed pieces during seed cutting. A knife that

> **Ring rot bacteria are capable of surviving 2–5 years in dried slime on the surfaces of crates, bins, burlap sacks, and harvesting and grading machinery, even if exposed to temperatures well below freezing.**

cuts one infected tuber can spread the pathogen to the next 20–100 seed pieces. Likewise, it can be spread during planting, particularly if a picker planter is used. Chewing insects, such as Colorado potato beetles and flea beetles, have been reported to transmit the pathogen, and it can also be carried by irrigation water.

After the pathogen becomes established in a plant, it multiplies and moves through the water-conducting tissues, where large populations of the bacteria develop. Infection usually occurs early in the life cycle of the plant, but visible symptoms generally do not appear until late in the growing season—about 80–120 days after planting. With the onset of symptoms, the bacteria move out of the vascular system and into adjacent tissues, and the vascular ring separates from surrounding tissue as a result.

In the field, ring rot bacteria are capable of causing disease only in potato. However, under experimental conditions they can infect tomato, eggplant, and other *Solanum* species. They have been reported to colonize sugar beet roots under field conditions but do not cause disease in this crop. The role of sugar beet in the epidemiology of potato ring rot in areas where both are grown is unknown.

The pathogen tends to spread more readily during seed cutting and planting if infected seed tubers are warmed before cutting. Planting in wet soil at temperatures of 64–72° F increases the chances of successful infection of contaminated seed pieces. During plant growth, dry soil conditions coupled with air temperatures of 75–90° F hasten the onset of symptoms. Air temperatures above 90° F retard the development of foliar symptoms. In growing seasons with cool, moist weather, foliar symptoms may be completely suppressed, because little moisture stress is placed on the diseased plants. Long days (over 14 hours) have also been reported to inhibit symptom development.

Tubers and plants may remain symptomless even though they are infected with the ring rot pathogen, in what are referred to as latent infections. Latent infections may be the result of environmental conditions unfavorable for symptom expression. They may also occur when the number of bacteria in an infected seed piece is too low for them to produce a population sufficient to cause symptom development. Ring rot in a seed lot may also remain undetected if only a few seed tubers within the lot are infected. In this case, detection of the disease during field inspection is extremely unlikely.

In general, early-maturing cultivars express ring rot symptoms earlier than late-maturing cultivars. A few cultivars have been developed (Merrimack, Teton, and BelRus) that do not show foliar symptoms of ring rot even though they are infected with the pathogen. Immunity to the ring rot pathogen has not been identified in *Solanum tuberosum*, but several sources of immunity have been found in *S. acaule*. Cultivars resistant to ring rot have not become commercially acceptable thus far, because of the concern that they may serve as symptomless carriers of the pathogen.

Management

Procedures for the management of ring rot must be part of every holistic health management plan. With most potato diseases, the management objective is to keep the pathogen population at a minimum to avoid losses. With ring rot, however, the goal must be to exclude the pathogen from all phases of potato production. Successful management of ring rot dictates the exclusive use of disease-free, certified seed potatoes. In addition, a strict sanitation program aimed at eliminating ring rot bacteria from all production surfaces must be maintained.

> ## Successful management of ring rot dictates the exclusive use of disease-free, certified seed potatoes and the maintenance of a strict sanitation program.

Certified seed potatoes grown in the United States and Canada are produced under regulations mandating zero tolerance for ring rot. This means that if only one plant or tuber is found with ring rot, the entire field or seed lot is not eligible for certification. An important point to keep in mind, however, is that *certification does not guarantee freedom from ring rot, but only that the disease has not been found in systematic inspections.* This regulation has been effective in minimizing the incidence of ring rot in seed potatoes throughout North America.

Certified seed potatoes should be purchased only from reputable seed growers who grow them from pathogen-tested seed stocks, preferably those derived from limited-generation programs using tissue culture. In a limited-generation program, seed lots are routinely flushed out and replaced with new pathogen-tested seed lots, so that the same seed lots are not grown year after year (Chapter 7).

Sanitation during seed handling is an important part of ring rot management. Before any seed lot is handled, all containers, tools, and implements, such as cutters, planters, graders, and diggers, should be thoroughly washed with detergent applied by a high-pressure washer (Fig. 4.1), rinsed with clean water, and then sanitized with a suitable disinfectant. Quaternary ammonium compounds, hypochlorites, polyphenolic compounds, and iodine compounds are all effective (Table 4.1). All of these, however, must be present for a minimum of 10 minutes on the surface that is being treated. Open-cell foam rubber rollers can be a significant source of contamination with the ring rot pathogen. They are extremely difficult to sanitize effectively and thus should be replaced with closed-cell types.

Because of the serious potential of ring rot, potato health managers should always be vigilant for any signs of this disease. An initial diagnosis is usually based on the characteristic foliar or tuber symptoms. Laboratory tests, however, should always be performed to confirm a diagnosis of ring rot. The Gram stain has been used for many years as an easy confirmatory test. The appearance of blue-stained cells of the correct size and shape in the exudate squeezed from a suspect stem or tuber is regarded as a positive test. In the last decade, serological assays (immunofluorescence, double diffusion, enzyme-linked immunosorbent assay, and latex agglutination) have become standard as conclusive tests for the ring rot pathogen. Pathogenicity tests with eggplant are sometimes employed.

> ## Seed lots known to be contaminated with the ring rot pathogen should never be planted.

Seed lots known to be contaminated with the ring rot pathogen should never be planted. Each U.S. state and Canadian province involved in seed potato certification has rules and regulations regarding the disposition of seed lots from farms where ring rot has been found. It is recommended that seed lots exposed to the disease not be used for seed but rather be sold through commercial markets.

If ring rot is confirmed to be present on any commercial potato farm, a thorough cleanup must be undertaken to reduce the risk of carrying the pathogen over into next year's crop. All infected tubers should be disposed of as soon as possible. It is prudent to delay harvest of fields known to be infested in order to allow infected tubers to decay in the field rather than be brought into storage. Fields with a high incidence of ring rot should not be harvested at all. Marketable tubers harvested from infested fields should be moved through acceptable market channels as quickly as possible. Cull tubers should be burned, taken to a commercial landfill, or spread thinly on the surface of nonproduction fields, if several cycles of freezing and thawing are certain to occur.

Commercial fields in which less than 5% of the plants are known to have ring rot can usually be harvested and the tubers stored and marketed with few problems. Actual disease incidence should be determined by competent professionals and laboratory testing. An integrated management approach involving delayed harvest, careful grading to remove any decayed tubers when the crop is placed in storage, and proper storage management can make a commercial crop with a low level of ring rot manageable with little economic impact.

After all stored tubers have been removed from the farm, crop and soil debris should be scraped from the surfaces of all potato-handling equipment and storages. All production surfaces should then be further cleaned with a strong detergent in hot water (above 100° F) applied by a high-pressure washer. This process should effectively remove all organic debris from equipment and storage surfaces, to prepare them for being sanitized. Details on chemical disinfectants and sanitizing procedures are discussed in Chapter 4.

After the occurrence of ring rot has been confirmed, potatoes should not be planted for two seasons in any field in which the disease has occurred. Strict control of volunteer potato plants in these fields is necessary to ensure the elimination of the pathogen.

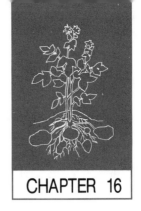

CHAPTER 16

Walter R. Stevenson
Department of Plant Pathology
University of Wisconsin, Madison

Management of Early Blight and Late Blight

Early blight and late blight are major foliar diseases of potato that pose significant risks to field productivity and later to the stored crop. Both diseases can limit yield, tuber quality, tuber size, tuber dry matter content, and crop marketability. In some areas, depending on environmental conditions and fungicide requirements, expenses for the control of these two diseases alone exceed 10% of total production costs. Growers must periodically assess the production risks associated with early blight and late blight and adjust their management decisions accordingly.

In some respects *early blight* and *late blight* are misnomers, which may lead to confusion about when these diseases occur. Early blight is usually first observed during the middle of the growing season, and late blight often appears near the end of the season. However, it is not uncommon in some areas for late blight to occur prior to flowering and for early blight to occur only after vines have begun to senesce. The timing of these diseases and associated crop losses vary regionally, with yearly weather patterns, and with the effectiveness of control measures instituted by potato health managers.

Early Blight

Although early blight occurs in most production areas to some degree every year, the disease has a significant effect on yield only when frequent wetting of the foliage (by rainfall, fog, dew, or irrigation) favors early and rapid symptom development. Under these conditions, yields may be reduced by 20–30% if protectant fungicides are not applied. Losses on fungicide-treated acreage usually do not exceed 5%. During years with infrequent rainfall and dew, disease progress is slowed, and the impact on yield is insignificant. In eastern North America, both foliar and tuber infections are important, but in the West (especially the Rocky Mountain production areas) tuber infection is of greater economic importance than foliar infection.

Symptoms

Foliar symptoms of early blight first appear as small (1/16 inch in diameter or less), circular, dark brown spots on the lower (older) leaves. As these spots enlarge to 3/8 inch in diameter (in rare cases up to 1/2 inch), they become restricted by leaf veins and take on an angular shape (Plate 50). The surface of leaf lesions is characterized by a series of dark concentric rings, for which they are known as target spot or bull's-eye lesions (Plate 51). A narrow band of chlorotic tissue often surrounds each lesion, and extensive chlorosis of infected foliage develops with time. Elongate brown or black lesions may also form on stems and petioles. The lesions are generally largest on the lower leaves. Numerous small lesions may pepper the upper leaves by the end of the season. As the disease progresses, leaf lesions enlarge and may join together. Severely infected leaves eventually wither and die but usually remain attached to the plant. Premature loss of healthy foliage due to early blight may result in smaller tubers and lower dry matter content.

Early blight lesions on tubers are circular to irregular in shape, slightly sunken, and often surrounded by a raised purple to dark brown border (Plate 52). The underlying tissues are leathery to corky in texture, dry, and usually dark brown. These lesions reduce the quality and marketability of tubers and are most troublesome on white- and red-skinned cultivars used for chip processing.

The Pathogen and Disease Development

Early blight is caused by the fungus *Alternaria solani*. This pathogen survives between cropping seasons as spores and mycelia in infested plant debris and soil and in potato tubers and other solanaceous crops and weeds, such as hairy nightshade (*Solanum sarrachoides*). These overwintering stages of *A. solani* can withstand a wide range of environmental conditions. In spring, the fungus produces spores that serve as primary inoculum to initiate the disease. Plants grown in fields where potatoes were infected with early blight during the previous season are the most liable to infection, since large quantities of overwintering inoculum are likely to be present from the previous crop. The inoculum is readily moved within and between fields, as the spores are easily carried by air currents, windblown soil, splashing rain, and irrigation water.

Spores of *A. solani* are produced on potato plants and plant debris within a temperature range of 41–86°F (the optimum is 68°F). Alternating wet and dry periods with temperatures in this range favor spore formation. Few spores are produced on leaves that are continually wet or dry. The dissemination of inoculum follows a diurnal pattern in which the number of airborne spores increases as leaves that are wet with dew dry off and wind speeds increase. The number of airborne spores peaks in the morning and declines in late afternoon and at night.

Spores landing on susceptible leaves germinate and penetrate tissues directly through the epidermis, through stomata, and through wounds such as those caused by sand abrasion, mechanical injury, or insect feeding. Free moisture (from rain, irrigation, fog, or dew) and favorable temperatures are required for infection, but fewer hours of leaf wetness are required at higher temperatures (for example, infection occurs after 12 hours at 50°F but after only 8 hours at 59°F).

Many cycles of early blight can occur within one growing season. Secondary spread of the pathogen begins when spores are produced on foliar lesions and carried to neighboring leaves and plants. This process is favored by alternating wet and dry conditions with long periods of high relative humidity and leaf wetness. The secondary spread of *A. solani* can be confirmed by trapping airborne spores with sticky spore traps. Early in the growing season the disease develops slowly, but the rate of spread of the pathogen increases after flowering and can be quite rapid later in the season, when early blight lesions are often found on most foliage of unprotected plants.

The pathogen penetrates tubers through lenticels and mechanical injuries to the skin, and infection requires free moisture. Tubers often become contaminated with spores of the pathogen during harvest. Viable spores may have accumulated on the soil surface or are dislodged from dead vines. Infection is most common in immature tubers and those of white- and red-skinned cultivars, since they are highly susceptible to abrasion during harvest. Coarse-textured soil and wet harvest conditions also favor infection. Lesions may continue to develop in storage, and infected tubers may shrivel, depending on storage conditions and disease severity. Early blight lesions on tubers, unlike late blight lesions, are usually not sites of secondary infection by other decay organisms.

Late Blight

Late blight is one of the most devastating diseases of potato worldwide. It is a limiting factor in potato cultivation in many developing countries and was responsible for the infamous Irish Potato Famine of the 1840s. In uncontrolled late blight epidemics, losses can reach 100%, particularly when extensive tuber infection and subsequent deterioration occur in storage.

Late blight is most serious where the weather is consistently cool and rainy in late summer and fall. In North America, the disease is of particular concern in eastern production areas. In the northeastern states and the Canadian Maritime provinces, temperature and moisture conditions generally favor late blight, and the disease is present nearly every year. In the North Central states and provinces, late blight occurs sporadically, depending on seasonal weather patterns. It has generally not been a significant disease in production areas in western North America, except in some valleys west of the Cascade Mountains, along the Pacific coast. In recent years, however, epidemics of late blight have developed on occasion in crops under center-pivot irrigation in arid production areas of the Pacific Northwest.

Symptoms

Symptoms of late blight appear on leaves as pale green, water-soaked spots, often beginning at the leaf tips or edges. The circular or irregularly shaped lesions are often surrounded by a pale yellowish green border that merges with the healthy tissue. The lesions enlarge rapidly and turn brown or purplish black. During periods of high relative humidity and leaf wetness, they may be bordered by a cottonlike white mold growth on the underside of the leaf (Plate 53). In dry weather, infected leaf tissues turn brown and quickly dry up (Plate 54). Infected stems and petioles turn brown to black, and entire vines may be killed and blackened in a short time when damp

weather persists. Decaying vines may be recognized by the foul odor characteristic of rapidly dying potato foliage.

Infection of tubers results in a shallow, coppery brown dry rot that spreads irregularly from the surface through the outer $1/8$ to $1/2$ inch of tissues (Plate 55). The boundary between healthy and diseased tissue is not well defined and may vary in depth in parts of an individual lesion. On the tuber surface, lesions appear brown, dry, and sunken, while tissues immediately beneath them appear granular and tan to copper brown. When tubers are stored under cool, dry conditions, lesion development is retarded, and lesions may become slightly sunken and desiccated during prolonged storage. Late blight lesions on tubers frequently become infected by various bacteria and fungi, which often cause a slimy, secondary breakdown of the tissues.

The Pathogen and Disease Development

Late blight is caused by the fungus *Phytophthora infestans*. In North America, the late blight fungus does not survive outside a living host plant for more than a few days. This major limitation in its life cycle is exploited in all late blight management strategies. Because of this characteristic, the fungus survives between potato crops mainly in infected potato tubers. These may be infected seed tubers, infected tubers that were removed during grading and dumped outdoors in cull piles, or unharvested infected tubers that were left in the field.

Whatever the source of infected tubers, if they survive the winter and then sprout the following spring, the late blight

> In North America, the late blight fungus does not survive outside a living host plant for more than a few days. This major limitation in its life cycle is exploited in all late blight management strategies.

pathogen can grow systemically from the tubers into the newly forming stems and leaves. Under cool, moist conditions, the fungus can form spores on the foliage of these plants. These spores (the primary inoculum) are easily dislodged and can be moved by the wind into neighboring potato fields and infect plants, thus beginning another cycle of late blight.

Besides potatoes, *P. infestans* can infect only a few other closely related solanaceous plants, including tomato, eggplant, pepper, and nightshade. These plants can serve as sources of primary inoculum, but they are generally not important in this respect in commercial potato production.

An outbreak of late blight generally follows a pattern in which the disease may take more than a year to develop fully and cause serious economic losses. It begins with a source of the pathogen. Because of the long distances over which seed potatoes are shipped and the large volume planted per acre, there is always a risk of introducing the late blight fungus into a production area on a few infected seed tubers, even in an area where the disease is not a commonly recognized problem. A combination of weather conditions favorable to late blight and lack of attention by growers to disease symptoms may result in unnoticed, sporadic late-season infection of foliage and tubers. If cull potatoes removed during grading are dumped into piles rather than buried or properly handled prior to the beginning of the next growing season, spores of the late blight fungus may be produced on sprouts from culls that survive the winter. This primary inoculum may then be widely disseminated throughout the production area, and if cool, moist weather prevails, a late blight epidemic can develop. Unless growers react quickly with intensive use of fungicides, losses can be high. This scenario is most obvious in areas where late blight is only a sporadic threat. In areas where weather conditions favor the disease almost every year, this pattern may be masked by a series of overlapping epidemics resulting from several sources of inoculum.

> **Because of the long distances over which seed potatoes are shipped and the large volume planted per acre, there is always a risk of introducing the late blight fungus into a production area on a few infected seed tubers.**

P. infestans is most active during periods of cool, moist weather. Cool nights and warm days accompanied by fog or rain are ideal conditions for late blight. The pathogen commonly infects potato leaves directly, by penetrating the epidermis, but occasionally enters through stomata to cause infection. Under favorable conditions, lesions may appear on leaves 3–5 days after infection, and spores begin to form in

lesions on the undersides of leaves soon thereafter. The spores are spread from leaf to leaf and plant to plant by irrigation, rain, heavy dew, and even equipment. They have been carried up to 40 miles by the wind, but they are very sensitive to changes in relative humidity and die rapidly when it drops below 95%. If conditions remain favorable, the disease may progress through many cycles during a growing season (Box 16.1).

Infection of tubers by the late blight fungus arises from spores that develop on foliage. Tubers exposed by soil cracking or erosion of hills may come in contact with spores washed down from infected leaves and stems by rainfall or irrigation. Tubers infected during the growing season may partially decay before harvest. Tubers may also become infected at harvest when they contact viable spores remaining on infected vines. Little if any tuber-to-tuber spread of late blight occurs in storage if proper storage management practices are followed.

Management Strategies for Early Blight and Late Blight

An effective blight management program is an essential part of holistic potato health management in most production locations. Management of early blight and late blight requires an integrated program of cultural procedures designed to minimize sources of the pathogens and the development of these diseases in the crop. This includes important preplant decisions, appropriate management strategies during crop

---

Box 16.1

The Key Role of Temperature in the Development of Late Blight

Understanding the effects of temperature on the germination of spores of *Phytophthora infestans* is necessary in order to fully appreciate the role of temperature in the development of late blight. Spores of the late blight fungus (properly called sporangia) are formed on the undersides of infected leaves at relative humidities above 90%, within a temperature range of 37–79°F (the optimum range is 64–72°F). Sporangia germinate by two different methods, depending on temperature (see the illustration). Between 70 and 79°F (optimum of 77°F), they germinate directly, forming a germ tube that penetrates host tissues. Below 65°F (optimum of 54°F), the contents of each sporangium divide into six to eight swimming spores, called zoospores, which escape through a hole in the end of the sporangium. Zoospores are very sensitive to drying, but they move freely in any water film on the plant surface. Eventually, they settle down and then germinate and penetrate host tissues. The optimum temperature range for zoospore germination is 54–59°F. Once host tissues have become infected, the optimum for fungal growth within the host is 64–70°F. Temperatures above 86°F are unfavorable for disease development, although the pathogen may survive higher temperatures.

The significance of these two methods of germination in the epidemiology of late blight is that when temperatures are in the 70s, each sporangium germinates directly and thus can cause only one infection. However, when temperatures drop below 65°F, the six to eight zoospores released

from each sporangium are each infective, thus potentially causing six to eight separate infections.

Ideal conditions for a late blight epidemic are night temperatures of 50–60°F along with fog, rain, or heavy dew and day temperatures of 60–70°F for four or five consecutive days. Under these conditions, late blight can "explode" and cause extensive damage in a very short time.

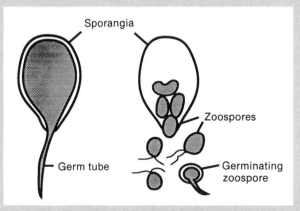

Sporangia of the late blight fungus, *Phytophthora infestans*, germinate directly (left) at temperatures of 70–79°F or by forming swimming zoospores (right) at lower temperatures. (Drawing by Cindy Gray)

growth, and careful harvest procedures. The application of foliar fungicides is usually a critical component of integrated management programs for early blight and late blight.

Preplant Management Decisions

Cultivar Selection. Selecting a cultivar with the highest level of available disease resistance that is compatible with marketing needs is an important part of any integrated disease management program. This can affect the selection of an appropriate fungicide. It may also significantly reduce the rate or the number of fungicide applications needed for successful control, thus lowering total management costs. Some cultivars can be harvested when the weather generally does not favor the development of early blight or late blight or before problems with these diseases have progressed to the point of affecting yield or quality. The total amount of fungicide applied can be reduced by using these cultivars, and in some locations they can be grown without fungicides.

Because early blight is most prevalent on lower, older leaves that are beginning to senesce, the disease generally progresses faster on early-maturing cultivars than on late-maturing ones. However, differences in foliage susceptibility to the early blight pathogen occur within each maturity class (Fig. 16.1).

No cultivar is immune to all races of the late blight pathogen, but several possess resistance to the common race 0 as well as some other races (Fig. 16.2). Some cultivars have sufficient resistance to slow the development of late blight, depending on the races of the pathogen that are present.

The selection of potato cultivars is discussed further in Chapter 3.

Field Selection. Select fields with good drainage and fertility that will promote overall crop health. Fields bordered by trees and other natural obstructions to air movement make control of foliar blights more difficult and should be avoided, as should small, irregularly shaped fields that are difficult to spray with fungicides. If aerial application of fungicides is planned, it

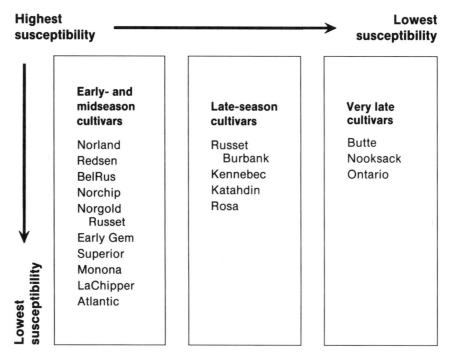

Fig. 16.1. Susceptibility of some potato cultivars to early blight.

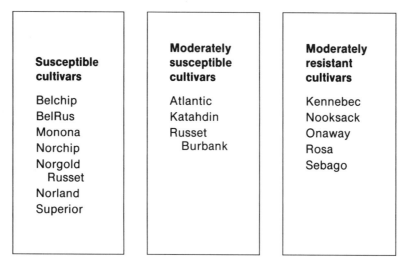

Fig. 16.2. Susceptibility of some potato cultivars to late blight.

is especially important to avoid fields with bordering trees or power lines.

Select fields that have been out of potato production for at least 2–3 years. Long rotations with cereals or legumes minimize the amount of overwintering inoculum of the early blight fungus from previous crops.

If potato early dying has been a problem at a potential production site, soil samples should be collected and assayed for populations of plant-parasitic nematodes and the fungus *Verticillium dahliae*. Infection by these pests stress a potato crop and may increase the susceptibility of the plants to early blight. Ideally, soil assays should be completed the summer before the intended planting, so that appropriate steps can be taken if soil populations of these pathogens warrant (Chapters 17 and 18).

Elimination of Overwintering Inoculum. Potential sources of overwintering inoculum of the pathogens causing early blight and late blight should be identified and destroyed or controlled before the new crop is planted, and definitely before it emerges. These sources include cull piles, volunteer potatoes, alternate weed hosts, and potato debris from a previous crop left on the surface of the field.

Only certified seed tubers should be planted. This is important in order to minimize the risk of bringing new inoculum of the late blight fungus into the production area and may help reduce the need for fungicides and other pesticides. Tips for choosing a healthy seed lot are given in Chapter 3.

Improper disposal of cull potatoes is often a major factor in initiating late blight epidemics.

Improper disposal of cull potatoes is often a major factor in initiating late blight epidemics. Blighted tubers that survive the winter and sprout the following spring are a major source of spores. Blighted potatoes should not be dumped into cull piles, because some of them will be protected from freezing and survive the winter. The safest method of disposal is to spread cull potatoes sparingly during the winter months on the surface of fields not intended for potato culture the following spring, where they are exposed to several cycles of freezing and thawing. Alternative methods are to haul culls to a commercial landfill or bury them on-site at least 3 feet deep. Feeding culls to livestock may be appropriate as long as the tubers are completely consumed and manure is not returned to fields used for potato production. Existing cull piles should be destroyed by burning or burying, or at least by treatment with a general herbicide to prevent any sprout formation. Tubers remaining on the surface of the field after harvest should be left to freeze and not disked or plowed under. Tubers that are disked or plowed under often survive the winter. Destruction of volunteer potatoes in the spring is also important in minimizing sources of primary inoculum.

Management During Crop Growth

Disease and Pest Control. Plants that are stressed by other diseases, such as early dying, Rhizoctonia stem canker, plant-parasitic nematodes, and seed piece decay, are more susceptible to early blight than healthy plants. Likewise, the stress associated with insect feeding, especially by Colorado potato beetles and leafhoppers, promotes the development of early blight. In addition, these pests may also play a role in local dissemination of inoculum. Weeds increase crop stress by competing for space, light, nutrients, and water. Excessive weed growth may also reduce air movement over the crop canopy, prolonging the duration of leaf wetness and thus favoring the forma-tion of spores, spore germination, and infection by both the early blight and the late blight pathogens. Hilling helps to control weeds early in the season and covers the developing tubers with sufficient soil to minimize infection later in the season by spores that are washed down from the foliage.

Plants that are stressed by other diseases are more susceptible to early blight than healthy plants.

Fertilization. Host nutrition has a great effect on the development of early blight. Deficiencies of nitrogen and phosphorus increase susceptibility to this disease. Overfertilization with nitrogen, however, stimulates excessive vegetative growth, delays maturity, and reduces yield. Thus a balance in fertility must be reached, in which sufficient nitrogen is provided to satisfy the demands of the crop without delaying maturity or enhancing susceptibility to early blight. Petiole analysis for nitrate content may be useful in monitoring the crop's needs and making adjustments in fertilization rates (Chapter 9).

Irrigation. Irrigation plays a key role in the development of both early blight and late blight. Sprinkler irrigation periodically wets foliage and, along with rainfall and frequent dews, creates the alternating wet and dry periods favorable for early blight. Overhead irrigation in arid areas increases the likelihood of both diseases and thus the need for fungicides. Excessive irrigation can erode hills, thus exposing shallow-set tubers to infection. In addition, excessive irrigation, which provides more water than is lost through evapotranspiration, removes nitrates from the root zone of the crop, as does rainfall heavy enough to cause runoff or soil leaching (Box 9.2). Nitrogen deficiency severe enough to cause premature senescence of potato plants increases their susceptibility to early blight and the difficulty of controlling the spread of the disease. The depletion of nitrate in the root zone depends to a large extent on soil characteristics. On sandy soils with low organic matter content, several inches of rainfall in a short time can often lead to problems with early blight as a result of nitrate leaching. Relationships between water management and early blight are discussed further in Chapter 8.

The duration of periods of uninterrupted leaf wetness is a critical factor in successful infection by the late blight fungus. To minimize the length of time during which foliage remains wet each night, it is important for it to be allowed to dry prior to dew formation and to dry as quickly as possible in the morning. Timing overhead irrigations to allow for drying before evening and adequate weed control to facilitate good air movement through the crop both help to minimize leaf wetness and thus the duration of potential infection periods.

Monitoring Blight Development. Routine scouting of potato fields for early blight and late blight increases the likelihood of identifying disease problems before they are beyond control and provides information on the effectiveness of current management practices. Scouting should begin just before crop emergence, to check for sites where overwintering inoculum might be present. After emergence, scouts should visit each field at least weekly until harvest, to evaluate crop and disease development at representative sites throughout the field. They should give special attention to areas most prone to disease development—so-called blight pockets, where blight is likely to appear first. These are usually near windbreaks, woodlots, or other obstructions to air movement, where plants tend to dry out more slowly; near the center of pivot irrigation systems; and near bodies of water, such as farm ponds and streams. Areas of fields where fungicide application is difficult (such as areas beneath power lines, next to utility poles, or next to highways and residential properties) should also receive special attention.

Disease Prediction Programs. Several disease prediction programs have been devised that can help scouts and crop managers determine if weather conditions have been favorable for disease development and when foliar blights are likely to appear. Some are based on weather data (temperature, humidity, and amounts of rainfall and irrigation) collected with a rain gauge and a hygrothermograph placed in the field (Fig. 16.3) and then entered into a microcomputer. Others use self-contained data-collecting and forecasting equipment situated in the field.

A simple degree-day model was developed in Colorado to predict the appearance of the first lesions of early blight. Degree-days are calculated from emergence, with a base temperature of 45° F. The first early blight lesions are observed at 650 degree-days in the San Luis Valley (a high mountain valley) and at 1,125 degree-days in north central Colorado. With this system, fungicide spray programs are initiated at these degree-day thresholds.

> **Routine scouting of potato fields for blight increases the likelihood of identifying problems before they are beyond control and provides information on the effectiveness of current management practices.**

Another predictive model for early blight, developed in Wisconsin, predicts the first seasonal rise in the number of airborne spores of *A. solani* based on the accumulation of 300 physiological days (a type of degree-day unit, referred to as P-days) from emergence. Application of fungicides is initiated at 300 P-days, and subsequent spray recommendations are based on P-day accumulation plus data on daily temperature, relative humidity, rainfall, and irrigation.

Either of these programs should be tested on small acreages before implementation in other areas. Predictive programs for early blight are especially useful in deciding when to begin applying fungicides in areas where early blight is the primary foliar disease and late blight is rare. Significant savings in spray costs for early blight control can be achieved by delaying fungicide applications until just prior to the predicted rise in airborne inoculum.

Several systems for forecasting late blight have also been devised. These include the Hyre system (based on temperature and rainfall), the Wallin system (based on temperature and humidity), and the BLITECAST system, developed in Pennsylvania, which integrates the Hyre and Wallin systems into a computer program. BLITECAST forecasts disease development on the basis of temperature, the duration of periods of relative humidity above 90%, and rainfall during the previous week. Guidelines for scheduling protectant fungicide sprays to control late blight are then given to growers. Since disease forecasts and spray recommendations made by current forecasting programs are based on historical data, there is an assumed risk on the part of the grower who uses these programs.

Forecasting systems for both foliar blights have been incorporated into integrated programs for use on microcomputers (such as POTATO CROP MANAGEMENT, developed in Wisconsin) and self-contained units available commercially from several companies. Disease-predictive systems for early blight or late blight may result in improved control, fewer fungicide applications, and less total fungicide applied. Successful use of these systems depends on sound management by all the growers in a locality.

Fungicides. Although the cultural management program described above minimizes the development of early blight and late blight, fungicide applications are usually still necessary in most production areas. Several protectant fungicides, such as chlorothalonil and mancozeb, are labeled for control of both of these diseases. To be effective, protectant materials must be applied before infection and must be reapplied regularly during the season as the plants grow. Complete coverage of all potato foliage is the key to successful use of protectant fungicides.

The number of fungicide applications required for control varies regionally. Growers in the West usually make only one to three applications per year, but it is not uncommon for growers in the central and eastern production areas to make eight to 10 applications on late-maturing cultivars. In spite of intensive use of protectant fungicides for the past 40 years, strains of the early blight and late blight pathogens resistant to these fungicides have not been detected.

The first systemic and curative fungicide for the control of late blight, metalaxyl, was introduced commercially in 1982.

Fig. 16.3. A, Rain gauge and weather shelter for a hygrothermograph situated in the canopy of a potato field. **B,** Temperature, humidity, and rainfall and irrigation data are collected and used to forecast the development of early blight and late blight. (Courtesy R. C. Rowe)

It has the advantage of being absorbed by the plant and translocated through the tissues. Metalaxyl is highly effective against *P. infestans*, but in contrast to the protectant fungicides used on potato, it is not effective against *A. solani*. When applied after infection, metalaxyl suppresses the enlargement of late blight lesions on leaves and the development of *P. infestans* spores on lesions.

Because of the very specialized activity of this fungicide, there is a risk of selecting metalaxyl-resistant strains of the late blight fungus out of the general population. Strains of *P. infestans* that cannot be controlled by metalaxyl have been found in some areas of Europe and North America. Metalaxyl is currently available in the United States in prepackaged mixtures with broad-spectrum protectant fungicides, to reduce the risk of selecting resistant strains. Growers are urged to apply these mixtures no more than twice each year according to label directions, to reduce this risk even further. Metalaxyl should never be applied alone, without a protectant fungicide.

Early detection of foliar blights through intensive scouting greatly improves control of these diseases, especially late blight. Various management options can then be considered—increase the rate of protectant fungicides, increase the frequency of application, change protectant materials, or apply a combination of a protectant and a systemic fungicide. If an outbreak of late blight is observed in or near metalaxyl-treated fields, scouts should collect samples of infected leaves for laboratory evaluation of the isolate's susceptibility or resistance to known concentrations of this fungicide.

Management During Harvest and Storage

Because the late blight fungus does not remain alive very long after the foliage dies, it is essential that the vines be *completely dead* for 2–3 weeks before harvest, to reduce the possibility of contaminating tubers with spores of the pathogen. Fungicide applications should continue until all vines are dead. Tubers should be harvested only after the skins are well set and should be handled gently to avoid abrasions, which increase the risk of infection by the early blight fungus (Chapter 6). Wherever possible, growers should avoid harvesting under wet conditions. If wet tubers are harvested, precautions must be taken to remove free moisture from their surfaces as quickly as possible. If significant blight infection is found in tubers at harvest, as many blighted tubers as possible should be graded out before the crop is placed in storage. These culls should be disposed of properly, so that they do not become a source of inoculum for the next year's crop.

Storage is difficult if a high percentage of the tubers are blighted. Storage under normal chip-stock conditions of 50–55° F and 90–95% relative humidity is nearly impossible, because these are also ideal conditions for further disease development. Contaminated tubers should be cooled to as low a temperature as is practical, preferably 38–40° F, as quickly as possible after digging. Good circulation of air through the pile must be maintained to keep the relative humidity below 85% and thus dry out infections. Blighted potatoes should not be held any longer than is absolutely necessary, as they generally do not store well.

Mary L. Powelson
Department of Botany and Plant Pathology
Oregon State University, Corvallis

Kenneth B. Johnson
Department of Botany and Plant Pathology
Oregon State University, Corvallis

Randall C. Rowe
Department of Plant Pathology
Ohio State University, Wooster

CHAPTER 17

Management of Diseases Caused by Soilborne Pathogens

Diseases caused by soilborne pathogens, most of which are fungi, pose one of the most difficult problems for the potato health manager. To a large degree, the difficulty can be attributed to the very persistent nature of these organisms, coupled with the fact that few fungicides, aside from fumigants, are effective in soil. It is difficult to limit the spread of soilborne pathogens, because they are easily moved with seed tubers, irrigation water, plant debris, windblown soil, and farm equipment. Moreover, these diseases often go unnoticed for several years, building slowly with each successive potato crop. Growers who suffer the greatest financial losses from diseases caused by soilborne pathogens are often those who produce potatoes under the most intensive management regimes and thus have invested the most in crop protection, nutrition, and in some cases irrigation.

In North America, there are many diseases of potato roots and tubers that are caused by soilborne pathogens. Those of major concern are potato early dying (also called Verticillium wilt), Sclerotinia stalk rot (also called white mold), Rhizoctonia canker (also called black scurf), pink rot, Pythium leak and seed piece decay, common scab, and Fusarium dry rot and seed piece decay. All these diseases cause significant economic losses annually, although rarely do they all cause losses in any one field in a single season. Geographic location, soil characteristics, and production practices usually favor specific diseases. For example, pink rot and Pythium leak are problems mostly in fields that are waterlogged for periods during the season because of overirrigation or poor soil drainage. Rhizoctonia canker is more severe in fine-textured soils. Common scab is more severe in coarse-textured, slightly acid, neutral, or alkaline soils than in fine-textured acidic soils. Potato early dying and Sclerotinia stalk rot are problems mostly under intensively managed irrigated cropping systems.

Successful management of diseases caused by soilborne pathogens requires a thorough understanding of each disease. Most diseases caused by soilborne fungi have a simple or mono-cyclic disease cycle, meaning that only one cycle of infection, pathogen growth, and reproduction occurs during each cropping season (Fig. 17.1). The disease cycle begins with infective propagules of the fungus (overwintering inoculum) lying dormant either in the soil or in association with seed tubers. Infection occurs during the development of the potato crop. Each of these diseases typically begins at a characteristic growth stage of potatoes. Symptoms are occasionally visible soon after infection, but they usually develop slowly as the season progresses. The fungus produces new infective propagules in or on infected plant tissues, usually as the tissues die, and these propagules either are returned to the soil during harvest and tillage operations or become associated with the tubers. This newly formed inoculum usually can survive in soil for several years in a dormant state. The cycle is completed when potatoes or another susceptible crop is planted again in the infested field, and the dormant inoculum then germinates and causes new infections.

Several strategies must be combined in a totally integrated approach in order to successfully manage this group of diseases. Two of the most important strategies involve the principles of exclusion and eradication of inoculum. Planting high-quality certified seed potatoes reduces the number of propagules of soilborne pathogens introduced into the field with the seed tubers. Practices that reduce populations of these pathogens include crop rotation, soil fumigation, and the removal or destruction of infested crop residues. Diseases caused by soilborne pathogens can be suppressed by limiting the number of successful infections or by restricting or slowing the rate of symptom development. Practices that may limit the number of infections per plant include cultivar selection, proper handling of seed tubers, shallow planting in warm soil, alteration of plant spacing and row orientation, and fungicide applications. Symptom development may be restricted or slowed by appropriate management of irrigation and fertility.

In this chapter, the important potato diseases caused by soilborne pathogens are discussed individually, together with specific management practices that are effective for each. Since potato health managers must deal with these diseases as a group, however, a totally integrated management strategy is presented at the end of the chapter.

Potato Early Dying

In fields where potatoes have been part of the production cycle for several years, a pattern of premature vine death and declining yields often develops. This syndrome, called potato early dying, limits production in many areas, especially in the North Central states, the Red River Valley, the Pacific Northwest, and Colorado.

Symptoms

Symptoms of potato early dying are difficult to distinguish from normal senescence. The disease may initially only retard the growth of infected plants. Foliar symptoms appear as uneven chlorosis and some wilting of the lower leaves (Plate 56). Areas between leaf veins turn yellow and later brown, often at the leaf tip first (Plate 57). Leaf yellowing and death proceed up the stem, which often remains erect. Wilting and yellowing occasionally affect leaflets on only one side of the petiole or leaves on only one side of the stem. A tan discoloration of the vascular tissues can usually be seen when a stem is cut in cross section near its base. Potato early dying may cause vascular discoloration at the stem end of tubers, but this symptom may also result from other causes.

Pathogens and Disease Development

The primary cause of potato early dying is the soilborne fungus *Verticillium*. Two species, *V. dahliae* and *V. albo-atrum*, are involved. They are distinguished from each other by the type of infective propagules produced on dying vines. *V. dahliae* forms tiny, nearly round, black bodies called microsclerotia, whereas *V. albo-atrum* forms dark, thickened fungal strands termed melanized hyphae. *V. dahliae* is widespread in the United States and predominates in production areas where average daily summer temperatures commonly exceed 80° F. *V. albo-atrum* grows at lower temperatures and is involved in potato early dying in production areas where average daily temperatures normally do not exceed 70° F during production, such as areas in Maine and southeastern Canada and winter production areas in Florida. Both fungi are easily isolated from infected stems or tubers.

Although *Verticillium* is the primary pathogen involved in potato early dying, co-infections with root-lesion nematodes, primarily *Pratylenchus penetrans*, have been implicated as an important part of this disease (Chapter 18). Infection of roots with both *V. dahliae* and *P. penetrans* can result in severe symptoms and markedly lower yields, even when the population densities of these pathogens in the soil are low enough that each pathogen would cause little or no damage if it were present alone.

Noninfested fields can become contaminated with *Verticillium* carried in or on the surface of seed tubers or in soil particles transported by the wind or by mechanical means. Once established in a field, the fungus can persist in the soil for many years as microsclerotia or melanized hyphae, either free or embedded in bits of plant debris. Also, because of their wide host range, the two species of *Verticillium* can maintain themselves at low populations on the roots of many symptomless crop and weed species, such as wheat and sunflower.

The dormant propagules of *Verticillium* germinate in the presence of growing roots of susceptible host plants and penetrate the outer root cells. The infection soon proceeds to the xylem (water-conducting tissue), where the fungus establishes itself. Spores are formed within this tissue and are transported in sap, and thus the fungus can achieve a systemic invasion of the plant. Symptoms of potato early dying eventually develop in infected plants. As these plants die, the fungus grows throughout all the dying tissues and forms infective propagules, either microsclerotia or melanized hyphae, which are released into the soil as the tissues decay.

The role of nematodes in potato early dying is poorly understood. Because root-lesion nematodes burrow through young root tissues and create many wounds, it has been thought that this might aid the entry of *Verticillium*. The fungus does not require wounds for entry, however, and recent studies have shown that the interaction between *Verticillium* and root-lesion nematodes varies considerably with the species of nematode and possibly with different strains of *V. dahliae*. These facts suggest that the interaction is probably more complex than simply the creation of wounds as infection sites. It may involve effects of nematode feeding on the potato that alter the plant's susceptibility to infection by *Verticillium* or facilitate more rapid invasion by the fungus.

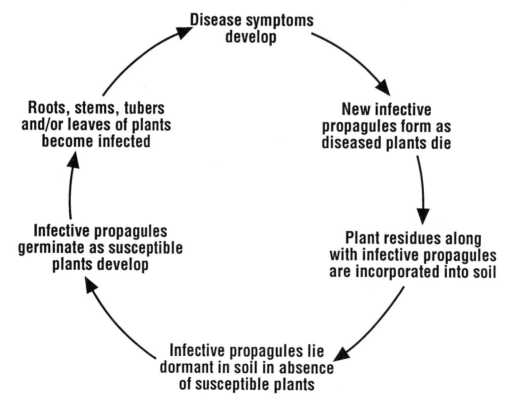

Fig. 17.1. A generalized monocyclic disease cycle, in which the pathogen has only one reproductive cycle per season. This is typical of most diseases caused by soilborne fungal pathogens. A disease cycle is the sequence of events that occurs during the development of a disease in a population of plants. In this situation, the disease cycle parallels the growth and development cycle of the crop.

Management

The amount of potato early dying that develops in a given crop depends upon the population densities of *V. dahliae* and associated pathogens, such as *P. penetrans*, in the soil at the time of planting. Population densities of *Verticillium* commonly found in soil, however, vary widely among geographic areas, being generally higher in the Pacific Northwest and much lower in the North Central states. In general, populations above 10 propagules per cubic centimeter (about 165 per cubic inch) of soil are required for significant amounts of disease to develop, and this can be considered an appropriate action threshold. Other factors, however, also affect disease development, including the susceptibility of the potato cultivar to *Verticillium* and fertility and irrigation practices.

> **Most management strategies effective against potato early dying are focused on reducing the amount of initial inoculum in the soil and thus the number of root infections by *Verticillium* and root-lesion nematodes.**

Most management strategies effective against potato early dying are focused on reducing the amount of initial inoculum in the soil and thus the number of root infections by *Verticillium* and root-lesion nematodes. Crop rotation has long been regarded as an important method for managing populations of soilborne pathogens. Inoculum of *Verticillium*, however, particularly that of *V. dahliae*, is relatively persistent in soil, and root-lesion nematodes have a wide host range among potential rotational crops. Short-term rotations of 2 or 3 years are useful as part of a total management scheme for potato early dying only in fields where the population density of *Verticillium* is near the action threshold. Crop rotation is always a valid potato health management practice for many other reasons, but its value and practicality in managing potato early dying are lessened in fields where the population density of *V. dahliae* greatly exceeds the action threshold at the beginning of a rotation.

Several soil fumigants have been widely used to control potato early dying. Metham sodium products applied through sprinkler irrigation systems are effective in many areas with coarse-textured soils. Where potatoes are grown in fine-textured soils or in areas where the crop is not sprinkler-irrigated or where sprinkler-applied fumigants are not acceptable, metham sodium or other fumigants such as 1,3-dichloropropene (1,3-D) with chloropicrin can be shank-injected, if this practice fits into the overall crop management system. Nonfumigant nematicides applied in-furrow at planting effectively suppress potato early dying in some locations. These materials primarily affect the nematode component of the disease and have no direct effect on *Verticillium*.

Soil fumigants control the disease by reducing the initial population density of *Verticillium* or root-lesion nematodes (or both). They do not completely eradicate these pathogens from infested fields, and economically damaging populations of *Verticillium* and root-lesion nematodes usually redevelop after one or two potato crops. Because soil fumigation is expensive and can have unwanted side effects (Chapter 2), the decision to fumigate should be based on an accurate diagnosis of the problem, the crop history, and perhaps an assay of the soil to determine the population of *Verticillium* and identify the species of root-lesion nematodes present. Some crop consultants and plant diagnostic clinics provide services that measure *Verticillium* and nematode population densities in a given field and can advise growers on management options.

In conjunction with practices that reduce the population densities of the early dying pathogens in soil, other management strategies focus on minimizing stresses on the crop in order to promote uniform and continuous plant growth. A balanced fertility program based on soil and foliar analyses helps maximize yield despite the presence of potato early dying in the field. Manipulating the amount of irrigation water applied can also limit the severity of the disease. Avoiding overirrigation or even keeping soils a little dry early in the season (through growth stage II) may reduce the amount of root infection by *V. dahliae*. On the other hand, carefully avoiding any plant water stress during growth stage IV, when tubers are bulking, which usually coincides with the warmest part of the season, may help decrease the severity of the disease.

If soil fumigation or a long crop rotation are not feasible and a summer fresh market exists, production in fields infested with the early dying pathogens can be maximized by planting moderately resistant cultivars and harvesting the crop before maturity. This practice is effective because potato early dying affects yield mostly at full crop maturity, when infection and symptom expression have had maximum time to develop. Another benefit is that potato crops killed early and harvested for fresh or seed markets do not contribute as much new inoculum to the soil as do late-season crops grown to maturity.

Planting resistant cultivars is ultimately the most practical method for management of potato early dying. Potato cultivars that are currently available differ considerably in their susceptibility to *Verticillium* (Fig. 17.2). Those with the greatest resistance, however, are presently not widely used in commercial production.

Even as resistant cultivars with improved horticultural qualities become available, control of potato early dying will continue to rely on an integrated management approach. Improved systems for predicting potential production losses due to this disease in a given field are being developed. In the future, these systems will be coupled with sound management programs for potato early dying that include appropriate cultivar and site selection, optimal irrigation and nutritional management, crop rotation, and in some situations soil fumigation.

Sclerotinia Stalk Rot

Sclerotinia stalk rot, also called white mold, occurs in most temperate areas where potatoes are grown. It is a serious problem in Maine, Florida, and the Pacific Northwest. This disease has become increasingly important where production practices include sprinkler irrigation and high nitrogen fertility. These practices promote lush, dense canopies of foliage, which maintain high relative humidity or free moisture for long periods—environmental factors that favor the development of the disease.

Symptoms

Sclerotinia stalk rot is usually first noticed by the presence of individual wilted plants within a canopy of otherwise healthy-looking plants. Closer inspection of the wilted plants reveals soft, watery lesions on the main stem near the soil line and on lateral branches that contact the soil. As these lesions dry out, they turn a bleached beige or tan (Plate 58). Under humid conditions, lesions may expand and eventually girdle the stem, causing the plant to wilt. White mold growth (Plate 59) and hardened, black, irregularly shaped fungal structures called sclerotia (Plate 60) commonly develop on or in decaying stems.

The Pathogen and Disease Development

The fungus that causes this disease, *Sclerotinia sclerotiorum*, can easily be identified on infected potato stems in the field. Under warm, moist conditions it forms a white cotton candy–like mold, usually accompanied by the black sclerotia, which most commonly develop in the hollowed-out centers of infected stems. Sclerotia generally range from ¼ to ½ inch in diameter.

Sclerotia survive in the soil for several years between susceptible crops. Those lying within 1–2 inches of the soil surface usually germinate when the crop canopy shades the surface and soil moisture remains high for several days. If enough moisture and organic matter are available, they can germinate directly to form a mat of white mold. In most production regions, however, small, funnel-shaped, mushroomlike structures called apothecia develop from sclerotia. Apothecia are produced over a period of 2–8 weeks, usually beginning at row closure, and eject windborne spores called ascospores.

Healthy, vigorous foliage is usually not infected directly by ascospores, but rather they germinate and colonize dead or dying tissues, usually from leaves or blossoms. From this food base, the fungus can then penetrate healthy potato tissue that is in direct contact with colonized tissues, causing the typical water-soaked lesions and then often forming a mat of white mold growth. As infected stems decay, new sclerotia are formed in the expanding lesions. These new sclerotia are returned to the soil following the decomposition of decayed plant material, and they can survive there for at least 3 years.

Sclerotinia can attack many broad-leaved crops and weeds, and it can grow on residues of several nonhost crops in wet, mild winter and spring weather.

Management

Foliar fungicides, crop rotation, and modification of the crop microenvironment are ways to limit Sclerotinia stalk rot. In production areas with severe disease pressure, control is achieved mainly by the application of protectant fungicides. In some areas, ascospores are discharged only within a short period, and thus a single fungicide application at row closure may be sufficient. In areas where ascospores are discharged over an extended period, however, repeated applications may be necessary, beginning at row closure.

Crop rotation with cereals or grasses for four or more years limits the incidence of Sclerotinia stalk rot. Rotation is of little value, however, in production areas where fields are planted every other year with potatoes or other susceptible broad-leaved crops, particularly dry beans or sunflowers.

Knowledge of the effects of irrigation on disease development has enabled some growers to manage irrigation timing to avoid stimulating this disease. Light, frequent irrigation of coarse-textured soils and heavy, less frequent irrigation of fine-textured soils both encourage dense canopy growth and long periods of leaf wetness or high relative humidity within the canopy. These conditions favor the production of apothecia, the germination of ascospores, and subsequent infection. Because ascospores are produced over a 2- to 8-week period beginning at row closure, alterations in irrigation frequency or duration must be made during this period to be effective in disease management. Care must be taken in restricting irrigation during this period, however, because plant water stress may lead to high numbers of malformed tubers and lowered yields, making this practice unworkable in production areas with a high water-use demand.

Susceptible cultivars	Moderately resistant cultivars	Resistant cultivars
BelRus	Allegany	Abnaki
Butte	Atlantic	Century Russet
Hilite Russet	Centennial Russet	Desiree
Irish Cobbler	Frontier Russet	Elba
Kanona	Hampton	Gemchip
Kennebec	Katahdin	Ranger Russet
Lemhi Russet	MaineChip	Reddale
Norgold Russet	Monona	Rideau
Onaway	Norchip	Russette
Russet Norkotah	NorKing Russet	Targhee
Sangre	Portage	
Shepody	Prestile	
Superior	Russet Burbank	
Viking	Russet Nugget	
White Rose		

Fig. 17.2. Susceptibility of some potato cultivars to *Verticillium*. Cultivar response to this pathogen is related to the maturity type and varies somewhat both regionally and seasonally. The placement of cultivars in the categories shown here is based on several published sources as well as the opinions of several authorities. Local advisors should be consulted for information on how particular cultivars might react in a particular production area.

Changing the canopy environment to reduce the duration of leaf wetness may be a useful management tactic in some production areas. One approach is to orient potato rows parallel with the direction of the prevailing winds. Planting cultivars that do not produce extensive vines or cultivars that have an upright growth habit may be of value in regions with a history of severe disease. Another alternative is to stop irrigation in early afternoon, to allow the plants to dry before evening.

Rhizoctonia Canker

Rhizoctonia stem and stolon canker, also called black scurf, can delay emergence, reduce stands, and in extreme cases limit yields. Equally important, however, is that crops severely affected by the *Rhizoctonia* fungus often produce a high percentage of tubers that are misshapen, cracked, nonuniformly sized, or discolored by sclerotia on their surfaces. Poor stands are produced when cankers form on emerging sprouts, and the problem is particularly severe when emergence and early crop development are retarded by cold, wet conditions, especially in fine-textured soils. The stolon canker phase of the disease develops during early tuber initiation, when young tubers can actually be "pruned off" by the pathogen.

Rhizoctonia canker occurs wherever potatoes are grown, but the disease is economically most important in the north central and northeastern United States and in southeastern Canada. Some western production areas are also affected, but the damage is usually limited to a decline in tuber quality.

Symptoms

Brownish black, sunken lesions on underground stems and stolons are characteristic of Rhizoctonia canker (Plate 61). The disease may cause nonuniform stands and weak, spindly-looking or late-emerging plants. Sprouts attacked before emergence are often killed, which leads to delayed emergence by weaker sprouts. Infected sprouts that do emerge often remain stunted. Early-season infections often result in the pruning of very young stolons where lesions girdle them completely. Lesions on more-developed stolons may cause malformation and abortion of developing tubers. Deep, sunken cankers may girdle main stems, causing yellowing, purpling, upward curling of leaves, and the formation of aerial tubers. These symptoms can be confused with those of purple top (Chapter 14 and Plates 39 and 40).

During midseason in the high-humidity environment under a dense canopy of foliage, the *Rhizoctonia* fungus may develop into its sexual phase (*Thanatephorus cucumeris*), which forms a white, powdery mold growth on stems, extending just above the soil line (Plate 62). This is often associated with typical dark brown stem lesions belowground. The fungus forms individual sclerotia or masses of sclerotia on mature tubers. These vary in appearance, from dark, netted or scurfy residues on tuber surfaces to individual black masses ranging from pinhead- to pea-sized (Plate 63). Growers often refer to *Rhizoctonia* sclerotia as "the dirt that won't wash off." Russeting or surface cracking of tubers has also been associated with this disease.

The Pathogen and Disease Development

Rhizoctonia canker is caused by the soilborne fungus *Rhizoctonia solani*. There are several strains of this fungus, and the one that attacks potato (usually anastomosis group 3, referred to as AG-3) is often well established in most fields used for potato production. *Rhizoctonia* causes diseases of a wide variety of crops, but the strains found in association with potato generally do not attack and reproduce on other plant species. Weeds and crop plants closely related to potato,

such as black nightshade, jimsonweed, tomato, and eggplant, are possible exceptions.

The fungus survives in soil as mycelium associated with decomposing plant residues. In addition, the sclerotia can survive on infected tubers and can persist free in soils for extended periods. Field populations of *R. solani* often decline in the absence of susceptible host plants, but survival rates may vary among different soil types. The acute phase of the disease, in which emerging sprouts are attacked, is usually caused by inoculum carried on seed tubers. The chronic phase, resulting in stem cankers, stolon infections, and the formation of sclerotia on tubers, usually develops when these tissues grow in proximity to inoculum in the soil. Cool (55–60°F), moist soils are optimal for infection. The fungus can penetrate tissues directly and form typical *Rhizoctonia* lesions. Once green leaves develop on sprouts, stem tissues are much less susceptible to infection. Sclerotia form on the surfaces of mature tubers under cool, moist conditions, generally after vine senescence has begun.

Management

An integrated approach must be used in the management of Rhizoctonia canker, as no single practice is effective. Both a proper crop rotation and the planting of seed tubers free of *Rhizoctonia* sclerotia are necessary to reduce the initial amount of inoculum of the pathogen. *Rhizoctonia*-free seed tubers are particularly important, because tuber-borne inoculum is most likely to result in serious sprout infection. Planting seed potatoes with *Rhizoctonia* sclerotia covering as little as 5% of the tuber surface often leads to serious damage. Rotation out of potatoes for 2 or 3 years, preferably to grasses or cereals, can reduce disease incidence. Growing sugar beets just prior to a crop of potatoes tends to increase problems with Rhizoctonia canker.

> **Because potato stems are much less susceptible to attack by *Rhizoctonia* after green tissue has developed following emergence, any practice favoring rapid emergence is useful in disease management.**

Because potato stems are much less susceptible to attack by *Rhizoctonia* after green tissue has developed following emergence, any practice favoring rapid emergence is useful in disease management. Such practices include planting in warm soil (above 60°F), warming seed tubers before planting, and preirrigation of dry soil. Caution should be exercised with preirrigation in cool weather, however, as wet soil may remain cool longer, resulting in increased disease incidence. Regardless of the seeding depth, seed pieces should not be covered with more than 2 inches of soil if problems with *Rhizoctonia* are anticipated. This shallow covering promotes rapid emergence.

Seed and furrow treatments with registered fungicides provide some control of Rhizoctonia canker, but only when the disease is initiated from inoculum on seed pieces that are planted in soil not heavily infested with the fungus. Using fungicides at planting provides no more control of *Rhizoctonia* than using disease-free seed potatoes. Planting potatoes directly in standing cereal stubble, as might be done in a minimum-tillage production system, may result in less disease than planting in the same soil prepared by deep plowing. Harvesting tubers quickly after vine desiccation and death limits the development of sclerotia on tuber surfaces.

Pink Rot, Pythium Leak, and Pythium Seed Piece Decay

Pink rot and Pythium leak, sometimes collectively called water rot, occur sporadically wherever potatoes are grown. They are usually of economic concern only when tubers are exposed to saturated soils for several days in succession during maturation and soil temperatures are above 70° F. When seed pieces are exposed to these same conditions, Pythium seed piece decay can be severe. Substantial problems with these diseases are usually associated with excessive precipitation or irrigation either early or late in the season, especially on poorly drained soils.

Symptoms

Delayed emergence and poor stands are often associated with Pythium seed piece decay. Infected seed pieces become a soft, watery mass.

Symptoms of pink rot in mature plants include brown or blackened roots or stolons and, in severe cases, leaf chlorosis, stunting, wilting, and even death of the plant. Water-soaking and light brown discoloration of vascular tissues may be observed in belowground stems of infected plants. The pathogen generally enters tubers through diseased stolons, but tuber infections occasionally occur at buds or lenticels. The decay spreads through infected tubers, with the advancing margin of the rot usually sharply delimited by a dark line, which may be visible through the skin (Plate 64). Eyes of infected tubers are often dark brown. Decaying tubers remain intact but are spongy and odorless. If an infected tuber is squeezed, a clear liquid exudes. The internal tissues of a cut tuber turn salmon pink after exposure to the air for 15–20 minutes (Plate 64) and then turn brownish black.

Pythium leak usually develops at breaks in tuber surfaces following harvest. The disease begins as a discolored, water-soaked area. As with pink rot, the advancing margin of the rot is usually bounded by a dark line. The most characteristic tuber symptom is an extremely watery condition of diseased tissues, which turn brown or gray and are reduced to a soft, watery paste of uniform texture.

Pathogens and Disease Development

Pink rot is caused by several species of the soilborne fungus *Phytophthora*, most commonly *Phytophthora erythroseptica*. Pythium leak is caused by several species of the closely related soilborne fungus *Pythium*, such as *Pythium ultimum*. All these fungi are widely distributed in both water and soil throughout North America, and their behavior is generally similar. They survive in soil as mycelium in decaying plant material or as resistant spores called oospores. In warm, moist soil, oospores of *Phytophthora* and some species of *Pythium* germinate to form swimming spores called zoospores, which move in water films. Mycelium of these species produces specialized structures that also release zoospores. Oospores of *P. ultimum* do not form zoospores but germinate directly.

Roots can be infected by *Phytophthora* at almost any stage of plant growth, but the symptoms are more severe in young roots. Both groups of fungi infect tubers through wounds, but *Phytophthora* generally infects tubers before harvest, whereas *Pythium* usually infects them through harvest wounds, especially at temperatures above 70° F. Seed pieces can be infected by *Pythium* as soon as they are planted.

Management

Pink rot and Pythium leak and seed piece decay are managed primarily by cultural practices. Crop rotation away from potatoes for at least 4 years may reduce the number of *Phytophthora* and *Pythium* oospores in infested soils. Because these diseases are most severe under warm conditions when soils remain wet for prolonged periods, the selection of well-drained planting sites is important. Pythium seed piece decay can be severe when green manure crops are plowed in immediately ahead of planting. Populations of *Pythium* can increase dramatically on this fresh vegetation incorporated into the soil. Delaying planting for at least 2 weeks after plowdown or killing vegetation with an herbicide a week or so before plowing may reduce the amount of seed piece decay.

In some production areas, pink rot and Pythium leak have been controlled by the systemic fungicide metalaxyl applied at late flowering and again 2–3 weeks later. Metalaxyl should always be applied in combination with a protectant fungicide, to avoid selecting metalaxyl-resistant strains of the late blight fungus (Chapter 16).

Leak and pink rot in tubers are most severe when warm, wet conditions prevail late in the growing season. Nitrogen fertility should be monitored to avoid stimulating excessive vegetative growth, as soils tend to remain wetter under a heavy plant canopy, especially under humid conditions. Care should be taken to avoid excessive irrigation in the weeks prior to harvest.

If considerable pink rot is present in the field, it is advisable to delay harvest to allow the full development of symptoms in infected tubers, so that they can be graded out before the crop is placed in storage. Low spots in fields should be left unharvested if they have been waterlogged. Because tuber wounds from harvest and handling are the main infection sites for *Pythium*, delaying harvest until soil temperatures are below 60° F results in less disease in storage than harvesting and transporting potatoes during warm weather. If tubers are windrowed on warm (above 70° F), moist soil, they should be removed from the field immediately. If left on the soil surface overnight, severe damage from Pythium leak may result.

If a significant amount of pink rot or Pythium leak has developed in a particular lot of tubers, it should be stored separately from healthy lots. Good airflow through the pile should be provided, to dry out leaky tubers. The tubers should be held at 50–60° F only long enough to allow suberization, after which the tuber pulp temperature should be decreased to 38–40° F. Any tuber lots with significant disease should be marketed as soon as possible or, preferably, sold straight from the field.

Scab

Scab is a serious disease of potato tubers. It has no aboveground symptoms. The main effect of the disease is lowered tuber quality. It is usually of greater economic importance in tubers grown for the fresh market than in those grown for processing. Two forms of scab occur in North America. Common scab occurs in all North American production areas and is most severe in soils above pH 5.5. Acid scab is important in acidic soils (below pH 5.5) in the northeastern United States and possibly elsewhere.

Symptoms

Scab symptoms are quite variable. Usually, roughly circular, raised, tan to brown, corky lesions of various sizes develop randomly across the tuber surface (Plate 65). Sometimes a rather superficial layer of corky tissues is produced, covering large areas of the tuber surface. This is referred to as russet scab. In cases in which lesions up to ½ inch deep are formed, the disease is called pitted scab. These deep lesions are dark brown to black, and the tissues underneath are often straw-colored and somewhat translucent. More than one of these lesion types may be present on a single tuber. Although scab symptoms are usually not noticed until late in the growing season or until harvest, small, brown, water-soaked, circular lesions are evident on tubers within a few weeks after infection (Fig. 17.3).

A few other conditions can be confused with scab. Tubers harvested from wet soil frequently have white, enlarged lenticels (Fig. 10.1), which can be mistaken for scab symptoms. *Rhizoctonia solani* causes a patchy russeting, checking, or cracking of the tuber surface, which may be confused with russet scab symptoms. In a few production areas, powdery scab, a different disease, caused by the fungus *Spongospora subterranea*, produces symptoms very similar to those of scab. Laboratory confirmation may be necessary to distinguish this disease from scab.

Pathogens and Disease Development

The pathogens causing scab belong to a group of microorganisms called actinomycetes, which are filamentous bacteria commonly present in soils. In soils above pH 5.2, *Streptomyces scabies* is usually responsible for common scab. It is capable of causing all three types of lesions (raised corky lesions, russet scab, and deep-pitted scab). In soils below pH 5.5, the acid-tolerant species *S. acidiscabies* causes acid scab. Although this species is distinct from *S. scabies*, the two diseases cannot be distinguished on the basis of symptoms. There are unconfirmed reports that other species of *Streptomyces* may be able to cause russet scab symptoms.

S. scabies is usually introduced into fields on seed potatoes. It survives indefinitely once the soil is contaminated. There have been reports that *Streptomyces* species pathogenic to potato were present in some native soils before potatoes were ever grown there. *S. scabies* can survive in soil on decaying plant debris, in old feed lots, or in fields heavily manured with animal wastes. It survives passage through the digestive tracts of animals and is distributed with manure. It can be disseminated further in infested soil adhering to implements or transported by wind or water. *S. scabies* has also been reported as a pathogen of other root crops, such as beet, turnip, rutabaga, radish, carrot, and parsnip. The acid scab organism, *S. acidiscabies*, has a similar host range but is usually tuber-borne, since it does not survive well in soil.

S. scabies usually survives best in soils at pH 5.5–7.5. *S. acidiscabies* occurs in soils with a pH as low as 4.5, but it generally produces the most severe disease at pH 5.0–5.5. Continuous cropping with potatoes, especially scab-susceptible cultivars, often increases the populations of these pathogens, with a resultant increase in disease severity.

Newly forming tubers are susceptible to infection as soon as tuberization begins (Fig. 17.3). Tubers are infected through stomata and immature lenticels. Mature tubers with a well-developed skin are no longer susceptible to infection, but existing lesions continue to expand as the tubers enlarge, so disease severity increases throughout the growing season. The disease is most severe in tubers that develop in warm, dry soils. Wet soils inhibit the activity of the pathogens. Coarse-textured soils that dry out quickly are therefore more conducive to scab than are fine-textured soils.

Resistance to scab appears to be related to the ability of tubers to form corky layers that effectively wall off the lesions as they develop. In susceptible cultivars, successive corky layers form as the pathogen penetrates progressively through tissue layers, causing deep lesions. In resistant cultivars, a single layer seems to prevent further invasion by the pathogen.

Management of Scab

A management program for scab should emphasize planting scab-free seed potatoes in soils that are not heavily infested with scab pathogens. A broad-spectrum chemical seed piece treatment also provides some control, especially of acid scab, in which the pathogen is mostly tuber-borne. Where soils are known to harbor high populations of scab pathogens, a 3- to 4-year rotation with nonsusceptible crops should be established, to reduce these soil populations. Alfalfa, rye, and soybeans are good rotational choices. Rotations with carrot, beet, spinach, turnip, and radish should be avoided.

Cultivars that are moderately resistant to scab should be

Fig. 17.3. Scab lesions on newly formed, rapidly expanding potato tubers.

Susceptible cultivars	Moderately resistant cultivars
Centennial Russet	Atlantic
Chippewa	BelRus
Denali	Conestoga
Elba	Crystal
Hampton	Islander
Irish Cobbler	Kennebec
Jemseg	LaRouge
Kanona	Monona
Katahdin	Norchip
Red Pontiac	Norgold Russet
Rosa	Norland
Shepody	Onaway
Steuben	Ontario
White Rose	Pungo
Yukon Gold	Rideau
	Russet Burbank
	Sebago
	Superior
	Viking

Fig. 17.4. Susceptibility of some potato cultivars to common scab.

planted whenever possible. Lesion types and potential scab severity vary among cultivars (Fig. 17.4). Russet-skinned cultivars are generally more resistant to pitted scab, but some red- and white-skinned cultivars are also resistant. High levels of resistance to scab are not available in current cultivars, and even the most resistant can become infected if conditions are highly favorable for disease development. Local information should be obtained on scab-resistant cultivars adapted to specific production areas.

Various cultural practices can be significant in a scab management program. In fields where common scab is a problem, soils should be maintained at or slightly below pH 5.5. The incidence of common scab may be reduced by applications of sulfur or acid-forming fertilizers, such as ammonium sulfate, which lower the soil pH. Manganese applications have been reported to limit the severity of common scab without lowering the soil pH. Consideration should be given to the potential for common scab before liming the soil, because raising the soil pH may aggravate a problem with this disease. If soil calcium is needed, gypsum can be applied without raising the soil pH or aggravating scab. When this management option is used, it should be kept in mind that low soil pH may affect the choice of rotational crops and alter the availability of certain nutrients in soil (Chapters 2 and 9 and Fig. 9.2).

Because the activity of the common scab pathogen is inhibited in moist soils, careful timing of irrigation to maintain 80–90% of available soil water during growth stage III and for the next 6–8 weeks can limit the severity of the disease. High soil moisture must be maintained throughout the entire period for this to be effective. This management technique is most useful with cultivars that are moderately resistant to scab. It should be used with caution, because extensive irrigation may promote diseases such as late blight, aerial stem rot, and Sclerotinia stalk rot.

Green manure crops, such as rye, millet, and oat, have been reported to reduce the incidence of scab. Plowed-down legumes, particularly red clover, encourage the development of the disease. Growers should also avoid applying animal manure or other animal wastes to soils where potato production is intended. Animal wastes raise the organic matter content of the soil and provide a food base for the common scab pathogen, which survives well in soil. Common scab is often severe in potato crops planted soon after manure application.

Successful management of scab requires several cultural practices, since no single one can provide complete control. Planting scab-resistant cultivars and scab-free seed potatoes, instituting a good crop rotation, and maintaining the soil at or slightly below pH 5.5 are the most important management steps.

Fusarium Dry Rot and Seed Piece Decay

Fusarium dry rot probably causes greater losses in storage and transit of both seed and commercial potatoes than any other postharvest disease. It is also a major cause of seed piece decay after planting.

Symptoms

The disease causes a dry rot of infected tubers, although a moist rot may occur if secondary infection with soft rot bacteria is also involved. The surfaces of infected tubers are sunken or wrinkled, and rotted tissues are brown or gray to black (Plate 66). White or pink mold growth may be visible on tuber surfaces. Internal cavities often develop in rotted tissues and contain white, yellow, or pink molds that are visible when tubers are cut (Plate 67). In storage, blue, black, purple, gray, white, yellow, or pink spore masses may form in these cavities. At low storage temperatures, internal tissues often become firm and dry or even powdery.

Pathogens and Disease Development

Fusarium dry rot is caused by several species of the soilborne fungus *Fusarium*. These fungi are common in most soils where potatoes are grown. They survive as resistant spores or mycelium in decayed plant tissue in the soil. Some infections develop on tubers before harvest, causing a stem-end decay, but most occur at harvest wounds. Small, brown lesions appear at wounds 3–4 weeks after harvest and continue to enlarge during storage, taking several months to develop fully. Infection proceeds fairly rapidly at temperatures above 50°F but ceases if they are lowered to 40°F. The fungus is dormant below this temperature but resumes growth when the tubers are warmed.

Fusarium seed piece decay is really the same disease. Seed tubers may be infected prior to shipment, and rotting in transit or storage often accounts for poor-quality seed tubers (Plate 66). When the pathogens are present on seed pieces or in the soil, poor stands may result, especially if the cut surfaces of the seed pieces are not properly suberized. Fusarium seed piece decay begins as reddish brown to black depressions on cut surfaces. These may expand to cover the entire seed piece. A slimy rot often develops when secondary soft rot bacteria take over.

Management

Fusarium dry rot is managed mostly by appropriate harvest procedures to minimize bruising and proper storage operation to promote rapid healing of harvest wounds (Chapter 6). Tubers should be harvested only after the vines are completely dead, to ensure skin maturity. Harvest machinery should be designed and operated to minimize bruising during harvest and handling operations (Box 6.2).

> **Fusarium dry rot is managed mostly by appropriate harvest procedures to minimize bruising and proper storage operation to promote rapid healing of harvest wounds.**

Application of the fungicide thiabendazole to harvested tubers going into storage should be considered if problems with Fusarium dry rot are anticipated. When this treatment is applied, all tuber surfaces must be covered. This is best accomplished during bin loading, by applying the fungicide as a fine mist at some point on the conveyor line where the tubers are tumbling. It is best if the application area is covered to encourage swirling of the fungicide mist. Some strains of *Fusarium* are resistant to thiabendazole and are thus not controlled by this treatment. If the presence of thiabendazole-resistant strains is suspected, samples of infected tubers should be submitted to a qualified pathologist for laboratory confirmation.

Care should be taken during bin filling to ensure that excess soil and debris do not accumulate within the pile. Pockets of soil block the circulation of air through the pile and may favor disease development in adjacent tubers. After being placed in storage, newly harvested potatoes should be held at 55–60°F and 90–95% relative humidity for the first 1–2 weeks, to promote rapid wound healing. Dry rot does not spread in storage if the potatoes are properly healed. Following

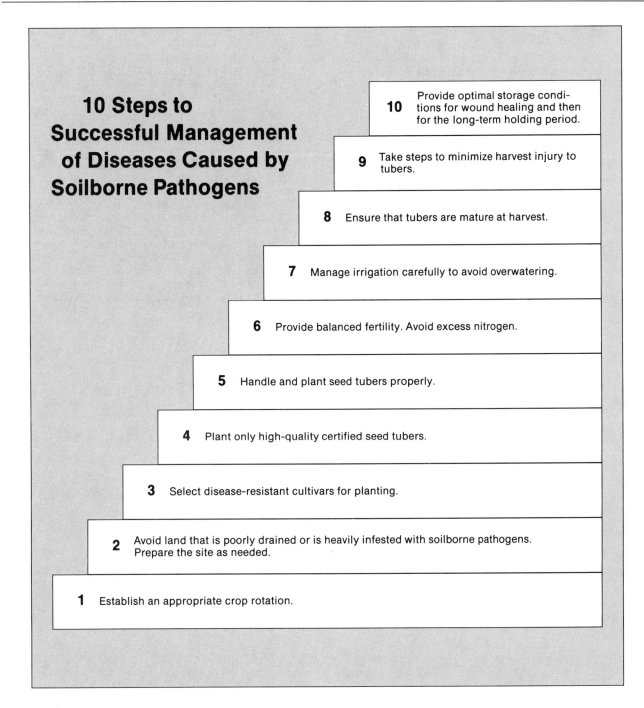

10 Steps to Successful Management of Diseases Caused by Soilborne Pathogens

10 Provide optimal storage conditions for wound healing and then for the long-term holding period.

9 Take steps to minimize harvest injury to tubers.

8 Ensure that tubers are mature at harvest.

7 Manage irrigation carefully to avoid overwatering.

6 Provide balanced fertility. Avoid excess nitrogen.

5 Handle and plant seed tubers properly.

4 Plant only high-quality certified seed tubers.

3 Select disease-resistant cultivars for planting.

2 Avoid land that is poorly drained or is heavily infested with soilborne pathogens. Prepare the site as needed.

1 Establish an appropriate crop rotation.

the curing period, temperatures should be lowered to a level appropriate for long-term storage (Table 6.1).

To avoid Fusarium seed piece decay, seed tubers that are cut for planting should be treated with a fungicide seed piece treatment and then either planted immediately under appropriate field conditions or allowed to suberize at 55–60° F and 95–99% relative humidity if they are to be stored as precut seed. A detailed discussion of these procedures is in Chapter 4.

An Integrated Management Strategy for Diseases Caused by Soilborne Pathogens

Successful management of diseases caused by soilborne pathogens requires that several practices, conducted at various times, be integrated into the holistic health management plan for the crop. An appropriate crop rotation scheme should be established to minimize populations of soilborne pathogens, weeds, and insect pests in the soil and to maintain or improve soil structure and fertility. Site selection and preparation are important. If possible, land heavily infested with soilborne pathogens, especially those causing early dying and scab, should be avoided. Adequate soil drainage is critical to reducing infection by many tuber-rotting organisms. Applications of lime or animal manure should be avoided, as they may aggravate scab. If appropriate to the production system, preplant soil fumigation should be considered if potato early dying has been a problem at the production site.

Cultivars should be selected with disease resistance in mind (Chapter 3 and Figs. 17.2 and 17.4). Potato cultivars vary in susceptibility to various soilborne pathogens, and it is wise to avoid highly susceptible cultivars, particularly if a specific disease problem is anticipated on the basis of past experience. Only high-quality certified seed tubers should be planted.

Proper handling of seed tubers prior to planting is an essential step in disease management. Seed should be inspected upon receipt, and any seed lot with visible frost injury or with *Rhizoctonia* sclerotia or scab lesions covering any significant amount (definitely no more than 5%) of the tuber surfaces should be rejected. In some areas it may be beneficial to treat freshly cut seed pieces with a fungicide formulated for the control of *Fusarium* or *Rhizoctonia*. Treated cut seed should be planted immediately or held at 55–60° F and high humidity, with good air movement through the pile to hasten the healing process.

To promote quick emergence, planting should be delayed until soil temperatures are above 55° F. Shallow planting at a depth of 2–3 inches rather than 5–6 inches allows quicker emergence and reduces stand loss to Rhizoctonia canker. A balanced nitrogen fertility program should be maintained— one that provides for the nutritional needs of the crop but does not stimulate excessive vegetative growth. Irrigation should be managed to prevent overwatering, which along with a lush canopy of foliage promotes the development of Sclerotinia stalk rot and tuber rots such as pink rot and Pythium leak. Consideration should be given to the use of appropriate foliar fungicides if severe problems are expected from any of these three diseases.

To ensure that tuber skins are mature and harvest injury is minimized, harvest should be delayed until the vines have been dead for 1–2 weeks. If possible, harvesting should be postponed when soil temperatures are above 70° F, to minimize problems with Pythium leak. All precautions must be taken to minimize bruising of tubers during harvest and handling operations. Grading tubers as they are placed in storage should be considered, especially if a significant amount of tuber rot has occurred in the field. Thiabendazole, applied as a mist on the tubers as they fall onto the bin pile is effective for the control of Fusarium dry rot in most cases. Storage facilities should be operated to provide optimal conditions for wound healing immediately after the bins are filled. Then the environment should be adjusted to provide conditions appropriate for storage, according to whether the tubers are to be used as seed or for fresh-market or processing purposes. An integrated disease management program such as this will minimize problems from soilborne pathogens and improve the overall health of the potato crop.

CHAPTER 18

Ann E. MacGuidwin
Department of Plant Pathology
University of Wisconsin, Madison

Management of Nematodes

Nematodes are tiny wormlike animals. They are the most numerous multicellular animals on earth and are present in nearly all ecosystems. Some beneficial nematodes feed on bacteria and aid in nutrient cycling or are natural enemies of some insect pests. Harmful nematodes include species that parasitize people, animals, or plants. Nematode pests of agricultural crops feed exclusively on plants, with most species attacking roots and belowground plant structures.

Plant-parasitic nematodes are microscopic, ranging from 0.004 to 0.04 inches in length. Their life cycles, which include egg, juvenile, and adult stages, are completed in about 20–50 days, depending on temperature. The extent and severity of damage resulting from nematode parasitism is related to the number of nematodes present and additional stresses to which the host plant is exposed. Plant-parasitic nematodes feed on plant roots in several ways (Fig. 18.1), but all have a needle-shaped mouthpart, called a stylet, that is inserted into plant tissues (Fig. 18.1D). Some species affect root growth by destroying cells and interfering with the uptake of water and nutrients. Others stimulate physiological changes that upset the balance of hormones and other metabolic systems in the host plant.

Nematode damage to potato ranges from a very subtle restriction in plant growth to severe stunting of plants (Plate 68) or obvious disfiguration of tubers (Plate 69). These pests are so common that nematodes of some type are present in nearly every field where potatoes are grown in most production areas of North America. Some species are limited in geographic distribution, whereas others are found in all areas. Some are highly detrimental to potato production; others do no damage. A few may pose little threat by themselves but may influence the severity of certain diseases caused by other pathogens, such as potato early dying, caused by the fungus *Verticillium* (Chapter 17). Some nematode species can serve as vectors to transmit virus pathogens, such as tobacco rattle virus (Chapter 14), while feeding on roots.

Of the many types of nematodes that can infect potatoes (Table 18.1), the four most widespread and economically significant in North America are root-lesion nematodes (*Pratylenchus* species), root-knot nematodes (*Meloidogyne* species), sting nematodes (*Belonolaimus* species), and stubby-root nematodes (*Paratrichodorus* species). Two others, which are important in only a few localities in North America, are significant pests in other potato production areas of the world. These are cyst nematodes (*Globodera rostochiensis* and *G. pallida*) and the potato rot nematode (*Ditylenchus destructor*).

Root-Lesion Nematodes

Root-lesion nematodes are found in all potato production areas in North America, and more than 40 species have been described. *Pratylenchus brachyurus* and *P. zeae* are found in production areas in the southern United States, and *P. crenatus* and *P. alleni* in the northern states and Canada. Species present throughout North America include *P. penetrans*, *P. neglectus*, and *P. scribneri*. Identification of species of root-lesion nematodes is a complex and laborious process, primarily based on morphological features, such as tail shape, the number of indentations on the lips, and stylet length. Because species identification requires much expertise, it is rarely offered in standard assay services.

Root-lesion nematodes have wide host ranges, including vegetable, forage, and fruit crops as well as many types of weeds. These nematodes can reproduce rapidly on some host plant species, and thus these hosts facilitate a considerable increase in the nematode population. Other host species, however, support only enough nematode reproduction to maintain the population.

Symptoms of damage due to root-lesion nematodes are similar on all hosts and include retarded growth of roots, stunting of plants, and chlorosis of foliage. The entry and movement of these nematodes within root and stolon tissues often result in browning and the formation of elliptical lesions. This symptom is variable, however, and similar lesions can be caused by other root-colonizing pathogens. Therefore root samples must be assayed for definitive diagnosis of these nematodes. Tubers usually show little visible damage, but small lesions sometimes form on the surface where nematodes have entered.

The effects of root-lesion nematodes on potato and the extent to which they interact with other pathogens differ among species. For example, *P. penetrans* alone at populations greater than 100 per 100 cubic centimeters of soil (about 17 nematodes per cubic inch) can limit potato yields, especially those of early-maturing cultivars. This species can also interact with *Verticillium* to cause potato early dying. In contrast, *P. crenatus* must occur at much higher populations to affect yields and does not interact with *Verticillium* in potato early dying.

The involvement of root-lesion nematodes with *Verticillium* in potato early dying is well documented. Co-infection by root-lesion nematodes (primarily *P. penetrans*) and *V. dahliae* may result in severe disease, including premature senescence, and low yields (Chapter 17). In some cultivars, certain root-lesion species have a synergistic relationship with the fungus: the damage caused by co-infection with both is greater than the sum of the damages that would be caused by each organism alone.

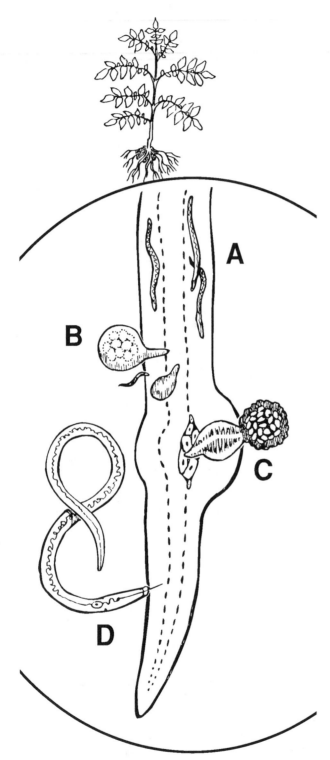

Fig. 18.1. Feeding habits of plant-parasitic nematodes. **A**, Root-lesion nematodes (endoparasites) burrowing in the host root cortex. **B**, Cyst nematodes (endoparasites), including a mature female with an internal egg mass. **C**, Root-knot nematode (endoparasite) with an attached egg mass, feeding on giant cells. **D**, Sting nematode (ectoparasite) feeding on root cells through its long stylet. (Drawing by Kandis Elliot)

Root-lesion nematodes are categorized as migratory endoparasites—they usually reside inside roots but move freely between root and soil habitats (Fig. 18.1A). Eggs deposited in plant tissue or soil hatch as second-stage juveniles. These molt (shed the cuticle) twice to develop into third-stage and then fourth-stage juveniles, before molting again to reach the adult stage. Only adults can reproduce. Juveniles and adults feed on root surfaces and in the root cortex. When plant cells die in response to feeding, the nematodes move in and out of roots in search of new feeding sites. Some species comprise both males and females; others are composed exclusively of females that reproduce without males. All stages are capable of infecting potato roots, stolons, and tubers.

The number of root-lesion nematode generations per year varies from one to three, depending on the species and the climate. All stages persist between cropping seasons, but fourth-stage juveniles and adults are the most important overwintering stages. In the spring, females reproduce as soon as roots are available for infection. A large increase in root-lesion nematode populations is generally noted about 2–3 months after planting. These nematodes use several strategies to survive harsh environmental conditions. They are capable of surviving dehydration when moisture becomes limiting, and northern species can survive soil freezing. Populations of root-lesion nematodes fluctuate seasonally. Between cropping seasons they are reduced by environmental factors and mortality associated with natural enemies in the soil.

Root-Knot Nematodes

There are more than 60 described species of root-knot nematodes. Although these pests damage a wide range of crops, only a few species cause serious losses in potato (Table 18.1). In the northeastern and north central United States and in eastern and central Canada, the northern root-knot nematode (*Meloidogyne hapla*) is the predominant species associated with potato. In the Pacific Northwest, both the northern root-knot nematode and the Columbia root-knot nematode (*M. chitwoodi*) attack potato. The southern root-knot nematode (*M. incognita*), the Javanese root-knot nematode (*M. javanica*), and the peanut root-knot nematode (*M. arenaria*) are associated with potato in the southern United States.

Although all of these species attack potato, their preferences for other host plants differ. For example, the northern root-knot nematode attacks most vegetable and fruit crops and alfalfa but does not infect corn, grasses, and cereals. In contrast, the Columbia root-knot nematode infects corn, grasses, and cereals, but most populations do poorly on alfalfa. There are two races of the Columbia root-knot nematode, however, and race 2 infects alfalfa. The southern and peanut root-knot nematodes are also divided into races that differ in host specificity.

The identification of root-knot nematode species is based on their morphology, physiology, gall characteristics, and host range. Like the identification of root-lesion nematode species, it is a time-consuming procedure that is not generally offered as a standard service by nematode diagnostic laboratories. However, information on the species of root-knot nematodes present in a field can sometimes be deduced from the cropping history, geographic region, and host plant symptoms. Species identification is important for planning crop rotations in regions where more than one species of root-knot nematode is present.

Root-knot nematodes are so named because of the common response of roots to infection. Invasion and feeding by these nematodes cause a swelling of cells at the feeding site and an increase in cell multiplication around the site. This results in a visible root swelling, or gall. The formation of root galls

Table 18.1. Nematodes associated with potato in North America

Scientific name (common name)	Feeding type[a]	Tuber infection	Damage potential[b]	Other pathogens interacting with nematodes
Pratylenchus (root-lesion)	ME			
P. crenatus		Yes	3	...
P. neglectus		Yes	3	...
P. penetrans		Yes	4	*Verticillium*
P. scribneri		Yes	3	*Verticillium*
Globodera (cyst)	SE			
G. pallida (white potato cyst)		Yes	5	...
G. rostochiensis (golden)		Yes	5	...
Meloidogyne (root-knot)	SE			
M. arenaria (peanut root-knot)		Yes	5	...
M. chitwoodi (Columbia root-knot)		Yes	5	...
M. hapla (northern root-knot)		Yes	5	...
M. incognita (southern root-knot)		Yes	5	*Pseudomonas*
M. javanica (Javanese root-knot)		Yes	5	...
Nacobbus aberrans (false root-knot)	SE	Yes	5	...
Belonolaimus longicaudatus (sting)	EC	No	5	...
Ditylenchus destructor (potato rot)	EC	Yes	5	Fungi
Helicotylenchus (spiral)	EC	No	1	...
Longidorus (needle)	EC	No	1	...
Paratrichodorus (stubby-root)	EC			
P. minor		No	1	Tobacco rattle virus
P. pachydermus		No	1	...
Paratylenchus (pin)	EC	Yes	1	...
Rotylenchus (spiral)	EC	No	1	...
Tylenchorhynchus (stunt)	EC	No	1	...
Xiphinema (dagger)	EC	No	2	...

[a] ME = migratory endoparasite, SE = sedentary endoparasite, and EC = ectoparasite.
[b] 1 = Low, 2 = moderately low, 3 = moderate, 4 = moderately high, and 5 = high.

in host plants is not essential to the nematode's life cycle. The location, shape, and size of the galls are peculiar to each root-knot species and each host crop. On potato roots, for example, moderately large galls form in response to infection by the southern root-knot nematode (Plate 70A) but very small ones in infections by the northern root-knot nematode. Gall formation on tubers also varies with the nematode species. Infection by the Columbia root-knot nematode and the southern root-knot nematode often causes bumpy tubers (Plate 69A), but infection by the northern root-knot nematode usually does not. Other symptoms associated with root-knot nematodes include internal browning of tubers (Plate 69B), small tubers, poor shoot growth (Plate 68B), and chlorosis of foliage.

Root-knot nematodes may also interact with other potato pathogens. Some studies have suggested that they may contribute to damage by *Verticillium*, but more recent research does not support this conclusion. In the southern United States, however, associations between the southern root-knot nematode and the wilt bacterium, *Pseudomonas solanacearum*, have been demonstrated, in which the presence of the nematode increases the incidence and severity of bacterial wilt, even when the population of the primary pathogen is low.

Root-knot nematodes are classified as sedentary endoparasites—once they are in position and commence feeding, they remain permanently attached to tissues inside the root and cannot leave the root (Fig. 18.1C). Like other plant-parasitic nematodes, they hatch from eggs as second-stage juveniles. The eggs are held together by a sticky substance produced by the female. The egg mass adheres to the posterior end of the female (Fig. 18.1C) and may be embedded in root tissue, exposed on the surface of the root, or detached and free in the soil.

Hatched second-stage juveniles migrate through the soil in search of infection sites on host roots. After penetrating a root, each juvenile establishes a feeding site composed of two to six cells. The bodies of juveniles enlarge as they feed. They soon lose the muscles necessary to leave the roots, and after this point in their development only the stylet and head move during feeding. Feeding by a root-knot nematode triggers physiological changes in the host plant that cause nutrients to accumulate at the feeding site. The root cells at the feeding site are physiologically highly active and become enlarged (Fig. 18.1C) and hence are called giant cells. These cells provide nutrients to the nematode for the remainder of its life.

Second-stage juveniles, like those of root-lesion nematodes, mature through the third and fourth juvenile stages before reaching adulthood. Most root-knot species are composed entirely of females. Adult females are swollen and round or oblong. Each female produces one egg mass, which may contain from 200 to 1,000 eggs. Males, when they are produced, are wormlike and do not feed.

The duration of the root-knot life cycle is related to temperature. One to five generations may be produced per year. These nematodes reproduce inside roots and tubers. Eggs and second-stage juveniles persisting through the winter in soil, root debris, and tubers act as inoculum in subsequent crops. Root-knot nematodes may be located quite deep in the soil. The Columbia root-knot nematode, for example, has been recovered from as much as 5–6 feet below the soil surface and is therefore difficult to control with soil fumigation.

Root-knot nematodes are adept at surviving harsh environments. The eggs are particularly well suited for survival. Second-stage juveniles can withstand desiccation and freezing. Both eggs and juveniles are susceptible to various natural enemies, such as egg-parasitic fungi and predators. The extent of mortality in root-knot nematode populations between seasons varies in different years and locations, generally ranging from 20 to 90%.

Stubby-Root Nematodes and Sting Nematodes

Stubby-root nematodes (*Paratrichodorus* species) are found in all potato production areas in North America. The most common stubby-root species associated with potato is *P. minor*. Closely related species in the genus *Trichodorus* are also present in potato production areas.

Sting nematodes (*Belonolaimus* species, primarily *B. longicaudatus*) are also commonly associated with potato. In North America, these nematodes are limited to sandy soils in the southeastern and south central United States.

Sting and stubby-root nematodes both have very wide host ranges. The names *sting* and *stubby-root* aptly describe the damage caused by these species. Root tips swell and stop growing as the nematodes feed, so that the root system remains small and poorly developed, and the roots are sparse, short, and clublike (Plate 70B). The injury is most severe in plants in the seedling stage (Plate 68B), when they are highly susceptible to drought stress. In some crops, such as corn, symptoms of damage due to these nematodes may resemble those of herbicide injury.

The number of nematodes necessary to damage crops varies with the species. In general, relatively few sting nematodes can have significant effects on yield. On the other hand, crops can usually tolerate a high population of stubby-root nematodes if no other pathogens are present. Aside from direct injury, nematode feeding often opens wounds, which provide entry sites for plant-pathogenic bacteria and fungi. Furthermore, stubby-root nematodes feeding on potato roots can act as vectors of tobacco rattle virus, the cause of corky ring spot (Plate 69C and D) (Chapter 14).

Sting and stubby-root nematodes are ectoparasites—they live in the soil and feed on plant roots without entering them (Fig. 18.1D). They hatch as second-stage juveniles from eggs deposited in the soil or close to root surfaces. Like root-knot and root-lesion nematodes, ectoparasites develop through two additional juvenile stages before reaching full maturity. All stages inhabit soil and feed by inserting their stylet mouthparts into roots. The feeding process empties and kills cells. Stubby-root nematodes use their short, curved stylets to feed on cells on the root surface. Sting nematodes have long, straight stylets, which pierce and penetrate deep inside roots (Fig. 18.1D). Both types prefer to feed on growing root tips, and they tend to move downward in the soil as root systems develop. It is not unusual to recover these species from soil at depths of 8–10 feet. Most populations of ectoparasitic species are composed of both males and females, and reproduction occurs by cross-fertilization.

Sting and stubby-root nematodes can survive dehydration when low soil moisture limits their movement. When the temperature or the oxygen concentration falls below a certain level, the nematodes slow down their normal life processes and become dormant. When favorable conditions return, they can recover and resume normal activity. Eggs of sting, stubby-root, and almost all other plant-parasitic nematodes are better adapted to survive harsh conditions than the other life stages. Stubby-root nematodes have been noted to quickly resurge to a high population after their numbers have been reduced by soil fumigants.

Cyst Nematodes and Potato Rot Nematode

The golden (potato cyst) nematode (*Globodera rostochiensis*) and the potato rot nematode (*Ditylenchus destructor*) damage potatoes only in highly localized areas of North America, but they are important pests in many other potato-growing regions of the world. In some areas of North America, potatoes harvested from fields known to be infested with these nematodes are subject to regulatory restrictions. The infested acreage and economic impact of these nematodes in North America have not been extensive in recent years, because of enforcement of quarantines and sanitation measures designed to limit their spread. Early detection of infestations by either of these species is essential to ensure that their impact on North American potato production remains low.

The golden nematode can severely damage potato if it is allowed to become established and increase its numbers. Although it has a fairly limited host range, restricted to plants closely related to potato (tomato, eggplant, and some weeds), this species has a strong ability to survive. It causes aboveground symptoms similar to those caused by root-knot nematodes. The most diagnostic feature of infection by the golden nematode is round, pinhead-sized females (cysts) on potato roots around the time of flowering (Plate 70C). The females are white when alive but turn yellow as the cysts mature. In the white potato cyst nematode (*G. pallida*), a closely related species that has been reported in Canada, the mature cysts remain white.

The golden nematode is a sedentary endoparasite with a life cycle similar to that of root-knot nematodes. Infection by the golden nematode does not cause roots to form galls. Rather, the body of the female breaks through the root surface as it grows and matures (Fig. 18.1B). Eggs are retained inside the female's body, which then becomes a cyst, serving as a protective covering for the eggs. Eventually, the cyst separates from the root and is free in the soil. Thus, although the presence of cysts on roots confirms infection by the golden nematode, their absence from roots does not necessarily indicate the absence of this nematode.

The potato rot nematode has been reported in nine states scattered across several potato production regions of the United States and in Prince Edward Island in Canada. Severe problems with this species have been documented in only a few areas. However, it is likely that damage and losses due to this nematode have been underestimated, because of difficulties in recognizing and identifying it and a limited understanding of its life cycle. The potato rot nematode has a wide host range and can feed on fungi under laboratory conditions. Infestations have been reported in fields planted with potatoes for the first time in 20 years or more, which indicates either that the nematode can persist on hosts other than potato or that it can establish a population very quickly from infected seed tubers.

The potato rot nematode causes no symptoms on aboveground parts or roots of potato. Its presence is recognized only by the symptoms it causes in tubers. In the early stages of infection, small, white, chalky lesions can be seen in peeled tubers. As the nematode reproduces, cracks appear on the tuber surface, and a progressive dry rot develops inside tubers (Plate 69E and F). These symptoms can occur anytime from midseason until the potatoes have been in storage for several months.

The life cycle of the potato rot nematode can be completed very rapidly (10–14 days), but it is unpredictable. The biology of this species is poorly understood, and recommendations for sampling and management are therefore made with less certainty than those for any other nematode pest of potato.

Management of Nematode Pests

Symptoms of nematode damage are often nondescript and similar to injuries caused by other biological and environmental factors. Stunting, chlorosis, wilting, and premature senescence—typical aboveground symptoms resulting from nematode infection of roots—may be due to other causes. Although some belowground symptoms are more distinctive (for example, root lesions, galling, and swollen root tips), even these are not unique to nematode damage. Proper diagnosis is therefore essential before any nematode management program is considered.

Proper diagnosis is essential before any nematode management program is considered.

To obtain an accurate diagnosis of a suspected nematode problem, soil and root samples should be submitted to experienced professionals who offer nematode assay services. Onsite diagnosis is usually difficult, if not impossible. Cooperative efforts between the person collecting samples and the diagnostic laboratory are necessary to detect and estimate the size of a nematode population and to evaluate the economic feasibility of implementing management strategies.

Estimating Nematode Populations

Obtaining an accurate estimate of a nematode population involves three steps: collecting soil and root samples, extracting and counting nematodes from the samples, and using the data to estimate the size of the population and the potential for crop damage.

Sampling. Collecting samples that accurately represent the nematode population in a field is the most time-consuming and important step in this process. Local crop advisors or assay laboratories should be asked to recommend sampling procedures. Appropriate methods depend on the nematode species present in the field, taking into account the unique biology and life history of each species. Different sampling schemes may be required at different times of year or for different crops. Soil samples are collected with soil core sampling tubes, trowels, or shovels. Separate samples should be collected from areas of the field that differ in soil type, topography, or cropping history. The samples should be collected from the root zone, including areas between rows, when the crop is well established. Some labs extract root pieces from soil samples for analysis. Others prefer separate root samples collected from the field. A sampling depth of 1 foot is adequate to detect most types of nematodes, but some, including the sting nematode and the Columbia root-knot nematode, may be situated much deeper in the soil.

Nematodes are generally not randomly distributed across a field but rather are clumped in areas of greater concentration interspersed with areas of lesser concentration. Because of this aggregated distribution pattern and the small size of these organisms, intensive sampling is generally needed in order to accurately and reliably estimate nematode populations in a field. Population estimates can be improved by collecting a large number of samples or by combining a large number of soil cores in each sample. These two alternatives each require about the same amount of effort, and since processing may be costly, it is generally more economical to bulk a large number of soil cores in a single sample. A common recommendation is to collect 20 soil cores for every 5 acres. Representative 5-acre sections should be sampled in large fields. The cores can be combined, mixed well, and then subsampled before submission to an assay lab. Most laboratories process only 1 pint of soil or less per sample.

The timing of sample collection depends on the objectives of the assay. Sampling to detect and monitor nematode populations is best done at midseason, when their numbers are usually greatest. If decisions must be made regarding postseason treatments or cover crops, samples should be collected at least 1 month before harvest. Decisions regarding at-plant or postplant treatments usually require sampling in the spring or the previous fall. In northern areas, samples should be collected after the ground has thawed to a depth of at least 6, and preferably 12, inches.

Proper handling of soil samples after collection is critical to obtaining reliable information on nematode populations. Different labs use different extraction methods, and some techniques recover only living nematodes. These organisms are quite sensitive to rapid desiccation and extreme heat, and they quickly die if soil samples are exposed to sun and air. In the field, samples should be placed in sealed plastic bags and kept out of direct sunlight in order to maintain the proper moisture and temperature. If they must be stored prior to shipping to the diagnostic lab, they should be refrigerated at about 40° F.

Assay Procedures. Numerous methods for extracting nematodes from soil and roots have been devised. Some methods require a greater amount of specialized equipment, but in all cases the end result is a suspension of nematodes in water. This is then examined under a microscope so that the nematodes can be counted. Since no extraction technique can recover all the nematodes in a sample, the number counted is usually adjusted to correct for the recovery efficiency of the procedure. This varies tremendously with the extraction technique, the soil texture, and the nematode species and life stages present.

Some diagnostic labs vary their procedures, depending on the objective of the assay, the nematodes they expect to find, or other factors. For example, samples submitted in the fall or spring following fumigation usually contain many dead nematodes. Since it is often difficult to distinguish between dead and living nematodes, the diagnostic lab may use a technique that recovers only those capable of movement. If samples were collected to evaluate pesticide efficacy, the lab should be alerted, to ensure that proper methods are used. To obtain information on root-inhabiting nematodes (root-lesion and root-knot species), both soil and root assays should be requested, even for samples collected after harvest and before planting. Many nematodes overwinter in roots and must be included in population estimates.

Interpreting Assay Results. Nematode management decisions are based on the anticipated risk of damage due to estimated populations of particular nematode species. There is a close relationship between crop performance and nematode numbers when the crop is planted. Data from samples collected shortly before planting a potato crop can be interpreted by comparison with locally adapted action thresholds established for particular nematode species.

Predicting the effect of nematode populations on the performance of subsequent crops is more complicated. Samples may be collected during a growing season to predict the following year's preseason nematode population. To do so, it is necessary to estimate changes in the population during the present season and during the interval between harvesting the current crop and planting the next crop. Nematode overwintering is poorly understood, so estimates of future populations may be inaccurate.

Advice on interpreting nematode assay results can come from many sources. The extent to which laboratories offer recommendations varies and should be understood before samples are submitted. Specialists from the Cooperative Extension Service or local crop consultants can often aid in interpretation or refer potato health managers to appropriate extension bulletins or other written resources. Information submitted with the sample (such as the purpose of collecting it, soil characteristics, the size of the sampling site, the sampling methods used, and cropping history) can simplify and aid in the interpretation of results. For example, information about the sampling depth is important in interpreting assay results when samples are collected for estimating populations of both nematodes and *Verticillium*. These pathogens may be distributed at very different depths in the soil, and as a result the population of either one may be over- or underestimated, depending on the sampling depth.

Information about the methods used to estimate nematode populations should be obtained from the laboratory performing the assays. The laboratory report should indicate whether an estimate is based on raw or adjusted counts of nematodes and whether the extraction technique excluded dead nematodes. The units (for example, numbers per pint of soil) and habitat (soil or roots) represented by the counts should also be clearly stated.

Integrated Nematode Management

After nematode population estimates have been obtained, the potato health manager can decide whether to implement a nematode management program. Different strategies are appropriate for different types of nematodes and for populations of different sizes. It is unusual for any field in agricultural production to be totally without plant-parasitic nematodes. Each species has a unique life cycle, capacity for increase, host range, and survival strategy that must be considered when a management program is being planned. Knowledge about the relative pathogenicity of each species is required in making informed management decisions. It may be necessary to devise a nematode management strategy aimed at a single key pest rather than try to control all nematode species present. Whatever strategy is chosen, it must fit well within the holistic health management plan for the crop.

> **It may be necessary to devise a nematode management strategy aimed at a single key pest rather than try to control all nematode species present.**

Consideration must also be given to the presence of other soilborne pathogens and insects, especially if pesticides are to be used as part of the management program. Some pesticides have both nematicidal and insecticidal properties. Thus a single material applied at a high rate may be more efficient and effective than a combination of one pesticide having only nematicidal properties and another having only insecticidal properties. Fumigant biocides may be warranted if soilborne fungal pathogens, such as *Verticillium*, are also present.

Although the aim of any nematode management program is to maximize economic returns from the immediate crop, long-term goals and benefits must also be considered. The main objective should be to reduce the populations of nematode pests already present to levels that the potato crop can tolerate, rather than to eliminate nematodes altogether. Other appropriate goals include preventing the introduction and spread of nematode pests not already present and encouraging diversity in the total community of organisms inhabiting production soils, which includes many natural enemies of

nematodes. Some types of fungi, bacteria, insects, and other invertebrates kill nematodes. Increasing or at least maintaining the populations of these natural enemies should be an objective of all management strategies, to take full advantage of these organisms and thus augment other control tactics. Another long-term objective should be to maintain genetic diversity in nematode populations and thus safeguard against the buildup of strains able to tolerate particular pesticides or overcome specific host resistance. Because no one management tactic can attain all these goals, several of the tactics described below must be incorporated into an integrated nematode management program.

Preventing the Introduction of Nematode Pests. In some areas, certain regulatory restrictions are imposed to prevent the introduction and spread of highly damaging nematode pests. All potato production regions in North America restrict the sale and movement of tubers infected with the golden nematode. In some areas, restrictions also apply to the Columbia root-knot and potato rot nematodes. Most regulations are intended for potatoes grown for seed.

Even if not formally mandated, efforts at early detection and restriction of the movement of these three species should be a part of any nematode management plan. Seed potatoes should be examined for galls or internal browning, and samples submitted to an assay lab if nematode infection is suspected. Noninfested fields in regions where these nematodes are known to be present should be sampled at regular intervals to ensure early detection. The diagnostic lab to which samples are sent should be asked to check specifically for cyst or potato rot nematodes, because cysts and potato rot juveniles may be missed by routine extraction methods.

The exclusive use of certified seed tubers is another tactic for avoiding the introduction of nematode pests. The risk of introducing ectoparasitic species, such as sting and stubby-root nematodes, in infected seed is small. However, some endoparasitic species, such as root-knot and root-lesion nematodes, do invade tubers and may survive overwinter storage to serve as inoculum in a potato crop when infected seed tubers are planted. The potato rot nematode invades and reproduces inside tubers, and thus infected seed tubers are the most important means of dispersal of this pest.

Growers should be alert for symptoms of nematode infection in tubers, including dark, dry lesions on tuber surfaces (root-lesion nematodes), bumps or swellings (root-knot nematodes), and surface cracking and internal dry rot (potato rot nematode). Suspected tubers should not be planted, and samples should be sent to a diagnostic lab for confirmation. Although most certified seed is free of nematodes, not all types of nematodes are considered in the certification process (Chapter 7). It is always wise to avoid planting seed tubers grown on land known to be infested with tuber-infecting nematodes.

Cultural Practices. Appropriate crop rotation is an important part of all nematode management programs. Varying the host crop from season to season promotes genetic diversity in nematode species and maintains a diverse biological community of nematodes and associated organisms in the soil, including natural enemies of nematodes. The cropping sequence and the number of years between potato crops needed to reduce populations of damaging nematodes depends on the species present and its population density. Because all plant-parasitic nematodes are obligate plant feeders, rotation is effective in reducing the populations of species with limited host ranges, by allowing time for natural mortality factors to be effective. For example, populations of the golden nematode and the northern root-knot nematode starve and are destroyed by natural enemies in the soil when corn and cereal crops are planted. However, these crops are good hosts of root-lesion nematodes and most ectoparasitic species and favor the reproduction of these pests. Thus, cropping decisions in fields infested with several types of nematodes must be based on management of the key nematode pest—the species that is economically most limiting.

Weed control is also important between potato crops, since many types of weeds can serve as reservoirs for populations of important nematode pests. Even rotational crops that are good hosts can be used to manipulate nematode populations. Planting a shallow-rooted crop prior to a planned soil fumigation ensures that the majority of the nematode population feeding on that crop will be in the upper soil layers, where the chemical is most effective. The number of nematode generations in a season, and hence the population density, can be altered by selecting short- or long-season rotational crops.

> ## It is always wise to avoid planting seed tubers grown on land known to be infested with tuber-infecting nematodes.

Cover crops can also be used to manipulate nematode populations. Although no one crop affects all nematode species, potato health may be significantly enhanced by reductions in populations of certain key species. Pangola digetgrass in southern regions and sudax (sorghum × sudangrass) and sudangrass in northern regions have been successfully used to manage one or more nematode species. Pangola digetgrass is a host of sting and stubby-root nematodes but not the southern root-knot nematode. Sudax and sudangrass are nonhosts of the northern root-knot nematode and poor hosts of the Columbia root-knot nematode and some root-lesion species. However, even a poor host can maintain a nematode population if the crop is planted at a high density or has a prolific root system.

Complete fallowing of production land may also reduce nematode populations but is less preferable than planting nonhost and nematode-resistant crops, because it is expensive and has adverse affects on soil structure. Most nematodes starve under clean fallow, but egg hatch is usually greater when plants are again allowed to grow in the field. Because the egg stage is well suited for long-term survival, a nematode population may persist until a crop is planted.

Soil flooding is used as a nematode management tactic in some potato production areas, mostly in the southern United States. Flooding kills nematodes by reducing the amount of oxygen available for respiration and increasing concentrations of substances toxic to nematodes, such as organic acids, methane, and hydrogen sulfide. A period of 7–9 months of continuous flooding or multiple flooding and drying cycles is required to kill eggs of root-knot nematodes. Flooding is most effective when the soil and air remain warm. Several cycles of flooding (for a minimum of 2 weeks) alternating with drying and disking may be as effective as continuous flooding. Using this tactic unsuccessfully, however, may prove to be harmful, since water is an excellent means of dispersing nematodes.

During production of a potato crop, maintaining plant health through proper irrigation and fertilizer management can alleviate much of the stress from nematode infection. In some situations, optimal nitrogen and phosphorus fertilization may be as effective as nematicides in limiting the detrimental effects of nematodes. Plants with vigorous root systems, however, offer a highly suitable habitat for nematode reproduction. Therefore, fertilization may favor reproduction and growth of nematode populations as well as the ability of potato plants to withstand their deleterious effects.

Several sanitation measures and postharvest practices are important for effective nematode management. The ability of many nematode species to survive desiccation and freezing facilitates their dispersal with soil and plant debris. Because nematodes can be transported into fields in soil clinging to machinery, equipment should be cleaned after use in fields known to be infested. Water alone is adequate if all soil is removed. Removing culls from harvested fields or exposing culls and roots to the weather by postharvest cultivation can substantially reduce the population of nematodes carried over into the next crop.

Host Plant Resistance. Planting resistant cultivars is a more viable strategy against sedentary endoparasitic species (root-knot and cyst nematodes) than against ectoparasitic species, because the former rely on specialized cells for feeding. These nematodes enter roots of resistant host plants but then become trapped after the feeding cells necessary for their survival fail to develop. Resistant cultivars yield well, but they may develop symptoms of infection (such as galling) before the nematodes are killed.

At present, only a few potato cultivars are available that have genetic resistance to specific nematode pests, but prospects are good for the development of many more. Resistant cultivars are already an essential component of management schemes for the golden nematode. If resistant cultivars are planted as part of a nematode management plan, it is best to alternate the use of several such cultivars in a field from year to year or to include susceptible cultivars planted in nematicide-treated soil in the rotation. This strategy avoids the selection of nematode races that can overcome specific host resistance.

Most potato cultivars now in commercial use are susceptible to nematode pests, but the effect of infection on yield varies among cultivars. For example, population densities of root-lesion nematodes (*P. penetrans*) that would affect yield in Superior are tolerated with little effect by Russet Burbank. If certain nematode species are known to be a potential problem in a production location, the selection of a less susceptible cultivar can be an important management decision. Because reactions of potato cultivars to nematode infection are affected by temperature and the presence of other organisms, information about the response of particular cultivars to particular nematode species should be obtained from local crop advisors.

Chemical Control. Pesticides have been used to control nematodes for more than 40 years. At one time, the cost of pesticide treatments was equal to or less than the cost of sampling and processing samples to estimate nematode populations. This led to indiscriminate "insurance" applications of nematicides with some crops.

There are many problems associated with nematicides. These products are toxic chemicals that, if misused, pose great risk to human health and the environment. Many nematicides are nonspecific in their activity and thus also reduce populations of natural enemies and competitors of nematodes. This sometimes allows nematode populations to later resurge to densities greater than those before treatment—the so-called rebound effect. Nematicides, particularly soil fumigants, are costly and require specialized equipment and expertise for application.

Despite their economic and environmental shortcomings, nematicides remain an important component of potato health management in some situations. To ensure the continued availability and effectiveness of nematicides in potato production, and to avoid human health problems and environmental contamination, it is important that they be used only when needed, and always with utmost care according to the label directions.

Pesticides used for nematode control are classed as fumigant and nonfumigant nematicides. Fumigants are volatile compounds that may be true nematicides (for example, 1,3-dichloropropene [1,3-D]) or broad-spectrum biocides (such as chloropicrin, methyl bromide, and methyl isothiocyanate). Biocides kill soilborne fungi, weeds, soil-dwelling insects, and other invertebrates as well as nematodes. Nonfumigant nematicides are nonvolatile organophosphate or carbamate compounds applied to the soil in granular or liquid form. Some nonfumigants have both nematicidal and insecticidal properties if applied at appropriate rates. The decision whether to use fumigant or nonfumigant nematicides depends on the soil texture, the vertical distribution of nematodes in the soil, the presence of other organisms, potential environmental effects, and the cash value of the crop.

Most soil fumigants are applied as liquids. They move through the soil profile, dissolved in soil water or in a gaseous state, and kill nematodes on contact. They are most effective in well-drained, porous soils. The residual life of fumigants ranges from several days for highly volatile compounds to 2 weeks or more for less volatile compounds. Fumigants are usually applied in the fall or spring, preceding a potato crop (Chapter 2). Most growers find fumigation more effective and convenient in the fall than in the spring.

Fumigants are highly effective in killing nematodes at depths of about 2–10 inches. Nematodes residing deep in the soil profile at the time of application but migrating to the soil surface later, when a crop is planted, may escape fumigation. For this reason, it is likely that some portion of most nematode populations survives after fumigation. The percentage of the population surviving may be quite high for sting and stubby-root nematodes and other species that reside deep in the soil. Increasing the rate of application does not necessarily increase the depth to which fumigants penetrate the soil.

All fumigants can be injected into the soil, and some must be applied in this manner. Chisel equipment is used to deliver a fumigant to a depth of 4–12 inches, either in the row or broadcast. Prior to fumigation, the soil should be in seedbed condition and free of clods and undecomposed plant material. The best results are obtained when the soil is moist and between 50 and 70°F at a 6-inch depth. Methyl bromide and chloropicrin are highly volatile materials, and when they are applied the soil must be covered with tarps to prevent premature escape of the gas. 1,3-D and methyl isothiocyanate mixtures are less volatile, and the soil may be sealed with a cultipacker or a similar implement after treatment.

All fumigants damage plants, but they dissipate from the soil in about 2 days (methyl bromide) to 2 weeks (1,3-D). Dissipation occurs more quickly under warmer and drier conditions. Metham sodium degrades into methyl isothiocyanate after application. It can be injected into the soil or applied through a sprinkler irrigation system, and the surface is then sealed with water. Metham sodium can be applied in irrigation water on cultivated fallow soil or over a fall cover crop. The cover crop is killed by this treatment, but the residual stubble provides overwinter protection from erosion. Regardless of whether a crop cover is present, the soil should be moist when the fumigant is applied. Application with irrigation water is most effective when the air is moderately cool, because less of the fumigant is lost through evaporation. In some areas this application method may be inappropriate because of potential groundwater pollution or contamination of nearby nontarget areas with windblown fumigant.

Nonfumigant nematicides are usually applied at planting. They have longer residual action than fumigants and protect potato plants during the early stages of growth. Some nonfumigants affect nematodes directly, by contact action, and others are taken up systemically by the plant and affect nematodes after feeding or infection has occurred. Nonfumigants, in granular or liquid formulations, are applied to the soil surface and incorporated or banded in the row or furrow. Thorough mechanical incorporation and adequate moisture are needed to promote solubilization and movement of the nematicide and thus ensure that it comes in contact with root systems and nematodes.

Nonfumigant nematicides sometimes only paralyze rather than kill nematodes. Those receiving a high dosage are probably killed outright, but those receiving less than a lethal dose may recover when pesticide levels in the soil diminish. For this reason, nonfumigant nematicides can result in increased yields by protecting plants at critical stages of growth, even though they do not eliminate nematode populations.

Nonfumigant nematicides have some advantages over fumigants. They are cheaper and easier to apply and, unlike most fumigants, do not require specialized application equipment or custom application. Some nonfumigants are also insecticidal and protect against both insects and nematodes at rates used for nematode control. However, the reverse may not hold true; materials used at rates recommended for insect control may not protect against nematodes. Nonfumigants are applied in the spring and do not require cultivation other than that needed for planting.

Several disadvantages associated with nonfumigant nematicides have led to a decrease in their use in recent years. They have high mammalian toxicity and potential for polluting groundwater. Granules of some nonfumigants, if left on the soil surface, attract birds, which will be killed if they eat them. There is growing evidence that because some nematodes survive the application of these products, pesticide-resistant nematode strains can develop after repeated exposures. There is also evidence that microbial communities in the soil can be altered by intensive use of nonfumigant nematicides, so as to increase the rate of biodegradation of these compounds in the soil.

> **It is important to adopt integrated nematode management programs that include several control strategies, instead of relying exclusively on nematicides.**

New classes of nematicides (such as avermectins) and chemicals aimed at disrupting nematode life cycles (such as hatch inhibitors and pheromones) are being developed to augment currently available pesticides. However, existing nematicides are being withdrawn from registration or are being placed under use restrictions faster than new products are being made available. Because of these trends, it is particularly important that potato health managers adopt integrated nematode management programs that include several control strategies, instead of relying exclusively on nematicides to protect potatoes or rotational crops. It is also essential to take all necessary steps to prevent environmental contamination with nematicides and other pesticides and hazardous human exposure to these chemicals.

Sources of Additional Information

General

Anonymous. 1992. Potato Statistical Yearbook. National Potato Council, Englewood, CO.

Burton, W. G. 1989. The Potato. 3rd ed. John Wiley & Sons, New York.

Harris, P. M. 1992. The Potato Crop. 2nd ed. Chapman and Hall, London.

Kahn, E. J., Jr. 1984. Profiles: The staffs of life. II. The potato—Man is what he eats. New Yorker, Nov., pp. 56-93.

Li, P. H., ed. 1985. Potato Physiology. Academic Press, Orlando, FL.

National Research Council. 1989. Alternative Agriculture. National Academy Press, Washington, DC.

Salaman, R. N. 1949. The History and Social Influence of the Potato. New ed., 1985. J. G. Hawkes, ed. Cambridge University Press, Cambridge.

Thornton, R. E., and Sieczka, J. B., eds. 1980. Commercial potato production in North America. American Potato Journal 57, supplement.

Seed Certification

Anonymous. 1982. Seed potato certification: Its purpose, capabilities, and limitations. American Potato Journal 59:231-236.

Knutson, K. W. 1988. Implications of new technologies for seed potato certification programs and seed growers. American Potato Journal 65:229-235.

Mellor, F. C., and Stace-Smith, R. 1977. Virus-free potatoes by tissue culture. Pages 616-637 in: Applied and Fundamental Aspects of Plant Cell Tissue and Organ Culture. J. Reinert and Y. P. S. Bajaj, eds. Springer-Verlag, Berlin.

Slack, S. A. 1980. Pathogen-free plants by meristem-tip culture. Plant Disease 64:15-17.

Slack, S. A., and French, E. R. 1982. New disease elimination techniques in seed production programs. Proceedings of Research for the Potato in the Year 2000. International Potato Center, Lima, Peru.

Cultivars and Seed Handling

Anonymous. 1991. Potato Varieties in Canada. 4th ed. New Brunswick Department of Agriculture, Perth-Andover, New Brunswick, Canada.

Chase, R. W. 1989. North American Potato Variety Inventory. Certification Section, Potato Association of America, and Department of Crop and Soil Sciences, Michigan State University, East Lansing.

O'Keefe, R. B., Sterrett, S., Chase, R. W., and Sieczka, J. B. 1990-1991. North American Potato Variety Handbook. Potato Association of America and University of Maine, Orono.

Extension Publications

Maine
Bull. 2241. Improving potato stands.

North Dakota
PP 877. Disease control guidelines for seed potato selection, handling and planting.

Washington
PNW 248. Potatoes: Influencing seed tuber behavior.

Irrigation

Adams, S. S., and Stevenson, W. R. 1990. Water management, disease development and potato production. American Potato Journal 67:3-11.

James, L. G. 1988. Principles of Farm Irrigation System Design. John Wiley & Sons, New York.

Wright, J. L., and Stark, J. C. 1990. Potato. Pages 859-888 in: Irrigation of Agricultural Crops. Agronomy Monograph 30. B. A. Stewart and D. R. Nielsen, eds. American Society of Agronomy, Madison, WI.

Extension Publications

California
ANR 2264. Questions and answers about tensiometers.
ANR 21403. Everybody's guide to water terms.
ANR 21454. Irrigation scheduling: A guide for efficient on-farm water management.

Colorado
Bull. 522S. Weed seed and trash screens for irrigation water.
Bull. 4.700. Estimating soil moisture for irrigation.
Bull. 4.707. Irrigation scheduling: The water balance approach.

Idaho
MS 39. Soil moisture scheduling procedure.
PNW 288. Irrigation scheduling.

Minnesota
AG-FO-1322. Irrigation scheduling—Checkbook method.

North Dakota
AE 1040. Growing irrigated potatoes.
AE 100. Tensiometers—Their use, installation and maintenance.

Ohio
AEX-370. Irrigation in Ohio: Eight major factors.

Wisconsin
A2839. Sprinkler irrigation in Wisconsin.
WISP. Wisconsin Irrigation Scheduling Program—A computer aid for growers scheduling crop irrigation. Available from Wisplan Computing Services, 302 Hiram Smith Hall, 1545 Observatory Drive, University of Wisconsin, Madison, WI 53706.

Fertility and Soils

Extension Publications

California
ANR 1881. Compaction of soil by agricultural equipment.
ANR 21136. Nitrate losses from irrigated cropland.

Idaho
CIS 743. Tissue analysis—A guide to nitrogen fertilization for Russet Burbank potatoes.
CIS 757. Fertilizer placement.
CIS 787. Liming materials.
CIS 863. Fertilizer primer: Terminology, calculations and application.
CIS 872. Quality water for Idaho—Nitrate and groundwater.
CIS 903. Phosphorus nutrition of potatoes.

Maine
Bull. 2056. Fertilizing potatoes.
Bull. 2091. Liming potatoes.

Michigan
E0909. Tile drainage for improved crop production.
E1460. Compact soil—Visual symptoms.

Minnesota
AG-BU-3115. Soil compaction—Causes, effects and control.
AG-BU-3166. Understanding nitrogen and agricultural chemicals in the environment.

North Dakota
SF 715. Fertilizing potatoes.
SF 990. Soil sampling for fertilizer recommendations.

Ohio
AEX301. Soil compaction and drainage.
AEX510. Soil compaction and heavy machinery.
Video VT15. Land drainage: A dominant cropland need.

Washington
WREP 9. Principles of soil sampling for Northwest agriculture.

Wisconsin
G3432. Effect of tillage on erosion, runoff and runoff water quality.
A2100. Sampling soils for testing.
A3367. Soil compaction: Causes, concerns and cures.
G3054. Nitrate in Wisconsin groundwater: Sources and concerns.

Harvest and Storage

Cargill, B. F. 1986. Engineering for Potatoes. Michigan State University and American Society of Agricultural Engineers, St. Joseph, MI.
Rastovski, A. van Es, et al. 1981. Storage of Potatoes: Post-Harvest Behavior, Store Design, Storage Practice, Handling. Centre for Agricultural Publishing and Documentation (PUDOC), Wageningen, Netherlands.

Extension Publications

Idaho
CIS 297. Potato storage—Construction and management.
CIS 759. Potato vine killing.
CIS 814. Disposal of cull and waste potatoes.
CIS 835. Potato harvesting and handling operations for quality, efficiency, and safety.
Bull. 725. Bruise-free potatoes: Our goal.
PNW 257. Potatoes—Storage and quality maintenance in the Pacific Northwest.
Videotape 275. Potato bruise prevention: The harvester.
Videotape 471. Potato bruise prevention: Harvester chain adjustment.
Videotape 586. Potato bruise prevention: Handling.

Maine
Bull. 1023. Designing forced ventilation systems for potato storages.
Bull. 1090. Potato harvester chain-speed adjustments for bruise reduction.
Bull. 1091. Potato harvester modifications for bruise reduction.
Bull. 1092. Potato storage design and management.
Bull. 1093. Potato storage ventilation—Storage environment.
Bull. 1095. Preventing fresh bruise in potato packing operations.
Bull. 1097. Proper operation of grading tables.
Bull. 1108. Selection of potato grading and handling equipment.
Bull. 2101. Managing potato storages for better potato appearance and quality.
Bull. 2149. Potato bin piler selection and operation.
Bull. 2213. SPEED: A computer program for potato harvester adjustment.
Bull. 2214. BELTS: A computer program for economic analysis of potato harvester bed changeover.

Michigan
E-2074. Potato bruising.

Minnesota
Video AG-VH-5523. Designing potato ventilation systems.
POTATO: A computer program to help design ventilation systems for new or existing potato storage buildings.

North Dakota
Video 187. Potato bruising prevention.

Washington
EB 646. Reducing potato damage during harvest.
EB 1080. Reducing potato harvesting bruise.
EB 1558. Potato harvester chain speed adjustment.
EM 2799. Potato storage and ventilation.
PNW 236. Designing bulk potato storage structures.
PNW 295. Insulation and vapor barriers in potato storage buildings.

Physiological Disorders

Bould, C., Hewitt, E. J., and Needham, P. 1984. Diagnosis of Mineral Disorders in Plants. Vol. 1, Principles. Chemical Publishing, New York.

Hiller, L. K., Koller, D. C., and Thornton, R. E. 1985. Physiological disorders of potato tubers. Pages 389-455 in: Potato Physiology. P. H. Li, ed. Academic Press, Orlando, FL.

Scaife, A., and Turner, M. 1984. Diagnosis of Mineral Disorders in Plants. Vol. 2, Vegetables. Chemical Publishing, New York.

Extension Publications

Idaho
CIS 136. Thumbnail cracks in potatoes.
EB 717. Sugar development in potatoes.
EXT 691. Brown center and hollow heart in potatoes.
MS 24. Translucent-end of potatoes in southwestern Idaho.

Washington
SP 7267. Understanding the potato.

Pest Management

Boiteau, G., Singh, R. P., and Parry, R. H. 1987. Potato pest management in Canada. Proceedings, Symposium on Improving Potato Production, Fredericton, New Brunswick.

Fry, W. E. 1982. Principles of Plant Disease Management. Academic Press, New York.

Hollingsworth, C. S., Ferro, D. N., and Coli, W. M. 1986. Potato Production in the Northeast: A Guide to Integrated Pest Management. Publication C-178. Massachusetts Cooperative Extension Service, Amherst.

Zehnder, G., Jansson, R. K., Powelson, M. L., and Ramon, K. V., eds. Advances in Potato Pest Biology and Management. American Phytopathological Society, St. Paul, MN. (Forthcoming.)

Extension Publications

California
ANR 3316. Integrated pest management for potatoes in the western United States.

Idaho
EXT 528. Soil fumigation: How and why it works.

Michigan
WQ30. Manage pesticides on potatoes—Avoid contaminating water.
E2042. Soil fumigation.
E2099. Using chemigation safely and effectively.

Ohio
L249. Soil fumigation.

Washington
EB 753. Concepts of integrated pest management in Washington.

Wisconsin
A2330. Soil fumigation and sterilization.
G3213. Pesticides in groundwater: How they get there; what happens to them; how to keep them out.
Video VA0049. Calibrating your field sprayer.
PCM. POTATO CROP MANAGEMENT—A computer program using an integrated systems approach to management of the potato crop that includes modules for emergence prediction, irrigation scheduling, and management of insects and disease (early and late blight). Available from Wisplan Computing Services, 302 Hiram Smith Hall, 1545 Observatory Drive, University of Wisconsin, Madison, WI 53706.

Weeds

Anonymous. Weed Identification Guide. Southern Weed Science Society, 309 West Clark Street, Champaign, IL 61820.

Lanini, T. W., and Wertz, B. A. 1986–1987. A Weed Identification Series. Pennsylvania Cooperative Extension Service, Pennsylvania State University, University Park.

Miller, J. F. Common Weed Seedlings of the United States and Canada. Georgia Cooperative Extension Service, University of Georgia, Athens.

Stucky, J. M., Monaco, T. J., and Worsham, A. D. 1980. Identifying Seedling and Mature Weeds Common in the Southeastern United States. North Carolina Agricultural Research Service and North Carolina Cooperative Extension Service, North Carolina State University, Raleigh.

Extension Publications

California
ANR 4030. Growers' weed identification handbook.

Colorado
Bull. 521A. Weeds of Colorado.
XOM-147. Weeds of the West.

Idaho
CIS 864. Herbicide carryover in potatoes.
PNW 352. Nightshade—Biology and control in cropland of the Pacific Northwest.
ESB 737. Diagnosing herbicide drift and carryover injury in potatoes.
EXT 695. Cultural and chemical practices for commercial potato weed control.

Michigan
E0791. Problem perennial weeds in Michigan.
Video VT026. Weed seedling identification.

Minnesota
AG-FO-2280. Application of herbicides through irrigation systems.
AG-FO-2928. Broadleaf weed seedling identification key.
AG-FO-0815. Herbicide spray drift.

North Dakota
NCR 218. Controlling Canada thistle.
NCR 281. Weeds of the North Central states.
NCR 377. Herbicide mode of action and injury symptoms.

Ohio
Video VT33. Identify grass and broadleaf weeds.

Washington
EB 1060. Quackgrass control in croplands.

Wisconsin
NCR 89. Annual broadleaf weed seedling identification.
NCR 90. Annual broadleaf weed identification.
NCR 91. Annual grass and perennial weed seedling identification.
NCR 92. Annual grass and perennial weed identification.

Insects

MacGillivray, M. E. 1979. Aphids Infesting Potatoes in Canada: Life Cycle and Field Key. Publication 1678. Agriculture Canada, Ottawa, Ontario.

Mackauer, M., and Way, M. J. 1976. *Myzus persicae* Sulz., an aphid of world importance. Pages 51-122 in: Studies in Biological Control. V. L. Delucchi, ed. Cambridge University Press, New York.

Radcliffe, E. B., Flanders, K. L., Ragsdale, D. W., and Noetzel, D. M. 1991. Potato insects—Pest management systems for potato insects. Pages 587-621 in: CRC Handbook of Pest Management. 2nd ed. D. Pimentel, ed. CRC Press, Boca Raton, FL.

Extension Publications

Colorado
Bull. 5.541. Potato or tomato psyllids in commercial fields—Characteristics and control.

Idaho
MS 109. Field keys to damaging stages of insects commonly attacking alfalfa, beans, cereals, corn, mint, peas, potatoes and sugarbeets in the Pacific Northwest.

Maine
Bull. 5012. Colorado potato beetle.
Bull. 5018. European corn borer on potatoes.
Bull. 5043. Wireworm on potatoes.
Bull. 5078. Green peach and potato aphid.

Michigan
E0584. European corn borer: Corn/peppers/potatoes/snapbeans.

North Dakota
E 901. White grub management.
E 1001. Potato leafhopper biology and control.
NCR 327. European corn borer development and management.

Washington
EB 919. Colorado potato beetle.
EB 955. Wireworm control in potatoes.
EB 1198. Potato flea beetle: Biology and control.
WREP 64. Management of potato insects in the western states.

Wisconsin
NCR 327. European corn borer development and management.

Diseases

Agrios, G. A. 1988. Plant Pathology. 3rd ed. Academic Press, San Diego, CA.

Bagnall, R. H., and Tai, G. C. C. 1986. Field resistance to potato virus Y in potato assessed by cluster analysis. Plant Disease 70:301-304.

Bagnall, R. H., and Tai, G. C. C. 1986. Potato leafroll virus: Evaluation of resistance in potato cultivars. Plant Disease 70:621-623.

Descriptions of Plant Viruses. Commonwealth Mycological Institute and Association of Applied Biologists, Kew, England.
No. 4. Potato virus X.
No. 54. Potato virus A.
No. 60. Potato virus S.
No. 66. Potato spindle tuber viroid.
No. 87. Potato virus M.
No. 242. Potato virus Y.
No. 291. Potato leafroll virus.

Franc, G. D., Harrison, M. D., and Lahman, L. K. 1988. A simple day-degree model for initiating chemical control of potato early blight in Colorado. Plant Disease 72:851-854.

Hooker, W. J., ed. 1981. Compendium of Potato Diseases. American Phytopathological Society, St. Paul, MN.

MacKenzie, D. R. 1981. Scheduling fungicide applications for potato late blight with BLITECAST. Plant Disease 65:394-399.

McDonald, J., et al. 1991. Tobacco veinal necrosis strain of potato virus Y (PVY[N]). AGDEX Factsheet 181/630. Ontario Ministry of Agriculture and Food, Ottawa.

Powelson, M. L., and Rowe, R. C. 1993. Potato early dying: Causes and management tactics in the eastern and western United States. Annual Review of Phytopathology 31. (Forthcoming.)

Pscheidt, J. W., and Stevenson, W. R. 1986. Comparison of forecasting methods for control of potato early blight in Wisconsin. Plant Disease 70:915-920.

Rich, A. 1983. Potato Diseases. Academic Press, New York.

Rowe, R. C., Davis, J. R., Powelson, M. L., and Rouse, D. I. 1987. Potato early dying: Causal agents and management strategies. Plant Disease 71:482-489.

Extension Publications

Colorado
Bull. 536A. Current status of potato leafroll virus disease in the San Luis Valley.
P114. Early blight of potato.

Idaho
CIS 262. Potato ring rot.
CIS 669. The blackleg–soft rot disease complex in potatoes.

Maine
Bull. 2248. White mold.
Bull. 5003. Bacterial ring rot.
Bull. 5013. Common potato scab.
Bull. 5014. Controlling Fusarium tuber rots.
Bull. 5016. Early blight of potato.
Bull. 5023. Fusarium tuber rots.
Bull. 5027. Late blight.
Bull. 5033. Potato virus diseases.
Bull. 5035. Silver scurf.
Bull. 5041. Verticillium wilt.

Michigan
E1763. Diseases of potato: Early blight.
E1801. Diseases of potato: Bacterial ring rot.
E1802. Diseases of potato: Late blight.
E2221. Diseases of potato: Common scab.
E2309. Blackleg and soft rot of potatoes.

Minnesota
AG-FS-1147. Late blight of potatoes.
AG-FS-1160. Verticillium wilt of potatoes.

New York
Bull. 205. Detection of potato tuber diseases and defects.

North Dakota
PP 507. Ring rot of potatoes.
PP 903. Blackleg and soft rot of potatoes.
PP 1039. Fusarium dry rot.

Ohio
Bull. 734. Potato tuber diseases: Management before and after harvest.
V28. Early blight of potato.

Washington
EM 2704. Potato leaf roll.
EM 2936. Sclerotinia stem rot on potato.
PNW 387. Powdery scab of potato.

Wisconsin
A2788. Potato disorder: Common scab.
A3243. Potato ring rot.

Nematodes

Barker, K. R., and Campbell, C. L. 1981. Sampling nematode populations. Pages 451-474 in: Plant Parasitic Nematodes. Vol. 3. B. M. Zuckerman and R. A. Rohde, eds. Academic Press, New York.
Brown, R. H., and Kerry, B. R., eds. 1987. Principles and Practice of Nematode Control in Crops. Academic Press, San Diego, CA.
Riggs, R. D., ed. 1982. Nematology in the Southern Region of the United States. Southern Cooperative Series Bulletin 276. Arkansas Agricultural Experiment Station, Fayetteville.
Sasser, J. N., and Carter, C. C., eds. 1985. An Advanced Treatise on *Meloidogyne*. Vol. 1, Biology and Control. North Carolina State University Graphics, Raleigh.

Extension Publications

California
ANR 4045. Phytonematology study guide.

Idaho
CIS 868. The potato rot nematode.
PNW 190. Root-knot nematodes of the Pacific Northwest.
EXP 614. Root-knot nematodes in agricultural waste.

Michigan
E2199. Detecting and avoiding nematode problems.

Washington
EB 1379. Sampling for nematodes in soil.
EM 2938. Root knot in potatoes.

Wisconsin
A2994. Nematodes and the damage they can cause to plants.

Sources of Extension Publications

California
Division of Agriculture and Natural Resources
ANR Publications
University of California
6701 San Pablo Avenue
Oakland, CA 94608-1239

Colorado
Colorado State University Cooperative Extension
Bulletin Room
Colorado State University
Fort Collins, CO 80523

Idaho
University of Idaho Cooperative Extension System
Agricultural Communications Center
Ag Publications Building
Building J40, Idaho Street
University of Idaho
Moscow, ID 83843-4196

Maine
University of Maine Cooperative Extension
State Publications Office
Room 202
5741 Libby Hall
Orono, ME 04469-5741

Michigan
Michigan State University Cooperative Extension Service
Bulletin Office
Room 10-B Agriculture Hall
Michigan State University
East Lansing, MI 48824-1039

Minnesota
Minnesota Extension Service
University of Minnesota Distribution Center
3 Coffey Hall
1420 Eckles Avenue
St. Paul, MN 55108-6064

New York
Cornell Cooperative Extension
Resource Center
Cornell University
7 Cornell Business and Technology Park
Ithaca, NY 14850

North Dakota
North Dakota State University Extension Service
Distribution Center
Morrill Hall, P.O. Box 5655
North Dakota State University
Fargo, ND 58105-5655

Ohio
Ohio State University Extension
Publications Office
385 Kottman Hall
2021 Coffey Road
Ohio State University
Columbus, OH 43210-1044

Washington
Washington State University Cooperative Extension
Bulletin Office
Cooper Publications Building
Washington State University
Pullman, WA 99164-5912

Wisconsin
University of Wisconsin Cooperative Extension
Extension Publications
Room 245
30 North Murray Street
Madison, WI 53715

Index